William Munshaw

Robert Gordon

Tho.s Armstrong

William Robinson

Eber White

Oliver

GREEN BUSH INN

Geo. Crookshanks

I.S.S.

Geo. Crookshanks

W.m Robinson

John Woods

POTTERY

Geo. Crookshanks

Jo.s Shepard

Scholfield, Property

Newtonbrook

Nicholas Munshaw

Jos. Neel

Geo. Davis

M. A.R.

Rich.d Montgomery

W.m Street

David Mulholland

W.m James

Agar Jo.H.

Rob.t Wentworth

Thomas Humberstone

Geo. Davis

Tho.s Harper

M.r Sigworth

POTTERY W.M.Ch.

Tho.s Davison

Tho.s

Joseph James

George Routliff

Ashton Fletcher

WILKET CREEK

Peter Lawrence

John Wilson 4.th J.P.

Lackie & Johnson

Ashton Fletcher

John.

Finck

HOTEL

W.m Tonson

Jos. Davis

Emanuel Bowes

W.m Holmes

Jonathan Dunn

Dav.

John Kirby

Abraham Johnson

John Kirby

Jonathan Dunn

Tho.s J. Lackie

E.M.Ch.

Joshua Cummer

John Cummer

Joshua Cummer

Nicho.s

David Gibson P.L.S.

Samuel Cummer

WILLOWDALE

Heirs of Daniel McBride

Michael Shepard

Heirs of Daniel McBride

Jacob Miller

Joseph Shepard

McBride

David Gibson

WAGGON S. STORE

Edw.d Pease

John Sheppard

Edward Pease

Andrew McGlashan

Christopher Harrison

John Bales

I West

I Con East

McDougall

Andrew McGlashan

James Harrison

John Vannostrand

John Bales

J. Steward

John Vannostrand

Moffatt Murray & Co

STAFFORDSHIRE HOUSE

Capt Peebles

W.

John Armour

M.M. & Co

M.rs Cameron

W.m Smith

Josku

W. Goodwin

John Armour

J & W Hogg

W.m Green

W.m Smith

M.rs Johnson

John

Joseph Penrose

TANNERY

Thomas Mercer

John Lawrence

os Lackie

Andrew McGlashan

YORK MILLS

STEAM & WATER G. M.

os Lackie

Rich.d L. Denison

Daniel Brooks

W.m Bell

Alex.r Patterson

Dr. Cowdry

Alex.r Whitney
Geo. Grainger

John Street

Home Avenue

Library

Board of
Education

Civic Square

Parking / Market

Communications
Tower

Existing
Borough Offices

Government
Centre

Empress Avenue

Schools

Elmwood Avenue

High Density Residential

Doris Avenue

Kenneth Avenue

Wilket Creek
Recreation Area

Beecroft Road

Yonge Street

Junior High
School

Elmhurst Avenue

Greenfield Avenue

Office and
Retail Centre

Bus Terminal

Sheppard Avenue

Poyntz Avenue

Anndale Avenue

Postal
Terminal

Pioneering
in
NORTH YORK

Pioneering

in

NORTH YORK

A HISTORY OF THE BOROUGH

by

PATRICIA W. HART

CONSULTING EDITOR

Frederick H. Armstrong

GENERAL PUBLISHING COMPANY LIMITED

TORONTO

*The endpapers show Tremaine's Map, 1860,
and a design illustration of the
proposed Yonge Redevelopment Area.*

*Published by General Publishing Company Limited
for the* North York Historical Society
in co-operation with the Borough of North York

Printed in Canada
by T. H. Best Printing Company Limited

To my husband, J. Gilbert Hart,
who has been so helpful, patient and understanding.

Contents

Maps

The dates on the maps indicate the date of indenture.
People in most cases settled four or five years earlier.

AUTHOR'S NOTE: Streets went unnamed in the early years. The names of houses and farms, as well as concession roads, served for addresses. To help the reader identify the sites of pioneer communities, mills, churches, schools, and buildings, present-day names have been used throughout.

The correct spelling of family names is difficult because so many names, spelled in various ways, are found in directories, maps, books, Registry Office records and other documents. An attempt has been made in the index to pull these names together through cross-references.

List of Illustrations

Newtonbrook Wesleyan Methodist Church manse, 1908.
Newtonbrook store and post office in 1920.
Keele Street, 1902.
Fairbank Wesleyan Methodist Church, Dufferin Street.
The Mulholland house, Bathurst Street.
John Perkins Bull's house, Downsview.

PAGES 200-201

Robert Clarke's house, Paxtonia Blvd.
The John Goulding family in front of their house, Keele Street.
Keele Street and Wilson Avenue, York Wesleyan Methodist Church
in the background.
First Weston (later Downsview) Station, Lawrence Avenue.
The Downsview Gun Club.
Isaac Harrison's barn, Dufferin Street.
Dublin House, Dufferin Street and Sheppard Avenue.
Cherry's Hotel in Fisherville, Dufferin Street and Steeles Avenue.
Elia Episcopal Methodist Church, Finch Avenue.
Centre of Elia, about 1920.

PAGES 232-233

Collecting sap from the maple trees in 1890.
Emery Station on Finch Avenue, east of Weston Road.
Emery schools at Weston Road and Finch Avenue.
Jennie Crosson with her Claremont Wesleyan Methodist Church
Sunday school class.
Rowntree Mill Road bridge over the Humber River in Humber
Summit.
John Crosson's log cabin, Victoria Park.
Milneford Mills.
Milneford Mill dam.
The first Don School, Don Mills Road.
Aggie Hogg's general store, Don post office, and library.

Acknowledgements

Throughout my work on this book the encouraging assistance and co-operation from members of the North York Historical Society has been invaluable. I would now like to express my deep appreciation to each of them, including the following manuscript workers:

Mrs. David Gardner provided information on Don Mills and the early organizations, and helped with the manuscript; Mrs. Jack Milne compiled material on the early settlers, churches, L'Amaroux, and O'Sullivan's Corners; Charles Proctor supplied material on the early schools, Mrs. Maurice Hecht on Lansing and Willowdale, Mrs. Henry Turman on Newtonbrook, Mrs. Grant Harper on transportation, and Ted Chirnside on the Indians.

Grateful acknowledgment is also due to The Conservation Authorities Branch of the Ontario Department of Energy and Resources Management for allowing me to quote from the Humber and Don Valley Conservation Reports; to the Perkins Bull Foundation for allowing quotation from Perkins Bull's volume on Downsview, *From Oxford to Ontario*; to Mrs. H. A. S. Molyneux and Dr. F. H. van Nostrand for the use of family documents and letters; to the Mulholland family for allowing the inclusion of a letter from Henry Mulholland to his wife; to G. Elmore Reaman for allowing me to quote from *The Trail of the Black Walnut*; and to the Ontario Historical Society for permission to include David Gibson's letter. My efforts to reach the copyright owners of Mrs. Hopper's book, *Primitive Methodism*, failed; I would appreciate any help in contacting her relatives.

I am indebted to the North York Public Library Board and John E. Dutton, Chief Librarian, for offering to provide marketing outlets for the book after publication; the Toronto Public Libraries, the Archives of the Province of Ontario, Black Creek Pioneer Village, and Upper Canada Village for their valuable assistance, and to The Imperial Oil Company Limited for allowing me to use numerous of their historical illustrations by C. W. Jefferys, and to Ted Chirnside for his line drawings and maps.

All the early settlers contributed to the development of the Township. North Yorkers can be proud of their fortitude and accomplishments. Hence, I have tried to mention all the old families of the area. I hope I have succeeded. I thank the many descendants of the early settlers who have supplied countless details and pictures. My sincere thanks also to the Centennial Committee members for their support, as well as the Mayor, Board of Control, and Council, who made it possible for this book to be published.

Roads and communities in 1825.

Introduction

The history of what is now the Borough of North York, or the northern part of the Township of York as it was called officially until 1922, is in many ways the story of a typical, prosperous, central Ontario farming community. It is in one respect unusual, however, for from the very founding of the Township of York in 1793, the community formed the hinterland of the Town of York (today the City of Toronto), which has been the Province's political and social capital almost continuously from the day it was founded concurrently with the Township. Also, from at least the mid-1820's the Town of York was the economic centre of the Province, a magnet which influenced the Township to the north particularly and dominated it as its market centre. In the early years the political connection was also very close because the town and township governments were combined up until the 1830's and urban and rural politics became closely intermixed.

After Toronto and York Township separated governmentally, the physical growth of Toronto began to affect the Township; sections were gradually nibbled away as the city expanded. Sometimes this took place in the form of direct annexation, a process which ended with the inclusion of the Eglinton area in 1912. At other times expansion resulted in the urbanization of sections of the township which became in themselves distinct satellite communities around Toronto. In this manner, the lakeshore was eventually cut off from the Township, which in time included only the area north of the city. Even here, such growing towns as Weston have established themselves as separate entities.

The early 1920's saw the culmination of this process of political evolution as far as York Township was concerned when, in 1922-1923, the rural areas to the north were constituted as the Township of North York and the urbanized south was divided into the Township of York proper and the Village of Forest Hill. Once separated, the north was able to retain its rural character for another thirty years, but was then suddenly swept into the city during the post-war construction boom. In 1953, North York became one of the thirteen municipalities which were joined to form Metropolitan Toronto; in 1967, with the revision of the Metropolitan Toronto Act, North York became one of the five new boroughs which surround the core city of Toronto in a revised metropolitan system. The change that North York has undergone in these few years has been so drastic that it has almost completely severed the Township from its past. For 150 years it has been a farming community; now it has suddenly become one of the most populous municipalities of the nation. As its past is so rapidly disappearing before the bulldozers in the continuing wave of urbanization, it is appropriate that North York should celebrate the Canadian Centennial by recording this past before it is not only gone but also forgotten.

PART ONE

SOCIAL AND ECONOMIC DEVELOPMENT

Pre-Settlement
Early Conditions in North York
Agriculture
Aspects of Early Country Life
Bees, Church Socials and Temperance Meetings
Mills and Distilleries
Inns and Taverns
Education
Early Industries
Trades and Professions, 1799-1878
Postal Services and Currency

Pre-settlement

To form a sound foundation for an understanding of the development of North York, it is important to know something of its land formation. The bedrock geology[1] is covered with a thick blanket of till left behind as the last glacier melted. The material comprising the till is rock ground to various sizes by the abrasive action of glacier flow over rock surfaces. Outwash deposits of sand and gravel were formed by water melting from the ice, flooding over the flat ground, washing out the clay sized particles, and leaving sand and gravel bars. The till tended to smooth out any great irregularities that may have been left of the old land surface, so that most of the till surface has a gently undulating topography and is fairly fertile. The till plain has been dissected by a branching pattern of young streams—the Humber and Don Rivers and their tributaries—which have cut down into the till and produced many delightful valleys. As a result, North York possesses 44,442 acres of gently rolling country with an elevation variance of 150 feet.

INDIANS

A narrow foot-path through the woods on the east side of the Humber River, known as the Toronto Carrying-Place, saved the Indians[2] and fur traders a voyage of hundreds of miles over exposed Great Lakes waters as they travelled to the upper lakes.[3] The western boundary of North York extended along part of the twenty-eight mile track from the mouth of the Humber to the west branch of the Holland River. This heavily wooded, fertile district, with its streams of fresh water, appealed to various migrating tribes of Huron Indians; so they set up encampments along the banks of the Black Creek between 1400 and 1650 **A.D.** Evidence of the existence of these stone-age people was found when ploughs turned up bones, arrowheads, potsherds, and other artifacts, marking the sites of their villages.

An Indian camp was a clear level space of from about five to seven acres containing a number of longhouses[4] twenty-one feet wide, and about the same in height, ranging from eleven to two hundred and twelve feet in length. Walls were formed by placing sturdy saplings upright in the ground and covering them with strips of bark carried up and over to make a low, domed roof. Large holes in the roof allowed the smoke to escape from open fires on the earthen floor. Although two families used the same fire, there might possibly be a dozen fires in one longhouse. As a result of the concentration of smoke in the longhouses all year, the Indians suffered constantly from eye trouble.

According to Champlain an aisle from ten to twelve feet wide ran down the centre of each cabin. Along the walls, sleeping platforms about four feet high were used in summer so that the occupants might escape the fleas.[5] In winter they slept on mats near the fire. Pieces of wood suspended from the roof served as conveniently high hangers for clothes and provisions that would otherwise have been lost to the hordes of scampering mice and famished dogs.

Part of A PALISADED HURON-IROQUOIS VILLAGE

C. W. Jefferys, Imperial Oil Collection

Men and women performed specified tasks. The longhouse was filled with firewood gathered continually by the women during the spring, summer, and fall to provide the next winter's supply. Within the dark, smoky confines of these drafty shelters, they worked at spinning hemp, preparing animal skins for clothing, and making baskets, sleeping mats, and pottery vessels which were shaped by hand and baked in an open fire. Broken or useless articles they discarded in dumps which were often situated over the bank of the plateau, to be discovered by modern archeologists. Indian men reserved to themselves the role of defenders as well as constructors of their villages. They cultivated tobacco, leaving the planting, cultivation, and harvesting of corn, beans, and squash to the women; they fished (an occupation even more important than hunting) and traded their surplus corn for skins provided by the Algonkians. They also made canoes, nets, and weapons. Their tools (wooden stocks with shell or stone edges) were very primitive; but they sufficed for the production of their diet,[6] which consisted mainly of corn supplemented by the beans and squash raised by the women and such fish, small animals, and birds as the men could obtain. Mongrel dogs, their sole domestic animals, were useful chiefly for the hunt; still, in time of food scarcity they tasted good boiled or roasted.

The threat of attack always loomed over Black Creek Valley, so the longhouses of the larger villages were protected by a multiple palisade[7]—three rows of interlaced stakes from eight to nine feet high, lined with heavy strips of bark reinforced at the base with large trees laid lengthwise. This palisade was topped with watch towers stocked with stones for ammunition and water to put out the fires which constantly threatened all the villages. From the watch towers, the fields and the women working them were guarded. About seven hundred and fifty acres of cultivated land[8] outside the palisade was needed to support a large Indian community. Every square inch was precious as the task of clearing was formidable; it must have taken two or three days to chop down one tree with a stone axe. The corn grown on this land was stored, dried, for winter use at one end of the longhouse in large bark casks placed away from the walls and mice. Enough was harvested in good years to provide a surplus for trading and for the next year's seed. After ten or twenty years the soil became exhausted and timber, used in great quantities for fire wood, disappeared along with the wild life it had sustained. Large village sites had then to be abandoned. Nature soon took over these empty sites; growth and decay provided a rich layer of dark topsoil covering the only evidence that a human culture had ever existed there.

INDIAN SITES

North York boasts of three ancient village sites, all explored by Dr. J. N. Emerson of the University of Toronto and all on Black Creek, a tributary of the Humber River. The five acre Black Creek Site on the west side of Jane Street north of Wilson Avenue, officially explored in 1948, was on the flat river bed by a low hill. Exposed parts of the palisade reaching half way up the slope revealed "a double row of posts with each row having large posts one foot in diameter spaced every five feet and connected by smaller posts."[9] Today the site is covered by earth fill and buildings for Crang Plaza.

The Downsview site[10] explored in 1950, also covers some five acres. These lie south of Sheppard Avenue and west of Keele Street on high ground by Downsview Dells Park above Black Creek. No settlement was disclosed, only the usual midden deposits; slim evidence of cannibalism was found in a mandible pendant.

The seven acre Parsons site officially excavated in 1952, is situated north of Finch Avenue west of Keele Street on a plateau of light, well-drained soil flanked on two sides by the steep ravines of Black Creek. "A multiple palisade as well as portions of house structures was exposed. Of particular interest was the abundance of fragmented human remains in the middens and the presence of mandible and skull gorgets, all of which suggested cannibalism."[11] An ossuary or Indian burial ground was discovered nearby.

INDIAN RELICS

Only the most durable artifacts remain; animal and human bones, stone objects, and broken pottery. Sprinkled through the site about six inches beneath the surface are hundreds of small flint chippings, the residue from the manufacture of arrowheads, scrapers, and other small tools. Whole arrow and spear points, stone axeheads, and needle sharp sewing awls of bone are still being found. On the other hand, though easily recognized by their light yellowish or reddish colour, remnants of early pottery are rarely more than two inches square. Their rough edges reveal the grit added to the wet clay as a tempering medium. Perhaps because their use made them harder, unbroken baked clay tobacco pipes are sometimes found. The short stem was made hollow by encasing a twig in the plastic clay; when baked, the twig was burned, leaving a clear passage from the bowl. Pipe bowls vary in shape and design; they include animal, bird, and human features. The Indian was an inveterate smoker, but not for pleasure. To him, tobacco held a quasi-religious significance and was reserved for occasions of solemnity.

Etienne Brûlé

Etienne Brûlé, the first European to master the Algonkian and Huron languages and enter Ontario, was also the first white man to set foot in North York. In September 1615 he and twelve Huron companions with two canoes left Champlain at the northern outlet of Lake Simcoe and travelled south along the Carrying-Place to the mouth of the Humber River. From here they journeyed to the Carantauans or Andastes in the Upper Susquehanna River district to obtain help against the Iroquois. By the time they returned, however, Champlain had been driven back by the Iroquois and had returned to Quebec; Brûlé was captured, tortured, and released by the enemy. After many years more spent in exploring the Indian country, he was killed and eaten by Hurons who accused him of crime.

NOTES

1 Courtesy of Peter A. Peach, Associate Professor of Geology, University of Toronto and Research Associate, Royal Ontario Museum.

2 J. N. Emerson, "The Archeology of the Ontario Iroquois", University of Chicago PhD. Thesis, 1954. Microfilm Copy, North York Public Library.

3 P. J. Robinson, *Toronto During the French Regime* (Toronto: Ryerson, 1933), pp. 5-7.

4 J. V. Wright, *The Ontario Iroquois Tradition* (Ottawa: Queen's Printer, 1966), National Museum Bulletin 210, pp. 81-83.

5 Diamond Jenness, *The Indians of Canada* (3rd ed.; Ottawa: Queen's Printer, 1955), p. 88.

6 Wright, *loc. cit.*

7 *Ibid.*

8 *Ibid.*, p. 81.

9 *Ibid.*, p. 69.

10 *Ibid.*

11 *Ibid.*, p. 70.

Early Conditions
in York County

EARLY LIFE IN UPPER CANADA IS VIVIDLY DEPICTED IN THE LETTERS
of some of the more literate settlers. The accounts of Anna Langton
and the Strickland sisters, Susanna Moody and Catharine Parr Traill,
are probably the best known, but York County possessed its own
chronicler in David Gibson, a surveyor who emigrated to Canada in
1825 (see Willowdale), whose account of pioneer life in the region
forms a fitting opening for our story of early social conditions. The
following letter[1] was written to a friend in Scotland:

Markham Mills,[2]
27th April, 1827.

My Dear Friend, —

It is now two years since I parted with you at Bolshan,[3] and I
beg you will excuse me for not writing sooner. I might have written
you last harvest by post, after I got a little information with regard
to the Cradle Scythe, but surveying was so pushing with me that I
did not like to stop business until the snow fell and I considered you
would receive this letter before the harvest of 1827, by the Dundee
Ships from Quebec. I have sent you a description of the Cradle
Scythe and also the manner of taking up the grain as near as I
possibly could from the little information I had last year which may
be of some benefit to you. Had I seen your Cradle I would have
been better able to instruct you as there are a good many different
kinds of them, but this which I had described is the most common.
I shall give you a short account of my life since I parted with you. I
sailed from Dundee a few days after I parted with you on board the
Gratitude, Captain Gellatly. We lay in Stromness[4] fourteen days, it
is a poor, barren country and not a single tree to be seen but high
barren mountains, with bent and short heath, the first week on the
Atlantic I was occasionally sick, but afterwards I could stand it

very well, our time was generally spent in reading books. I studied Navigation and got some instructions from the Captain which have been of considerable benefit to me. On my arrival at Quebec I delivered my introductory letters and was very kindly received by Mr. Robinson and the Surveyor General. Fourteen days afterwards the Surveyor General sent me out with another Surveyor on an exploring Survey to the head Waters of the River St. John, our party was four Indians, the Surveyor and myself. We were out thirty two days, the half of the time we could not see the least appearance of any human beings ever having trod those lonely woods, when any person travels in the woods of Canada into such lands as is not surveyed they carry an axe along with them and make marks on the trees that they may find their way back again. But Surveyors take the courses and distances as they go along and keep their reckoning similar to a ship out at sea, and we run from a clearing that one settler has made to another clearing as a ship would sail between two islands.

The Indians carried our provisions on their backs, and when we came to a Lake we cut down a dead tree and cut off five or six pieces about six feet long and lashed them together with alder branches, put our provisions on the raft, got on ourselves and with the assistance of young trees made flat like an oar at the root we paddled ourselves across lakes, rivers, Beaverdams, etc., etc. It [took] only about 15 or 20 minutes to fix such a conveyance. I did not like the thought of having a few alder branches lashed round a few dead trees and our lives depending on the twisting them together at first, but I got hardened to it and thought nothing more of it than if I had got into a good boat. At night we built what the Indians call a Cabin, but in U.C. they call it a Bark, our bed is of Sapon or Hemlock branches. Our rations is 1 and a half lbs. of bread, 1 lb. of pork and one half pint of peas (English pint) per day; when near any river we generally have plenty of trout, whitefish, suckers or eels and when back from rivers we shoot Partridges, they are so tame that if you whistle or make a noise they will let you within two or three yards of them, but if you don't make any noise to attract their attention they will fly away. After the Survey was over I stayed with the Surveyor out in the country and assisted him in drawing out the plans and reports. I lived very cheap in the country but when in Quebec I paid one pound-per week for board, a few days before the arrival of the Governor I came to Quebec, and met with my Cousin who had left his situation in Montreal and got one in Quebec with near twice the salary being 70 pounds a year, bed, board and washing. I stayed in Quebec until the arrival of the Earl of Dalhousie. Mr. Robinson, his steward, stated to his Lordship that I was in Quebec. His Lordship desired Mr. Robinson to send me to him. I went and his Lordship used me very kindly. He stated that he was to see the Surveyor General in a few days, and that I should call in a few days after and he would be able to say what could be done for me. (When I went again he told me that he had tried to get me in as a clerk in the Surveyor General's office, but the Surveyor General was averse to it and said there was not employment for another then). His Lordship did not insist on it. After I found there could be no situation got for me I stated to his Lordship that I had friends in Upper Canada that I intended visiting. His Lordship then said that he would give me Introductory Letters for the Upper Province that might be of service to me. He asked me to leave my address with him and call in two days and the letters would be ready for me, he also stated that if any situation appeared he would write me to come down if I did not succeed in U. C. My Cousin introduced me to a merchant in Montreal who I stayed four weeks with. He offered me 40 pounds the first [year] and 50 the second, board, washing and lodging. I was to return in the spring to his situation, but was to write him from U. C. if I accepted his offer, but I saw too good prospects in U. C. for returning to Montreal to be head clerk in any back store. I would have had two men to work in the store along with me taking in and delivering out goods of which I had to keep a strict account.

In travelling up the country I never stopped night nor day until I came to Kingston, taking the stage where there were rapids in the river and steamboats where they run. When I arrived in Kingston I found it very pleasant weather although the snow was lying six inches deep in Montreal fourteen days before I left it. When I came to Kingston I found but one schooner lying in the Harbour bound for York but was not to sail for fourteen days after, and no certainty of her sailing that fall if it came hard weather, so I left my little trunk in charge of Mr. McLoud, Kingston, who I had been recommended to by letters from Mr. Torrance in Montreal and as there was no passage to be got either by water or stage coach, I put a clean shirt and pair of stockings in my pocket and six days afterwards I arrived in the Township of Markham about eighteen miles north east of York in U. Canada where I was kindly received by my friends. They wrote me when in Quebec to come to Upper Canada, that they had no doubt but that I would get plenty of employment, and gave me great encouragement. My friends were very glad to see the letters I had along with me from the Governor of Lower Canada. I went to York a few days after and delivered my Introductory Letters, the one was to the Rev. Dr. Strachan, the other to the Lieut. Governor, they both advised me to get appointed a Deputy Surveyor of Land. I was examined by the Surveyor General, found competent and got a commission written out in the usual form signed by the Lieut. Governor (after I found security in the amount of 500 pounds for my good behaviour, my friends in Markham were my Securities) the Lieut. Governor gave me back Lord Dalhousie's letter and stated that there was no situation vacant then but as soon as I saw a situation vacant that I would like to apply for it and again show Lord Dalhousie's letter. Since I was appointed a Deputy Surveyor I petitioned the Magistrates of the Home District to appoint me a Surveyor of Highways for the Western Division of the

Home District which they granted, the clerk of the quarter Sessions
then stated to the Magistrates that the Surveyor of Highways for the
Eastern Division of the Home District was a very illiterate sort of
a man and that they never got a proper report from him and also
asked if they would have any objection to appoint me for the Eastern
Division also which they readily granted since I have been appointed
Surveyor of Highways for the Southern division of the Home District
I have as much business as I can attend to. A Surveyor of Highways
has 7/6 per day from the time he leaves home to the time he
returns, and has always to have a Surveyor of land along with him,
he can call whom he pleases, so I can call myself. Government gives
surveyors 15/- and rations but by an Act passed in 1818 a surveyor
of land when surveying roads has but 10/- so when I act in both
capacities I have 17/6 per day, and when surveying for private
people I have 15/- per day or 5/- for every 50 chains I run along
the side of their lot, when a Township is surveyed the ends of the lot
are only staked off, the farmer has to find the side lines of his lot
himself. The lots are generally two hundred acres near York which
measure a 100 chains long. Each line is then 10/- and I can run
two lines per day with freedom, but there is a great deal of lost time
in travelling between places. Land can be bought not far from York
from 10/- to 25/- per acre. The price varies according to the quality
of the lot. Land with maple, basswood, beech and a few pine, on it
is thought to be the first rate sort of land in the Home District, but
where it is most of pine or hemlock it is most commonly too much
sand. The other is chiefly sand and Clay, when it is chiefly beech it
is generally a very hard clay bottom. In low swampy places, where
generally grows White Cedar, in other low ground that is wet in
spring and fall grows Blackash, Basswood and sometimes Hickory.
The price of land varies considerably if there is any mill seat to be
got on it or good spring water, as every one likes to build near a
running stream. The farmers in Canada have to work hard during the
summer but in winter there is not much work, those that are clearing
off land generally do their heavy chopping in winter, and thresh out
their grain, take it to the Mill, then carry their flour to market, which
is put up in barrels, Pork, etc., is also put up in barrels. They thresh
with oxen or horses, by laying the barn floor all over with sheaves,
then get the horses or oxen into the barn, shut the door and make
them walk around amongst the untied sheaves, when it will be to
their belly, until the animals are quite fatigued, then let them stand
until they turn it over and throw it up slack again, and continue to
drive them until it is threshed. I have not seen a threshing mill in
Canada. The winter is considered the most pleasant season for people
travelling, for when the snow falls it seldom goes away until spring.
In winter the farmers use sleighs instead of wagons or carts. The
runners of the sleigh are of wood shod with iron, and bent up at
front so as to rise over any log that may be in the way. They carry
heavier loads with the sleighs in winter than they do in summer with
the wagon. In winter the snow fills up the little hollow places and

makes it nearly level. After harvest, but before the snow falls, the farmers cut out all the underwood and lay it into heaps, and cut the fallen dead trees into pieces from twelve to twenty feet long according to their thickness. They go over the ground in this way cutting all that will be covered with snow, then when the snow is deep in winter they have the large trees to cut down, they cut the trees so that their top will fall near a brush heap, they first cut up the body of the tree in lengths from twelve to twenty feet in proportion to their thickness, then pile up the branches on the nearest adjoining brush-heap, letting the large logs or body of the tree lie scattered on the ground until during the summer when they burn off all the brush-heaps. In a very dry time the fire will run over all the patch that is cut down, burning the leaves and Vegetable mould between the brush-heaps which is considered to injure the land very much. The next piece of work is to roll the large logs into piles, which they call logging. It requires three men, a yoke of oxen and a driver. The oxen is yoked with the yoke and bow and having a chain from the middle of the yoke coming between the oxen which fastens round the log, the oxen are taught to start both at once with a sudden jerk which starts the log out of its bed and draws it to the pile, the other three men during that time are carrying the small logs and putting them on the pile until it is three or four logs high and about the same breadth at the bottom. Logging is very hard work having so many heavy lifts, and the men are as black as chimney sweeps when at this work, the logs get burned on the outside when the brush is burning. After the log heaps are burned they collect the ashes and take them to a potash work where they can get a little whiskey, Tea, or Cloth, in exchange but cash is never given on account of its scarcity here; They then sow the ground with wheat in the fall without ploughing it. Their harrow is made in the form of a wedge having about twelve teeth, six on each side, each tooth is about 1 and a half inches square and about twelve inches long, this form of a harrow never sticks in a stump although they stand about three feet above the surface of the ground, when it has been maple or beech the stump will come in in about seven years, in the spring when the frost is coming out of the ground they take a yoke of oxen and fixing the chain round the top of the stump, then make the oxen go forward with a sudden jerk, in this way a great many are drawn out, or in summer when the stumps are quite dry if they light a little fire on a dry part of the stump and the wind blowing a little it will burn it to the ground before the fire goes out, but pine and hemlock stumps will stand a man's life time I believe. The turpentine prevents them from rotting, on that account and the great expense of clearing renders that sort of land of less value. I don't think they have any regular rotation of cropping here, it is very common to sow Timothy grass with the first crop of wheat and let it lie in the grass as long as it will cut for hay. They seldom drive out their dung from the barn although the land would be much better of it, they consider it to be more expense than profit to carry it far from the barn so lay it on some place near that they think stands in need of it. They generally keep sheep so as to have wool for their own clothes. I believe that the following lines that are written of Scotland about two hundred years ago are very applicable to Canada at this present time.

> About two hundred years or mare sin sine
> When fashions werna half sa fine
> Hudden gray undyed or drest
> Was suncy weed to busk the best
> And lint was beaten wi' the mell
> And Ilk een singled to themsel'.

I have not heard of a mill for dressing flax in U. C. There was a Scotchman who petitioned the House of Assembly to grant a premium to the first one who would erect a mill for dressing flax but whether they granted it or not I am not able to say at present. Hudden Gray is a very common dress of the farmers in U. C. particularly the Dutch, there are a great many Dutch farmers that have excellent farms in the Township of Markham. It is settled chiefly with Dutch.[5] They are a very industrious set of people and attend to the improvement of their farms very much, indeed more so than any other set of people I have met with in Canada. I consider this a good country for the Labouring Class, it will not pay in this country to carry on farming as is done in Scotland, the price of Grain is so low and servants wages so high there is not a steady man to be got that will work for wages as every one wishes to be on land of his own, by going back from York thirty or forty miles good land can be got for 5/- an acre. There are many people in this country who came in only a few years since who have good farms, although they had to purchase land and pay the interest of the money and pay off as much of the stock as they could every year, that are now independent. They had to work hard for a few years, but who would not do so having such a prospect in view, rent day never comes in Canada, after they have paid for their land and their taxes are only 4/- or 10/- a year in proportion to their clearing and stock of cattle, and as to the management of the Government affairs, there is very little room for complaint, the House of Assembly men are put in by the farmers, or freeholders and everything is done agreeably to the desire of the generality of the people, more so than might be expected in a country that is composed of all nations. The rate of wages of the different professions to the best of my information is as follows:

> Mill Wright from 7/6 — to 10/- per day.
> House Carpenter from 5/- to 6/3 per day.
> Saw Mill Attenders from 2 pounds 10 shillings to
>   3 pounds 15 s. a month.
> Farm Servants from 20 pounds to 24 pounds a year.
> Masons and Bricklayers from 5/- to 7/6 per day.

Weaving is from /6 to /7 and a half per yard for plain cloth.
They generally weave 8 or 10 yards a day. Women's wages are
from 1 pound to 1.10 pounds per month, all the professions above
stated are found board and lodging along with the rates of wages
as above stated. Boarding in farm houses is 5/- per week in York
from 10/- to 20/-. Oatmeal is sold by some of the storekeepers in
York but at a very high price. I don't think there is a mill for
manufacturing Oatmeal in Canada. It is brought from the United
States chiefly. But we have a very good substitute—the wheat loaf.
Every farmer has an oven which is built of brick and will hold six
or seven loaves at once, they light a large fire in it and after the
bricks get hot they take out the fire and put in the loaves then shut
the door of the oven quite close for about an hour, when it will be
baked, they make as good bread as any Scotch Baker. There is
seldom any other sort of bread used here. Indian Corn is used in the
same way as oatmeal in Scotland when it is made into potage. It
would be a great deal better if it were dried before being ground,
but there are no kilns here as in Scotland. Hogs are very little
expense in keeping as they run in the woods all the year except when
the snow gets 1½ or 2 feet deep they then have to be fed at the
barn. In the fall of the year they get plenty of beech and hickory
nuts which fatten them, but before they kill them they confine them
and feed them with Indian Corn for a few weeks which makes
the pork firm. The farmers here make their own sugar in March
when the heat of the sun melts the snow and at night hard frost,
the maple trees will run a pail full of sap during the heat of the day.
With a quarter of an inch Auger they bore about one half inch into
the tree, a little more than through the bark and with a gouge make a
little cut under the hole and put a little piece of pine board into the cut
projecting out from the tree so that the sap will run along the board
and drop into a block of pine which is cut out so that it will hold
a pail full of sap.

They carry the sap to a place where they boil it into molasses
in large boilers, then turn the molasses into a smaller kettle then
boiling it until it crystalizes they then pour it into something that is
wider at the mouth than at bottom (such as a basin) until it cools,
then tumbling it out when it is a firm lump of sugar, equal to any
Muscavado Sugar, and as clear in colour. It sells for about /4 per
lb. when they make it, but in winter from /6 to /7½ per lb. The
trees grow as well as any that have not been tapt, and a sugar bush
as it is most exposed to the heat of the sun. Making sugar is hard
work, as they have to walk through the snow carrying the sap
together, they sometimes draw it together with oxen on a sleigh,
but oftener they carry it in keals with a yoke on their shoulders.
Sugar time comes at a very convenient season, as it is before the
snow goes off the ground and there is not much work to do on the
farm then. After the sugar is made they set to repairing their fences
to defend the wheat.

My Dear Friend,—If there is any information you want with

regard to Canada, if you would be so good as to let me know, I should be glad to give you all the information that is in my power. Or if any of your acquaintances were coming to Canada to purchase land I should be glad to instruct them to the best of my skill and abilities. I occasionally reside in the Township of Markham with Mr. Peter Milne who is a cousin of my father's, has 200 acres of land, a flour mill with two run of stones, a saw mill, fulling mill, dying and clothing works, and keeps a store of dry-goods and spiritous liquors. He made his money in the United States and came into Canada a few years ago. His brother that is married to my aunt used to carry on his filling, dying, grist and saw mill with the assistance of his family but they have dissolved partnership this spring and now stays in the Township of York about seven miles up Yonge Street, and are putting up a saw mill and Fulling works of their own. I oftener stay with him in the Township of York. His name is Alexander Milne, Fuller and Dyer. His brother Peter got married this spring to an English girl, they then dissolved partnership.

N.B.—My Friend, A. Milne has been reading over this sheet and wishes me to state that eight gallons or two pail fulls of sap of the maple tree will make one pound of sugar in general and a farmer generally has between three or four hundred pounds of this sort of sugar for his own use every year. They very frequently sell it to the storekeepers in exchange for other store goods such as tea, spirits, etc., etc., everything for the use of man to make him comfortable is in plenty here, there is a good deal of business done here by way of barter on account of the scarcity of money. Anyone that comes to Canada with the thought of making money by farming will find themselves very much deceived as labour is so high and the price of produce so low, but they that are industrious can find by their labour to satisfy all their wants, as to eating, drinking and wearing apparel, and many of the luxuries of life. They have a house, and land of their own, and plenty of fire to keep them warm in the cold winter evenings. I hope you will be so good as to excuse this hurried scrawl when everything is confused with another just as it came in my head.

I remain your obt. serv't

David Gibson.

NOTES

1 David Gibson, "Conditions in York County a Century Ago", Ontario Historical Society, *Papers and Records*, XXIV (1927), 256-365.

2 This letter was given to the captain of an ocean vessel to deliver in Scotland. He failed to do so and on his return trip sent the letter back to Markham Mills.

3 Bolshan is an estate in the parish of Kinnell, Forfarshire.

4 In the Orkney Islands.

5 Dutch in this case meant the Pennsylvania Germans.

Agriculture

EVERY SETTLER BECAME A FARMER, NO MATTER WHAT OTHER LINE of work he undertook. Clearing a new tract of land followed a regular pattern. Neighbours were notified that a "bee" would be held to erect a small one-room log cabin, usually sixteen by twenty feet, and every one turned out to help. The logs for the walls were notched to fit snugly together at the corners, and the cracks were chinked, or filled with wedge-shaped pieces of wood plastered with clay. The roof was made of bark or small, hollowed, basswood logs laid in tile fashion, and a hole was provided to allow the smoke from the fire to escape until a chimney of logs plastered with a mixture of clay and straw could be built.

As there were no matches, it was necessary to keep a small fire burning constantly for cooking or heating purposes. Often on bitterly cold winter mornings the family awakened to find the fire out, and the farmer or one of the children had to slog his way through heavy snow drifts to a neighbour's cabin, perhaps a mile or so away, to fetch a pail of live coals in order to rekindle the fire for breakfast.

The only light in the cabin was provided by a small window covered by a shutter, oiled paper, or glass if it was available. The door was made by splitting logs into rough boards and attaching wooden hinges and latches. Usually the settler had to content himself for a time with a cabin floor of bare earth, packed down hard. But before long a cellar would be scooped out and a permanent, plank floor would be installed made from logs split into puncheons.[1] The furniture consisted of crude log benches or stools, a table, plank beds, and shelves set on pegs to hold the dishes.

The underbrush, consisting of small trees and bushes, was cut away

Squared Logs

C. W. Jefferys, Imperial Oil Collection

from the cabin and thrown into piles to be burned. All winter the sound of the settler's axe and the crashing of falling trees could be heard ringing through the forest. Trees were chopped so that they fell together in piles that were later burned on dry evenings when the wind had died down. The logs that remained after the burning were cut into lengths, draw by oxen into heaps, and again set on fire. The chunks left after this second burning were collected again into piles by all members of the family, and a final burning left the land with only the stumps. The ashes were sold to an ashery to make potash, the making of which constituted one of the most flourishing business ventures of the early 1800's.

The farmer planted potatoes, turnips, pumpkins, and Indian corn between the stumps. Often the corn did not ripen and, although the potatoes were plentiful, they were not always of good quality. After an early frost the harvest was very poor, resulting in a shortage of wheat for bread making. However, fish, partridges, pigeons, salmon, and deer helped to supplement the diet the following winter.

The stumps usually rotted after four or five years and became loose enough to be pulled out by oxen. This method required a good, strong logging chain, a pole of from twelve to fifteen feet in length and six to eight inches in diameter that acted as a lever, and a yoke of oxen, which were driven ahead with a jerk to twist the stump out of the ground. The pine stumps, not so easily uprooted, required blasting or the use of a stumping machine. The latter consisted of a large screw fastened both to a framework placed over the stumps, and to chains which bound the stumps and its exposed roots. Horses or oxen were hitched to a long pole which rotated the screw upwards as the animals were driven around the framework, the taut chains gradually prying the stump from the ground.

Prowling wild animals were a constant menace. Bears and squirrels destroyed the wheat by eating off the heads, wolves killed the sheep and hogs, and the foxes preyed upon the chickens, lambs, and small pigs. Trapping and shooting with an old-fashioned, flint-lock army musket was an important means of keeping alive.

All such formidable common obstacles tended to encourage co-operation among the settlers, and a rapport emerged which bound social and economic aspects of community life together. But even with the generous aid of neighbours a large family was an invaluable asset for obvious reasons; the more hands employed in the continuous, arduous tasks of cultivation and establishing the homestead, the better. The family was not so mobile as it is today, and the necessity for eking a life from the soil prevented the patterns of family life from being as fluid. Often when sons married they brought their wives to live with the family until they establish themselves on their own. Grandparents tended to move in with their off-spring, and unmarried daughters and sisters were similarly integrated into the family unit. Almost invariably one off-spring stayed on the homestead with his or her parents. Regardless of the composition of the family at any one time there was always enough work to keep everyone busy.

Conditions improved gradually with the arrival of new settlers, men of substance, who bought improved farms from the original owners. New houses were built and mills established in convenient locations. These cash transactions helped to boost the economy during the lean years after the War of 1812.

WATER

Drinking-water was obtained from the clear, running streams until locations for surface wells ten or twelve feet deep could be investigated. Because of the dense forests water was very close to the surface of the ground, and wells were dug near the log houses. These, lined with un-mortared stone, had a wooden box or stone arrangement on top about three feet high to prevent children and animals from falling into them.

To obtain water a bucket was thrown into the well with a rope tied to the handle, and when filled it was hauled up hand-over-hand. The weight of the bucket and the difficulty of leaning over the wall to guide it as it was pulled upwards led to the development of pole or sweep wells. A log with a crotch or fork at one end was set in the ground near the well. A sweep, or long pole, lay in the crotch with the long end of the pole over the well attached to an additional pole with a hook for the bucket; the short end of the sweep was constructed with a box or container for rocks to balance the weight of the bucket full of water. This arrangement provided such good leverage that a child could fetch the water, if need be.

Later the farmers dug deep wells where heavy pails of water were hauled to the surface by ropes attached to a windlass. Gradually various types of pumps were invented to bring the water to the surface. In the 1860's Charles Powell of Newtonbrook invented the swing pump with a handle at one side that swung up and down; on the downward stroke the water poured out of a spout into a bucket.

FARM ANIMALS

Farm animals were essential both for food and helping with the heavy work. To begin with, a few chickens supplied eggs and poultry, and a cow provided milk, cream and butter. Milking first thing in the morning and again in the late afternoon became one of the women's chores; they enjoyed their walk to the small clearing, carrying their three-legged milking stools and pails. When full, each pail was covered and carried to a "spring" house hidden among the trees, where chilly spring-water flowed around the containers keeping the milk cold. When removed later the cream would be skimmed off the milk to make butter.

As fields were cleared, more cows were added to the establishment, and often children could be seen, with their dog running beside them, bringing the cows each evening from the pasture to be milked in the barn. However, chasing the cows or making them run was forbidden as it would invariably spoil the milk.

Horses were not used in the beginning, but were acquired later. One or two good oxen were far superior for bush work as they needed less care, their food was less expensive, and they could handle heavy work. Before starting to work on the farm, however, their small cloven hooves had to be fitted with shoes made in two pieces. Being tremendously heavy animals, weighing between one thousand and two thousand pounds, they could not stand on three feet; so the blacksmith placed a sling under their bellies and, with a series of pulleys and a windlass, took the weight off their legs while fitting the shoes.

The oxen were indispensable for the heavy work in the clearing of new land. After having provided power for the stumping machine, they were used to haul the loose uprooted stumps to one side of the clearing where a stump fence was arranged. Large stones had to be loosened and pulled on a sled to a location where they would not be an obstruction, and logs were dragged into positions for the out-buildings. When the new field was finally ready for planting, and the oxen slowly drew the plough through the first furrows, the family, lined up along the new stump fence, beamed with delight.

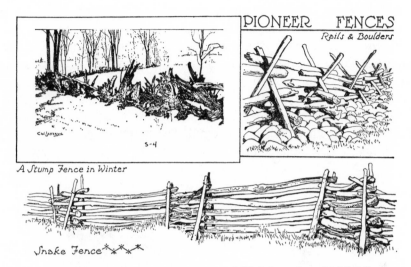

PIONEER FENCES

Rails & Boulders

A Stump Fence in Winter

Snake Fence ✕✕✕

C. W. Jefferys, Imperial Oil Collection

Hogs, sheep, geese, ducks, and turkeys were added as the farmer became more affluent. In 1806 the majority of the inhabitants agreed that hogs and cattle should be marked for identification and run at large in the country. Any stock trespassing on fenced land could be impounded, but the complaint had to satisfy the fence-viewer, who required that all fences be five feet high, constructed of vertical stakes and horizontal riders, and the bottom three feet of the fence should allow not more than four inches between rails. Before being butchered for market, the hogs were placed in pens and fattened. Those belonging to a miller were usually well fed with bran from the mill or the mash thrown out at the distillery.

Each spring the farmer pulled his sheep into the farm pond or a nearby stream or trough and scrubbed them thoroughly a few days before clipping off their winter fleece, which was then turned over to the women of the household, so that they could prepare the wool. The women also fed the geese, ducks, turkeys, and hens and collected the eggs, but the men kept the hen house clean with new straw. Each evening the women or children would shoo the ducks and geese found swimming in the pond and the hens pecking grain around the barn door into the hen house, to protect them from the skunks and weasels lurking around the farmyard.

IMPLEMENTS

All the early farm implements were very simple and made by the farmer, who took them to the blacksmith only to have the iron work added. Minor farm implements included long handled shovels, spades, hoes, garden rakes, and pitchforks, all made of iron and very clumsy and heavy. The forks for pitching hay were light and of wood; the manure forks were usually very heavy and made with broad tines.

The chief implements used by the farmers were the plough, harrow, roller, sickle, scythe, and scythe cradle, with the reaper and thresher coming later. The plough, used to turn up the ground in preparation

Early Harrow Frame & Teeth of Wood

C. W. Jefferys, Imperial Oil Collection

for planting, was first made of bent oak covered with iron; the harrow, used to break up the clods and cover the scattered seeds with soil, was originally a bunch of brush tied together and run over the loose ground. It was followed by a three-cornered drag, or V-shaped framework of wood, strengthened by cross-bars and fitted with iron teeth that scratched up the earth and was very manoeuvrable around the stumps still in the ground. After the stump removal, a square harrow made of wood with iron teeth was used.

A roller made of a heavy log with a tongue attached to hitch an ox or horse was very successful in levelling off the lumpy ground. The scythe, a long-handled implement with a one-edged cutting blade was used for mowing grass. The sickle, a short-handled knife with a two-foot semi-circular blade, was used for many years to cut grain. It was superseded by the scythe cradle, consisting of a scythe with a cradle, or framework, of wood attached for gathering the grain together as it

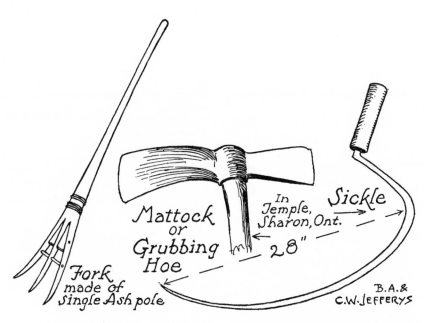

Fork made of Single Ash pole

Mattock or Grubbing Hoe

In Jemple, Sharon, Ont.

Sickle

28"

B.A.& C.W.JEFFERYS

C. W. Jefferys, Imperial Oil Collection

was cut. The farmer swung the cradle with a sweeping stroke cutting a swath of grain two-thirds of the scythe's length at one cut; the width of the cut was as far as he could stretch.

Men and women followed the cradler with a wooden hand-rake with long teeth. After pulling forward the sheaf that had fallen from the cradle, they raked under it and then went on to the next sheaf. When each person had enough for a bundle, a handful of stalks was twisted into a strand around it, binding it into a sheaf that was placed on end to dry. Ten or twelve of these sheaves made a shock. According to David Gibson in 1827 eight persons "in one afternoon . . . cut and bound one hundred shocks making twelve and a half sheaves to each, and four of us had only been a few days at such work."[2]

In 1831 the cradles were superseded by reaping machines that cut the grain while a man followed behind to rake it into sheaves. In 1845 a seat was added to the rear of the reaper for the man who raked, and in 1863 a self-raking attachment was used. Later machines cut the grain and bound it into sheaves; the modern combine has replaced all these old models.

After the grain sheaves had been stacked in the barn, threshing was undertaken by oxen tramping on the grain as described by David Gibson in the last chapter, or by men beating the grain with a hand

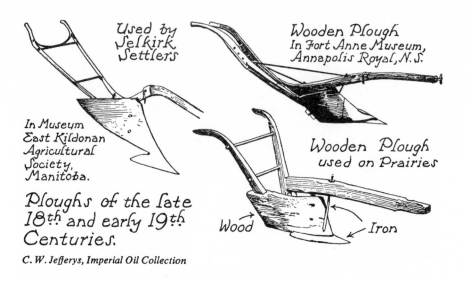

Used by Selkirk Settlers

Wooden Plough
In Fort Anne Museum,
Annapolis Royal, N.S.

In Museum
East Kildonan
Agricultural
Society,
Manitoba.

Wooden Plough
used on Prairies

Ploughs of the late
18th and early 19th
Centuries.

Wood   Iron

C. W. Jefferys, Imperial Oil Collection

flail to separate it from the shocks. Before starting the operation, how-ever, it was necessary to enclose the farm animals. The sheaves were spread over the barn floor and the barnyard rang with the "thud . . . thud" of the flail, a long stick joined with leather at the end, as the farmer swung it over his head and hit the heads of wheat time after time until all the grain was threshed out of the stocks. It was neces-sary, however, to turn it over with a fork and beat it again before the straw was gathered and stored to provide bedding for the animals and the grain was put into containers for winnowing.

A breeze was necessary in the early days for winnowing and clean-ing the grain as it was often accomplished by opening the barn door and tossing the grain into the air in a winnowing basket or blanket so that the grain fell back into the basket and the chaff was blown away on the wind. The grain was then stored in the granary until taken to the mill to be ground into flour.

The first threshing machines, requiring eight men to operate, were fitted with a narrow cylinder containing iron spikes to shake out the grain, which landed in a heap at the rear with the straw and chaff. The straw was raked, shaken, and piled outside, leaving the grain and chaff to be put into a fanning mill where they became separated after being run through the mill a second time.[3]

Thresher 1890

C. W. Jefferys, Imperial Oil Collection

Later on the steam engine and the separator were introduced. This new process required twelve men, not counting the thresher and his helper. As one man cut the bands on the sheaves, four or five others in the mow passed the sheaves to the man feeding the machine, who spread out each sheaf so that it fed into the cylinder evenly. Two or three men carried away the boxes of grain as they were filled by the machine and dumped them into the granary bins. If the remaining straw was placed outside in a stack, four or five men were needed to build it.[4] This machine was later replaced by the self-feeding separator that cut the bands and fed the sheaves into the cylinder, while the tractor took the place of the steam engine. Today this equipment, also, has been replaced by the combine.

The following account, part of the *Humber Valley Conservation Report*[5] published in 1948, is so complete in detail and gives so accurate a description of the phases of agriculture in North York that it has been included here:

> The development of agriculture in the Humber Watershed, although it resembled that of most of Ontario, was influenced by factors which did not operate elsewhere, or which did not have the same weight. The proximity of Toronto, with its market, and the relatively easy access to the Great Lakes-St. Lawrence export route determined to an appreciable extent what should be produced; the varied topography and soil types found in the watershed tended to diversify production.
>
> It is convenient to divide the development of farming into four phases—the pioneer stage, an era of grain growing, the transition to mixed farming, and the varied agriculture of the present day.

Assigning exact dates to these periods is difficult, since changes were made by individuals acting more or less independently of each other, and the over-all transitions were gradual.

The pioneer phase overlaps the grain growing period through much of its course. Clearing and cultivation spread generally northward from Lake Ontario and westward from Yonge Street, and its pace was that of the manual worker, so that, while the earlier settled portions of the watershed were already engaged in grain growing for export, the axe of the backwoodsman could still be heard ringing through the forest, perhaps only one concession farther back.

Farms were opened up more or less haphazardly, beginning with a few grants to discharged soldiers in 1794, but agriculture was not extensive until after the larger grants of 1819. Immigrants were counselled to choose their land according to the type of forest cover growing on it; stands of mixed hardwoods, with maple, elm, and beech predominating, were considered to indicate the best soil, while pine, hemlock and tamarack were to be avoided if possible. The oak plains, of which Scarlett's Plains on the Humber were an example, were generally regarded as less desirable, because of the scarcity of timber for building, fencing, etc. as well as because of supposedly inferior soil. The Humber Watershed contained rather large stands of the "undesirable" type than many other parts of Ontario. These considerations were in turn influenced by proximity to roads, Crown regulations regarding the cutting of pine, Crown and Clergy Reserves, and personal predilection; the total effect was to produce a patchwork of farms and woodland which existed for some time.

Once located, the settler commenced to clear his land, if possible starting in the spring. He would plant his first crop, usually potatoes and a little Indian corn, together with squashes and pumpkins, among the stumps of his first clearing, as soon as possible. It was customary not to cultivate at all; more could be accomplished by clearing further land, and the newly bared soil was usually rich enough and free enough from weeds to give a fair return without much attention.

Fall wheat would probably be sown among the stumps of the land cleared during the first summer, and then scratched into the unstirred soil with a harrow, made triangular for easier passage between the stumps, and with teeth slanting slightly back to facilitate dragging it over the roots. The rest of the first year would be fully taken up with the building of a log house, and a little fencing. Spring wheat might be sown the following year where the corn and potatoes had been the first.

After one crop of wheat, clearings were usually left in hay or pasture while the tree roots rotted; or they might be sown with oats, rye or buckwheat. Some farmers sowed wheat after wheat, but it was generally considered best to sow fall wheat on four or five acres of newly cleared land each year.[6]

After four or five years, the tree-roots in the earliest clearing would have decayed sufficiently to admit of a primitive sort of ploughing and another crop of wheat would be taken off, followed again by oats or rye or pasture. Finally about ten years after settlement, the stumps could be pulled by oxen, and the land taken into permanent cultivation under recognized methods.

During the period of twenty years or more characteristic of the pioneering phase, the farmer's income would be largely from his small wheat crops, supplemented by lumber, pork, potatoes and peas. Sawmills and grist mills were soon numerous on the Humber and its tributaries, in many cases preceding any great amount of settlement. Most of these, however, used timber from their own grants, so that the farmer's income from lumber was not great. The greater part of the timber from his clearings was burnt, usually at one of the old-time "logging-bees"; its ashes were another source of income as the Canadian potash industry expanded.

The early settler kept only enough livestock for his own needs, and gave them a minimum of care. A yoke of oxen were the customary work animals; most settlers preferred them to horses for bush work, and they required less care and expensive feed. A few cows, sheep and poultry completed the list of domestic animals. The early Canadian hog could only with difficulty be termed domestic. He ran almost wild in the forest, feeding on kitchen waste, or whatever he could find, and was often hunted with a rifle, like game, at killing time. Sometimes a settler would catch and pen his hogs about a month before butchering, to be fattened on corn, potatoes, or more probably peas. Millers were among the larger pork producers. Their pigs fed on mill waste, principally bran, for which there was almost no market in the early nineteenth century; if the mill, as was often the case, was associated with a distillery, there was also the spent mash for feed. In general, these hogs were far inferior to those of more settled areas, but were a mainstay of the backwoodsman. The Honourable Adam Fergusson, speaking to the Provincial Agricultural Association in 1849, claimed that: "Of all our domestic animals there are none in Canada to which we are all more indebted than the Hog. Without his aid, small progress could have been made in clearing the forest, by supporting the hardy pioneer of the backwoods."[7]

The market at York, organized in [1803], created a demand not only for pork and beef, but also for such commodities as oatmeal, potatoes and peas. It is known that farmers had raised pork for town consumption as early as 1794, as well as some fruit, most of which was grown around the mouth of the Humber.

The War of 1812 created an extraordinary demand for every kind of farm produce. The local supply was inadequate in any case and was further handicapped by the calls on farm labour for militia service and by destructive enemy action. Prices became prohibitive and government action became necessary. Distilling was forbidden for a time in an attempt to increase the quantity of wheat for milling. Large quantities of grain and cattle were imported, mostly from enemy territory. Nevertheless prices had finally to be "pegged" to prevent profiteering. The following are the official prices of farm products at York in 1815.[8]

PRICES OF FOOD AND FORAGE IN THE HOME DISTRICT

December 22nd, 1815

Flour – per barrel	£3.	10s.
Wheat – per bushel		12s. 6d.
Pease – per bushel		10s.
Indian Corn – per bushel		10s.
Barley – per bushel		10s.
Rye – per bushel		10s.
Oates – per bushel		5s.
Hay – per ton	£5.	
Straw – per ton	£3.	
Beef, on the hoof	£2.	1s.
Beef, Slaughtered, per pound		7½d.
Pork, Slaughtered, per pound		1s.

In spite of the difficulties under which the settlers were working, this extraordinary demand [for farm produce] had a favourable effect in some areas, which were not directly affected by the fighting. Farmers had every encouragement to improve their holdings and increase their production. The war prosperity helped to increase the demand for land in the Home District when immigration began again after the war. The inevitable fall in prices did not check this development to any noticeable extent.

As York grew into Toronto, this demand continued to increase, and its pressure was reflected by high prices in years of crop failure, as for instance after the "cold summer" of 1816, when flour sold at $16.00 a barrel.[9]

As larger and larger areas passed over from the clearing stage to settled agriculture, it became possible to produce crops for export. The Toronto area had a surplus of grain as early as 1804, and production increased steadily. Both York and Peel Counties came to regard wheat as their staple crop, and as long as the market remained reasonably good, there was little tendency to experiment with other lines. After the postwar depression and the bad years of

1819-22, conditions improved, and by early 1830's the prosperous wheat farmer was a typical figure in the Humber Watershed.

However, the market was subject to wide fluctuation; Britain, the principal importer of Canadian wheat, was committed to the protection of the British farmer, and good crops in England would reduce imports to almost nothing, as for instance in the years following 1832. In 1834-5 the price of wheat in Toronto dropped to a low of 32 cents a bushel, and the export demand did not resume its former proportions till after 1840.[10] Hard times were slightly alleviated by American demand caused by crop failures in the northern states, but the agricultural depression was severe. Nevertheless, farmers continued to rely on wheat. Livestock did not seem to offer a solution of their difficulties; American breeders could produce beef, mutton and pork for export at far lower prices; other lines could not be developed quickly enough to be of much help.

The 1840's brought a return of prosperity. Crops were good, and acreage increased. Preferential treatment under new British Corn Laws and small protective tariffs against American products helped. At the same time, the eastern portions of Ontario were forced to abandon wheat as a staple crop, because of the westward advance of the wheat midge, which is estimated to have reached the Bay of Quinte by 1849; this left the farmers of Central and Western Ontario at an advantage. The blight, which ravaged the potato crop from 1843 on, also resulted in higher prices for grain.

Although the early 1850's were not marked by prosperity, a general European crop failure in 1853 sent the price of Canadian grain skyrocketing, and the Crimean War, by cutting off supplies of Russian wheat, kept quotations high. Boom times continued until 1857, with wheat selling for anything up to $2.40 (in 1856). Farmers built new barns and houses, and acquired a considerable amount of the new farm machinery which had been developed over the past two decades. But this four year boom was in many senses the end of an era. The panic of 1857, coupled with a poor crop, plunged Ontario back into depression, and wheat growing, although it remained a major part of Ontario farming for a further twenty years, was never again to assume the relative prominence it had formerly held.

There were several reasons for this. During most of the wheat-growing period, the farmers of Peel and York Counties had had about a third of their cleared land in wheat, and it was necessary to practise very short rotations to maintain this figure. Some farmers used an exhausting rotation of wheat and naked fallow, while others continued to sow wheat year after year on the same fields, although this practise was not common in the Humber Watershed. In spite of the efforts of progressive agriculturists, and the publicity given them by the Provincial Agricultural Association after its formation in 1847, farmers continued these debilitating methods. Although intensive cultivation was not the rule, since labour was expensive and land cheap, there were evident on many farms the signs of soil exhaustion. Manure was little used, and such crop rotations as were practised were frequently abandoned in favour of sowing more wheat when the market was good. The wheat midge had advanced in Central Ontario by 1856, and was seriously reducing harvests. To many farmers it was already apparent that wheat could no longer be the mainstay of the agricultural community.

The lure of high prices continued to operate, however, after a dip in the early sixties, fall wheat rose to well over $1.50 and remained high until 1868, when it fell to ninety cents within a year. This was only a temporary drop; even during the depressed years following 1873, wheat rarely fell below $1.00, and was usually higher.[11]

The Census of 1871 shows a drop of almost a third in the proportion of land in wheat from 1861; but this does not appear to be a true picture. The fall in price of nearly $1.00 in 1868-70 undoubtedly caused farmers to curtail wheat production; and this assumption is borne out by the fact that while townships in the Humber Watershed had an average of 18.7 per cent of their land in wheat during this depressed period, the figure had risen by the time of the Census of 1881 to 25 per cent.[12] It seems evident, therefore, that the effects of soil exhaustion had been somewhat exaggerated by the farm publications of the fifties and sixties, although they were undoubtedly present.

PERCENTAGE OF IMPROVED LAND IN WHEAT

Township	1861	1871	1881	1891
Adjala	31.2	29.8	32.8	26.0
Albion	34.1	18.1	24.8	18.8
Caledon	35.1	24.1	29.2	19.0
Chinguacousy	33.5	18.0	22.7	14.5
Etobicoke	19.3	11.9	15.3	9.2
King	30.0	18.0	22.7	14.5
Mono	29.2	31.3	29.9	22.1
Toronto Gore	25.2	13.5	23.5	15.2
Vaughan	13.4	13.9	21.7	16.0
York	19.5	9.1	17.1	9.9
Average	27.0	18.7	24.4	16.7

Additional evidence of the situation prevailing is found in the increased acreage devoted to oats and barley. Barley replaced wheat in many instances, partially as a result of the wheat midge, partially because of the growing American demand for brewing, and continued to be grown in enormous quantities until the McKinley Tariff of 1890 reduced the trade to a fraction of its volume. This was particularly true·on the morainic soils of the upper watershed, which were better suited to coarse grain.

Since barley is a more debilitating crop than wheat, it seems evident that economic factors, rather than soil exhaustion, were primarily responsible for the change to mixed farming. However, it would not be untrue to say that many, if not most, of the farms on the watershed were deteriorating rapidly, and that harsh economic necessity saved them from inevitable ruin. For some areas, the change came too late, and the exhausted soil has not yet recovered.

The final blow to Ontario wheat farming came from the Canadian West. After 1880, Manitoba wheat came into the Toronto market (as well as the export trade) in competition with the local product, and consistently found preference, even at ten to twenty cents a bushel more than the best grades of Ontario fall wheat. Under these circumstances the Central Ontario farmer reduced his land in wheat to between five and fifteen per cent of his holdings, depending on the current price; this situation has continued to the present day. Barley, as has been noted, was not a large item of production after 1890, and oats, which continued to be produced as a major crop for a further thirty years, lost some of its importance with the passing of the horse but is still an important crop in the area.

The Growth of Mixed Farming

Just as grain growing overlapped the pioneer stages on the watershed, so the development of other lines began long before "wheating" had started to dip from its zenith. Potash became negligible as a source of income after 1850, when intensive exploitation of the Strassfurt deposits in Germany began; in addition to this, the timber was outstripping ashes in value as trees became scarcer. The farmer's self-sufficiency was rapidly disappearing; cookstoves, manufactured lamps, imported cloth, luxury items of food, farm machinery and all other appurtenances of a spreading civilization replaced the earlier home-made articles, and they had to be paid for in cash, sooner or later. The farmer began to cast about for sources of income beyond his annual crop returns.

Fairly large numbers of stock had been kept on some farms from the thirties, especially in the Black Creek area. One or two of the roomy log barns built about 1830 are still in use. Considerable numbers of working oxen were kept at that time, the number of oxen in Upper Canada in 1831 being greater than the number of horses. Good work oxen were nearly as valuable as work horses. The number of milch cows had increased considerably. The settlers in the Black Creek area were mostly from Pennsylvania where dairy-ing was well established before the Revolution and in some cases had brought cattle with them when they came to Canada. These cattle were of nondescript breed, however, and though hardy were not good producers of either milk or beef. On the less developed parts of the watershed stock-keeping was still in the primitive stage.

Livestock improvement began fairly early; the more well-to-do colonists had imported blood horses from England in the 1830's, and the breeding of light draught horses began soon after. Clydes-dales were imported from 1836 on, and had produced a strain of heavy draught horses generally conceded to be among the best in America. Cattle were improved rather more slowly. Grade Durhams and Devons were not uncommon in the early days, but were not bred in any great numbers. The state of cattle breeding was sum-med up in 1846 by the Honourable Adam Fergusson: "We find everywhere a mongrel mixture of Devons, Herefords, Lancashires and Normans, frequently indeed producing good milkers, and useful cattle for the yoke, but entirely devoid of any established qualities upon which the breeder can rely . . ."[13] Swine improvement was very slow; the Berkshire and Essex types eventually became well estab-lished, but buyers continued to complain of their quality until late in the nineteenth century.[14] Sheep received more attention, and good breeds were common in the forties, with Leicesters and Southdowns the favorites. This provided a profitable winter line for farmers of the Humber Valley from about 1850 on—the stall feeding of sheep for the Toronto market.[15]

Poultry improvement began about 1852, with the spread of the "hen fever" from the United States; eight or ten varieties of hens were introduced, as well as new types of ducks, geese and turkeys. It should be emphasized, however, that all the early improvements were on the farms of the well-to-do or the progressive farmer; the average Canadian was content with the native hybrids.

The American market stimulated livestock breeding; especially after the advent of the Reciprocity Treaty. The 1850's saw a steady rise in prices; even during the depression following 1857, prices were double those of the forties. Improvement in cattle, sheep and horses was rapid, as it became apparent that good breeds com-manded better prices, and actually cost less proportionally to feed for the market.

By the time of the Royal Commission on Agriculture of 1880, Ontario farms could boast of purebred Durhams, Devons, Ayrshires, Polled Angus, Herefords, Holsteins, Jerseys and other breeds. Horses and sheep were represented in equal variety. The Commissioners note, however, that a number of Ontario farmers, while realizing that higher prices would result, refused to improve their stock, because their assessment would be raised!

The extent of the over-all change in farming is indicated in the preamble to the chapter on General Farming in the Commission's Report:

> . . . the person to whom these remarks are more directly addressed is the man who carries on a system of mixed farming, working probably from one hundred to two hundred acres of land, raising just such crops as his soil seems best adapted for or his convenience demands, keeping his fifteen to twenty head of stock, and a few sheep and hogs, using the milk of his cows for the cheese factory or home dairy, and fattening two or three beasts annually for the market. Such men as these form by far the larger portion of the farmers of Ontario.

A foreign market for cattle developed after 1870 to replace the American, largely lost with the end of Reciprocity. Shipments of cattle to England were 32,680 head in the year 1879-80, and 50,000 in the calendar year 1880. A few horses were also shipped, but the bulk of the trade in other animals were in sheep, with shipments rising from 3,170 in 1877 to 109,506 in 1880.[16] Lambs continued to go to American buyers. The main cattle-raising section of the province did not include the Humber Watershed, but Peel and York Counties made considerable contributions to the trade. Its importance was largely in enabling the farmer to free himself from dependence on grain.

The breeding of horses for American mines and of lighter draught animals for street railways were two profitable lines. However, by the 1890's American needs were being supplied locally, and the electrification of street railways about the turn of the century cut off the other main demand. Sales of horses from Peel and York Counties fell to 2,469 in 1900. The demand for other draught animals went on, and increased until the years before the Great War, when York and Peel Counties were marketing about 5,000 horses annually. Since then there has been a gradual decline; the average number of horses sold in the 1920's was about 2,500 per annum.

It was the rise in the dairy industry which gave the farms of the Humber Watershed their largest single source of income in the twentieth century, and which materially aided in getting the farmer over the economic dislocation occasioned by the collapse of the grain market. Cheese and butter had been made for the Toronto market from the earliest days of settlement, on a home dairy basis, and small quantities were even exported. By 1850, dairying was becoming fairly important, although its profits were not to be compared with those of wheat farming. In the years from 1847 to 1851, butter production in the United Counties (York, Peel and Ontario) jumped from 428,297 lbs. to 1,877,577,[17] and a contemporary writer says that in Peel County "there are no large dairies, but most of the farmers manufacture considerable quantities of butter and cheese for sale."[18]

The factory system of cheese-making was introduced in 1864,[19] and although Peel and York Counties were never among the largest cheese producers, they did produce more than half a million pounds of cheese in the peak years of the mid-1890's. After that, the industry declined rapidly; Peel County is dropped from the returns shortly after the turn of the century, and York County just before the Great War, although the total production for the province continued to rise.

Creameries were founded in the late seventies, but were hampered by having to compete with the cheese factories; they had more success in the Toronto area than in other districts, but for a long time their production was small. The sale of milk in the city was almost completely unorganized, and even the most elementary sanitation was neglected. Gradually, however, better systems evolved. The livestock breeders looked with suspicion on the growth of the dairy industry, because it tended to make farmers neglect stock improvement, or to make them look for milking qualities rather than beef-producing strain.

The Royal Commission of 1880 tended rather to look on beef cattle as the most important aspect of cattle raising. In assessing various breeds of cattle, they remark: "For family use, or where the sole object is to command a high price for very choice butter, the Jerseys are a useful breed of very docile and manageable little animals, but to the ordinary farmer they are, and are likely to remain, practically unknown." Under the prevailing circumstances, it is understandable that they were unable to foresee the herds of Jerseys and Guernseys which dot the fields of milk-producing areas.

Their views would have been particularly applicable at the time to the Humber Watershed, where the proportion of milch cows was well below the provincial average in 1880. It was not, in fact, until after the Great War that farms in Peel and York Counties passed the average number of milch cows, although dairying was definitely a major source of income two decades before. The great specialization in dairying in the Eastern Counties and parts of Western Ontario made the provincial average fairly high, so that, although the farms on the Humber only average five or six milch cows per hundred acres in the thirty years before 1919, they were producing more milk and butter than many other parts of Ontario.

The Present State of Agriculture

Present day farming on the Humber follows the lines indicated by the transition to mixed farming.[20] It exhibits a well-balanced economy, with emphasis on dairying and dairy products both for the Toronto market and for export. Stock is produced for the packing houses, and market gardening is carried on to some extent. Horses continue to be bred in small quantities. With the advent of dairy farming, the farmer has had a fairly steady source of income, free from the wide fluctuations of a one-crop economy. Some farms have not yet recovered from the exhausting grain growing period, but there is a little improvement brought about by the increased amounts of manure available, and the retirement of precultivated land to pasture, which has tended to check erosion and rebuild to some extent the worked-out soil. Poultry are kept in increasing numbers, rising from 400,000 in 1896 to 1,500,000 in 1943,[21] and both eggs and fowl are another steady source of income.

No account of the development of agriculture would be complete without some mention of the part played by the Agricultural Societies, beginning with the formation of the Home District Agricultural Society in 1830, and carrying on to the present day, when Societies flourish in almost every township. These groups consistently worked for better farming practices, sponsored competitions, arranged for the importation of better seed and purebred stock, and in general aided the progress of agriculture. Although occasionally hampered by local jealousies and rivalries, their contributions have been of great value to the farmers of the Humber Watershed, as well as to Ontario as a whole.

NOTES

1 Split logs, three or four inches in thickness, hewn smooth on one side by a broad axe.
2 David Gibson, "Conditions in York County a Century Ago", Ontario Historical Society, *Papers and Records*, XXIV (1927), 364.
3 M. G. Sherk, ("A Canuck", pseud.), *Pen Pictures of Early Pioneer Life in Upper Canada* (Toronto: William Briggs, 1905), pp. 179-180.
4 Courtesy Mr. Harold Gray.
5 Ontario Department of Planning and Development, "Agriculture", *Humber Valley Conservation Report*, 1948, pp. 136-56.
6 R. L. Jones, *History of Agriculture in Ontario, 1613-1880* (Toronto: University of Toronto Press, 1946), p. 72.
7 Province of Upper Canada, Board of Agriculture, *Journals and Transactions*, I.
8 Public Archives of Canada, *Upper Canada Sundries*.

9 Jones, *op. cit.*, p. 37. As this is about the price fixed in 1815, the regulations may have still been in force.

10 *Ibid.*, p. 123.

11 "Commercial Reports", *Globe*, (1861-1891).

12 The lack of data between years in which the decennial census was taken makes the progress of agriculture a subject of conjecture. However, after 1882, when full data are available, there is a close correlation between the market price of grain and the proportion of land devoted to it by farmers, with the percentage of land in wheat rising the year following a price rise, and vice versa. It seems reasonable, therefore, to attribute the sharp drop in 1871 to the price fall just preceding. A complicating factor in estimating the importance of soil exhaustion is the fact that newly cleared land, or land formerly not used for wheat, was probably taken into cultivation and other land retired to pasture.

13 Province of Upper Canada, Board of Agriculture, *Journals and Transactions*, 1855-6.

14 Ontario, Royal Commission on Agriculture. Report (1881).

15 Woollen mills are found on the Humber from 1825. After 1845 several of these mills were cloth factories of some size.

16 Ontario, Royal Commission on Agriculture, Report (1881).

17 Province of Upper Canada, Board of Agriculture, *Journals and Transactions*, 1855-6, p. 332ff.

18 *Ibid.*

19 There was a cheese factory at Eversley by 1878.

20 1948; date of report's publication.

21 Figures quoted are for Peel and York Counties combined.

Aspects of Early Country Life

LIFE FOR THE FARMER AND HIS WIFE AND FAMILY WAS A CONTINUAL round of chores from the time they rose at dawn until they went to bed by candlelight.[1] Besides the regular farm work, carried on primarily by the farmer and his sons, and the smooth operation of the household by the women, there were also seasonal tasks which made systematic perseverance from day to day all the more important.

MAPLE SUGAR TIME

In late February and early March when the sap began to flow in the sugar maple trees, the settlers had one of the busiest seasons of the year obtaining their only sugar supply. In the early days maple sugar was the product rather than the syrup, and the whole family spent days in the sugar bush collecting and boiling the sap. A fence usually enclosed the area to prevent the cattle from upsetting the troughs or drinking the syrup, which could prove fatal to them.

With an axe a slit was made in the bark of the tree a few feet from the ground, and a wooden spout wedged into the hole carried the sap on warm, sunny days to a hollowed log trough or sap bucket. Sometimes a sugar house or rough shed, open on one side and covered with brush and boughs, was put up to provide shelter for the workers and watchers during cold weather. A large fire was built near it under a cross limb between two trees, from which two or three kettles were hung. When the troughs were nearly full of sap it was collected in pails or in a barrel on a sled and dumped into one of the large, iron kettles. As the sap began to boil it was watched closely by the workers, who stoked the fire to keep it boiling. They waited patiently for it to reach just the proper consistency when it could be poured into the moulds to harden. The children enjoyed the excitement of the occasion and were sometimes given a spoonful of syrup or had some ladled onto the snow to harden into maple sugar. *(Taffy)*

FLAX

About an acre of flax was sown by the settler to provide his family with linen for clothing and other necessities. The plants were pulled up by the roots, and the seeds were rippled or separated from the stalks. The latter were then soaked in soft water or exposed to the dew at night in order to "ret" or rot them. Water retting took from about eight to twenty days, and dew retting several weeks depending on weather conditions. During this process the true flax fibre remained uninjured. After a period of being spread out on the grass to dry, a handful of stalks was scutched or pounded between two beams called a flax brake, or "crackle," in order to crush and loosen the woody part of the stalk from the true flax fibre; then it was swingled, or beaten, by a large sword-shaped piece of wood to remove the remaining broken stalk. Finally the fibre was heckled, or hatcheled, by drawing the ends through strong heckle-teeth inserted in an oblong board. By the processes of combing and cleaning, the long fibres became dressed flax; the short or broken fibres became tow. The spinners of the family made these gray fibres into linen thread to be woven into cloth.

BUTCHERING AND THE SMOKE HOUSE

Butchering day was a very important and busy one on the farm, with all hands helping to get through quickly. A neighbour with a knack for butchering arrived early to help with the operation shortly after the farmer had put large kettles of water on the fire built in the yard and had sharpened his knives for the occasion. During the day six or eight pigs and cattle were killed. Hams, bacon, and other kinds of meat were cut in pieces and salted down in big tubs or barrels, while liver was cooked and made into liver-wurst and the meat around the bones of the feet and head was made into head-cheese. Finally meat for sausages was stuffed into its casing. After six or seven weeks the farmers took the hams, bacons, and sausages out of the brine and washed and hung them on the rafters in a small log or brick smoke house built for the purpose. A smouldering fire of beech, maple, or dried corn cobs was kept burning for about a week, filling the room with a pungent smoke that cured the meat. An ample supply was thus provided for the winter.

Other families hung their hams on ropes near the stove pipe which supplied heat to the second floor of the house. On one occasion a maid stoked the kitchen stove to do some baking in John Hogg's farm house in Don Mills, and because of the excessive heat the house caught on fire. The ropes holding the hams gradually burned through, causing them to thump to the floor and so warn the family below that the house was on fire.

CIDER MILLS AND CIDER MAKING

As soon as the settler was able to clear his land, orchards were set out. Although the quality of fruit was improved later with the introduction of grafting techniques, with the availability of apple seed brought from Pennsylvania a reasonably successful fall harvest could be expected. A portion of the harvest was stored for winter; another was set aside to be made into cider. The milling process was relatively simple but not all farmers had the time or the resources to construct one. Here the sour apples were washed and dumped into a hopper where they were crushed between large wooden wheels driven by horsepower. The pulp remaining was placed in a press which squeezed out the juice. At one cent per gallon of cider produced, milling became a profitable enterprise.

Henry Snider, of Elia, built a screw-press cider mill in 1840 (now at Pioneer Village) that had a capacity of five hundred gallons a day. After the apples were crushed in the grinder the crushing box was loaded alternately with straw and crushed apples. When filled "two or four men walking on a raised platform rotated the huge iron screw downward."[2] As the cider poured out of the mill it went through a hair sieve partly filled with straw, removing all impurities.

Most of the cider was used for making apple-sauce or apple-butter. The housewife oversaw the long day's process of boiling down the cider while stirring it constantly with a paddle. Sweet apples, pared, cored, and sliced, were added periodically during the day until a syrupy consistency was reached. Then cinnamon, nutmeg, or other spice was added to taste, and the finished apple-butter stored in stone crocks for future use. Some of the cider, however, was stored in wooden casks, and after several months of fermentation it provided a refreshing drink at bees and other gatherings, that is, until many of the persons who frequented them were influenced by temperance sentiments. The temperature of some of the stored cider was allowed to rise above fifty-nine degrees to provide vinegar for cooking.

CUTTING ICE

Each winter ice was cut out with a hand-saw on the mill ponds of the Don and Humber Rivers, though never on still water ponds, which were relatively impure. After having been cut, it was hauled by sled to an ice house built on the farm close to the homestead, and as each block was stored it was covered with several inches of sawdust. When needed for household or dairy use, the chunks were pulled out, chopped to the required size, thoroughly washed, and carried pinched in ice tongs to the ice box or milk house.

THE BAKE-OVEN

In many respects the kitchen was the centre of family life, and a large kitchen with a brick fireplace and a built-in bake-oven was the joy of every housewife who had previously baked her bread in a long legged bake-kettle surrounded by red hot coals. With the new bake-oven, a fire was kindled inside and kept burning for two or three hours before the oven was to be used. When the dough was ready the coals were raked out with a scraper and broom, and the lady of the house tested the temperature by placing her hand in the oven. If she could not keep it there until she counted to twenty, the dough was shovelled into the oven on a long-handled, wooden peel and placed on the oven floor to bake. When the batch was finished the peel was used again to draw the bread out, and the pleasant aroma from the kitchen put the whole family in a happy frame of mind.

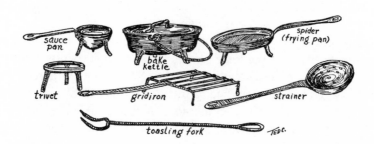

BUTTER MAKING

After the farmer had acquired a cow, butter, like bread, was easily made, and butter making was added to the women's chores. Cream is made up of tiny globules of fat that float to the top when milk has been standing for any length of time. The housewife skimmed the cream from the milk pails and poured it into a churn. In pioneer days this was a slender, round, wooden utensil made by the cooper, with a dasher, or rod, that slipped through a round hole in the tightly fitted cover. Attached to the end of the dasher was a round piece of wood with holes in it. As the rod was lifted up and down with a regular motion the cream was stirred and beaten until the fat particles, or butter, began to collect and float to the top. The process continued until as much of the cream as possible had been churned into butter, and when the cover was removed the butter was lifted out with a large, wooden ladle. The buttermilk remaining was poured into waiting cups for the children who had taken part in the churning.

Mrs. Watson, who lived in Emery, was an expert butter maker and on cool days made many trips on foot to the St. Lawrence Market with a basket of butter on her head. The distance was sixteen miles, and she returned home the same day.

PRESERVING

During the summer and early fall the women collected vegetables from the garden and berries and fruit from the bushes and trees and spent many days over a hot fire preserving them. The winter supply of food depended on what could be prepared at this time, as it was impossible to run to the store for fresh fruit and vegetables. Jams and jellies were made and stored in a cold location in the cellar; barrels of apples were placed in a dry, cool place away from rats and mice. Vegetables such as potatoes, carrots, and turnips were stored in root cellars built for the purpose underground, below frost level.

CANDLES, CANDLE MAKING, AND LANTERNS

The women of each household had to keep a constant supply of candles in the house to provide light for their families and for the barnyard every night. The first candles, tallow dips, were made by twisting strands of cotton twine, attaching them to a stick dipped in melted beef or sheep tallow, and hanging them up to harden. The process was repeated over and over again during the day until the candle attained the proper size.

The pioneer women were familiar with the small, grayish bayberries that could be boiled down into a pure, clear tallow. Bayberry candles kept their shape during the hot summer, and the spicy aroma given off when they were extinguished made them very desirable.

Fortunately for the women, before very long, candles were made

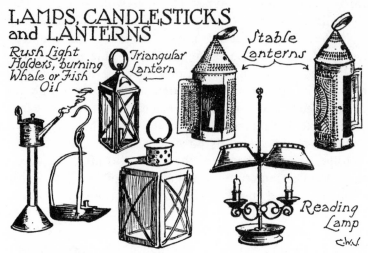

C. W. Jefferys, Imperial Oil Collection

in tin moulds. A cotton wick was stretched through the mould, tied in a knot at the pointed end, and attached to a stock at the large end. The mould was filled with melted tallow and set to cool; when hardened the candles were drawn out and put away in a candle box. Snuffers were used to cut off the charred part of the wick to make the candle burn brighter; an extinguisher was available to place over the flame to snuff out the light.

Tin lanterns provided with a tallow candle and holes for the light to shine through were used in the barns and stables. Lanterns with glass sides were developed later, but both were very dangerous because so much dry hay was stored around the barn.

SOAP MAKING AND WASHING

The housewife threw all scraps of grease, fat, and pork rinds in a barrel; when enough had accumulated, a whole day was spent in making a batch of soap. According to an old superstitution the moon had to be just right or the soap would not have the proper consistency.

Lye was made in an ash leach or barrel in the yard. To make a leach the farmer knocked the bottom out of the barrel, placed it on a board raised above the ground, and tilted it so that the finished lye ran into a pail placed underneath. Lye was made by putting a layer of straw in the barrel, then a quantity of lime, and finally hardwood ashes. Water was poured over the mixture; as it soaked through, it dissolved the caustic potash so that the lye ran through to the pail.

A pole hung between two crotched posts held a large, iron kettle of lye and grease over a brisk fire. As the mixture boiled the housewife stirred it constantly; if hard soap was required rather than soft, jelly-like soap, a little salt and resin were added and the mixture had to be boiled longer. Twenty pounds of grease added to lye made from about six bushels of ashes, yielded a small barrel of soft soap.

On washday, buckets of water had to be hauled from the well to the house and heated over the fire before the housewife could do the washing. The same applied to the luxury of hot baths for the family. It is no wonder that bath night occurred but once a week on Saturday nights so that the family might clean up before going to church on Sundays. A tub was placed in front of the blazing fire, and as the members of the family immersed themselves one after the other the water became increasingly murky. It is doubtful if the last person in the tub was any cleaner when he came out. In the early days troughs of water in the yard were used for daily cleanliness, while in winter the kitchen supplied the same convenience. In later years bedroom washstands equipped with basins and pitchers of water made the adage "cleanliness before Godliness" a little easier to achieve.

Spinning and Weaving

With the introduction of sheep, spinning wheels and looms were set up, and wool was spun into yarn for weaving and knitting. After the wool was cleaned, sheared, sorted, greased, and carded as described in the chapter on the woollen mill, spinning or twisting the wool into yarn was accomplished with the aid of the spinning wheel, which provided a mechanical way to rotate a spindle. The spinner paced back and forth beside the large wheel which she whirled with her right hand after guiding a length of carded wool on the spindle with her left hand, drawing the wool out into yarn.

When the spindle was full, the wool was wound off on a niddy-noddy, or hand reel, ready to be knit into garments or woven into blankets or cloth to be made into clothing. This was done by the family, an itinerant weaver, a neighbour with a loom, or a woollen mill which also handled the fulling and dressing of the cloth. After spinning for a full day and, in the process, walking four miles pacing back and forth handling the yarn, the housewife had prepared enough wool to weave from two to four yards of cloth or knit ten pairs of mittens and eight pairs of stockings.

A smaller wheel used for spinning flax had a treadle worked by foot, so the operator was able to sit down while spinning. A bunch of flax was fastened to the distaff, pulled off by the spinner, attached to the spindle, and gradually lengthened. This thread became pure linen which was woven into cloth for shirts, pantaloons for men, sheeting, table cloths, and napkins.

CLOTHING

The articles of clothing which the settlers brought with them gradually wore out and had to be replaced with clothing made from leather or fur. When the early pioneers settled in North York coats and breeches were made of deerskin, caps of some thick fur like raccoon, while shoes were replaced with buck moccasins like those worn by the Indians. Heavy bear skins kept the family warm on cold winter nights until sheep could supply wool to be woven into blankets and geese could furnish down for eiderdowns.

With the introduction of wool and flax new garments were made of homespun grey; linsey-woolsey, a very scratchy, coarse mixture of linen and wool, was a favourite cloth for women's dresses and children's clothes. Grandmothers and aunties sat before the fire on cold winter nights, their knitting needles clicking continuously as they tried to supply the demands of the family for stockings, mittens, caps, mufflers, and sweaters.

Men and boys dressed alike in roomy box-coats with big pockets and brass or horn buttons. Their pantaloons or trousers were sometimes made by an itinerant tailor. On the farm they dressed for comfort in overalls tucked into calf-high, laced boots, collarless shirts worn open at the neck, and red bandanas knotted tightly to prevent the beards of barley from crawling down their necks during the threshing season.[3] In winter some men wore cloaks with bright red Russian cravats and sealskin caps with ear flaps pulled down.[4] Settlers arriving from England wore knee breeches and long stockings.

The women's hair was styled in plaits, waterfall curls, or in a coil on the nape of the neck. Ear-rings were popular; poke bonnets, or beaver, leghorn, or straw hats were worn in the city according to the season. Mary Gapper mentions in her diary that "the women here rarely wear caps except the very old ones and tie a handkerchief over their heads when they go out, unless formally dressed for the occasion in which case they wear bonnets of an ugly fly-away fashion—their winter gowns are generally dark flannel of the country."[5]

The Primitive Methodist women wore plain dresses. A collar or square of white Brussels net was doubled in half under the dress and laid in folds above it at the neck. Plain attire was suitably in keeping with Godliness; frills, flounces, flowers, feathers, ornaments, or jewellery of any kind except a wedding ring, were to be avoided. Lilac and buff caps were later replaced by black ones. A fine woollen shawl was worn as an outer garment in winter; a black satin shawl, either brocaded or plain, served the same end in summer. Coats were never worn until late in the century, and then a shawl was often put over them so that the women would not appear too giddy.[6] As infants always wore caps people were scandalised if a child's head was bare. Older women also wore white caps during the day and special night caps for sleeping. Great pains were taken to iron and starch the frills on the borders of the cap and the ribbons that tied in a bow under the chin.

FURNISHINGS

In the 1860's carpets were seldom seen, and the women of the neighbourhood vied with each other as to who would have the whitest floor. It was scrubbed weekly whether it needed it or not, and cleaning went on all the year round. The bricks around the fireplace were reddened every two weeks with Venetian red mixed with buttermilk, while the andirons were polished with blacklead.

The brass candlesticks, snuffers, and trays "were like beaten gold, ready and waiting for company."[7] Two candles with their flickering yellow light were thought enough to illuminate a room; the best candlesticks held "number six" candles, which meant that there were six candles to a pound of wax. When coal oil lamps appeared they were very dangerous as they might explode without warning, so only grown-ups were allowed to light them.

A couple of carpet strips, if available, were used to furnish the spare bedroom. Also featured were a chair, a small washstand with a large wash basin, a huge pitcher filled with water when a guest was about to arrive, a soap dish containing a cake of homemade soap, and a matching chamber pot kept in the cupboard underneath. The bed was a delight to childish eyes; in summer it had a white roof with a deep wide-fringed valance at front and back. The winter curtains of drab moreen trimmed with blue velvet surrounded the bed and reached to the floor. They could enclose the guest or could be looped back at the head and foot.[8] The spare room was cleaned regularly. In the winter rugs were cleaned by pulling them outside, whisking snow on each one, and then sweeping them briskly.

EARLY HARDSHIPS

William Marsh and his wife Susannah emigrated to Canada from England, and like all early settlers had to overcome many hardships during the first years. Marsh worked at the Narrows of Lake Simcoe, while his wife remained in York Mills near St. John's Church and ran a small school. Excerpts from a letter to her husband depict early living conditions in 1830.

> I have not been able to get the wheat thrash'd yet and am obliged to borrow flour, I tried to get a Barrell or half a barrell of flour of Mr. Shepard and told him I would pay him in wheat but he wanted to make up all he could to send to Montreal so did not accommodate me. Mr. Sheppard at the Tavern sent me a load of wood, he has engaged Mr. Ricketts to help him make brick. Mr. Van Nostrand has engaged to plough the garden for me and I applied to Mr. Ricketts to plant it but did not get an answer. Eber White has a good cow and calf to sell Mrs. Van Nostrand tells me age between 6 & 8 price 20 dollars, Bull calf 2 or 3 weeks old weaned—he is obliged to sell to make up money to pay for a horse he has purchased, do not intend keeping her to wait your answer if he finds a purchaser before. Mrs. Sheppard and her brother Paul gone up to old David Wilsons feast. Mary and Anna must have some shoes ?where had I best get them—.
>
> Cornelius and John Van Nostrand is going up to the landing on Tuesday with an English familys goods who is going to settle the other side of the lake, he wants four waggons I have not heard his name or whose waggons is going besides theirs—. I have been to a quilting and 2 picking bees since you left.[9]

In another letter to her sister in England a week later Mrs. Marsh tells of the kindness of her neighbours.

> Marsh was taken with intermitting fever which was followed

by the ague which laid him by the whole of last summer—but
nothing could exceed the kindness of the people to us in our poor
afflicted state—and they secured our crops for us whilst Marsh lay
sick in his bed (notwithstanding the high price of labour at that
season of the year) without a farthing expense to us—and we had
more than 120 bushels of the finest wheat you ever saw—brought
home to us as our half of the crop. . . .

   Tavern keeping is good business here also storekeeping wearing
apparel very reasonable, labour dear—a dollar a day in harvest,
half a dollar at other seasons of the year, always board—I wish
thousands of our English poor were here.[10]

NOTES

1 Sherk, *op. cit.*

2 Dorothy Duncan, *Pioneer Village, Black Creek Conservation Area*, p. 10.

3 Ontario, Department of Tourism and Information, Centennial Planning Branch,
   A Century of Fashion.

4 Mary Gapper O'Brien, journal, February 3, 1829.

5 *Ibid.*, January 14, 1829.

6 Jane Agar Hopper (Mrs. R. P.), *Old-Time Primitive Methodism in Canada* (Toronto:
   William Briggs, 1904), pp. 254-255.

7 *Ibid.*, p. 231.

8 *Ibid.*, p. 64.

9 Susannah (Susan) Brown Marsh, correspondence, 1819-1836. Transcript copy in
   The North York Historical Society files, courtesy of Mrs. H. A. S. Molyneux.

10 *Ibid.*

Bees, Church Socials, and Temperance Meetings

AMUSEMENTS WERE SIMPLE; THEY CENTRED IN THE HOME AND varied with the season of the year. They included bees of various kinds[1] as well as horseback riding, skating on the ponds, sleighing parties, taffy pulls, and church socials. Most such events ended with games or dancing, much to the delight of the young people. Temperance meetings held in the schoolhouse or Temperance Hall took the form of speeches, debates, and hymn singing.

THE LOGGING BEE

The logging bee was one of the first community efforts. All the men in the neighbourhood were invited. The settler provided a jug of whiskey for refreshment as well as iron-wood handspikes prepared a day or two beforehand to make it easier for the men to roll the logs into piles. Each guest brought his oxen, with a big logging chain draggind behind. The chains were placed around the logs which were then dragged between the stumps to a designated pile. These were set on fire when stacked to a height of three or four feet; the youngsters gathered around and roasted ears of corn, cracked jokes and told stories. If the field were large, the host divided the men into two gangs each with a section of ground to cover. A jug of whiskey or a new yoke for the oxen was offered as a prize for the gang that finished first. Excitement ran high as the jug of grog was passed among the men tackling the job. Often these bees ended in a spree or dance that lasted till three or four in the morning.

THE RAISING BEE

The raising bee always caused great excitement. If the barn or house were large, from fifty to a hundred men were invited as well as their wives and families. The housewife spent days beforehand preparing a feast that was served outside near the new building on saw-horse tables made of boards. Whiskey was always provided until temperance sentiments prevailed and tea, coffee, and temperance beverages became the accepted liquid refreshment. The master-builder, a man with a powerful voice that could be heard by all, did the calling and directing. If it were a large barn, captains were appointed and sides chosen with one team racing the other to see which could complete the work first, and be allowed to go to dinner first. When the hearty meal of meat pie, ham, sausages, potatoes, corn, turnip, bread, fruit pies, and cakes was devoured, a dance was held on the floor of the newly-raised barn.

THE HUSKING BEE

In autumn, after the corn was stripped off its stocks and hauled into the barn, the neighbours—men, women, boys, and girls—were invited to a husking bee. The guests arrived at about six or seven o'clock and spent the evening husking the corn. The ears were thrown in piles on one side of the barn; the husks, piling up in front of the workers, were carried out periodically by a member of the host's family as they accumulated. Tin lanterns with candles hung around the barn furnished light for the occasion. About ten o'clock everyone adjourned to the house for refreshments: cider, cookies and cakes were enjoyed, and dancing or a few rounds of charades. Romance flourished, adding to the excitement of the younger children, who teased and played pranks on the young couples. After the husking, the corn was placed in a corn crib built on posts, several feet from the ground, covered with sheet iron or tin to form a flange so that the rats and mice could not reach the corn. The sides made of slats allowed the air to circulate and prevented the corn from heating or moulding. The ears of corn were left in the crib until needed to feed the pigs and fatten the poultry for market.

THE PARING BEE

The paring bee was very popular in the fall of the year when apples had to be pared and cored for drying, making applesauce, or apple-butter. Young and old entered into the fun, seeing who could peel the most apples or who could get the peeling off in one piece. Anyone who succeeded twirled the peel over his head and let it drop. The letter which it resembled as it lay on the floor was supposed to be the initial of his, or her, future spouse. Paring machines were in use by 1870, and team competition became popular. The boys operated the paring machine; the girls did the coring. After those present finished their work, tea, cakes, and cookies were enjoyed; then the fun began. Sides were taken for "Jenkins Says," a game in which one side tried to guess which hand of the opposing team held a penny after the Captain called "Jenkins says hands up" and then "Jenkins says hands down." The noise always added to the occasion so that the opposing side could not hear the penny hit the table as hands were flattened out on it. "Musical Chairs" followed if there was a fiddle in the house, or "Spoons," another favorite game beautifully portrayed in one of Goya's paintings. This was supposed to be a very quiet game, but giggles and squeals helped the blindfolded person identify his prisoner as he felt her with a long handled, wooden spoon.

THE QUILTING BEE

The women as well as the men helped each other with certain chores which provided enjoyable social gatherings for every one concerned. The quilting bee was held in the early afternoon; the married and single women gathered at a friend's house and spent the afternoon quilting a complete piece of patchwork. When they arrived they found the frame set up and ready with the patchwork laid over a lining filled with layers of wool or cotton and fastened to a frame of four long wooden bars set on chairs. Quilting was pleasant work because the women had a good gossip; their husbands and young men were usually invited for tea, cookies, and cake.

THE PLUCKING BEE

Every farmer kept a flock of geese to provide down for pillows and feather ticks. Beginning in June the geese were generally plucked once every seven weeks by the women of the family. Afternoon bees were often held, when the neighbour women arrived to help with the plucking. A stocking was placed over the head of each goose as it was plucked, to stop the poor creatures from biting. The feathers were put into pillowcases or ticks which were sewn across the ends when filled. Afterwards the guests enjoyed tea and cakes and a good laugh with the husbands who came to the festivities.

CHURCH SOCIALS

Tea and missionary meetings held in church halls were outstanding events for feasts, music, and speeches. People from other church congregations journeyed by sleigh to these meetings to enjoy the fine food, visit with friends, and catch up on all the news. Rivalry burned fiercely between communities as to who could supply the best oyster supper or the most elaborate tea table. The suppers were held in winter when the oysters could be shipped in barrels from the Atlantic coast. Those attending paid just twenty-five cents for all that they could eat, as at this time oysters were only twenty-five cents a quart. Speeches and singing followed these events. Newtonbrook Methodist Church once held a social at which the table was adorned with nine three-layer cakes and between three hundred and four hundred puff pastry tarts.

In June strawberry festivals were held in the church driving shed. The cost again was twenty-five cents and it included games such as the three-legged race, the potato race, football, tugs-of-war, supper with strawberries, ice-cream and cake, and speeches. The following night the charge was ten cents when every one came back to eat the left-over food.

The Baptist picnics in the York Ridge Road area were very popular among the young people. In the afternoon games were played including throwing the bean bags through a hole, the sack race (when legs were tied into a sack and one had to hop from one end of the field to the other), the egg and spoon race, and relay races. By the end of the afternoon everyone was ready for the hearty picnic supper spread out for all to enjoy.

For many years the Bethesda Presbyterian Church held a garden party each summer, by turn in the gardens of various members of the congregation. For twenty-five cents a supper of sandwiches, pickles, salads, pie, or strawberries with ice-cream and cake was served following an evening of recitations and speeches. If a field were available, a soccer match between the local boys and a team from another area was arranged.

Various Primitive Methodist Church congregations met occasionally for field meetings[2] in a grove of trees. A farmer's wagon was used as a pulpit, and the worshippers sat on plank seats built for the occasion. Wagons filled with young people drove miles to these outings where all enjoyed themselves telling stories, laughing and joking with their friends. Families brought baskets of food for dinner and supper as the services continued throughout the day and early evening.

A Christmas tree party took place each year with the children taking part in a programme and the adults entering into the fun. Mrs. Timothy Gray of Don Mills was particularly fond of Spanish onions, a fact well known by some of the local farmers, who wrapped a few and placed them on the Christmas tree for her. Not to be outdone by these pranksters, the next year Mrs. Gray decided to take revenge on them. She made a batch of tarts. The filling was in a pot on the back of the stove when her son Harold came in. His mother asked him to bring in from the wood shed some thin chips of wood and some sawdust, which she placed in the filling. When the tarts were finished, they were wrapped and finally placed under the Christmas tree for a couple of farmers. Imagine their surprise when they bit into them!

TEMPERANCE MEETINGS

Excessive drinking was prevalent among the pioneers. It served as an escape from the rigours of clearing the land and making homes in the wilderness; men enjoyed a well-earned drink after a building or logging bee. Many early settlers were unsuited to the lonely and demoralizing existence; others were plagued with shortage of money. The inn which provided food, drink, and lodging for the traveller was also the community centre for the settler. Poor roads meant that only short distances could be travelled in a day; so before the building of the railroads, the taverns in Upper Canada averaged about one to a mile.

Drunkenness and its results became such a serious social problem that a spontaneous wave of temperance swept North America during the second quarter of the nineteenth century.[3] Temperance organizations in the United States soon extended their work into the British provinces. In Upper Canada alone in 1842 there were 147 distilleries and ninety-six breweries serving a population of less than 500,000. After the organization of the first temperance society in Upper Canada in 1828, the movement soon gained quite a following until, by 1832, approximately 100 societies were recorded with a membership of 10,000.

Attendance at temperance meetings ranged from seven to twenty-five. A reading from the Bible began every meeting; accounts were approved and new members proposed and subsequently initiated if accepted by ballot. Singing of songs and hymns provided the settler with an outlet for his emotions. Social evenings were arranged with "ice-cream, bananas and lemons as refreshments."[4] Accounts covering oysters and biscuits suggest oyster suppers from time to time. Many families really did benefit from the movement, but perhaps its greatest value was its meeting of the settler's need for social life. The programme at these socials included mouth organ solos, readings, songs, recitations, debates, and speeches. The speakers covered a wide variety of subjects ranging from the federation of Upper and Lower Canada to whether farmers should keep or sell their stock and crops and a debate on marriage *versus* bachelordom.

NOTES

1 Sherk, *op. cit.*
2 Hopper, *op. cit.*, pp. 118-119.
3 M. H. Garland and J. J. Talman, "Pioneer Drinking Habits and the Rise of Temperance Agitation in Upper Canada prior to 1840". Ontario Historical Society, *Papers and Records,* XXVII (1931), 341-361.
4 Records available courtesy of Miss Marion Coulson.

Mills and Distilleries

IN 1793 WATER-POWER WAS PLENTIFUL AND LAND OWNERS WERE permitted to use their water-rights for mills, provided that navigation was not hindered or the passage of fish blocked. Speculation no doubt developed because a new regulation was initiated in 1820 prohibiting "Land Boards from locating any mill sites until security had been given for the erection of mills."[1] Obtaining a mill site was a tremendous boon to the fortunate settler lucky enough to be granted one.

SAW MILLS

In 1793 York Township was a dense forest of huge "pine, beech, hard and soft maple, white and red oak, black and white birch, basswood, ironwood, hickory, cedar, elm, ash, cherry, tamarack,"[2] and many other varieties of trees.

Pit-sawing was the first method used by the settler to convert timber into boards. He dug a large pit, or used the bank of a river, built a platform above it, and pulled a log forward over the edge. The log was cut with a two-handled, six to eight foot whipsaw by a pitman standing beneath it in the pit, and a friend, the top sawyer, standing on the platform. Eye shields were found indispensable because sawdust dropped constantly into the eyes of the poor man in the pit. The top sawyer had to be a skilled workman who could direct the saw along a chalked line. To saw twenty-five boards was a heavy day's work for two men.

Saw and grist mills sprang up along the Black Creek and the Don and Humber Rivers, often together with a pond supplying the power. By first erecting a simple frame saw mill, the miller could later provide lumber for a grist mill, a much more substantial building. During spring freshets the saws rasped and screamed out over the country side twenty-four hours a day, but in the summer, when the water was low, it became necessary to shut off the saw mill to provide enough power for the grist mill. Mill· ponds with dams constructed of posts, logs layered at right angles, mud, and planks, held the water supply for the mill. They also stored the heavy logs, water-cured them by removing the sap or pitch, prevented the ends from cracking, and minimized insect damage by loosening the bark under which the insects burrowed. The maintenance of the mill-dam entailed great expense and hard work as it was washed away frequently due to frost action and the force of the water during spring freshets or a flood.

Operation of the new mill itself, while an improvement over pit-sawing, was still strenuous and sometimes hazardous. First, a man jumped into a small punt tied near the mill, chose his log, and floated it to a wooden ramp by pushing it with a long, hooked pole. Here it was chained at the butt and drawn by a windlass to the sawing floor of the mill, where the miller rolled it onto a movable cradle or carriage on which it would be cut. In later years the log was floated onto a submerged cart just off the ramp and then hoisted up to the saw.

Power to drive the saw was obtained from water flowing down a wooden mill-race (or flume) through the lower floor of the mill to a penstock, a kind of miniature dam, above the water-wheel. When ready to saw the miller raised the sluice on the penstock, and, the water flowed downward pushing on the wooden blades or buckets, thus turning the wheel. As the wheel turned, an axle was rotated which moved the gears and belts of the wooden-framed, vertical muley saw. The water-wheel, although sometimes exposed, was often boxed in to protect it from excessive dryness in summer and from frost and snow in winter.

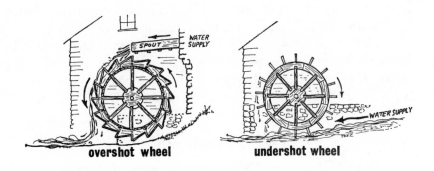

overshot wheel　　　　　**undershot wheel**

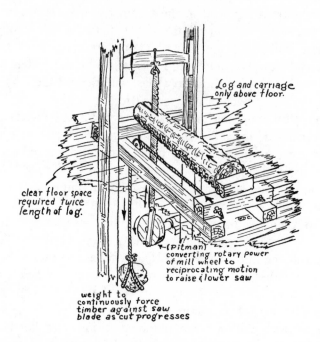

As the saw moved up and down cutting the huge log, the movable cradle carried the log forward drawn by a couple of weights hung on ropes, or a ratchet which took its power from the wheel. The sawing area had to be more than twice the length of the timber to be cut. The water spilling over the water-wheel flowed quickly along a tail-race until it met the river below the dam.

Houses, furniture, and domestic fuel were necessary in the beginning and as commerce developed the demand for fuelwood increased. In order to operate brick factories, bakeries, breweries, distilleries, the blacksmiths', steamboats on the lakes, and finally railway engines, great quantities of wood were required for fuel. Other important uses for lumber included wooden utensils, agricultural implements, barrels, pails, staves, laths, vehicles and boats, as well as planks for various plank roads in the Township, fences to keep the animals from wandering, and railway ties.

The Grist Mills

The grist or flour mill was usually a three- or four-storey building, about forty-five by thirty-five feet with one, two, or three run of mill-stones. Until a convenient mill was erected, the settler was forced either to carry his grain considerable distances, or crush it himself in a hollowed-out stump using a wooden masher.

Horses were scarce and roads too full of stumps for wagons to travel, so the farmer wanting his grain ground properly spent most of the day trudging to and from the mill through the forest trails or along Yonge Street carrying the sack of grain across his shoulders. Since these early grist mills operated along side of saw mills, the distant whine of the saw through the woods must have been a welcome sound as the settler approached his destination. While he waited for his flour he dropped in to chat with the cooper, who was making barrels, tubs, and pails in his workshop, and he visited the blacksmith, who was busy fixing equipment for the mill and making edge tools, ploughs, harrows, and cooking pots for the neighbourhood settlers. Sometimes when it was too late to return home the same day, the settler spent the night with the miller.

The journey home from the mill was made a little easier by the subtraction of the miller's fee from the settler's load of meal. Because money was scarce the rate of toll or payment in kind at the mill was set by the Legislative Assembly, giving the miller a definite percentage of flour for his labour. This system of bartering, with no money exchanged, continued for many years.

As the roads improved and the farmers were able to buy horses, wheat was hauled to the mill in wagons, unloaded at a large side door,

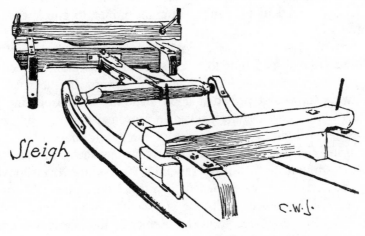

Sleigh

C.W.J.

C. W. Jefferys, Imperial Oil Collection

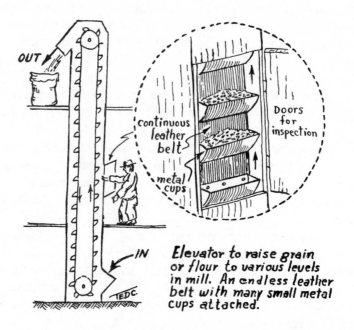

OUT

continuous
leather
belt

metal
cups

Doors
for
inspection

Elevator to raise grain
or flour to various levels
in mill. An endless leather
belt with many small metal
cups attached.

IN

and weighed on a beam scale before being hoisted to the top floor
where it was cleaned and stored in bins or put immediately into the
hopper for grinding. Occasionally, when the mill was very busy, the
farmer's wagons had to wait in line for the miller to check each load
of grain.

As early as 1817 Thomas Arnold advertised that one floor of his
Millford Mills contained bins to store each farmer's grain. If delivered
to the mill in winter when the holes and stumps in the road were
covered with snow and provided good sledding with oxen, the grain
could be ground and carefully packed in seasoned barrels made by the
cooper at the mill, and thus be ready for the spring market.[3]

The principle involved in operating the water-wheels of the average
grist mill was similar to that of the saw mill. As the large overshot water-
wheel turned when the gate opened, it rotated the upper millstone, or
runner, against the lower millstone, or nether, which remained stationary. The clean grain fed from the hopper to the stones was crushed
between them and spilled off the edge into a chute connected to a bin,
or in later years into tiny metal cups fastened to leather belts that
conveyed the flour from under the stones to a storage bin.[4]

In the centre of each millstone the miller pierced a hole, or eye, to provide for the spindle, or shaft. The grinding surface of each stone was cut, or dressed, by the miller with deep furrows which extended tangentially from the eye to the edge of the stone; the pattern of the grooves was made clockwise on one stone, counter-clockwise on the other for maximum abrasion of the grain between them. The upper stone sat on the spindle and could be raised or lowered in relation to the stationary stone by a hand wheel, depending on the coarseness or fineness of meal the settler required. By rubbing a little flour under his thumb a good miller could easily judge the would-be results of its baked products, the coolness of the stones, and the sharpness of the furrows. Spring wheat, or wheat planted in the spring of the year, was best handled by these mills because it was hard and otherwise had to be tempered or softened by moistening before being ground. All flour was whole wheat because there was no separation of bran and shorts.

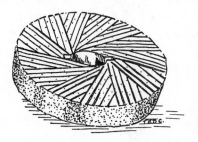

By 1850 steam-mills were increasing in number, water-power was not essential, and the small water-mills found it difficult to keep pace with modern improvements. A reel about forty or fifty feet long and two and a half feet in diameter was introduced to make white flour. The reel was made up of sections covered with silk or bolting cloth, as it was called, and sections of wire screen. The flour was still ground on the old mill-stones and then elevated to the reel to separate the bran and shorts from the flour.

The next stage in flour-grinding came following 1875 with the introduction of the roller-mill consisting of double stands of rollers. Here the grain was ground by being passed through the series of rollers and separating reels. Each stand had two pairs of rollers, one on each side of a real. Each reel was covered with bolting cloth of the proper gauge for the exact separation it was intended to make on the ground stock. As flour went through one reel it was sifted off, and the balance of the meal proceeded to the next stand for further separation.

The sifter system followed. There were different types of sifters; the one at Gray's Mill was called a plansifter and consisted of a box about eight feet long, about five feet wide, and deep enough to hold six sifting screens. This machine was hung from the ceiling on wooden rods and was set on one side of a balanced wheel so that it sifted with a circular motion, about ninety revolutions a minute. It did all the work of the cumbersome reels with their yards of expensive bolting cloth. The mill under this system was able to make a barrel of straight grade flour from four bushels and twenty pounds of wheat. It was rated as a "forty barrel" mill, that is, it could produce forty barrels of flour in twenty-four hours.

The steel plate chopper was used only for grinding feed for cattle and other live stock. There were only two of these devices on the Middle Don in later years; one at Gray's Mill and the other at Schmidt's Mill on Steeles Avenue. It consisted of a set of eight steel sections, four bolted to each head. Some choppers had one head running, and one stationary head; others had two running heads, one running in opposition to the other at about 1500 revolutions per minute.[5]

The wheat ground around Don Mills in later years was mostly fall wheat, or wheat planted in the fall of the year, which because of its softness, was made into flour for pastry.

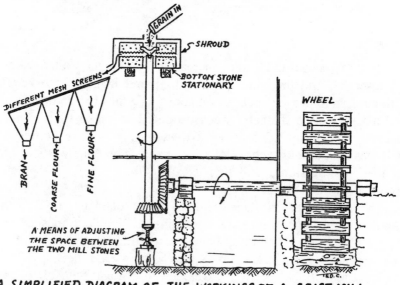

A SIMPLIFIED DIAGRAM OF THE WORKINGS OF A GRIST MILL

DISTILLERIES

Distilleries for producing spirituous liquors developed with the mills and were often connected to a grist mill because they were able to use the farmer's inferior grain. The farmer hauled his grain to the mill to be ground, and after cleaning up the load of wheat, a bag of trailings consisting of small grain remained. This was generally traded for whiskey, and the farmer's ten-gallon barrel was almost filled.

Since grain was essential for the distilling business, during the War of 1812 the distilleries were closed for a time in order to provide enough wheat to overcome the shortage of flour. As early as December 22, 1821, A. N. McNabb advertised in the *Upper Canada Gazette* for a thousand bushels of wheat for his still in Markham and offered half cash and half whiskey as payment, as well as stating that any quantity of whiskey would be exchanged for wheat or other grain.

The person who could extract the most alcohol from a given amount of grain was most sought after and could command a large wage. On August 21, 1839, Thomas Hodgson, distiller for James Hogg, advertised in the *British Colonist* the results of a wager in which he "produced 271½ gallons of whiskey from 60 bushels of chopped barley, being 18 quarts to the bushel; the quantity specified in the wager, and six quarts over. The whiskey was the strength of 32 below hydrometer proof. Any person desirous of learning T. Hodgson's method of distilling, can be instructed for a reasonable consideration."

Each distillery owner was required to obtain a license for his still by the fifth of January each year, the fee being two shillings and six-pence per gallon according to its capacity. Cornelius van Nostrand, a miller and still-house owner in York Mills, had a large still holding eighty gallons of spirits; his license was five pounds a year in 1838.[6] Stores retailing wine, brandy, rum and other spirituous liquors "in quantities of not less than one quart, to be drank out of his House"[7] paid a license fee of seven pounds ten shillings in 1840 payable by March 28th. John van Nostrand, aged sixteen, was selling liquor in his store on Yonge Street in 1833 which cost two shillings for one quart of whiskey, five shillings for one quart of spirits, and five shillings for two gallons of wine.[8]

THE WOOLLEN MILL

There were two woollen mills in North York; one was in operation in the 1850's and 60's in Newtonbrook, and the other, established in 1827 by Alexander Milne of Don Mills, became a real family business, with every member responsible for some part of it.

The mill area was a hive of industry in the spring; the saw buzzing, the logs floating in the mill pond, and the miller's sheep white from their bath under the mill pond spill-off, grazing near the dam. An occasional "ba-a-a" was heard from the flock as each lamb was caught, pulled over on its back with its feet held in the miller's left hand while he clipped off its winter coat of fleece with large shears. Before being scoured in hot soapy water, the wool was sorted, and bits of sticks, burrs, pine tar and matted wool were pulled or cut out. The scouring removed the natural grease and oil from the wool and it could easily be dyed after being thoroughly rinsed. Iron vessels were used for dyeing most dark colours, and, later, brass or tin were used for delicate tints. "Indigo was used for dyeing blue, madder for red, butternut husks or sumach blossoms for brown, onion skins, waxwood or golden rod for yellow and beech tree bark for drab."[9]

Before carding it was necessary to saturate the dyed or washed wool with lard or oil by rubbing and working it into the wool which aided the combing or carding process by fluffing up and mixing the wool evenly. This was a pleasant, quiet task undertaken by the grandmother of each family. As she rocked in her corner beside the fire she pulled two rectangular paddles or cards containing a small ball of wool between them, back and forth in opposite directions. The paddles, less than a foot long and about five inches wide, contained thickly set, wire teeth that curved toward the handle in the centre. If worsted yarn was desired, however, it was necessary to straighten rather than fluff the fibres and pull out the short ones. In both cases the wool was rolled finally into a soft ball, or into a roving about twelve inches long and three-quarters of an inch deep, ready for the spinner.

After the women of the family had spun and woven their wool into cloth, they took it to the Woollen mill for fulling and in some cases for dyeing. During the fulling process the woven cloth was put into a container of hot soapy water and fuller's earth. A pestle or mallet, moving horizontally, knocked and rolled the cloth back and forth to shrink and thicken it, and the fuller's earth acted as a cleansing agent for removing the grease, stains, and dirt still in the cloth. When pulled out of the tub it was stretched on a tenter frame, held by hooks made by bending wrought-iron nails, and placed in the sun to dry.

Dressing or burling, the next process, meant removing any loose threads or knots of wool or flax from the surface of the material. The finisher of cloth had to know how to shear the surface evenly, and for this work he used huge shears with square instead of pointed ends. For raising the nap after pressing, the fuller turned to the thistle growing in his field, and with a handful he was able to raise the nap better than modern machinery!

In 1828 the Milne's Fulling Mill charged fivepence Halifax currency and eightpence New York currency to full a yard of cloth; and for fulling, dyeing and dressing Blacks, London Browns, Snuffs and other dark colours, one shilling six and three quarter pence Halifax currency or two shillings sixpence New York currency.[10]

MILLS IN NORTH YORK

Date	Saw Mills	Grist Mills	Woollen Mills
1825	10	1	—
1851	25	8	2
1860	20	8	2
1878	8	5	1

The decrease in saw mills from twenty in 1860 to eight in 1878 gives a clear indication of the depletion of timber stands throughout North York which resulted from clearing the land for general farming, growing wheat, barley and oats, and pasture land for dairy and prize livestock.

YORK MILLS

The Heron Mills

As Yonge Street descended the valley northward, it wound down Heron's Hill to the east, now Donwoods Drive, to Heron's Bridge on Donino Avenue. Samuel Heron, who operated a store on King Street in York, had owned property at York Mills as well as in Scarborough and West York. In 1803 he ran into financial difficulties and lost everything. John Gray, who took over his York Mills property, made an arrangement with Heron who then constructed one of the first grist and saw mills in York Township[11] on the West Branch of the Don River. By 1810 he had added a distillery to his establishment, and by February 26, 1812, he was trying to sell but no sale was recorded. The following advertisement was placed in the *York Gazette*, the York newspaper:

> Lot No. 9 East side Yonge Street: on the Premises there are a Saw Mill and Grist Mill, both in good order, and a Still House with two Stills, capable of making 18 gallons of Whiskey per day. The Mills with a portion of land will be sold separate if required or all together. There is a large improvement on said lot. . . .
> York 15th July 1811
>
> *Samuel Heron*

The Arnold Mills

Thomas Arnold, Township assessor in 1817, lived in a new frame house containing six rooms, a cellar and cellar-kitchen, on the west side of Yonge Street on a site which is now under the Macdonald-Cartier Freeway. Also on the property stood a large frame barn, fifty by thirty feet, and a new saw mill capable of cutting 2,000 feet of timber in twenty-four hours with a substantial mill-dam erected on the Don River.[12] It was offered for sale because Thomas had bought land and constructed a grist mill north of Heron's old mill.

The new property contained a three-storey flour mill, forty-five by thirty-five feet, with two run of stones capable of manufacturing from 200 to 300 bushels of wheat in twenty-four hours, a two-storey building of thirty feet square used as a house and store, a blacksmith shop, and a small log house for the miller.[13] Arnold called his property Millford Mills and advertised that "one floor of the mill shall be laid out in Bins for the purpose of keeping the grain separate which may be stored by each individual. . . ."[14] It was recommended that the farmer store his wheat in the mill during the sleighing season, when it could be ground and carefully packed in seasoned barrels for the spring market.

The Heron-Arnold Mill Site

James Hogg emigrated to Canada from Scotland and bought Thomas Arnold's mill and farm in 1824. Hogg advertised in the *Colonial Advocate* on February 28, 1828:

> Cash for merchantable Wheat will be paid during the winter by Subscriber at Milford Mills.

Gradually he extended his holdings by purchasing land on the west side of Yonge north of the Don River, and built a distillery to make whiskey out of the inferior grain sent in to be processed. He renamed his property York Mills and expanded his grist mill to include three run of Burr stones, driven by two water-wheels, a smut machine for cleaning grain, and a country and merchant bolt. Near the mills William Goodwin ran a carriage and wagon shop. William Mitchell had a blacksmith's shop, and John Hogg had a cooperage.[15]

In 1840 John Somerville took over York Mills, the Hogg property, and became miller and postmaster.[16] Four years later, Thomas Somerville acquired the property and operated a flourishing export flour business with Great Britain, as Canadian flour entered that country duty free. With the repeal of the British Corn Laws and the adoption of world free trade in 1846, the Canadian milling boom was very short-lived. Somerville, as well as Cornelius van Nostrand, also in York Mills, Benjamin Thorne in Thornhill, and William Kaitting in Humber Summit, found no market for their flour and many advertisements similar to the following of December 8, 1848, appeared in the *Globe*:

> In Bankruptcy. Thomas Somerville of York Mills in the County of York—merchant and miller. Meeting of Creditors 21st Dec. James Mitchell. Assignee of Estate and Effects.

An extensive credit sale followed which was advertised in the *Globe* on December 29, 1848. Fortunately, by 1850 Somerville was able to re-establish himself in Weston, where he opened a new grist mill known as the Glenbank Mills.

In 1851 the sons of James Hogg were old enough to take over their father's property. John and William opened a subdivision called Hogg's Hollow, and James, the youngest son, became the miller, with a water-powered flour mill having three pair of mill-stones and employing three persons.[17] In 1856 the mill was partially converted to steam, and a steam saw mill came into operation.

John Arkell bought the Hogg flour mill and saw mill and ran them and the post office from 1878-1886, when Joseph S. Pratt purchased them for his son George. In 1895 the mills were destroyed by fire, and George rebuilt on the same site. A few years later people began to demand more finely ground flour; new machinery and rollers were needed to improve the quality. The cost was staggering for a small miller, and trade on Yonge Street had dropped considerably. George Pratt was forced to give up the flour business and used the building only for a saw mill and cider press. In 1926, three years after the inception of North York Township, the mill ceased to operate. It was later turned into a riding stable, and the old iron wheel was buried under the floor of the west part of the building because it was too heavy for a scrap-metal dealer to cart it away. The dilapidated, empty mill building was finally torn down in 1959.

The Van Nostrand Mills

Cornelius van Nostrand built a large grist and saw mill in 1837 on the first Arnold property, west of Yonge under the modern Macdonald-Cartier viaduct, and the following year he erected an eighty gallon still-house, forty by thirty-four feet, near the mill. By 1840 van Nostrand had ordered an engine from St. Catharines to convert his mill to steam, and shortly afterwards the York Hill Steam Mills, named after the family property, were sending flour to Great Britain. Business was good and expansion necessary to meet the demand. As a result van Nostrand bought property to the south of the mill where James Hogg's old still-house had originally stood, and built another flour mill with a house attached for the miller. Both mills were in full operation and poor quality grain was sent to the distillery.

Britain's adoption of free trade in 1846 did not have its effect in Canada until about 1848, when Cornelius suffered severe losses. No bankruptcy notice appeared in the newspaper, but an indenture was registered dated February 19, 1849, in which all the holdings of Cornelius van Nostrand, miller, and Mary van Nostrand, his wife, were turned over to "Duncan McDonell of the City of Toronto, Merchant, and John Robertson of the same place, merchant, creditors of the said Cornelius and trustees named and appointed on behalf of themselves and the other creditors."

At the same time John van Nostrand, aged 25 years, was appointed the true and lawful Attorney for Duncan McDonell and John Robertson

> to do all acts which may be requisite and necessary for the management of the said property until the same can be disposed of with advantage to the estate . . . to take and keep possession of all and singular the aforesaid mentioned property and effects . . . keeping and rendering a true and proper account thereof . . . to manage the business of the Mills, Distillery, and other matters and business . . . keeping a proper account there.[18]

A few months later broadsides were posted for an extensive auction sale of farm stock, farming implements, dry goods, groceries, hardware, forty barrels of whiskey, a cooper's establishment, etc.; also for the private sale of a large grist mill with three run of stones, distillery and about 180 acres of land, and a grist mill with two run of stones, a brick house and eight acres of land.[19] Following the sale, van Nostrand moved to Springfield (Erindale), where he opened a small grist mill; his son, John, continued to operate the store under the creditors, and was finally able to repay the family debts.

Van Nostrand's Mill Site

Duncan McDonell and John Robertson, new owners of the van Nostrand York Hill Steam Mills, found that the old engine bought in 1841 needed extensive repairs and was not worth fixing. As a result they entered into an agreement with Joseph Shepard "to repair and complete the mill-dam on the West Branch of the River Don . . . to be built about the height and width of the dam standing before being carried away and to be completed and made a sufficient dam for the purposes of the mill."[20] The work was to be completed with a guarantee that the mill would not stand idle longer than three weeks.

In 1851 W. H. Savingny was listed as the miller employed at the Metcalfe Mills,[21] which were run by water-power and employed six persons, and the Red Flour Mill, also run by water-power employing four persons. These were the original van Nostrand Mills. In 1854 Louis Moffat, who held the mortgages, took over the mills in the name of Moffat Murray & Co., general merchants in Toronto, and a branch of the important Montreal firm. By 1860 John Lukes was miller for the lower mill, an oatmeal mill operated by water-power, producing 2,000 barrels per annum, and employing two persons; and William Lukes was miller for the upper mill, still operating with water-power and producing 5,000 barrels of flour and employing two men and a woman.[22]

The lower mill on the west side of Yonge[23] was bought by Wallace Carson in 1878 and milling was discontinued. The property around the upper mill[24] was sold in 1876 to David Boyle, an early York Mills blacksmith, who may have owned a saw mill on the site. The flour mill was run by Joseph Rumble and John Calvert who advertised in the Miles *Illustrated Historical Atlas of York County* in 1878: "Covertdale Mills. Millers & Grain Buyers." In 1887 the Sheddon Company was formed and continued to operate the mill until 1897, the year of Queen Victoria's Diamond Jubilee, when Colonel Sweeney bought it and turned it into a summer home. In 1929 it was destroyed by fire.

LANSING

Joseph Shepard owned a water-powered grist and saw mill in 1830 on the West Branch of the Don River north of Sheppard Avenue, east of Bathurst Street.[25] The grist mill run by his son, Thomas, was shipping flour to Montreal, and the saw mill run by his son, Michael, was casting bullets at the time of the Rebellion of 1837. Following the Rebellion and his return to Lansing, Thomas took over the old saw mill left to him by his father. In 1847 he placed the premises on the market; the advertisement offered a comfortable cottage of forty feet square, a barn and other out-buildings, three acres of excellent orchard, and a steam saw mill capable of cutting 4,000 feet of lumber in twenty-four hours.[26] Like many mills listed in the newspaper, this one did not sell, and by 1851 he was operating two mills; the saw mill in the ravine, and a grist mill to the north, just east of Bathurst, which provided flour for the stores on Yonge Street. In the spring the road leading down to the mill was so bad that it was impossible to haul the flour to the top of the hill even with a team of oxen, and Shepard had to carry 100 pound bags up the hill on his shoulders in order to get them to market.

In 1856 he sold the mills to his brother, Joseph, and bought the Oriole saw mill from his brother Michael.

Joseph Shepard II's mills were run by water-power and in 1861 they were handling 25,000 bushels of wheat at an annual value of $22,500, and 300 planks at an annual value of $600. In 1871 the mills were run by William Hortop and were called the Ripley Mills.

NEWTONBROOK

The Playter Mill

John Mills Jackson who owned the north-west corner of Drewry and Yonge leased his property to Robert Armour in 1820 and went to England. A short time later he returned to Canada and settled on his Newtonbrook property, which he advertised for sale in the *Upper Canada Gazette* on April 25, 1823.[27] In the intervening years a substantial saw mill close to Yonge Street had replaced a still-house built at an earlier date, and mention is made of "a considerable expense having been laid out on the Dam the last summer." George Playter, the sheriff's deputy, bought the property, and his brother Ely moved in and ran the mill in 1823. How long Wilket Creek was able to supply water for a saw mill is not known.

Both these men, and their other brothers, John, Watson, and James Playter played prominent parts in the affairs of the Township and County of York. Their father, Captain George Playter Sr., emigrated from England to Philadelphia, where he married a Quaker and became a Quaker himself. During the War of Independence, however, he felt constrained to become a Loyalist soldier, and in 1780 came to Canada with many other United Empire Loyalist families. He first settled in Kingston, but moved to York Township when York was selected as the capital of Upper Canada. A man of the old school, he was described as always wearing a three-cornered hat, broad-toed shoes with large silver buckles, and white stockings, and carrying a cane.[28]

The Cummer Mills

John Cummer, son of Jacob Cummer of Willowdale, owned a farm on the north-west corner of Finch and Yonge. A side road, later Cummer Avenue, ran east to the Don River in 1819 where John operated a saw mill owned by his father.[29] Many early religious camp meetings were held at these mills through the years.

By 1851 John Cummer and his son, Jacob, had added a grist mill and a woollen factory to the saw mill, and the mills became known as the Reading Mills, named for the city in Pennsylvania where the family originally lived. Jacob gradually took over the milling and lumber business from his father and built a brick house, still standing at the mill site near the dam. In 1851 the saw mill employed two men and cut 200,000 feet of lumber annually; the grist mill employed three people and shipped flour to Montreal; and Samuel Willis, an Irishman, and John Ure, a Scot, were the weavers. The woollen business, bought by Mr. McIntosh and James L. Vroom, closed about 1857.[30]

William Cummer, who had been taught the flour business by his brother Jacob, handled the Reading Mills for a short time after Jacob moved to Cadillac, Michigan.[31] Late in 1867, the year of Confederation, William took over the store and post office in Newtonbrook and turned the mills over to his brothers, Edwin S. and Albert Cummer, who in turn, sold to James Cooper, an Irishman, in 1878.

The Davidson and Hammil Mills

North of the Reading Mills on a small tributary of the Middle Don stood a saw mill owned by Thomas Davidson who employed three people in 1851 and produced 500,000 feet of lumber. This mill later came into the possession of John Sellers who ran it until about 1870.[32] Further north on the same tributary, on the north-east corner of Steeles and Leslie in Markham, Samuel Hammil operated a saw mill in 1860.[33]

The Fish Mills

Benjamin Fish built a distillery in 1828 at Steeles and Bayview in Markham, followed by a grist and saw mill about 1830.[34] In 1851 four people handled 9,000 bushels of wheat in the grist mill and 700 logs in the saw mill. Fire destroyed the mills, but Fish rebuilt, and in 1866 sold them to John Parsons who renovated the grist mill and employed George Morrison and Abraham Leonard as merchant and miller in 1871. James Reith became miller and grain buyer of the newly named Empire Mills in 1878.

H. B. Schmidt in 1883 bought the mills, made extensive alterations, and put in a system of rollers instead of mill-stones. The family lived in the house next to the mills and boarded the mill-hands. Because of ill health, Schmidt was forced to sell in 1920 to W. H. Lever. In 1938 when Lever sold to Angus A. Macdonald, an artist, the mill was turned into a house and finally pulled down in 1965 in order to straighten the corner. Bayview Avenue now runs over ground that once was the mill pond.

EGLINTON

The Don River crosses Bayview Avenue at Lawrence. Since 1929 a huge bridge has spanned the ravine, but prior to this a road descended the hill, crossed a small bridge over the river and ascended on the east side. In this picturesque ravine Eli Beman ran a saw mill as early as 1820, and Jacob Lawrence built another to the south of the Beman site in 1845.[35] According to the 1851 census two persons were employed at the Lawrence mill, which it labelled "old."

One of the most notable figures owning a saw mill east of Yonge in North York was the Hon. William McDougall, an attorney and solicitor in Upper Canada in 1847, who gave up law, became interested in journalism, and published *The North American*, which he sold to George Brown in 1855. McDougall employed one person in 1851 to run his saw mill and cut 200,000 feet of lumber per annum.[36] Entering the Legislative Assembly in 1858, McDougall became an eloquent and powerful speaker, a Father of Confederation and, briefly, lieutenant-general of the Hudson Bay Company territories when Canada took them over in 1869.

DOWNSVIEW

During the 1840's three saw mills were built along the Black Creek tributary of the Humber River. One belonged to James Lever,[37] an ardent Methodist layman from Pittsburgh, who was responsible for building a small log church in Weston about 1821. His mill was situated on the west side of Jane Street, north of Wilson Avenue, and to the north stood the Taylor Mill in 1846,[38] operated by the Snider family in 1860.

At this point the Black Creek crosses to the east side of Jane, where Jacob Stong erected a small saw mill in 1848.[39] This property was sold to Thomas Griffith who, in turn, rented the saw mill to a Mr. Richardson. John Boake finally bought it in 1854, and received a contract for sawing lumber for the new Plank Road. This mill was still operating in 1860 on the Boake's Silver Hollow Farm.

John Chew was running a saw mill on the Humber River north of Wilson Avenue in 1847.[40] On January 1, he ran the following notice in the *British Colonist*:

> Lumber For Sale. The subscriber offers for Sale at his Mill, Weston, River Humber, a large quantity of Pine and Oak Lumber of all the different kinds usually cut for the Toronto Market, partly seasoned, and of excellent quality, Cheap For Cash. Signed John Chew. Weston, Dec. 21, 1846.

Weston

The Humber River, named after a river in the north of England, forms the boundary between the Boroughs of North York and Etobicoke. The Village of Weston forms the southern boundary of Downsview, and the location of the Village was changed from the Etobicoke side of the Humber to the east side following the spring freshet of 1850.[41] The Weston mills are mentioned here because the settler in North York carried or drove his grain to the nearest mill, no matter where it was located.

In 1827 Joseph Holley opened a saw mill about a quarter of a mile south of Lawrence Avenue, and the property passed through many hands. It became James Magee's flax and saw mill in 1850, and John Dennis replaced the early buildings with a large woollen factory of brick and stone in 1853. Farren & Miles, the new owners, employed twenty-five hands to run eight power-looms and 500 spindles in 1867. It finally became the Weston Woollen Manufacturing Company, employing 100 people; its failure in 1895 was a local catastrophe.[42]

George Dixon built a saw mill on the Etobicoke side of the river north of the Holley saw mill in 1818. About 1840 this mill was bought by the Gibson brothers, who built a flour mill on the site. It was sold to Thomas Somerville and operated for twenty years as the Glenbank Mills, one of the larger flour mills on the Humber.[43] Somerville had previously run the Hogg mills in York Mills.

Nearly a quarter of a mile north of Lawrence, John Porter built a saw mill in 1830 that drew its water from a pond a quarter of a mile upstream by means of a long race. Rowland Burr bought it about 1840 and added a flour mill and woollen factory under one roof west of the saw mill. These were destroyed by fire and the property sold to Robert McDougall in 1850, who built a large four-storey flour mill with three run of stones. In 1861 it was producing 8,340 barrels of flour per annum and the mill was known as the Southwestern Mills. It was taken over by C. & W. Wadsworth in 1883.[44]

A Mr. Countryman built a grist mill at the north end of Weston, the fourth mill site in Etobicoke. It burned down and Joseph Holley rebuilt it and added a saw mill. In 1815 James Farr owned the mills and allowed Alexander Milne, later of Don Mills, and his partner Jacob McKay of Humber Summit to carry on a carding and fulling business in a portion of the new flour mill. C. & W. Wadsworth purchased the property in 1828, built a new saw mill in 1830, erected a distillery in 1840, and put up a new five-storey flour mill with six run of stones, south of the old building in 1856.[45]

ELIA

An early saw mill operating on Black Creek in 1851 stood on the Snider[46] property east of Jane Street, and their second house overlooked the mill pond.

The Willson & Wreggitt Mills

In 1851 John Willson IV, J.P. and clerk and treasurer of York Township, owned and operated a saw mill on the West Branch of the Don River north of Finch Avenue, east of Dufferin Street.[47] South of Finch, across from the Willson Mill, William Wreggitt[48] operated a water-powered flour mill in 1851 near a log house he built in 1835. The sawdust piles in the valley indicate that a saw mill was operating on the property also.

The James Mill

North of the Willson mill, about a quarter of a mile north of Finch and east of Dufferin, Joseph James operated a water-powered saw mill that employed one person in 1851. In 1860 Francis James was proprietor, employed two men, and cut 25,000 plank boards annually. In 1878 Arthur Cowan ran the business and advertised in the Miles *Illustraded Historical Atlas of the County of York*:

> A dealer in elm and basswood lumber as well as a maple timber suitable for axles, and money to loan on easy terms, at the James' Saw Mill, lot 22 Con. 2 West York.

FISHERVILLE

Steeles Avenue ran west of Yonge in 1820 to a saw mill run by Valentine Fisher on the West Branch of the Don River, south of Steeles, an area which later became known as Fisherville.[49] Prior to 1851 he had also built a new grist mill below the old saw mill site, and the mill-road entrance was on Steeles near the bridge. In 1854 George Knaggs was proprietor, and in 1857 Norman Millikin, from Markham, became the owner and established a steam and water grist mill employing two persons and producing 1,000 barrels of flour in 1861. Finally this mill, after passing through several hands, became the property of John Allan in 1891, who continued to operate it for a number of years; the children and young people of the neighbourhood enjoyed skating parties on his pond each winter.

In this modern age people who live in the city do not realize how dark a country road can be at night without a moon to guide them.

At least two accidents occurred at this Steeles Avenue mill pond; one involved a man returning home from Abner Cherry's tavern, and the other a seamstress delivering a wedding dress. In each case the victims wandered from the road, and were drowned in the pond.

KAISERVILLE

John Smith[50] owned a saw mill in Vaughan on the Black Creek at Jane and Steeles Avenue in 1820 which was taken over by the Dalziel (pronounced De el') family whose property is now part of Black Creek Pioneer Village.

HUMBER SUMMIT

The Rowntree mills were built about half way between Finch and Steeles, west of Islington Avenue. Joseph Rowntree built a saw mill on the York Township side of the Humber in 1843 and a grist mill on the Etobicoke side by 1848.[51] A small bridge straddled the river, and the Rowntree brick house, a storey and a half, stood half way up the hill in Etobicoke, north of the grist mill. In 1860 these mills were known as the Greenholme Mills, handling 30,000 bushels of wheat and employing four people; they continued to operate into the twentieth century. By the 1950's the property was a summer resort known as Riverbank Park, and houses lined the river road. Disaster hit the community in 1954 when Hurricane Hazel swept away twelve houses and damaged many others.

To the south, at the corner of Finch and Islington Avenue, William Kaitting ran a grist and saw mill prior to 1846 on the Etobicoke side of the Humber River. The grist mill had "two pair Burr Mill Stones, Merchant and Country Bolts, Smut Mill, Elevators, Conveyers, &c., everything complete for carrying on the business of a miller. A Saw Mill, and 120 acres of Land, mostly covered with Pine Lumber."[52] Kaitting, like Somerville and van Nostrand in York Mills, was shipping flour to Great Britain. When the British Corn Laws were repealed and free trade was established, Kaitting went bankrupt, and his mills were put up for auction in 1848. Three years later he was operating a saw mill on the east or York Township side of the river, at the corner of Finch.[53]

In 1851 Henry John Boulton, son of D'Arcy Boulton Sr., bought the Kaitting mills on the east and west side of the river, and in 1855 built a large house called Humberford on the Etobicoke side of the Humber. Boulton, after practicing law in Toronto, turned his attention to farming and introduced into Canada the tile system of land drainage which has proved so valuable to the rural districts.[54] His mills, known as the Humberford Mills, were sold to James Rowntree, a son of Joseph Rowntree, in 1875, but had ceased operations in 1878. Rowntree built a large brick farmhouse on the north-east corner of Finch and Islington Avenue and the property became known as the Italian Gardens in 1960. The house was destroyed by fire about 1965 and the land was taken over for subdivision.

William Crosson built and operated a saw mill in 1848 south of Finch Avenue on a part of the Humber called the Ox-bow[55] near John C. Devins' log house. This mill was still running in 1860, and the property was known as the Bow-Bend Farm. When the river was forced to change its course by Hurricane Hazel, North York lost forty acres of land to Etobicoke. Having a dense forest of white pine on his property, John Duncan, a brother of William Duncan of Dublin, built a saw mill on Duncan (or Burns) Creek, east of Islington Avenue, north of Finch.[56]

DON MILLS

The Milne Woollen Mill

In the spring of 1827 the Alexander Milne family moved to York Township and erected a saw mill and fulling works on the south-west corner of Lawrence and Leslie,[57] now Edwards Gardens. The three-storey building furnished space for carding and fulling on the lower floors and a saw mill on the third floor, with water flowing from the mill pond providing power for an eighteen-foot overshot paddle-wheel.

The following advertisement in the *Colonial Advocate* for August 2, 1827, lists interesting features as to cost, payment, and location of the woollen mill:

> Wool Carding; Fulling, Dyeing, and Dressing Cloth . . .
> The machinery is new and of the first quality, and he (the subscriber Mr. Milne) will Card Wool with neatness and despatch at Three Pence per pound. Customers living at a distance may depend on having their work done well and soon, and ready to take back with them. N.B. Wheat, Oats, Barley, and Corn taken in payment. The road to my establishment, from Scarboro' is by Pilkey's and Humphrey's saw mill: and on Yonge-Street, by Jonathan Hale's or Mr. Mercer's.[58]

After operating the woollen and saw mill for five years on this small creek, the water supply began to dwindle. In 1832 Milne was forced to move to a new location on the Middle Don River on the south side of Lawrence Avenue, and east of Don Mills Road, where the Don Mills Ski Club is now located.[59]

The new woollen mill, a long, rambling, single-storey building, and a saw mill were supplied with water from a single mill pond. Lawrence Avenue was not a straight road at the Middle Don. It led down the hill toward the river, turned south on the west side of the Don for about 150 yards, then east across a bridge and past the mill. It then wound north again to approximately where the present road runs east.

In February, 1846, Peter Milne wrote to David Gibson at Lockport stating that he had been to see Alexander Milne, his father, the week before, and that "they have a power loom agoing and Spinning & gitting along well, they half binn a buying 300 Sheep Skin at 3/4 cy per skins."[60] Alexander Milne also wrote to David Gibson at Lockport from Farmer's Factory, on September 29, 1847:

> We are all in good health I saw Peter yesterday he was in town from McKays his mother in law is dead and he was getting some things for the funeral he has some thought of coming over with me when I come for the sheep if I have six or eight good yeous with the rams it will answer I have thought of coming by bufflo and on the Saturday meet you on the cannal—to come down with you you will write when the sheep would be ready. . . . Write him immediately and also when I might come for the sheep. I am just as busy as ever appls to gather potates to dig and manny of them roten corn to gather buck wheat to take up ¾ acre of Beans see after Manufactry of cloth and lumber temperance lecturing and I expect to prech Glad tidings from heaven to some who may come to hear in toronto sunday first—the only way to live long is make use of our time.[61]

As the years passed, more money became available in the community, enabling the development of other processes at the woollen factory. By 1850, when hand-weaving was becoming less important, some of the early carding mills became weaving mills. By this time William Milne was proprietor of the woollen mill; a power-loom was in operation with two weavers, a spinner, and three other men, and the saw mill employed two men. In 1851 Milne Hollow was a thriving community with sixteen buildings, including Milne's house and barns on Lawrence Avenue, on the west side of the river.

Ten years later, in 1861, the woollen mill was producing 2,225 yards of cloth per year, which was sold in the family store on the west side of the Don, south of William's house, and the saw mill was producing 400,000 feet of lumber annually. Four males and one female were employed, and all the buildings were connected.

The great flood of 1878 fairly devastated Milne Hollow, sweeping away the mill-dam, the bridge, the logs in the pond, the saw mill, and the woollen mill. However, William Milne and his son, Alexander W., soon erected a new brick woollen factory, eighty by fifty feet, with three full storeys and a basement with casements well above ground. New, improved machinery was added and Milneford Mills began manufacturing rolls, yarns, cloths, flannels, and blankets which were sold on the local market.[62] The new mill stood on the east side of the river beside the oldest house in the area, William's first house, now owned by Alexander. A tenement for the workers and their families stood at the turn of the road to the north, as well as a house, and a wagon shop operated by John Gray.

Charles Milne, son of A. W. Milne, closed the woollen mill in the early 1900's. In 1921 fire destroyed the Milne house across the river on Lawrence Avenue; in 1946, when bricks were scarce due to the Second World War, the mill was torn down; in 1953 the houses were demolished; and finally in 1964, with the building of the Don Valley Parkway, the tiny bridge by the mill pond was pulled down leaving only one house to mark the site of the bustling activities of 1851.

The Humphrey Mill Site

Smith Humphrey erected a saw mill north of Lawrence and east of Don Mills Road as early as 1827. It was purchased in 1836 by John Hogg,[63] a brother of James Hogg of York Mills, who operated it for fifteen or twenty years.

The Gray Mills

The Gray Mills[64] were directly north of the Humphrey saw mill site. Prior to 1837 William Gray established a grist mill and his brother, James, built a distillery on the west side of the Middle Don River, and Alexander, another brother, built a saw mill on the east side. The water for both mills was supplied by the same mill pond, and frequently in the dry seasons, when the river was low, William would holler across the river for Alexander to cut off his water-supply to the saw mill in order to continue work in the grist mill. The four-storey frame grist mill in 1851 was operated by a turbine water-wheel, had one pair of stones, and employed two people. Shortly afterwards another pair of millstones was added, making one pair available for grinding feed for cattle and the other for grinding flour. By 1860 one man was still employed in the saw mill and they were cutting 250,000 feet of lumber annually, but the operation had to be discontinued as local timber disappeared.

Timothy Gray, William's son, took over Gray's Mill, and also owned and rented the blacksmith shop, which stood to the south of the hawthorn-lined road leading to the mill from Don Mills Road. Following the flood of 1878, a new mill-dam had to be built, and Gray's Mill continued to grind fine quality pastry flour. In 1900 its brand name was printed on a red and white label, "Wee MacGregor." In 1914 the mill property was turned into a dairy farm by its new owner, David Dunlap.

The Jones Mills

A saw mill was operating south of Eglinton Avenue near Leslie Street in 1851, on the property of Charles Snider.[65] By 1860 this mill had disappeared and William Jones had two saw mills on the west Branch of the Don River. One stood north of Eglinton Avenue in Wilket Creek Park, and the other was on his farm in the area now known as Glenorchy.[66]

The Taylor Mills

The property three-quarters of a mile north of Eglinton, east and west of Don Mills Road, and south of Eglinton to the Forks of the Don River,[67] as well as other Todmorden property, belonged to the Taylor brothers. John, Thomas, and George emigrated to Canada in 1825, spent nine years in Vaughan, and then moved to the Forks of the Don River where they established paper mills and saw mills. John Taylor in 1851 had a saw mill run by water-power and employing two men, cutting 350,000 feet of timber annually in Wilket Creek Park.[68] A solid belt of white pine extended from Don Mills Road along the present C.P.R. line to Woodbine. One white pine yielded 5,000 board-feet of lumber, and the tree was hollow twelve feet from the ground!

The brothers worked together farming, breeding cattle and horses, and building mills. In 1854 they bought John Eastwood's and Colin Skinner's York Paper Mill, grist mill, and distillery, and soon developed three paper mills. The "Upper Mill" was located on the West Branch of the Don River near the Forks, on the border of North York, with a mill pond which flooded about thirty acres of land east of the river. It was built in 1846-47 through the influence of the Hon. George Brown, who started the *Globe* in 1844. The "Middle Mill" became a unit of the Howard Smith Paper Mills in 1939 and is to be seen in the Valley today. The "Lower Mill" did a thriving business until it was finally destroyed by fire in 1900. During their period of prosperity, the three mills used hundreds of tons of rags, straw, esparto grass, ropes and canvas to manufacture newsprint, coloured paper, poster bills, books, tea and common paper bags. The output was four tons every twelve hours and one hundred men were employed.

ORIOLE

In 1814 when William Marsh, the younger, purchased the Mulholland property[69] he built a saw mill near the Macdonald-Cartier Freeway and east of Leslie Street. This mill site became the centre of Oriole and provided lumber and, later, flour for the area. The following notice in the *Upper Canada Gazette* for October 2, 1823, not only gives information about the saw mill, but shows what happened to property when influential merchants were not paid.

> Sheriff's Sale. Against the land and Tenements of William Marsh at the suits of Baldwin & Co. and Alex. Wood. I have seized Lot no. 14 in the 3rd concession East of Yonge containing 200 acres together with a Saw Mill and other Buildings thereon erected. To be Sold by Public Auction, Monday, December 1, 1823 at the Market Place.

In 1824 the mill was owned by Stillwell Willson, and in 1828 it was swept away by a flood. In 1846 Michael Shepard, having returned to Canada after receiving a pardon for his Rebellion activities, ran a saw mill on the site, and by 1851 employed two men and cut 600,000 feet of lumber annually. Thomas Shepard, his brother, who had been operating a grist and saw mill in Lansing, bought the Oriole site in 1856 and added a grist mill. Shortly afterwards, Thomas Summers opened a blacksmith shop on the south east corner of Leslie and Sheppard Avenue. When the mills burned in 1869, Shepard retired. Lumber, however, was still plentiful in the district, and Alexander M. Smith bought the Shepard property and ran a saw mill on the site from 1869-71. He was followed by Alexander Stewart who was operating it in 1878.

In 1822 Stillwell Willson and Jacob Notheart each had a half-interest in another saw mill south of Oriole north of York Mills Road[70] on the Middle Don River. James Hunter bought the Notheart-Willson site in 1838 and he and his son, Edward, built a saw mill to the south. By 1851 the mill employed two men and cut 300,000 feet of lumber annually. During the flood of 1878 the mill was destroyed and replaced with a steam-mill which was still operating in 1885.

Another saw mill developed north of Oriole in Flynntown where Almira Phillips cut 50,000 feet of lumber annually in 1851,[71] and by 1860 he had sold it to James Dunton, who ran it for a short time.

NOTES

1 January 12. Minutes of Council, Land K, p. 349. As quoted in G. C. Patterson, *Land Settlement in Upper Canada 1783-1840*, Ontario, Department of Archives, Sixteenth Report (Toronto: King's Printer, 1921), p. 134.

2 W. H. Smith, *Canada: Past, Present and Future* (Toronto: Thomas Maclear, 1851), I, 273.

3 *Upper Canada Gazette* (April 22, 1819).

4 M. N. Rawson, *Little Old Mills* (New York: E. P. Dutton & Company, 1935), pp. 158-159.

5 Courtesy Mr. Harold Gray.

6 Courtesy Dr. F. H. van Nostrand.

7 *Ibid.*

8 *Ibid.*

9 Sherk, *op. cit.*, p. 144.

10 *Colonial Advocate* (February 28, 1828).

11 Lot 9 1st concession east of Yonge Street. A grist and saw mill were advertised for sale in the *Upper Canada Gazette* on July 6, 1809, and again on February 7, 1810. Heron is also spelled Herron.

12 *Upper Canada Gazette* (July 16, 1818). Lot 13, 1st concession west of Yonge Street.

13 *Upper Canada Gazette* (April 22, 1819). Lot 10, 1st concession east of Yonge Street.

14 *Upper Canada Gazette* (October 30, 1817).

15 William Goodwin, or Godwin, and William Mitchell bought a few acres in 1827 on Lot 10, 1st concession east of Yonge Street and John Hogg bought an acre in 1834.

16 Lot 10, 1st concession east of Yonge Street.

17 Lot 10, 1st concession east of Yonge Street. Canada West, Census, York Township, 1851. Microfilm copy, North York Public Library.

18 Information about the van Nostrand mills was supplied by Dr. F. H. van Nostrand from his family documents.

19 *Globe* (March 28, 1848).

20 Information supplied by Dr. F. H. van Nostrand.

21 Smith, *op. cit.*, I, 75. Canada West, Census, York Township, 1851. Microfilm copy, North York Public Library. No information is available about the name "Metcalfe".

22 Canada West, Census, York Township, 1861. Microfilm copy, North York Public Library.

23 Lot 11, 1st concession west of Yonge Street.

24 Lot 13, 1st concession west of Yonge Street.

25 Lot 16, 1st concession west of Yonge Street.

26 *British Colonist* (April 2, 1847).

27 Lot 23, 1st concession west of Yonge Street.

28 H. Scadding, *Toronto of Old* (Toronto: Adam, Stevenson & Co., 1873), p. 288.

29 John Cummer lived on lot 21, 1st concession west of Yonge Street and his mills were on lots 22 and 23, 2nd concession east of Yonge Street.

30 *History of Toronto and the County of York, Ontario* (Toronto: C. Blackett Robinson, 1885), I, pt. III, 95.

31 W. W. Cummer, and C. L. Cummer, *Cummer Memoranda* (Cleveland: O. S. Hubbell Printing Co., 1911), p. 102.

32 Lot 24, 2nd concession east of Yonge Street.

33 Lot 1, 3rd concession east of Yonge Street, Markham.

34 Lot 1, 2nd concession east of Yonge Street, Markham.

35 Lot 6, 1st concession east of Yonge Street.

36 Lot 7, 1st concession east of Yonge Street.

37 Lot 12, 5th concession west of Yonge Street.

38 Lot 14, 5th concession west of Yonge Street.
39 Lot 14, 4th concession west of Yonge Street.
40 Lot 11, 6th concession west of Yonge Street.
41 *History of Toronto and the County of York, Ontario*, I, pt. III, 188-189.
42 Lots 4 and 5, 5th concession west of Yonge Street.
43 Across the Humber River from lot 5, 5th concession west of Yonge Street.
44 Lot 6, 5th concession west of Yonge Street.
45 Across the Humber River from lot 8, 5th concession west of Yonge Street.
46 Lot 18, 4th concession west of Yonge Street.
47 Lot 21, 2nd concession west of Yonge Street.
48 Lot 20, 2nd concession west of Yonge Street.
49 Lot 25, 2nd concession west of Yonge Street.
50 Smith was spelled Schmidt. John Smith was Johannas Schmidt.
51 Lot 23, 7th concession west of Yonge Street.
52 *Globe* (May 17, 1849). On the present Children's Hospital property. Kaitting was also spelled Keating.
53 Lot 21, 7th concession west of Yonge Street.
54 J. H. Beers & Co., *Commemorative Biographical Record of the County of York* (Toronto: 1907). Lot 21, 7th concession west of Yonge Street.
55 Lot 19, 6th concession west of Yonge Street.
56 Lot 23, 6th concession west of Yonge Street.
57 *History of Toronto and the County of York, Ontario*, I, pt. III, 95. Lot 5, 2nd concession east of Yonge Street.
58 Jonathan Hale: lots 4, 5, 6, 1st concession east of Yonge Street. Thomas Mercer: lot 10, 1st concession east of Yonge Street.
59 Lot 5, 4th concession east of Yonge Street.
60 David Gibson Papers. Microfilm copy, North York Public Library.
61 *Ibid.*
62 Miles & Co., *Illustrated Historical Atlas of the County of York* (Toronto: Miles & Co., 1878), p. 68.
63 East half of lot 7, 3rd concession east of Yonge Street.
64 Lot 9, 3rd concession east of Yonge Street.
65 Lot 10, 3rd concession from the Bay.
66 First mill: lot 1, 3rd concession east of Yonge Street; second mill: lot 4, 2nd concession east of Yonge Street.
67 Lots 1, 2, 3, 3rd conscession east of Yonge Street and lots 6, 7, 8, 9, 10, 3rd concession from the Bay.
68 Lot 2, 3rd concession east of Yonge Street.
69 Lot 14, 3rd concession east of Yonge Street.
70 Lots 12 and 13, 3rd concession east of Yonge Street.
71 Lot 18, 2nd concession east of Yonge Street.

Inns and Taverns

INTRODUCTION

THE EARLY INNS DOING BUSINESS AT THE TURN OF THE NINETEENTH
century as described by contemporary travellers, consisted of a kitchen,
a bar-room, and one bedroom containing four or five beds, each of
which, on occasion, accommodated two or more persons. The building
was generally a log construction, later to be rebuilt in frame or brick.
The exterior, ordinarily allowed to weather, was later painted, and the
interiors were often whitewashed and floors sanded and scrubbed. The
locally designed furniture was made of pine, and although there were no
washstands or basins, a log trough outside was made to serve the purpose for everyone. Most inns were granted licenses to sell liquor, but
only after the Court of Quarter Sessions was presented with evidence
indicating the necessity for a tavern at the specified location.

Upon arriving at an inn, hungry and exhausted from being jolted
all day in a springless coach, a traveller found he must share a room
with other guests. According to John Howison, an early visitor in Upper
Canada,

> most of the taverns in Upper Canada are indeed a burlesque upon
> what they profess to be. A tolerable meal can scarcely be procured
> at any one of them, nay, I have visited several which were not even
> provided with bread. It is immaterial what meal the traveller calls for,
> as the same articles will be set before him morning, noon, and night,
> not even excepting tea, which is considered so essential to comfort;
> for, if the mistress of the hotel has none of the Chinese plant, she will
> send one of her children into the woods to gather parts of the ever-
> green, hemlock, or other nauseous vegetables, and having made an
> infusion of the herb brought in, will perhaps inquire of her astonished
> and shuddering guest, if the tea is sufficiently strong. None of the

> minor public-houses are provided with servants to attend travellers who put up at them, and therefore, when the landlord is absent, or in an independent humour, one is obliged to unsaddle, feed, and take care of his own horse, otherwise the animal will be totally neglected, for the women disdain to do anything of this kind.[1]

The noise and confusion in the public room was also vexing for a weary gentleman. It "contained a wonderful medley of persons. They were drinking, talking, smoking, swearing, and spitting promiscuously; and the melting of the snow, which they had brought into the apartment upon their shoes, had deluged the whole floor."[2] Later upon going to bed the guest was prevented from sleeping "by the fumes of rum and tobacco, the bites of mosquitoes, and the hardness of the planks which formed"[3] his bed.

THE 1830's AND 40's

The rural inns surrounded by their farmyards were built in the 1830's and 40's to accommodate the large influx of immigrants arriving to settle on farms or establish trades, and those moving produce and goods to and from large centres. There were no railways, roads were bad, and the inns crowded. Visitors were rarely refused a bed. If the tavern were full, the hay loft was used for overflow sleeping accommodation, and often a chorus of snoring guests greeted a newcomer as he entered the barn. In order to guard against fire every house had to be equipped with two ladders, one to reach the eaves of the house and the other to be bolted or hooked on the roof near the chimney; and the owners had to have two buckets made of wood, leather, or canvas covered with pitch to hold two gallons of water. These, labelled with the owner's name, were to be used only in the event of fire.

The tavern sign, hanging high between two poles, waved in the breeze attracting tired farmers returning to and from market. The pump out in front was kept busy most of the day pumping troughs or pails of water for the horses while their masters refreshed themselves with a few glasses of grog while they discussed political matters involving the Family Compact and William Lyon Mackenzie, as well as local news items, with their friends. The horses of those wishing to spend the night were provided with good stabling and provender. The innkeeper was always pleased to promote pidgeon shoots and provide space for temperance and political meetings, dances, and Township Council meetings.

Meals were not always palatable except at the inns noted for their larders. Most food was cooked in a huge fireplace. Bread originally baked in iron bake-kettles was now done in a bake-oven, meat was stewed or minced in large pots or roasted on a spit about three feet long with a crank at one end. Prongs held the meat securely so that it would turn with the spit. The kitchen was the centre of activity, with visitors chatting before the fire and the innkeeper's household preparing for the next meal or getting things ready for the arrival of the next stage coach.

Following 1850

Following the passing of the Baldwin Municipal Act in 1849, each Township provided rules and regulations regarding the cost of inn licenses, the number of comfortable beds required, and the facilities for stabling horses.[4] Also, magistrates or the governor could grant certificates to each innkeeper only after a notice attesting to his integrity had been posted in a prominent location for eight days. He was liable to imprisonment for two to six months and a fine of twenty-five pounds to a hundred pounds paid to heirs and relatives for accidents to intoxicated persons. In York Township the license fee for innkeepers in 1860 was thirty-six dollars, and in 1863, thirty-one dollars. In 1866 the Temperance Society tried to raise the fee to one hundred dollars, but Council voted on a motion for a fifty-dollar license and it was defeated three to two. Temperance feelings apparently changed in the next few years, because by 1871 the fee had dropped to thirty dollars. Licenses for "temperance houses" at a cost of twenty-five to seventy-five shillings were given also to those who could produce proof of honesty and good moral character. Only those licensed as apothecaries or temperance hotel-keepers could sell temperance drinks such as "spruce beer, sarsaparilla, raspberry vinegar, ginger beer, essence of juice of lemons or of oranges or lemonade,"[5] if sold by others, the penalty was ten pounds.

A Survey of the Taverns

York Mills

Prior to 1835, rather than running directly north through York Mills as it does today, Yonge Street curved to the east down Donwoods Drive, along Donino Avenue and up Old Yonge Street, finally rejoining the present route north of York Mills. The early inns in York Mills were no doubt along this old route. We find indirect mention of one in Rev. Hunter's *The History of Simcoe County*. At one point he discusses an early trader named Cowan and his grandson, William Cowan, "who was brought up by his maternal grandmother, who kept a wayside hostelry at Hogg's Hollow [now York Mills], at the time of the War of 1812."[6] One of her sons, Joseph Rémi Vallière de Saint-Réal, became Chief Justice of Montreal. The widow Vallière's inn was in a convenient location to provide food, drink, and lodging for the ragged soldier-farmers returning to and from the battle area, as well as men with supplies going north to the Upper Lakes. Food was very scarce during this period, and flour was in short supply. Early harvesting was pre-vented by wet weather; the farmers were not available to store their wheat early enough; and the purchases of the commissariat were in-creased tremendously reducing the quantity of flour on the open market.[7]

Samuel Heron, the miller, also ran a tavern in the area in 1817, and a two-storey inn was erected about 1830 on Donino Avenue just north of Mill Street, with a Mr. Ross as proprietor. When the new Yonge Street was built straight through the valley, Ross's house lost much of its patronage, and James Hogg turned it into a home for his family. It was in this building that James Hogg's funeral service was held in 1839. Years later it was destroyed by fire.

Anderson's Tavern, the first hotel in York Mills on new Yonge Street was "not quite finished with driving house, etc."[8] when advertised by Mrs. Hogg in September, 1839. In 1838, it is recorded that the Township Council meeting adjourned to the tavern, "the first build-ing on the east side of the road at the bottom of the hollow,"[9] and next to it, on the north side, stood a store. A roomy stable and driv-ing sheds, an important part of any inn, were finally built across the road. When the store and hotel burned, around 1856, the stable and sheds were only saved from destruction by the efforts of members of the community who formed a bucket brigade from the mill pond to the buildings.[10] One of the early landlords, a quick-witted Irishman named William Hanlan, was so cheerful that travellers asserted he must have braved the dangers of kissing the Blarney stone. In 1851 William Richardson, an Englishman, was the innkeeper and lived with his family in the tavern.

It is not known when the second York Mills Hotel was built; only the store is shown on the W. & J. Hogg lot plan in 1856. However, James Bird may have been the first landlord in 1859. Alexander Hill is listed in 1860, John Ashton in 1861, and William Lennox, a native of North-ern Ireland, Worshipful Master of the Orange Lodge, and very popular with the brethren, in 1864. He was followed in 1869 by Michael Stew-art, an Irishman of Orange proclivities, who always celebrated "The Twelfth" with a host of friends, singing "The Protestant Boys" and other party songs. The hotel was vacant in 1870-71, and then Wallace Carson, another Irish Protestant, became landlord and stayed for seven-teen years. William, his son, became the official bouncer in case argu-ments turned into fights. By 1889 David Birrell, a Scot, had taken pos-session and ran it until 1936. Anyone driving on Yonge today knows

REDRAWN BY TED C. FROM
T.P.L. R.A. READ COLLECTION

this long-established hotel as the Jolly Miller. Its shape has not changed, it now has a skating rink and still stands beside the old Hogg store, built after the fire in the 1850's. A bridge, recently replaced, was constructed over the Don River on Mill Street in 1913, and named after Birrell.

The Half Way House[11] stood at the top of a hill on the east side of Yonge Street just north of the line of the Macdonald-Cartier Freeway on an acre of land bought by George Harrison from Joseph Harrison in 1841. A note in David Gibson's diary for May 22, 1849, says, "Measured off one acre at Tavern on No. 14 1st concession east for Harrison and Nightingale." The two-storey tavern was run by Matt Burk, an Irishman, in 1851.

In 1857, Thomas Leach, an Englishman, who had been owner of the White Horse Cellar in Toronto (William Baker's old livery stable), became proprietor of the Bellevue House.[12] Originally the van Nostrand store, the two-storey, brick and frame building stood south of the Half Way House near the top of the hill. But as well as acting as innkeeper, Leach was also a veterinary surgeon, mail-carrier, and an auctioneer handling many of the country's leading sales. Thomas Leach, Jr., a master mariner, owned the property following his father's death, and in 1864-65 John Leach was proprietor. In 1869 the building reverted to a general store run by Mrs. Thomas Leach.

Lansing

John Everson, an appointed constable, ran a tavern on the southeast corner of Yonge Street and Sheppard Avenue in 1802. Ely Playter, in his diary for June 4, 1802, says, "We soon got of jioned with Mr. B. Arnold and rode on, as fast as we could through the bad roads we ware joined by J. Wilson Junr. three of the Mr Johnsons, Hollingshead, Hoover, Hendrick, and some others, we all stoped at Eversons Tavern and drank some Whiskey, whare more company came up, making 14 Horsemen. Pass'd an number on foot all going into town." John Everson's wife, Helena, continued to operate the inn in 1805 after his death.

Across the road, on the south-west corner of Sheppard Avenue and Yonge Street, stood another tavern in 1802 run by Thomas Hill, who sold the property in 1805 and moved to the south-west corner of Lawrence and Yonge where he opened another inn in 1811. It is not known if the building at Sheppard Avenue continued as a tavern, but the property was bought by Thomas Sheppard in 1824, who built the Golden Lion Hotel[13] the following year, with large stables and barns to the south, and driving sheds that would accommodate a dozen horses and vehicles to the north. The inn was a large, square, frame building with verandas on its east and south sides, a kitchen constructed of mud brick which may have been the Hill's house, and accommodation for a score of people. Over the main doorway stood a life-size lion carved out of a pine stump, the work of Paul Sheppard[14] of Scarborough, who twenty years later carved another from oak, using putty to fashion a mane.

The Golden Lion played its part in the Rebellion of 1837. William Lyon Mackenzie obtained a horse there in order to escape from the loyalists; and Dick Frizzell, who had ridden into Toronto from Thornhill to give warning of the uprising to the Government, stopped there for dinner with friends on his way home in the evening of December 7, 1837.[15]

Thomas Sheppard and his sons were expert musicians and held regular band practices in the large room on the south side of the house. Before long a dance hall was built over the driving sheds and parties of young people came from Toronto to the inn for dances. Cheese and crackers were served free in the bar, and the following little ditty was often heard:

> Here am I
> On my way to Zion
> I find my sons
> In the Golden Lion.

Through the years there were a number of owners and proprietors,[16] and after the turn of the twentieth century the Golden Lion Hotel became the residence of the Rev. T. W. Pickett, a retired Methodist minister. A Sunday school was conducted in connection with the Willow-dale Episcopal Methodist Church in the old bar-room on the south side of the house, and became the nucleus of the Lansing United Church. The Rev. Mr. Pickett gave his daughter, Mrs. George S. Henry, the second Golden Lion statue and in 1953 it was presented to York Pioneers for the Sharon Temple Museum. When the North York Historical Society was formed in 1960, the lion was returned to North York. In 1922, when North York became a Township, the old hotel housed the municipal offices for a short time, and finally, in 1928 it was torn down. On the south-west corner of Bathurst and Sheppard was Morgan's Corners Hotel, and G. Weatheral may have been proprietor there in 1869-71. William Bourke, an Irishman who came to Canada with the 2nd Battalion of Her Majesty's 17th Regiment in 1862, became proprietor in 1871,[17] and four years later moved to a hotel in Thistletown and later to the Russell House in Weston.

Willowdale

James Davis, eldest son of Asahel Davis of the Township of Nelson, purchased the lot on the south-west corner of Finch Avenue and Yonge Street in 1825 and built a two-storey brick inn, forty-four feet by thirty-two, with a brick wing twenty-six by eighteen feet. There were seventeen rooms, three immense brick ovens, and the usual bar and wine cellar. Beside the inn stood two driving-houses, a shed, a wooden house, a garden and two good wells. On the farm were two large, frame barns, a shed and a stable, and near the barns was a never-failing pond, as well as an apple orchard with about seventy mature trees.[18]

Davis became a member of the executive of the first Temperance Society of the Township of York in 1831 and took a leading part in the movement. The *Christian Guardian*, on March 19, 1831, records a meeting of the inhabitants held at the Meeting House. Forty-one people and the Chairman "forcibly urged the necessity of counteracting the vice of intemperance which is making such inroads on the peace and happiness of society." Overwhelmed by the influence of the speaker, Davis returned home and dumped the contents of his barrels of beer, rum and whiskey in the garden. As a result, the bar and wine cellar were eliminated from the inn and it became known as Temperance Inn.

Newtonbrook

About a quarter of a mile north of Finch Avenue, on the east side of Yonge Street, stood John Montgomery's first tavern, The Bird in Hand Inn[19] built by John and his father, Alexander, about 1820. The house was a two-storey, frame structure with a centre hall similar to

Cook's Tavern at Upper Canada Village. In January, 1827, in the wake of disagreements between father and son, the two decided to separate and, following a legal procedure in which the house was divided, they sawed the house in two, from top to bottom and front to back.[20] John kept the south half of the house, which was being used as an inn, and Alexander lived in the northern half. When John opened his inn near Eglinton and Yonge in the 1830's he leased his Newtonbrook building to John Finch, who made a name for himself as an innkeeper. His hostelry was held in high esteem for its excellent cooking and was popular "among excursion parties from town, and among the half-pay settlers of the Lake Simcoe region".[21]

In 1845 after being pardoned by the Queen for his actions in the Rebellion of 1837, John Montgomery is again listed as an innkeeper at Newtonbrook. Shortly afterwards he apparently opened his second Eglinton hotel, because Sir Richard Bonnycastle writes, "We departed from Richmond Hill at half past five and waggoned on to Finch's Inn, seven miles, where we breakfasted. This is another excellent resting place, and the country between the two is thickly settled. . . . Finch's Tavern, where we breakfasted at seven o'clock, was formerly the Old Stand . . . of the notorious Montgomery . . . who moved to a place about four miles from the city."[22]

In 1847 John Finch bought the lot on the north-east corner of Finch Avenue and Yonge Street and erected a two-storey, frame hotel. On September 20, 1848, he advertised in the *British Colonist* stating that he had ". . . opened his new and capacious Hotel, on Yonge Street, situated within a quarter of a mile of the premises formerly occupied by the subscriber. . . . The house and outbuildings are entirely new. . . . The subscriber will always take care to have his larder well stored and his Wine and Spirit Cellar well supplied with genuine articles . . . his stabling shall be well regulated, so that every comfort . . . may at all times be depended upon at 'Finch's Hotel'." In 1851 Finch had a by-law passed in order to allow a travelling circus to perform on the grounds. Later the hotel was leased to various innkeepers[23] and, finally, in 1873 it was sold to Charles McBride, who tore it down and used the lumber to build the Bedford Park Hotel.[24]

The original Green Bush Inn stood on the north-east corner of Steeles Avenue and Yonge Street in Markham Township. It was opened in 1830 by Joseph Abrahams, and a large balsam tree in front of the hotel gave it its name.[25] One night the stables of this hotel were destroyed by fire, and eleven horses belonging to farmers from the north were killed while their masters slept in the house. Well-water was all that was available to quench the fire, the river being too far away. Abrahams

later moved with his painted signboard, designed after the balsam tree, to the outskirts of York on Lot Street in Toronto and opened another hotel by the same name.

John Morley, a Newtonbrook property owner, built a tavern on the north-west corner of Steeles Avenue and Yonge Street in Vaughan Township in 1847. This hotel was later called Steele's Hotel, Poplar House, and the Green Bush Inn, with Thomas Steele as proprietor. John C. Steele, a joiner and son of Thomas, took over the hotel in 1877, and the traffic was so steady on Yonge Street that John's son, as a boy, pumped pails of water for the horses from early morning until sunset while their weary owners refreshed themselves at the bar.[26] Thomas Collins purchased and lived in the hotel in 1938, after moving it around the corner on to Steeles Avenue. The driving shed on Yonge Street was incorporated into the house north of a service station. The old building still stands today, a sad, sagging, neglected frame structure on a commercially zoned lot next to the busy station. It awaits redevelopment, with nothing to indicate that in happier days it was a gracious building and a major resting point for travellers heading north on Yonge Street.

Eglinton

Montgomery's Tavern, of Rebellion fame, was built on the west side of Yonge Street near Montgomery Avenue in the early 1830's by John Montgomery, the former Newtonbrook innkeeper. It was a two-storey frame building and "around the front of the house, which faced toward Toronto, ran a platform or 'stoop' raised on three steps to avoid the slush in spring thaws. On one side of the door was the usual large bar-room, over the main entrance a lamp, and before the house a huge signboard raised on high bearing the usual hospitable announcement."[27] The inn was rented to John Linfoot a week before the Rebellion, when the Montgomery family moved back to Newtonbrook. Mackenzie's rebels made it their headquarters for the attack on Toronto and it was burned to the ground during the skirmish.

In 1843, Montgomery returned to Yonge Street, as he predicted when he was condemned to hang after the Rebellion, and rebuilt his two-storey hotel a little south of the first one. This second "house was of wood and of excellent construction. It was built of boards six inches wide laid flat and every other board lapped over. It was then plastered."[28] Sir Richard Bonnycastle when travelling to Toronto from Holland Landing in 1845 mentioned Montgomery: "His tavern was burnt to the ground by the militia during the action, on account of the barbarous murder there of Colonel Moodie, a very old retired officer who was killed by Mackenzie's orders in cold blood. It is now rebuilt on a very extensive scale; and he is again there having been permitted to return, and his property, which was confiscated, has been restored to his creditors."[29] Eventually Montgomery rented the house to his son, William, and opened the Franklin House at 141 Yonge Street in 1855, and the Robinson House on Bay Street about 1859.

Charles McBride, a resident of Willowdale, bought the old Montgomery Hotel and opened it as the Prospect House in 1858. John Miller rented it in 1863-64, and then McBride returned for five more years.[30] The York Township Council and the Masonic Temple Lodge meetings were held there until about 1871 when they moved into the Masonic Building next door. When Prospect House caught fire and burned to the ground on November 20, 1881, the site was bought by John Oulcott who came to Canada from Staffordshire, England in 1863. Oulcott House, a three-storey brick building with a forty-eight foot frontage and 100 foot depth, was built about seventy-five feet north of the old site, with extensive driving sheds and stables. Oulcott opened it in 1883 and ran it for twenty-nine years, though it became a temperance house when "local option" was passed in Eglinton in 1908. Richard Hull owned it in 1917 and it was tenanted by Joseph Reddy.

About a mile and a quarter north of the Montgomery's Inn, on the west side of Yonge, stood a well-known road house called Nightingale's Hotel, or The Durham Ox.[31] James Nightingale built a low, two-storey tavern about 1840 with driving sheds on the north side, and Thomas Nightingale was the landlord. John Miller took over the inn in 1857, and later it burned to the ground.

The area north of Lawrence Avenue gradually developed, and

following 1873 Charles McBride, previous owner of the Prospect House, bought Finch's Tavern at Finch Avenue and Yonge. He tore it down, and with the timbers built the Bedford Park Hotel on his farm south of Fairlawn Avenue, on the west side of Yonge Street.[32] In 1888 William Brunskill was proprietor, and after the local option act was passed, the hotel was run as a temperance house by Edward Jackson. It is still standing today encased in a store front.

Fairbank

In 1867 Francis McFarlane bought property from Thomas Gladstone, an innkeeper, and operated the York and Vaughan Hotel, a two-storey frame building at the corner of Dufferin and Eglinton.[33] About 1870 the hotel was destroyed by fire and replaced with a new building located 600 feet to the north which burned down in 1912. McFarlane, besides running the inn, became a district agent for agricultural implements, selling and servicing such items as drills, rakes, ploughs, fanning-mills, and harrows.

Downsview

The hotels of Weston, catering to the Downsview population, were on Weston Road and included the Farmer's Home Inn, a two-storey, brick building managed by John McDonough in 1851, and later by P. Chapman; John Little's tavern, the Weston Hotel owned by John Boynton of Elia and managed by his son-in-law, John Kemp, and John Eagle's hotel, still standing today on the north-east corner of Lawrence and Weston Road. The latter was a large two-storey building with a long ell, with veranda and balcony facing Lawrence Avenue. A huge stable and a brick blacksmith shop stood in the courtyard ready to cater to the needs of the traveller or neighbouring farmer. North of Weston, on the corner of the Albion and Weston Roads, east of the bridge over the Humber, stood Downsview's only inn, a brick tavern run by Robert Hiscocks in 1860.[34]

Elia

On old Dufferin Street, about three-quarters of a mile north of Finch Avenue stood Jacob Kurtz's inn,[35] built about 1848 for his wife, Mary Mabley, and containing fifteen rooms and three fireplaces. In the 1850's when the Gore Vaughan Plank Road was built to straighten Dufferin Street north of Finch, this hotel was too far off the main road for business, and Jacob moved to an inn on the south-east corner of Steeles Avenue and new Dufferin in Fisherville.

Fisherville

In 1855, after the Gore and Vaughan Plank Road was built, Jacob Kurtz moved his hotel south of Steeles in Elia to an inn on the southeast corner of Steeles and the Plank Road (Dufferin Street).[36] This building was a large two-storey frame house facing Dufferin, with a tall, hanging gate announcing the name, Fisherville Hotel, and a driving shed across the road, on the west side of Dufferin. Jacob sold the inn to his brother-in-law James Mabley in 1858, who died soon afterwards. His widow married Abner Cherry and the Cherry family ran the hotel for over fifty years. Cherry paid exceptional attention to a patron's horse. Upon the arrival of a traveller, the bar was closed tightly until the horse had been unhitched, watered, fed, and bedded down for the night. The old Cherry House was later bought by Thomas Potton, who built a pavilion dance hall on the grounds. In 1920, this inn was called Hanging Gate Inn, and its inviting sign read:

> This gate hangs high
> And hinders none
> Refresh yourself
> And carry on.

In 1945 the old buildings were demolished by the University of Toronto, which took over the property and established its Connaught Medical Research Laboratories east of the West Branch of the Don River.

Humber Summit

Very little is known of the inns at Humber Summit. Edward Phillips ran the Plank Road Inn, a one-storey log house south of Steeles Avenue. William McKay's inn on the north-west corner of Islington and Steeles Avenues in Vaughan provided a place of refreshment in the 1850's and sixties for those travelling on Islington Avenue, back and forth to Woodbridge and other northern areas.

Don Mills

A tavern[37] stood on the north-west corner of Lawrence and Don Mills Road on property first owned by John Elliott and later by John Carruthers of Toronto. During the years 1851-61, and perhaps earlier, many farmers stopped to chat and refresh themselves on their way north with grain to be ground at the Gray Mills or with wool to be made into yarn or cloth at Alexander Milne's woollen mill to the east.

L'Amaroux

Prior to 1851 a tavern[38] stood about a quarter of a mile north of Finch Avenue, on the west side of Victoria Park Avenue. It was vacant by then and not in use in 1860, but nothing else is really known about it.

Patrick O'Sullivan, a native of County Cork, Ireland, emigrated to Canada with his parents. In 1860 he married Ann O'Reilly and they opened a hotel with two bedrooms, a bar, and meal service. It stood on her father's property on the north-west corner of Victoria Park and Sheppard, formerly Lansing Cut-off, with driving sheds to the west of it, and a pump near the front door.[39] Patrick died the following year and his wife carried on the business. Their son, Michael, opened the O'Sullivan's Corners Post Office in the hotel and became its first postmaster in 1892. A Sunday drive with dinner at O'Sullivan's was a favourite treat until the post office and hotel building were demolished about 1954.

NOTES

1   John Howison, *Sketches of Upper Canada* (Edinburgh: Oliver & Boyd, 1821), pp. 118-119.

2   *Ibid.*, p. 207.

3   *Ibid.*, p. 42.

4   By-laws regarding inns for York Township, passed in 1851, were lost when the Masonic Hall at Eglinton burned to the ground in 1881. The municipal offices were in the building.

5   Province of Upper Canada, *Statutes*, 1850, 13 & 14 Victoriae. Cap. 27, pp. 1197-1200.

6   A. F. Hunter, *A History of Simcoe County* (Historical Committee of Simcoe County, 1948), p. 22. Joseph Rémi Vallière de Saint-Réal, 1787-1847.

7   E. G. Firth, *The Town of York, 1793-1815* (Toronto: University of Toronto Press, 1962), p. lxxxviii.

8   *British Colonist* (September 18, 1839).

9   T. A. Reed, "Yonge Street Highway", Toronto Public Libraries, T. A. Reed Collection.

10   *Ibid.*, p. 23.

11   *Ibid.*, p. 22.

12   Lot 13, 1st concession east of Yonge Street. Labelled "Staffordshire House" on the Tremaine Map, of York County (1860).

13   Lot 15, 1st concession west of Yonge Street. Sheppard is also spelled Shepherd, and Thomas may be related to Joseph Shepard's family.

14   Paul Sheppard who lived in Scarborough, carved the original steeple for St. Paul's Church, L'Amaroux, and also St. James' Cathedral steeple in Toronto. Knowledge of his work on the Golden Lion statue was told to T. A. Reed by Charles McBride.

15   J. R. Robertson, *Old Toronto*, ed. E. C. Kyte (Toronto: Macmillan, 1954), p. 112.

16   John Meek was proprietor in 1851, Charles Sheppard in 1857, Cornelius van Nostrand

and his wife Fanny Sheppard van Nostrand in 1869-70, John Anderson in 1870, Nelson Davis in 1870, Benjamin Pullinger in 1871, Francis Cosgrove in 1873, Richard Walkinshaw in 1875, and James Thompson in 1883 and still proprietor in 1890-91.

17 J. R. Nason, *Nason's East and West Riding of the County of York, or Townships of Etobicoke, Markham, Scarboro', Vaughan & York Directory* (Toronto: Dudley & Burns, 1871). Lot 15, 2nd concession west of Yonge Street.

18 B. P. Davis, and C. L. Davis, *The Davis Family and the Leather Industry, 1834-1934* (Toronto: Ryerson, 1934), p. 69. Lot 20, 1st concession west of Yonge Street.

19 T. A. Reed, *op. cit.*, p. 26. H. Scadding places this inn in York: H. Scadding, *Toronto of Old* (Toronto: Adam Stevenson & Co., 1873), p. 437. Lot 22, 1st concession east of Yonge Street.

20 John Langstaff, "Old Hotels on Yonge Street", The *Sun* (July 25, 1903).

21 H. Scadding, *op. cit.*, p. 447.

22 Sir Richard Bonnycastle, *Canada and Canadians in 1846* (London: Henry Colburn, 1846), pp. 188-190.

23 Lot 21, 1st concession east of Yonge Street. Innkeepers following John Finch were: Thomas Palmer in 1860, John Likens in 1864, James Fenley in 1869, and William Kirk in 1871.

24 T. A. Reed, *op. cit.*, p. 20.

25 H. Scadding, *op. cit.*, p. 403. Lot 26, 1st concession east of Yonge Street in Markham.

26 K. W. Jefferys, "Yonge Street in Olden Days", The *Enterprise* (May 2, 1935). Lot 26, 1st concession west of Yonge Street.

27 Lot 1, 1st concession west of Yonge Street. *History of Toronto and the County of York* (Toronto: C. Blackett Robinson, 1885), I, pt. I, 168.

28 T. A. Reed, *op. cit.*, p. 19.

29 Bonnycastle, *op. cit.*, pp. 190-191.

30 Charles McBride sold the Prospect House to Thomas Beatty of Leslieville in 1870 who sold it three years later to William Smith.

31 Lots 6 and 7, 1st concession west of Yonge Street. T. A. Reed, *op. cit.*, p. 19.

32 *Ibid.*, p. 20. Charles McBride owned a farm on lot 7, 1st concession west of Yonge Street.

33 Lot 1, 3rd concession west of Yonge Street. In 1873 Rhodolphus Wilson became proprietor, and in 1884 Francis McFarlane returned.

34 Lot 12, 6th concession west of Yonge Street.

35 Lot 23, 3rd concession west of Yonge Street.

36 Lot 25, 2nd concession west of Yonge Street.

37 Lot 6, 3rd concession east of Yonge Street.

38 Lot 22, 4th concession east of Yonge Street.

39 Lot 14, 4th concession east of Yonge Street. O'Reilly is sometimes spelled Reilly.

Education

IN 1798 THE EXECUTIVE COUNCIL OF UPPER CANADA RECOMMENDED the establishment of grammar schools in Cornwall, Kingston, Newark, and Sandwich. No schools were officially opened, however, until after the passage of the Grammar Schools Act in 1807 when eight were founded. The Common Schools Act of 1816 was the next step toward mass education, and the first attempt to provide for the wants of the people. It enabled local citizens to come together and pledge money to build and operate a school under the direction of "three fit and discreet trustees." For its part the Government granted a sum of not more than thirty pounds toward the teacher's salary.

Early settlers, particularly those who had emigrated to Canada from the more settled and organized areas of the United States, realized the importance of education for their children, and a log school was erected in Newtonbrook as early as 1801. Only a few farms were cleared so schoolhouses were built on the road or path, otherwise the parents worried that the children might get lost in the woods or be attacked by wild animals.

The log schoolhouse erected in the 1820's was about eighteen by twenty feet, built of chinked, unhewn logs eighteen inches in diameter with a fireplace at one end of the room. Its chimney, made of poles lying one on top of the other plastered with clay, frequently caught fire during very cold weather. A woodshed or lean-to stood near the door and logs supplied by the farmers were split by the older boys who tended the fire. Two outhouses stood behind the building, one for the boys and the other for the girls. One or two small windows with twelve six-inch panes provided the only light. Two rows of crude log desks, one on each side of the room faced the windows, and two rows of log benches or forms without backs were placed around the walls for the younger children whose feet dangled in the air most of the day. Sometimes, however, they found room to sit cross-legged with an elbow on one knee and a hand supporting their chin while the other hand held a book before their weary eyes. The pupils were usually from six to ten years old, but young men and women eighteen to twenty years of age often returned to school during the winter months if a competent teacher was employed. The girls sat on one side of the room dressed in stiff "linsey-woolsey,"[1] with white cuffs, petticoats, bodices, and white kerchiefs around their necks. The boys, wearing knee breeches that usually hung down below the knee, long-sleeved collarless shirts, and short jackets, sat together on the other side. The teacher's table and chair were placed near the warmth of the fireplace, and on cold winter days the poor pupils farthest from the fire could hardly hold pens in their stiff, frozen fingers. Standard equipment in every school included a lamp to provide light on dark rainy days, an eight-inch bell that clanged each morning and afternoon to call the children into school from outside, a pointer used to threaten the children if they did not behave themselves, and of course the tawse, or multithonged strap, for inflicting punishment. A pail and dipper for drinking-water sat on the floor near the table.

Itinerant teachers were often discharged British soldiers, worn-out tailors or shoemakers, or men who had failed in all other undertakings. It was not necessary to have a teaching diploma and many of the teachers had only a smattering of education. Their essential qualification was their "ability to suppress disorder while the pupils committed to memory the lessons of the text book and recited them."[2] In a few cases, however, men with the advantage of a superior education, like Elihu Pease in Newtonbrook, undertook the job, but rarely stayed for more than a year. The salary for these early teachers was meagre, about twenty-five cents a month per pupil, although free board and lodging were provided during the engagement by having the teacher move every two or three days from one student's home to another.

School opened and closed each day with a prayer, and religious and moral instruction consisting of reading the Bible and memorizing New Testament verses continued periodically throughout the day. About the only other subjects taught were reading, writing, spelling, and arithmetic because, for the most part, the schoolmasters themselves had very little training beyond that. There were only a few textbooks and they were extremely uninteresting. A slanted board for writing ran along the wall, and each student supplied any paper that could be found, his own slate and rag for cleaning, and home-made ink, pens and rulers. One way to make ink was by boiling the inner bark of the soft maple in water and adding a little copperas (iron sulphate) to the solution. Pens were made by sharpening the large quill feathers taken from the wing of the goose. People often kept a bundle of these on hand to fashion into pens with a small knife, later called a penknife.

The school hours in 1856 in some districts were 9 a.m. to 4 p.m., Saturdays included because the parents objected to paying tuition fees for holidays. It was 1860 before the children were given a half-holiday on Saturdays. Is it any wonder that they became bored and frequently turned their attention to stirring up a little excitement?

In the spring the roads became a slippery mass of mud and clay that clung tenaciously to each boot as the children and young people walked down the road to school. Hand-forged iron scrapers were provided outside the door, but the youngsters often wandered in without using them, tracking hunks of sticky mud into the classroom. Some teenagers, when lessons got a little dull, picked the mud off the floor and threw it at a friend, or on the wall or ceiling. This later dropped to the floor or on the head of some unfortunate pupil with a "plop" when it dried a little. The culprit, if caught, was severely switched or had his hands strapped with the tawse, much to the amusement of the older children and the horror of the younger ones. Since discipline was the order of the day, the strap was used when children did not learn their lessons or for misbehaviour; whispering was often stopped by gagging the offender with a small wooden board; and hot mustard was applied to the tongue of those who lied.

THE 1850 SCHOOLS

Following 1847 many of the old log schoolhouses were replaced with red brick structures that provided better light with two or three large windows along each side of the building. Others were replaced by frame buildings and the young children sitting on long benches around the walls shivered with the cold wind that whistled through the cracks at their backs.

One or two new box stoves that held two-foot logs were installed to replace the old fireplaces, but it was still cold inside. Each winter morning the ink had to be thawed out on top of the stove and often it froze again during the day. Occasionally some mischievous boy would leave the top on the bottle as it thawed resulting in an explosion and a large black blob of ink on the ceiling.

A huge bell placed in the tower on the roof could be heard three miles away when the heavy bell rope was pulled by the teacher to call the children to school each morning and afternoon. Many a straggler preferred to play hooky if he were still some distance away rather than face the wrath of the teacher.

Egerton Ryerson, an active Methodist minister and a constant visitor to North York churches, as Superintendent of Education from 1844 to 1876 developed the Ontario School System. A series of School Acts from 1841 on gradually eliminated the haphazard, inefficient school methods of the past. A normal school for teacher-training was opened in 1847; the Irish National School Books, a complete and admirable series, were recommended by the Ontario Board of Education; and the district and local superintendents made regular inspections and wrote reports on buildings and equipment.

During this period school was open all year round in some districts with the younger children attending school in the late spring and summer. In this way they avoided snow storms with their huge drifts, and daily long walks to and from school in cold weather. The teenagers attended in the winter months when the chores were light. Each morning the boys fed and watered the cows, horses, pigs, and chickens, and perhaps milked the cow before trudging off to spend the day in school. Upon returning home extra wood had to be chopped and the woodbox filled before supper. Is it any wonder that truancy became a severe problem and lateness plagued the classroom?

Parents also felt that school was not necessary for the older girls, since a future housewife did not need to know how to read or write. On the other hand, it was felt she must learn how to run the household by assisting her mother with the spinning and weaving; making clothes, as well as washing them; knitting sweaters, mittens, socks, caps, and mufflers; helping with soap and candle making; lending a hand with fruit-preserving in the fall; and, of course, preparing and clearing away the three daily meals, which in itself could prove a formidable task since families often included ten or twelve children.

Through Egerton Ryerson's public relations program on education, and the loss of many good teachers, parents began to consider seriously the qualifications of the teacher and the prospects of increased salaries. In 1853 teachers in the Don School received £60 a year. By 1856 salaries had risen to £105, but a drop occurred during the next few years indicating a period of poor crops or general depression.

New subjects, grammar and geography, were added to the curriculum and maps and blackboards were soon made available. In 1855 a school library was added in the Don School, and the boys found that some books about the size of Spenser's *Faerie Queen*, made splendid missiles for bombarding invading mice. The standards of conduct, clothing, and hygiene were still very low, and no games or amusements were added to break the long lesson period. Strict discipline was essential to keep order in the classroom, and teachers capable of being good disciplinarians were in demand. Good teachers often left one school to obtain a better salary somewhere else, and poor teachers were fired in expectation that another more competent one could be found quickly.

Because of the number of grades in the one-room schoolhouse it was a remarkable accomplishment for any teacher to have complete control over his classes. There was constant movement in the room. Some children were "asking permission to go out, others to get a drink, and many flocking to the teacher's desk with words to pronounce, sums to be examined and corrected, pens to be mended. . . . So that the place [was] filled with noise and disorder, rendering study impossible, and anything like the cultivation of cheerful and benevolent affections entirely out of the question."[4]

Educational standards were greatly improved following 1857 when regular quarterly examinations and a more interesting program for both teachers and pupils were introduced. Following test sessions relaxing parties were held in J. Perkins Bull's orchard in Downsview, and according to his account, cakes, pies, sardines and poultry provided a bountiful lunch, "and if a keen appetite be peculiar to children, we might infer that second childhood was overtaking many of the adults."[5] Races and games, played in the Bull's orchard, rounded out these enjoyable afternoons. A comprehensive carefully selected list of prize books was furnished for the trustees of the district and township schools from which they could select awards for outstanding pupils, thus providing incentive for the others. There were also merit cards, with beautifully illustrated mottoes, to be awarded weekly for punctuality, good conduct, diligence, and perfect recitations.

Regularly during the week temperance societies and school and church trustee meetings were held, as well as debates on "free education," with Superintendent Ryerson and many prominent citizens advocating the idea, and most of the farmers opposing it. Light was provided by candles or oil lamps on the window sills. Each Sunday, Methodist or Presbyterian church services were held in the school building and it became the centre for church socials such as teas, oyster suppers, strawberry festivals, and Christmas parties.

EDUCATION AFTER 1870

By 1870 the parents displayed much more interest and took an active part in the social activities of the school, including the spelling match. Those with daughters attending school began to promote the hiring of lady teachers. Larger brick schools were built in many areas, with a raised platform across the front of the classroom to elevate the teacher's desk, providing a better view of his pupils. Two doors were provided for fire safety, as well as small porches for protection in winter.

Although literature, history, music, and drawing were added to the curriculum, the school texts and teaching were still not interesting enough to hold the attention of a vigorous group of pent-up youngsters and teenagers who were mostly interested in farming. Pen nibs were often jabbed into the legs of reciting pupils, pigtails were frequently dipped into inkwells, and slates were broken over the heads of culprits, who thus earned a wooden collar, the broken edges of the slate threatening their necks. According to the Victoria Park School minute book "Stanley Smith brought an axe to school and chopped down the school steps." Children were soundly flogged for such actions, as well as for not learning their lessons, and many were sent to a stool in a corner with the dunce's cap on their heads. In one school the stove legs were very shaky and the boys soon discovered a good kick would separate the pipes sufficiently to fill the room with smoke, making it necessary to close the school for the rest of the day.

Because the teaching was so deplorable in the early years, strict rules and regulations went into effect in some areas. Each day the teacher was responsible for filling the lamps with oil, cleaning the shades or chimneys as they were called, and trimming the wicks. In one community the regulations stated that men teachers could take one evening each week for courting purposes, or two evenings a week if they went to church regularly. After their ten hours in school, the teachers were expected to pass the remaining time of day reading the Bible or other worthy books. Women teachers who married, or were engaged in unseemly conduct were dismissed. It was suggested also that every teacher should lay aside a goodly sum of his earnings for his benefit during his declining years so that he would not become a burden on society. Any teacher who smoked, used liquor in any form, frequented pool or public halls, or had a shave in a barber shop cast his worth, intentions, and integrity under suspicion. The teacher who performed his labours faithfully without fault for five years would be given a munificent increase of twenty-five cents per week in his pay providing the Board of Education approved.

INDIVIDUAL COMMUNITIES

York Mills

As York Mills[6] grew a schoolhouse became necessary for teaching as well as a meeting place for church services. Although its exact location is unknown, in 1807 a log school house probably stood on the hill behind the Jolly Miller Hotel, either just north or just south of Old Yonge Street. Seneca Ketchum may have purchased land from Thomas Mercer for the purpose, but in 1815 the building "was in a ruinous state. It had no chimney, but merely a large hole in the roof through which the smoke might escape when there happened to be any fire, and the furniture consisted of a short school form, a table and a broken chair."[7]

The second York Mills School, known as S.S. No. 3, was a red brick, one-room building with two doors facing south, located near the north-west corner of John and Yonge Streets. It was built in 1847 by the District Council of the Home District, who purchased the land from the widow of James Hogg, the miller.

In 1893 the third two-storey York Mills school was erected near the location of the present building on York Mills Road. The style of the building was similar to the Willowdale School built the year before, with a high bell tower and a large and small room on each floor. The lower floor rooms were used for classes, and according to Inspector D. F. Fotheringham's report on April 14, 1905, the premises were in fine condition, but he had a suggestion for the school authorities: "get a good long stand for your fine large dictionary in four volumes. It can hardly be used packed away as it is at present." Thirty-seven students attended school in 1908 and forty-seven in 1909. The top floor rooms were used for church and school socials, meetings, and dances, and on March 4, 1908, E. F. Wood, the Secretary-Treasurer, mentions in his minutes that the trustees' "meeting was called to discuss the Inspectors report and to see the new slate Black boards which have been put up." And "It was also decided to raise the rent of the hall for dancing parties thereby discouraging the same. Not less than $3.00 nor more than $5.00 according to the party wanting it." The building was destroyed by fire in November, 1924, and the fourth and present school was constructed in 1925. It is now known as York Mills Public School, but was called Baron Renfrew for many years. The old school still standing on Yonge just south of John Street was purchased, renovated and used for years by Frank Albutt, a cabinet maker.

Willowdale

A School Superintendent reported the existence of a log school in Willowdale[8] as early as 1801, indicating that the Cummer and Johnson families, the first settlers, were interested in providing education for their children soon after their arrival in Willowdale. However, this may have been the log school in the centre of the road in Newtonbrook, reported by John Stegmann the same year (see Newtonbrook). Early schools were built in the road allowance, or path cut through the trees, so that the children could easily find the building without going into the woods.

In 1842 a brick schoolhouse was constructed with 38,500 bricks made on the Gibson farm by Henry Neal. It became known as the Willowdale School, S.S. No. 4, and it stood near the corner of Ellerslie and Yonge on a tenth of an acre of land sold by Abraham Johnson for £10. Although serving the children from the surrounding neighbourhood, for some the building was a long distance away, particularly on cold mornings. The Bales and Jackson children had to walk all the way from Bathurst and Sheppard Avenue, and the Joseph Shepard, Elihu Pease, and Thomas Sheppard children, from Lansing.

In 1875 a two-storey schoolhouse replaced the 1842 building. It was erected on the Wallace property south of the first school and contained two large rooms, one on each floor. Several windows on each side of the building provided good light, and one wonders if the shutters on the first floor windows were an extravagant frill or just a protective measure against flying stones. A sturdy, wooden swing was put up, as well, to amuse the younger children. Edwin Ball taught at the school for twenty-five years, and as Superintendent of the Sunday school of Willowdale Methodist Episcopal Church he is said to have contributed much toward moulding the characters of his students.

In 1892 another larger, two-storey school was constructed with a handsome belfry rising above one of the front entrances. Although the exterior appearance gave the impression that it contained many classrooms there were actually only four rooms, a large and a small one on each floor, together with spacious cloakrooms. Also, the large room on the top floor was used as a public hall, and the small room provided a dressing room for entertainers. The classrooms were downstairs. The building cost approximately $5,000, was designed by Harold Gibson, and built on the same property as the first school. On the day of the opening, Schoolmaster Ball marched his pupils up the road to the new school.

During the First World War it was used as a barracks for the "land army" girls who were brought out to harvest flax on William Wallace's farm. When McKee Avenue School was built east of Yonge in 1927, the old school was used as an annex. The bell, which at one time called pupils to school, found its way to Africa due to the active missionaries in the district, and now serves native school children. On September 15,

1950, classes were discontinued; the building served as a Magistrates' Court and justice was administered there for thirteen years. On the completion of a new courthouse behind the school, the old building was razed in 1963.

Newtonbrook

John Stegmann, formerly a German officer in a Hessian regiment, was directed by Surveyor-General D. W. Smith to report on the condition of Yonge Street in 1801. His report stated: "[Lot] No. 25, west side, complied with, East side, complied with;—nothing done to the street, and a schoolhouse erected in the centre of the street. This is the end of the Township of York."[9] In 1820 Elihu Pease taught in this early schoolhouse.[10]

In 1847 a brick school, S.S. No. 5, was built on the north side of Drewry about half way between Yonge and Bathurst. Church services and Sunday school meetings were held in the new building rather than the old log schoolhouse. For evening services members of the congregation brought their candle sconces and hung them on the wall to light the room. These sconces were tin candle sticks with high backs which protected the wall and acted as reflectors. Another one-room brick school was built in 1878 just west of Yonge with space provided for the teacher to live in the building. This school still stands today converted into the Newtonbrook Gospel Tabernacle. A fourth school, built in 1928 across the road on the north side of Drewry, was a four-room structure erected at a cost of $35,000. As a school Trustee for thirty-eight years, G. R. Goulding was very prominent in its planning and development, and the school originally was named after him.

Eglinton

The first Eglinton school, a chinked, unhewn log building, twenty-eight by thirty-eight feet, was operating on the east side of Bayview Avenue in 1816.[11] The District Council finally bought the property, 406 square feet, from Alexander McCormick in 1847. Many heated discussions took place in the old school, often in regard to the question of free schooling. In this case, James Hervey Price and Jesse Ketchum, Jr., were the ones to press for its adoption; the farmers, by and large, remained adamant in their opposition. A new brick school was built in 1850, and finally another two-storey schoolhouse was erected on the west side of Yonge Street across from the post office in 1879 to accommodate the increasing population.

Fairbank

Fairbank's first log school, completed around 1825, was on the Dollery property, north of Eglinton, west of Dufferin.[12] Originally S.S. No. 16, it was later changed to S.S. No. 15 and called "Needhams" after the school teacher.[13] This log building was replaced in 1863 with a brick school built on the Watson lot across the road. In an entry for December 22, 1863, William A. Clarke mentions a social event in his diary: "We all at a Tea Party at Fair Bank School House."[14] Wild leeks grew in the district and the boys ate them on the way to school, much to the disgust of the teacher and other pupils; and strawberries growing wild on William Moore's farm were so plentiful a hat full could be picked in a short time.

Dublin

In 1829 when William Duncan's growing family reached school age, he built a log schoolhouse on his farm west of Dufferin Street and hired a school master.[15] The second school, another log structure, was erected by the community, half a lot east of Dufferin, on the north side of Sheppard Avenue. By 1872 a third brick school was built across the road. Apparently the Department of Health objected that the privy for the school was too near the building, although it was already on the very edge of the property. A meeting was held in the schoolhouse and a heated argument ensued. Finally Elizabeth Watson, feeling that it was not right to wrangle in a building used weekly as a church, announced that she would be willing to have the privy on her side of the fence to settle the dispute. With that there was a rush for the door, part of the fence was torn down, the privy was pushed through the opening putting the door in line with the fence, and peace was restored.[16]

A former teacher recalled a raised platform across the front of her room, a wood stove with an open woodshed on the west side of the school, and near the front door, a pump with a battered metal cup that everyone used. The school originally had one door, but a second was added in case of fire. The well-known "frog pond" at the rear of the grounds was always a centre of activity in winter and summer. As the community continued to grow, a new public school was built in 1944 with the old 1872 cornerstone mounted in the wall of the main entrance.

Downsview

LAWRENCE AND BATHURST CROSSROADS

As an enterprising neighbourhood leader with a family of ten children, Henry Mulholland was instrumental in establishing a school in this community.[17] By 1817 a log school stood on the south-east corner of Lawrence and Bathurst. It was replaced in 1864 by a new solid brick, one-room building at a cost of $655. The new school, S.S. No. 14, was later called Forest Hill School and stood on the south-east corner of Bathurst and Glencairn Avenue.

A two-room brick building replaced the second school in 1921. This building was located north of Lawrence on the west side of Bathurst, south of the church, on Fred Mulholland's farm and cost $46,000. At the opening ceremonies, James Graham, a teacher in 1863, gave the address, and the school's name was changed to Saranac. To-day this school is used by the Audio-Visual Department of the Board of Education and the Saranac pupils are accommodated in a modern building to the west on the same property.

KEELE AND WILSON CROSSROADS

An old log schoolhouse built about 1828 straddled Keele Street just north of Wilson Avenue.[18] A substantial building, constructed of logs eighteen inches in diameter, it served the Downsview children for many years. After the 1850 Wesleyan Methodist church was erected, however, the farmers decided that the teacher should hold his classes in the new building rather than in the crowded, unsanitary, log school-house. In 1857 Squire Bull appointed William Watson, Christopher's son, as teacher at $500 per annum. As well as being "strong on the strap," he provided regular quarterly examinations for his pupils. The school trustees officially purchased the old church for $515 in 1870 and the sum of eleven dollars was collected from the sale of the old log school. The new school was heated by two stoves, one at each end, and for Christmas entertainments parents brought oil lamps and placed them along the window sills. In 1887 it was enlarged and brick-veneered, and it was finally razed in 1948, when a seven-room brick building was officially opened by Reeve George Mitchell.

Elia

The first Elia log school stood on the north-west corner of Finch Avenue and Keele Street in 1830, on Jacob Stong's property.[19] It was replaced in 1851 by a frame structure, forty by thirty feet, known as S.S. No. 18, which was built on the same site with board siding. In 1873 a new brick school was erected across the road on the north-east corner, and the first teacher was Jacob Hoover. In 1956 this school was closed and the pupils were transported by bus to the Downsview School.

Emery

By 1834 school sessions were held in a log house on the farm of

Charles Grubbe south of Finch Avenue on Weston Road.[20] On January 1, 1851, the farmers met at a log pile on the corner of Finch and discussed a new school for the neighbourhood. It was decided to replace the old building with a more modern structure containing improved lighting and heating, and six months later a one-room brick school was opened, built on the property of John Crosson. The first teacher was well qualified, a Miss Scobey from Scotland. In 1886 continuation school classes were taught by Lizzie Robinson. By 1914 the community had outgrown its school and a new brick building was constructed beside the old one which was finally pulled down. This third school closed its doors in June 1958, and the old school bell was mounted in a cairn in the courtyard of the present Emery Collegiate Institute, south-east of the corner.

Kaiserville

Stong's schoolhouse was erected in 1824 just east of the present cemetery at Steeles and Jane Street in Black Creek Pioneer Village.[21] Because the settlers were Pennsylvania Germans the teaching was originally in German. The school was discontinued in 1839 when York Township was laid out in School Sections and the children attended school in the community of Edgeley, to the north.

Humber Summit

Considering the large number of children in the neighbourhood an early school was essential. Classes were held in a log building on the Parsons' property,[22] known as the Parsons' School, until after 1851 when the children attended the school at Finch and Weston Road.

Don Mills

The first Don school was a log house raised by means of a bee in 1837 and opened in 1838.[23] It was built on John Hogg's farm adjoining William Gray's property. One of the memorable features of this log schoolhouse was a loose board in the floor and a movable log in the foundation. On one occasion, the boys inside, tired of the strict discipline, quietly slipped through the hole, one at a time. Finally, alerted by the noise outside, the teacher realized his class had dwindled and out he went to chase the boys back inside. At each round of the building, the boys would slip in through the hole, one or two at a time, until soon the teacher found he was chasing himself. Upon entering the school, the distraught teacher found his pupils apparently hard at work.

In 1853, the school trustees decided to build a new school, S.S. No. 9, on the south-east corner of Lawrence and Don Mills Road on land donated by William Milne, and on December 1, 1853, Duncan Fitzpatrick marched his pupils down the Don Independent Road to the new red brick schoolhouse. Fees were 7½d. per month per pupil. In 1854 there were 155 children. The old log schoolhouse was hauled by oxen to John Hogg's farm and used as a stable.

Improved conditions did not inhibit this fun-loving class, and young Butler was an excellent ventriloquist. He imitated a cat and disturbed the class to such an extent that the teacher sent students out looking for the animal under the school building. Across the road from the school Charles Watson had considerable difficulty protecting his pear crop from the boys when the teacher went home for lunch.

In 1855 a school library was established and the teacher became the librarian and was paid by Council. According to the 1856 records, forty people circulated books and only 5% of the general population were unable to read and write.

The corner stone of the new Don school was laid on October 7, 1924, by Thomas Gray. Situated on the same site as the second school, it was officially opened on January 30, 1925, and the following Monday morning the children were marched from the old school to the new. The Public Library moved into the basement of the new school, but later, with the growing need for more classrooms, it was eventually disbanded and the books were given away. Joseph Watson bought the old 1853 school for $500 and had it moved to the north-west corner of Lawrence and Don Mills Road where it served as a granary.

Oriole

A School Superintendent reported a log school in Oriole as early as 1826, and the Harrison, Brock, Hunter, Wilson and Miller children all attended.[24] In 1848, the year the Toronto School Board had a row with the City Council over money for education, and closed all their schools for twelve months, a brick schoolhouse, S.S. No. 11, was built on the Clark property facing Sheppard Avenue to replace the old building. As there were thirteen children in each of the Clark and Mulholland families alone, the little log school must have been very crowded.

A new red brick school was built in 1874 on the north-west corner of the school yard and additional land was purchased. George S. Henry, trustee, secretary, and auditor of the school for forty years, offered to donate property for a consolidated school, but this generous offer was blocked by a few dissenters. Instead, a new brick school was built on the old site. Teacher Olive Keam closed the old school and opened the new one in 1910. This school was heated with a block stove that held logs of wood two feet long. In 1958 classes were terminated and the building was used as a residence and office until 1966 when it was demolished in order to widen Sheppard Avenue.

O'Sullivan's Corners

In 1856 S.S. No. 23 stood on Victoria Park, a quarter of a mile north of York Mills Road, on the property of William Sylvester.[25] In 1873 land was expropriated from George O'Reilly, who vigorously protested because his farm had only a narrow frontage on the town line. A white frame school trimmed in red was built on a half acre, enclosed with a red picket fence. The attendance was small. At one time the only pupil was Tom Phelan, now a Toronto lawyer, and a descendant of the O'Sullivans. The log-book of this school reports some unusual day to day incidents: "Ronald Muirhead broke his arm for the third time. . . . The flagpole fell, breaking Mr. W. Muirhead's leg. . . . Tom Phelan traded his tricycle with Dave Mason for his Shetland pony. The parents made them trade back."

In 1946 the school was rented from North York and operated by the Scarborough Board of Education. Later it was used as a residence, and in 1965 was razed to make way for the Macdonald-Cartier Freeway. Spencer Clark, owner of the Guild Inn in Scarborough, salvaged the school, including the bell, and plans to rebuild it as a pioneer exhibit.

L'Amaroux

The first Zion School was a small log structure built about 1829 on the north side of Finch Avenue, on Henry Scrace's farm.[26] In 1867 the school superintendent estimated the property to be worth $20, and it was felt that a new building was needed. In 1869 a fine, one-room brick school, S.S. No. 12, was built down the road on the south side of Finch, east of Leslie Street. Here Miss Helen Delury taught for seven years at a salary of $300 per annum, supplemented by $25 for janitorial service and stoking the pot-belly stove with coal. The older boys, some as old as 21, helped her lift the heavy scuttle. This, the last, unaltered, "little red schoolhouse," which served as a community centre for a number of years and closed in 1955, belongs at present to the North York Public Library.

NOTES

1   A rough cloth of half linen and half wool.

2   Ontario, Royal Commission on Education, *Report,* 1950 (Toronto: King's Printer, 1950), p. 11.

3   J. G. Hodgins, *Documentary History of Education in Upper Canada* (Toronto: King's Printer, 1900), VII, 107.

4   J. G. Hodgins, *The Establishment of Schools and Colleges in Ontario, 1792-1910* (Toronto: King's Printer, 1910), II, 85.

5   W. P. Bull, *From Oxford to Ontario; A History of the Downsview Community* (Toronto: Bull Foundation, 1941), p. 201.

6   First school: lot 10, 1st concession east of Yonge; Second: lot 11, 1st concession west of Yonge; Third: lot 10, 1st concession east of Yonge.

7   *The Church,* V (September 6, 1843). As quoted in M. A. Graham, *150 Years at York Mills* (Toronto: General Publishing, 1966), p. 20.

8   Second School: lot 19, 1st concession west of Yonge Street; Third: lot 18, 1st concession west of Yonge Street; Fourth: lot 19, 1st concession west of Yonge Street. Although the Willowdale School changed very little over the years, at various stages it was known as Willowdale School, Brown School, Yonge Street School, Willowdale Continuation School, Willowdale High School, Queen Mary Annex and McKee Annex.

9   Scadding, *op. cit.,* pp. 427-429. School was built in road allowance so that children could find it.

10 Second School: lot 23, 1st concession west of Yonge; Third: lot 22, 1st concession west of Yonge; Fourth: lot 23, 1st concession west of Yonge.

11 Second school: lot 1, 2nd concession east of Yonge Street; Hodgins, *The Establishment of Schools and Colleges in Ontario, 1792-1910,* I, 257. Third school: lot 2, 1st concession west of Yonge Street.

12 First school: lot 2, 3rd concession west of Yonge Street; Second: lot 3, 2nd concession west of Yonge Street in North York.

13 *Fairbank United Church, 1889-1939,* Golden Jubilee Anniversary Services, October 1, 3, 5, 1939. 50th Anniversary pamphlet.

14 *Ibid.*

15 First school: lot 16, 3rd concession west of Yonge Street; Second: lot 16, 2nd concession west of Yonge; Third: lot 15, 2nd concession west of Yonge; Fourth: same as the third.

16 Bull, *op. cit.,* pp. 69-71.

17 First school at Bathurst and Lawrence area: lot 5, 1st concession west of Yonge Street; Second: lot 4, 1st concession west of Yonge; Third: lot 6, 2nd concession west of Yonge.

18 Keele and Wilson: First school: lot 11, 3rd concession west of Yonge Street; Second: same.

19 Finch and Keele: lot 21, 4th concession west of Yonge Street.

20 First school: lot 17, 6th concession west of Yonge Street; Second: lot 21, 5th concession west of Yonge.

21 Lot 25, 4th concession west of Yonge Street.

22 Lot 22, 6th concession west of Yonge Street.

23 First school: east half of lot 7, 3rd concession east of Yonge Street; Second: east half of lot 5, 3rd concession east of Yonge; Third: same.

24 First school: lot 15, 2nd concession east of Yonge Street; Second: same.

25 O'Sullivan's Corners: First school: lot 12, 4th concession east of Yonge Street; Second: lot 13, 4th concession east of Yonge.

26 First school: lot 21, 3rd concession east of Yonge Street; Second: lot 20, 3rd concession east of Yonge.

Early Industries

Craftsmen or specialists in various trades came into being in order to fulfil the day-to-day requirements of an expanding society. Originally each settler made his own ploughs, wagons, buildings, bricks, churns, pails, and the harnesses for his horses. However, some men were more skilled than others and it was found profitable and more efficient for the farmers to accept the well-made products of others in place of their own. Gradually, as specialization increased, craftsmen built up trades and industries evolved. Some of the important early industries in North York are explained here in some detail, followed by a list of "Trades and Professions" in the next chapter.

BLACKSMITHING

The early farmers had their own forge buildings and did their own horseshoeing and repairing of equipment. The blacksmith, however, soon became an indispensable member of the economic community. Not only was he concerned with shoeing horses, but he was also responsible for the repair and manufacture of a wide range of farm and domestic equipment such as ploughs, harrows, runners, and tireing wheels, making edge-tools, cooking pots, hinges, and guns. The blacksmith often operated in conjunction with or in the vicinity of a wheelwright, a wagon maker, and a miller. This made it possible for the farmer to have new shoes put on his horses, his equipment made or mended, and his grain processed at one location.

Although the details of metalworking varied from article to article, as well as according to the patron's specifications, the general procedure was as follows: First, before placing the piece of metal in his fire the smith pumped his bellows to get the coals glowing red. Into this gleaming bed went the metal, where it remained until it became dead white in colour and, sprinkling sparks, it was pulled from the fire with long tongs. Like lightning the smith had it on his anvil and hammered it into shape, first with the sledge and then with a smaller hammer. After a quick, sizzling dip in the water barrel, it was re-examined, reshaped if necessary, then finished.

According to a day-book of 1874, blacksmiths were charging the following prices:

Hinges and springs on end board	$1.00
New irons to pump	.60
Ironing harrows	3.50
Ironing whipple tree	.20
Sharpening share	.10
Repairs to harrow	1.75
Setting 1 shoe	.12½
2 new shoes	.75
1 new shoe	.37½
Irons for sleigh box	1.25
3 hoops on hogshead	.60
Sharpening and putting in 36 harrow teeth	.90
Work to plough	5.00
Ironing neck yoke	1.25
Sundrie repairs to reaper	.40

BRICKMAKING

Some of the early houses were made of mud-blocks protected by stucco or wood siding. The method of making these bricks was very simple. An oval pit was dug and filled with pure clay, which was saturated with water for twenty-four hours. A yoke of oxen tread or tempered it, and during this operation short straw was added at the rate of four common bundles to a hundred bricks. The bricks were moulded near the pit by simply placing the mould on level ground and filling it with the tempered mortar. They were formed by drawing a straight-edged board across the upper surface and removing the mould. However, they were not moved until sufficiently dry to turn on edge, and then they were stacked to season, and protected from the weather by broad boards.[1]

Although not too many of these houses were constructed they were supposedly warmer, more durable, and also cheaper than frame. The

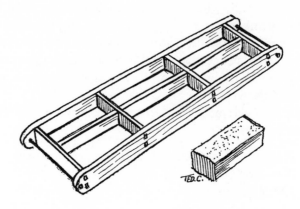

following advertisement appeared in the *British Colonist*, November 16, 1842:

MUD BUILDINGS

The Subscriber having made himself thoroughly acquainted with the construction of these very cheap and desirable Buildings, would call attention of the Public, as to their fitness for Churches, School Houses, and Gentleman's Cotages; and is prepared to take contracts in Town and Country for the erection and completion of any building of the above description.

The Subscriber is now erecting one of these buildings for himself on Yonge Street, five miles from Town, which can be seen and details explained to any Gentleman desirous of entering into a contract with the Subscriber. Letters (post-paid) to the care of Messrs. Bryce and McMurrich, will receive attention.

John Ross, House Carpenter
Yonge Street, July 5, 1842.[2]

Other houses were made of bricks burned on the farm. Wooden moulds were made, sometimes containing six compartments. A mould was thoroughly wetted, sprinkled with sand on all surfaces, and then tamped, a little more than full, with properly tempered clay. The surplus was scraped off, and the mould turned upside down on a board. When dry enough to handle, the bricks were put on racks with free access to air but protected from the sun and rain. When dry, they were stacked to make a kiln with flues near the ground for stoking the fire. The bricks were spaced so that the hot gas from the fire could circulate through the mass. A week was necessary to burn a kiln of brick, and ideally all parts of the pile should turn a cherry red with heat, a rare achievement. After cooling, the kiln was dismantled, and the soft or "slack burned" brick was taken out and refired in the next kiln.[2]

CARPENTRY

The broadaxe and adz were the tools used by the early carpenters to shape logs into posts, main beams and cross timbers. The siding was planed by hand, usually by young men learning the trade. Window frames, sashes and doors were made on the job. The floors were of broad boards, planed smooth and secured by pegs. As a farmer became more prosperous and could hire carpenters, he replaced his log cabin with a frame building.

COOPERING

Coopers, found at each mill site, made an amazing variety of household necessities. These included flour and cider barrels, "the old oaken bucket that hung by the well," sap buckets, pails, churns, butter and wash tubs and, in fact, anything formed of staves drawn together with wooden hoops.[4]

The "wet," or cask-making cooper was a man of skill who used only oak for his craft. He knew off hand the number and dimensions of staves required to make a vessel of a particular size. The cask had to be perfectly watertight and its capacity exact to specification. It was also required to be strong enough to stand the pressure of fermenting liquids and be durable enough to last for many years of hard use.[5]

The "dry" cooper, the least specialized of coopers, made casks for non-liquid substances such as flour. The work was less exacting than "wet" coopering and the barrels were less bulged, and bound together with wooden hoops. Douglas fir was used mainly for the staves but elm, spruce, poplar, beech and many others were also utilized.

The "white" cooper made pails, butter churns, washtubs and other household and dairy utensils, as well as bowls and rakes. Oak, sycamore and ash were his main materials. Great quantities of cheap, wooden sap buckets were required each spring, as maple sugar and syrup played an important part in the economy of the community. These buckets were shaped solely for utility and no unnecessary work went into their construction. The material used was almost invariably the very best, old, free-splitting white pine, although cedar was sometimes used. Six, light, wooden hoops held it together and the main concern of its maker was to see that it proved watertight.[6]

The work of the butter-tub artist, on the other hand, was to design

white oak butter firkins for marketing valuable products, so the external appearance was important. These firkins were given a smooth finish on all sides, and the outside was given a coat of varnish.[7]

HARNESS MAKING

Although the art of the harness maker was essential to the rural community, very few local men practised the trade. The best harness makers were located in Toronto within easy reach of North York farmers transporting produce to market. Their superior workmanship was preferred over that of the less experienced local craftsman. Some tanners doubled as harness makers, utilizing the surplus leather received from the farmers in lieu of payment for tanning.[8] In any case, great skill was required in making bridles, belts, straps, reins, breechings, binders and traces. The making of collars and saddles was especially difficult and required years of training. Work could not be interrupted, since the leather had to be kept at an even temperature for modelling.

POTASH MAKING

As a result of continued land-clearing in North York, asheries developed, making profitable use of the burnt timber. Potash proved to be a most important product and was even exported overseas. It was used in the manufacture of glass, soap, and fast-colour dyes. Pearl ashes, refined potash, were used in the making of baking soda.

According to John M'Gregor writing in 1832, "the pot and pearl ashes of commerce require little art in their preparation. The common wood ashes, especially those of the hard woods, such as maple, beech, birch, oak, or elm, are put into vats or large casks, over which water is poured. The water afterwards drains off through holes at the bottom, and carries away the salts in solution. This liquor, or ley, is then boiled in large iron pots, which causes the water to escape by evaporation, leaving the salts behind in the form which constitutes them the potash of commerce. In this state their colour is very rusty red, which by calcination, is turned into a pure white, and when thus refined, the salts are termed pearl ashes."[10]

In the *Upper Canada Gazette* for December 7, 1799, the following item was noted:

ASHES, ASHES, ASHES

The subscriber begs leave to inform the public, that he is about to erect a POT-ASH upon lot No. 7, West side of Yong-street; where he will give a generous price for ASHES;—for house-ashes NINE-PENCE per bushel, for field-ashes SIX-PENCE, delivered at his Potash. He conceives it his duty to inform those who may have ashes to dispose of, that it will not be in his power to pay cash, but merchandise at cash price.
York, Dec. 7, '99.   Duke W. Kendrick.[9]

POTTERY MAKING

The art of the potter consists in his ability to treat, as well as shape, clay. The texture of the clay is very important. It must be dug in the early fall before the winter rains, and then be left exposed to the winter weather for four months. During this time, the clay is broken up and turned periodically so that its weathering is uniform. It is next ground into a smooth paste, a process called pugging. Then mixed with water, the clay takes on a creamy, smooth consistency. This mixture, called "slip," is passed through a silk gauze, the water is squeezed out, and the slip is left stiff enough to be shaped into balls and thrown on the potters wheel.[11]

Thomas Humberstone was the first potter in North York, and his pottery continued at Newtonbrook through the nineteenth century. The Hogg brothers also made coarse, earthenware articles in their brick-yard in 1851. An advertisement in the *Colonial Advocate*, October 7, 1830, explains marketing procedures:

YONGE STREET POTTERY
FOUR MILES FROM YORK.

Wanted, a pedlar to hawk Brown Pottery Ware, through the country. He may either furnish a Waggon, or have one furnished him, on giving security. He will be required to receive orders for ware to be made at this pottery.

Merchants supplied Brown Ware at wholesale prices, with the usual credit; and their orders will be attended to at the shortest notice. An assortment of Crockery is constantly kept on hand. One or two Journeymen wanted, who will receive liberal wages.

Michael Whitmore
Yonge-Street. April 26, 1830.

SHINGLE MAKING

The first type of shingle, called "shake," was made by hand from short lengths, or bolts of pine or cedar, cut to the right thickness by an axe or frow. One end of the shingle was fastened to a shingle-horse and by means of a heavy drawknife the shingle was tapered to an edge. A good shingle maker could turn out eighty to a hundred hand-made shingles in an hour. By the 1870's these craftsmen were replaced with a machine.[12]

SHOEMAKING

Every community had a boot or shoemaker who, sitting at one end of his cobblers bench with built-in compartments for various sizes of pegs and nails at his side,[13] managed to keep the entire neighbourhood shod. In most cases boots were almost to the knee for men and somewhat lower for the ladies, and although the farmer wore heavy cowhide boots for day-to-day wear, he also needed a pair of fine calfskin for church and social occasions.

Many different qualities of leather were required by the bootmaker for his craft. The upper part of the shoe had to be soft and supple, and sheep skin or kid was needed for linings. Hard, durable leather was necessary for the sole. Considerable knowledge of hides was required to cut the skin to the best advantage and avoid unnecessary waste. The thickness, stretching quality and colour of the leather also had to be considered to ensure a matching pair of boots.[14] Although the cobbler's tools were simple and inexpensive, he required awls of many sizes and shapes, three or four thin knives, one or two of them curved, and all razor sharp.

After being cut, the upper parts of a boot or shoe were fitted together and stitched to make the complete uppers. The thread used was made by the craftsman from several straws of hemp twisted, waxed together, and pointed with stout pig bristles at both ends. The shaping of the insoles, heels, middle and outer soles, was the most intricate procedure. Then the boot was lasted, by straining the assembled uppers with pliers over the metal or beechwood last, which represented the shape of the customer's foot. The outer soles were attached with wooden pegs and then the boots were ready for sewing, lace holes and eyelets. When all irregularities were smoothed out, the finished boots were polished with great care. Well into the nineteenth century, country shoemakers were making pairs of (two) identical shoes, each modelled on the same last, rather than "rights" and "lefts."

TANNING

The tannery business is always mentioned in the histories of early Canadian communities but very little is told of the process. Since most farm butchering was done in the late fall or early winter the business was quite seasonal. As soon as the tanner received the hide he took his razor sharp knife and traced the initials of the owner on the flesh side of the hide, close to the tail. No matter how many different processes the hide went through, this equivalent of an indelible laundry-mark was absolute proof of ownership. The cowhides were split along the back line, making two identical "sides," but calfskins and sheep pelts were tanned whole. After trimming off the tail, legs, and ragged head, the hair or wool had to be removed. To facilitate the loosening of the wool of sheep and lamb, the skins were moistened and stacked in piles to "sweat." Cowhides were placed in a vat of milk of lime to loosen their hair, which was later used by masons to mix with their plastering mortar. Then, in order to obtain good, soft, durable leather, it was necessary to remove all lime by placing the hides to soak in a witch's brew of hen dung, salt, and water, known as "bate." The hides were later very thoroughly scrubbed and rinsed in pure, soft water.

Now the hides were ready for the tanning liquor. A layer of ground hemlock or oak bark was spread over the bottom of a plank vat about six feet square and four feet deep and it was covered with a hide. Two or three shovelfuls of bark were spread on top of this and then another hide; the procedure was repeated until the vat was full. Water was added to completely cover the skins. The hides were examined, and repiled from time to time, and more bark was added when necessary. This process usually required six months. Then the skins were thoroughly washed and hung over poles in the loft to dry. Sufficient ventilation was necessary to avoid moulding, but at the same time it was important that the drying process was not too rapid. The leather was now ready for the currier who scraped it, rubbed it with tallow and neat's-foot oil, blackened the hair side with lampblack, and then rubbed it smooth to give a slight polish.[15] The finished leather was divided equally between the farmer and tanner in lieu of monetary exchange.

An item of interest appeared in the *Upper Canada Gazette*, December 15, 1825. A notice under the name of B. Bull of Downsview stated that it was necessary to kill a heifer not his own that had been running with his cattle. The owner was requested to make himself known so that he could be paid her value, the hide having been taken to Jesse Ketchum's tannery in York. Jesse Ketchum also gave notice in the same paper to clear himself of any legal problems.

There were four tanneries on Yonge Street. Jacob Lawrence ran a tannery on the south-west corner of Lawrence Avenue, Andrew Mc-Glashan had one on the south-west corner of York Mills Road, Elihu Pease had one on the south-east corner of Sheppard Avenue, and Andrew Davis, Pease's son-in-law, had one on the south-west corner of Finch.

WHEEL MAKING

The wheelwright was responsible for building complete vehicles largely of white oak and white ash. His specialty, however, was wheel making. The diameter of the wheels on the early vehicles was much greater than those made today. Big wheels with high clearance enabled a wagon to straddle low stumps and boulders and roll more easily over the rough and muddy roads of North York.

Five stages were involved in wheel making. The first was hub making and morticing. A fourteen- or fifteen-inch length of tough white elm was needed for a hub twelve inches in diameter, and at least six years was required for seasoning. The hub was then cut, shaped with the hand ax and drawing knife, and bored to fit the axle. Mortices, or holes, were bored at an angle to receive the spokes, a very exacting job. The standard number of spokes for the front wheels was twelve and for the rear, fourteen. Next came the spokes which bear the greatest pressure on a wheel. These were made of seasoned, straight grained ash or hickory and shaped to the desired size and form. The felly, or rim, was sawed out of an oak plank, the pattern outlined so that the pieces would form a complete circle when put together with pin and dowel. A spoke auger bored the hole to fit the spoke in the felly.

Tireing with a hoop, or "ironing off," was the next process. A sixteen-foot bar of metal was measured for size, flattened at each end, heated, and passed through the rollers of the tire bender to obtain the desired shape, and the two loose ends welded together. The tire was heated until it was almost white hot, then it was taken off and dropped into position over the wheel. The rim sometimes burst into flames, but before any damage occurred, water was poured over it. Terrific crackling noises indicated that the tire was shrinking and the wheel was tightening under the enormous pressure of contraction.[16] Finally, in placing the wheel on the wagon the old wooden axles were lubricated with various homemade concoctions, the most common being a combination of tallow and pine tar,[17] which was mixed with lard in winter to prevent it from thickening.

Newtonbrook became a centre for blacksmiths and wheelwrights in the sixties and seventies. Sometimes the job was combined because the blacksmith often became a wheelwright.

NOTES

1 "Unburnt Brick Houses", *British American Cultivator* (March, 1843).

2 Lot 3, 1st concession west of Yonge Street.

3 Jared van Wagenen, Jr., *The Golden Age of Homespun* (New York: Hill & Wang, 1963), pp. 208-9.

4 *Ibid.*, p. 107.

5 J. G. Jenkins, *Traditional Country Craftsmen* (London: Routledge & Kegan Paul, 1965), pp. 82-3.

6 Van Wagenen, Jr., *op. cit.*, p. 108.

7 *Ibid.*, pp. 109-10.

8 *Ibid.*, p. 84.

9 Lot 7, 1st concession west of Yonge Street.

10 J. M'Gregor, *British America* (London: T. Cadell, 1833), II, 582.

11 Jenkins, *op. cit.*, p. 151.

12 Ontario, Department of Planning and Development, "Forestry", *Don Valley Conservation Report*, 1950, p. 13.

13 Van Wagenen, *op. cit.*, p. 198.

14 Jenkins, *op. cit.*, pp. 215-20.

15 Van Wagenen, *op. cit.*, pp. 186-9.

16 Jenkins, *op. cit.*, pp. 100-12.

17 Van Wagenen, *op. cit.*, pp. 116-21.

Trades and Professions
1799-1878

No LIST OF NAMES IS EVER COMPLETE; SOMEONE IS ALWAYS LEFT out unintentionally. The following names were compiled from various sources: a few available church records, land deeds and wills, family histories collected by the North York Historical Society, biographical accounts such the *History of Toronto and the County of York*, numerous directories covering the years 1837-1871, the Tremaine Map of 1860, the Miles *Illustrated Historical Atlas* of 1878, and the Census of 1851, 1861, 1871.

Agents
   J. C. T. Cochrane, William Harvey, John Lawless Jr., Francis McFarlane, William Nash, Albert C. Weed

Agricultural implement makers
   William Gooderham, Albert C. Weed, Tertules Weed

Auctioneers
   A. Andrews, William Brown, Thomas Leach, John Young

Bakers
   James Chadwick, Franklin Jackes, Robert Lackie, Alex Rennie, Robert Taylor

Berry picker
   Mrs. Jane Roberts

Blacksmiths
   Don Mills: Robert Crabtree, John Finn, Peter Milne

Downsview:	Robert Ashberry, Matthew Ashlee, Thomas Charlton, William Geddes, Nicholas Hare, Askelon Raynor
Eglinton:	David Campbell, James Campbell, Robert J. Campbell, Albert Childs, Alexander Hamilton, Patrick McCormick
Elia:	John Gram, William Troyer
Emery:	Henry Cousins, Isaac Devins, Vern Devins, Malcolm McCullen
Fisherville:	Anthony Bowes
Humber Summit:	Jesse Mabee
Kaiserville:	Benjamin Kaiser, Joshua Kaiser, William James Westwick, William Whitmore
L'Amaroux:	John O'Reilly, Jesse Richardson, Alex Rogers
Lansing:	William Duncan, Charles Shepard, Daniel Shepard
Newtonbrook:	Henry Dougherty, Charles Field, Charles Graham, Donald Graham, David Gray, John Gray, Thomas Horne, James Johnson, Thomas Johnston, James Jordon, James McDonald, Charles McNamee, Alexander Montgomery, William Summerville, William Troyer, Henry Walsley, Peter Weatheral
Oriole:	Thomas Johnston, John Reid, George Summers, Thomas Summers
Willowdale:	James Killoe, James Lindsay, John Lindsay, Gideon Phillips, Jacob Slinker, Alfred Tucker
York Mills:	Thomas Botham, David Boyle, Frisby Bull, William Curry, Charles Eden, William Gray, William Hunter, George Ireland, William Mitchell, —— Moore, Hugh Ross, Joseph Skinner, William Trayling, John Weir, Charles Wrothmall

Brewers

Charles Cull, John Edward Cull

Bricklayer

John Spence

Brickmakers

James Andrews, William Bowman, William Brown, George Cudmore, Henry James, Pat McCade, Henry Neal, James Walmsley, John Williams, —— Wreggetts

Builders

Eglinton:	John Fisher, Nicholas Maugham
Newtonbrook:	Richard Harris, John Sankey
Weston:	William Tyrrell
Willowdale:	John Cummer, James Fairbanks, Jr., G. W. Miller
York Mills:	George Gray, Robert Gray, Joseph Pennock, William Tuck

Butchers

W. J. Langrell, Henry Nightingale, George Routliff, James Tyler, John Whitton

Carpenters

Don Mills:	Thomas Boyd, John Craig, William Craig, Shadrach Davis, Albert Fitzpatrick, William Heron, Thomas Hollingshead, Smith Humphrey
Downsview:	Thomas Bull, John Wilmot
Eglinton:	Robert Clark, Thomas Erumens, John Fisher, Francis Grainger, Alex Hill, John Hill, Silas Hill, William Hill, Nicholas Maugham, John Ross
Fairbank:	Isaac Dollery
Fisherville:	James Green
Kaiserville:	Jacob Kaiser
L'Amaroux:	William Murphy
Lansing:	Angus Blue, Alonzo Weed
Newtonbrook:	Nathaniel Carrol, Richard Harris, William Pennock, John Sankey, Thomas Wiliams
Oriole:	Stillwell Willson
Willowdale:	David Cummer, James Fairbanks, Jr., —— Martin, G. W. Miller
York Mills:	Robert Curry, George Gray, Robert Gray, Stephen Kelly, James McDonald, Joseph Pennock, Henry Sylvester

Chemist

Joseph Beckett

Chopper

Phillip Maxwell

Civil Engineer

William M. Gibson

Clock and watch maker
  William Watson

Clog maker
  John Elliott

Coach maker
  Matthew Hutchinson

Colonization Roads
  David Gibson, supervisor, James W. Bridgland, inspector

Coopers
Fisherville:	James Green
Newtonbrook:	Alexander Dessco, John Joseph Drury, Michael Drury, William Drury, Cesaire Gayette, William Valliere
York Mills:	Robert Carmichael, John Craig, William Craig, William Graham, John Hogg, Robert Hogg, William Johnson, S. Keegrar, Jonathan Leader, Hugh McDonell, William McElhinney, William Millburn, James Mitchell, James Reynolds, William Watson

Cordwainer (shoemaker)
  William Millar

Coroner
  Thomas Armstrong

Curriers (leather dressers)
  Benjamin Ambler Allison, William Benson, James Hugo, Thomas Scully

Dentist
  George H. Husband

Distillers
Don Mills:	James Gray
Newtonbrook:	Benjamin Fish, David McDougall
York Mills:	Samuel Heron, Thomas Hodgson, James Hogg, William Marsh, Andrew Mercer, Cornelius van Nostrand

Doctors
  Thomas Armstrong, E. Bull, Thomas Cowdry, J. A. De la Hooke,

Alexander McMaster, George Parsons, O. S. Wainstanley, Joseph Williamson

Dressmakers
Eglinton:	Sarah Ann Boyd, Eliza Dixey, Jeannette Ramsey
Newtonbrook:	Mrs. Bloomer, C. Flynn, Miss McCague

Drovers
Thomas Buverley, William Langrell

Dyer
Peter Cole

Firemen
John Jones, Edward O'Brien

Gardener
John Zeagman

Grain dealers
Franklin Cummer, David McBride

Harness makers
Robert Bestard, Arthur Griffith, Elihu Pease

Insurance Agents
Jacob Cummer, E. H. Devins, Nicholas Shepherd

Inventors
Jacob Cummer, Sr., Jacob Kaiser, Charles Powell

Joiner
William Pool

Justices of the Peace
Don Mills:	Charles D. Maginn, W. H. Norris, James Taylor
Downsview:	Clark B. Bridgland, John P. Bull, Robert Clarke, W. A. Clarke, William Jackson
Dublin:	William Duncan
Eglinton:	Franklin Jackes, William Jackes, Peter Lawrence, Nicholas Maugham, James Metcalfe, Charles Snider, William Snider
Elia:	Jacob Stong
Fairbank:	Joseph Watson
Humber Summit:	William Adam Duncan
Lansing:	Joseph Shepard

Newtonbrook: John Cummer, William James, William Robin-
                son, John Willson IV
Oriole: William Mulholland
Weston: William Ellerly, William Tyrrell, W. Wadsworth
Willowdale: James Davis, Abraham Johnson, Arthur L. Will-
                son
York Mills: John C. T. Cochrane, John Hogg

Lawyer (see Solicitor)

Mariners
John Davidson, Thomas Leach, Jr.

Masons
Xavier Clinkinbroomer, John Noble, George Taylor, John Woods

Melodeon makers
William Norris, Frank Stevenson

Milliners
Sarah Ann Boyd, Eliza Dixey, Miss Langstaff, Jeannette Ramsey,
Miss Watson

Music professor
John Willson

Newspaper men
James Beaty, propr. *Leader*

Nursery man
Arthur Reynolds

Painters and glaziers
—— Murphy, —— Pearcy, Andrew Ross, Joseph Smith

Potters
James Andrews, William Bowman, William Brown, George Cud-
more, Simon T. Humberstone, Thomas Humberstone I, Thomas
Humberstone II, Henry James, James McClasky, James Walmsley

Pump makers
Thomas Langstaff, Wallace McBride, Edward Neely, Charles Powell

Railroad labourers
Patrick Colin, John Rian, Kennedy Rian, Michael Yeoman

Road builder
Duncan McCague, supt.

Sawyers

William Curry, Jr., John Dancy, George Keightly, Philip Leader, Robert Leader, Hugh McCulloch, John Malloy, Stephen Markwell

Shingle manufacturers

Henry Collins, Jacob Cummer, William Graham, Joseph Piper

Shoemakers

Michael O'Brien, —— Turner, James Walker

Don Mills:	John Barron, Daniel Castick, David Castick, Charles Cutting
Downsview:	Edward Bull, Thomas Hill
Dublin:	Tim the Irishman, Robert Morrow
Eglinton:	George Clark, John Clark, John Coulter, Edward Dack, Joseph Hargrave
Elia:	William Speight
L'Amaroux:	James Flynn, John Myers, Richard Skelton
Lansing:	James Flynn, William Miller
Newtonbrook:	Daniel Agar, James Agar, W. W. Cameron, Daniel Flynn, Jack Flynn, George Munroe, William Stubins
Oriole:	Martin Flynn
Willowdale:	James Garvin, Henry Gullinus, J. Gwynne, Samuel Harris
York Mills:	Robert Girvan, William Miller, Robert Munroe, William Munroe, Isaac Wallace

Solicitor

Arthur Lawrence Willson

Spinners

James Gray, James Ross

Stone cutter

Fris Hardy

Surveyors

David Gibson, James A. Gibson, Peter S. Gibson, W. G. Morrison, Henry Smith, John Young

Tailors

John Brown, William Howe, James Mitchell, Adam Witherspoon, Albert Witherspoon

Tanners

Eglinton:	Jacob Lawrence

Lansing:	Edward Pease, Elihu Pease
Willowdale:	Andrew Davis, James Hugo, Jacob Lawrence
York Mills:	Andrew McGlashan I, Andrew McGlashan II, Mrs. Andrew McGlashan, Gideon Murray

Teamsters

Andrew Forsyth, James Forsyth, John Forsyth, John Street, William Sylvester

Threshers

George Goulding, George Keightly, Robert Whittaker

Tile manufacturers

James Andrews, Thomas Nightingale

Tinsmiths

Archibald Campbell, Jacob Cummer II, Joseph Cummer

Veterinary surgeons

Jacob Cummer I, Thomas Goulding, Thomas Leach

Wagon makers

Don Mills:	John Gray, Charles Sanderson
Downsview:	Robert Clark, William Dobson, William Geddes, David Simpson
Eglinton:	William Douglas, John Lawrence
Elia:	John Gram
Emery:	John R. Devins
L'Amaroux:	Archibald Wright
Lansing:	Cornelius van Nostrand
Newtonbrook:	John Gray, James Johnson, James Macdonald, Joseph McDonnell, Alexander Montgomery, John Street, Henry H. Walker
Willowdale:	John Gwynne
York Mills:	Thomas Collins, William Foster, William Goodwin, Thomas G. Harvey, Thomas Johnson, William Robinson

Weavers

Don Mills:	James Mason, Alexander Milne, Samuel Poplewell, John Wilson
Eglinton:	Thomas Paisley
L'Amaroux:	Thomas Ogden
Newtonbrook:	John Ure, Samuel Willis

Well diggers
  Thomas Bagley, William Pell

Wheelwrights
  Kaiserville: Jacob Kaiser
  Newtonbrook: Alexander Anderson, Thomas Howe

Whip maker
  James Martin

Postal Services and Currency

BRITISH NORTH AMERICAN POSTAL SERVICES[1] WERE UNDER THE BRITISH postal authorities, who insisted that each mail route should be self-supporting. Profits were not available to extend services to frontier settlements, but had to be remitted instead to the British Treasury. A regular mail service to settlements west of Kingston was established after 1800 following receipt of a guarantee from the Legislative Assembly that the province would pay any deficit, and all postmaster appointments were made in England.

During this early British period the *Upper Canada Gazette* periodically listed the names of persons whose letters were waiting to be picked up at the York Post Office, the only post office in the area. If anyone in a neighbourhood collected his mail while in town, he also picked up letters for those living near him. Postal rates, determined in relation to the distance of delivery, were so high that writing home to Europe was virtually impossible for most settlers. Instead, letters were often entrusted to someone travelling to the vicinity of the intended recipient. The address was written on the back of a letter which was folded and sealed with wax. The following address,[2] dated May, 1824, indicates the lot where the receiver lived:

> *Mr. James van Nostrand*
> *Yonge Street No. 13*
> *York*
> *Upper Canada*
> *Politeness Mr. Milland*

and another letter[3] which went through the mails bore a round stamp "Queenston My 2 1835" and second stamp "Paid." In the upper right hand corner was scrawled "2/9," the cost of postage. It was addressed to:

Mr. Marsh
6th Mile Stone Yonge Street
Toronto late York
Upper Canada

On January 1, 1836, the British postal authorities established a post office and appointed a postmaster at York Mills. By that time post-boys on horseback had been replaced by William Weller's Royal Mail coach with four prancing horses, which carried the mail and passengers from Toronto to Holland Landing. Its arrival at York Mills was announced by a shrill blast from a horn. Hostlers at James Hogg's inn immediately appeared to take over the horses, providing water and a rub-down with straw. The driver pulled out the mail bag for the post-man and unloaded luggage belonging to passengers who had reached their destination. After refreshments all clambered into the coach, including any new passengers, and the trip up Yonge Street continued.

The Canadian provinces in 1851 were empowered to assume control of their own postal services provided they would agree to an efficient, uniform system. Upper and Lower Canada took over the operation of their own services on April 6, 1851, followed by Nova Scotia and New Brunswick, two months later. Postage stamps were introduced, and Sir Sandford Fleming, later chief surveyor for the C.P.R., inventor of standard time, and a Downsview landowner, designed the first Canadian stamp, the threepenny beaver, issued April 23, 1851. Postal service developed steadily as rates were reduced and service was extended to rural areas. North York is a good example of how rapidly services expanded. Three post offices were opened in the 1850's: Dublin in 1854, L'Amaroux in 1854, and Willowdale in 1855. During this period newspapers were handled free of charge or at very low rates; postal money orders and registered mail were introduced in 1855; and a parcel-post service was inaugurated in 1859.

Newspapers or magazines were treasured by all who received them, and were read, re-read, and eventually passed on to neighbours. They were distributed by the publisher, who sent a man around on horseback to deliver them or leave them with an agent along the route to be picked up by the subscribers. Often, to cut down expenses, six or seven neighbours subscribed to a paper together. The family living on the main road received it first and, after reading it thoroughly, passed it on to the next co-subscriber.

The Ontario, Simcoe and Huron Railway, later the Northern, began operations in 1853, extending and improving the mail service. Special mail cars, quite common by 1857, were built in which the mail was sorted en route. On its way north a mail bag for each postal district was thrown from the train by a postal clerk at a designated location along the line. The local postmaster on the other hand was responsible for hanging his bag of outgoing mail on a hook to be picked off by the clerk as the train slowed down on its return trip to Toronto.

The stage line on Yonge Street to Holland Landing was discontinued as train service was provided, but mail was still carried by omnibus as far as Richmond Hill. These enclosed wagons, pulled by two horses, were provided with four windows and seats along each side, and a door with steps at the rear. The driver was perched on a seat across the front of the roof with a stand at a forty-five degree angle below him to support his feet. Beginning about 1895 the radial street cars traveling northwood took over the North York-Yonge Street mail delivery.

THE CURRENCY

Halifax currency with its pounds, shillings, and pence became the official standard in the British Colonies in 1775, but it was not until 1821, and later in Upper Canada, that other currencies were deprived of legal recognition. The Halifax pound was equivalent to four dollars and the shilling to twenty cents, and there were no Canadian coins until 1858. Most of the early trading as we have noted was done by barter or exchanging farm produce for store goods, logs for shingles, and lumber and whiskey for grain. What silver there was in circulation consisted of American and British coins, as well as a few of Mexican, Spanish or French origin.

The Federal Government of the United States authorized the decimal system in 1793, but it was some time before it became universal. Previously each state had its own money system and a person travelling from one state to another had to compute in the currency of the state through which he was passing. The New York currency was frequently quoted in Canada and the pound was equivalent to two dollars and fifty cents, and the shilling to twelve and a half cents. Lower Canada finally adopted the decimal system as its official currency standard in 1853, Upper Canada followed in 1858, and Nova Scotia and New Brunswick in 1860. However, as in the United States, it took a number of years before it became universal.

NOTES

1   A list of North York post offices and postmasters appears in the Appendix.
2   Courtesy Mrs. H. A. S. Molyneux.
3   Courtesy Mrs. H. A. S. Molyneux.

PART TWO

THE GROWTH OF COMMUNITIES

INTRODUCTION

THE MANY LITTLE COMMUNITIES WHICH SPRANG UP IN THE NINE-
teenth century in what is now the Borough of North York had their
beginnings as service areas for the farms which surrounded them. Here
the farmers came to have their horses shod, to have their grain ground,
to visit the general store, or to collect their mail. Naturally, there was
a tendency for the neighbourhood churches and schools to concentrate in
the same area. These communities usually grew up around the busiest
concession-line crossroads. Yonge Street, Dufferin Street or the 3rd concession road, and Victoria Park Road called the 5th concession road,
or Dawes Road, became the major north-south routes of the Township, Finch and Sheppard side roads were the east-west arteries. Other
villages grew up around river crossings where mills could easily be
located.

Many of the activities of these centres have already been discussed
under the social and economic aspects of the community in Part I; their
individual growth as villages will be discussed here, including information regarding the early careers of their founders.

THE YONGE STREET COMMUNITIES

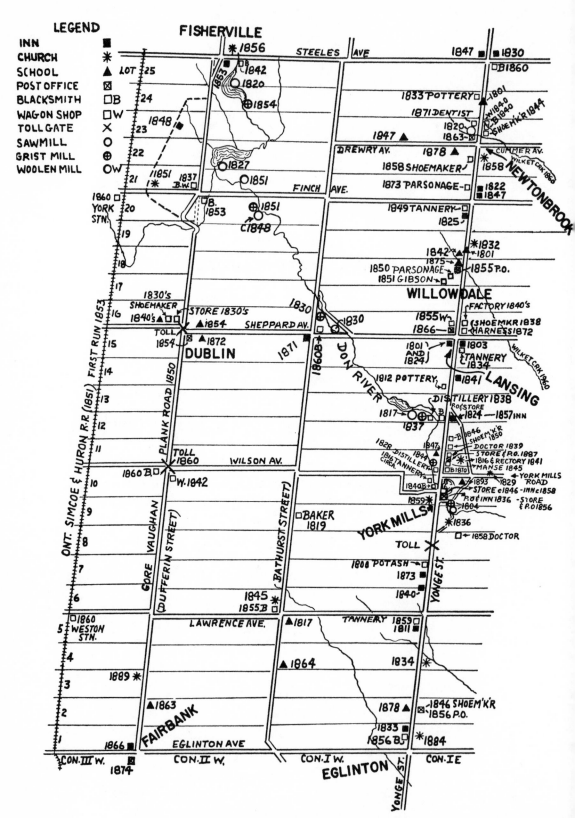

Communities in the Yonge Street area.

Yonge Street

IN 1793 LIEUTENANT-GOVERNOR JOHN GRAVES SIMCOE ADVERTISED free lots of 200 acres[1] to any settler coming to York. A plan was laid out in a grid pattern for the Home District[2] with concession lines a mile and a quarter apart. With Yonge Street as the centre north-south concession line, land grants were always designated in reference to concessions east and west of Yonge. On the east side of Yonge there were four concessions and four concession roads, and on the west side, seven of each. The east-west roads were a mile and a quarter apart and were known respectively as the side road between lot five and six, ten and eleven, fifteen and sixteen, twenty and twenty-one, and twenty-five and twenty-six. If a corner was owned by a prominent person, or the location of an inn, the name of the man or the inn was often chosen for the side road. Five lots, a quarter of a mile wide and a mile and a quarter deep, ran between each of these side roads. They were numbered from the base line, which was Eglinton, and ran northward.

To qualify for a grant of land a man had to prove he was a professing Christian, capable of manual labour, and a law-abiding citizen of the country in which he last resided. Before obtaining the final deed, however, the settler had to complete certain duties over a two year period. These included clearing the land for cultivation, building a frame or log house at least sixteen by twenty feet with a shingle roof, and fencing ten acres of land. All timber across the width of the lot had to be cut, with thirty-three feet levelled off for half the public road.

The most important highway surveyed and laid out under Governor Simcoe was Yonge Street, extending all the way from York to Lake Simcoe. Named in honour of a friend of Simcoe's, the British Secretary of War, Sir George Yonge, it was opened by Augustus Jones, Deputy

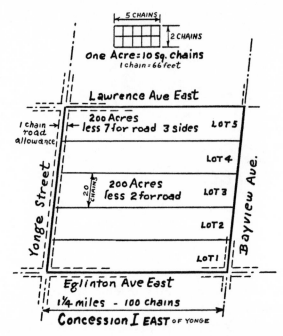

A Typical Survey of 5 Crown grant lots of approximately 200 acres each. Lots are numbered 1 to 25 beginning at Eglinton in each concession. Concessions are numbered 1 to 4 east of Yonge and 1 to 7 west of Yonge.

Provincial Surveyor, and a band of Queen's Rangers as far as Lot 17 or a quarter of a mile north of Sheppard Avenue, by May 1794. "Opening" a road signified that a path twenty feet wide had been cut through the woods, and the brush cleared away. Settlers travelled on foot or on horseback, except in winter, when snow filled the holes and buried the stumps making it possible to use sleighs to visit friends and attend social events.

When Jones reached York Mills he found he could not cut a road straight down the hill through the swampy marsh land, but had to follow the land contour, winding to the east down the side of the ravine (Donwoods Drive). The river bed was small and easily crossed at this point in the valley, but a very steep grade was unavoidable as he cut his way up the side of the ravine on the north side of the river (Old Yonge Street). From the top of the slope the trail followed the edge of the ravine back to the line laid out on the map for Yonge Street. Another detour was necessary in Newtonbrook. A small creek crossed Yonge Street just north of Drewry Avenue that was very boggy and needed draining. As a result the Queen's Rangers jogged the road to the west where an easier crossing was possible.

In 1800 a path through the woods represented Yonge Street as far north as lot 29, or almost to Thornhill. The larger trees were cut and some of the brush cleared, but there were no bridges over the streams. A bill passed in 1804 provided for the "improvement" and maintenance of Yonge Street, which meant building bridges and corduroying, or laying logs across the swamps. The upkeep of the roads was by statute labour requiring the settler to maintain the quarter mile stretch of road bordering his land.

In 1807 it was suggested that Yonge Street should be "turnpiked." This consisted of removing all stumps and boulders from the centre of the road and ploughing the edges to provide drainage by use of ditches and road-crowning. By 1816 some of the stumps and large roots had been removed, but wagon travel was still slow because there were far too many mud holes, and bridges were frequently washed out by floods.

The roads were still in a dreadful state in 1825, when a line of covered wagons operated commercially on Yonge Street carrying freight. Travellers on foot, however, often obtained rides. The drivers, as well as those on George Playter & Son's first stage coach line in 1829, stopped regularly at the inns along the route to refresh their horses and themselves. An advertisement in the *Colonial Advocate* for September 24, 1829, gives the hours and prices of trips running north:

> Newmarket Mail Stage. William Garbutt, haveing taken the contract for carrying His Majesty's Mails between York and Newmarket for the next four years, respectfully informs the public that The Mail Stage will start from Joseph Bloor's Hotel, York, on Mondays and Thursdays at 12 o'clock noon, and arrive at nine o'clock, the same evening in Newmarket;—and will leave Mr. Barber's Tavern, Newmarket, for York on Wednesdays and Saturdays, at 6 in the morning, and arrive in York at 2 p.m. on the same days. Prices for passengers conveyed between York and Newmarket, six shillings and three pence currency, and in proportion for shorter distances. Packages carried on this route at moderate rates.
>
> Mr. Barber will accommodate passengers arriving with the Mail Stage at Newmarket; and they may be comfortably conveyed to Holland Landing, or in other directions if required.
>
> *York, March 30th. 1829.*

William Weller of Cobourg, the most prominent stage coach proprietor in Upper Canada, purchased George Playter's line in 1832. His bright yellow stage coaches, each drawn by four, imported, Irish stock mares clattered daily along the rutted country lanes to Holland Landing, Hamilton, and Quinte, stopping at designated inns along the way to rest and feed the horses, or change to a fresh pair, before continuing on the next stage of the journey. The coach was filled with travellers on each trip, and the roof and large, wooden compartment behind the passenger's carriage were loaded with luggage and express. The driver's seat was on top of another high, wooden compartment, similar to the one in the rear, containing the Royal Mail bags for each postal community that the coach passed through. Privileged passengers were allowed to sit with the driver, an outstanding personage along his route, who bought and delivered many necessities for the farmers and their wives, and often carried confidential messages for them. Each stage was obliged to travel quickly in order to make connections with other lines or fulfil its contract with the Government for carrying the mails. When a farm wagon was seen in the distance in the centre of the road, loud tooting informed its occupants of the coach's approach, and the farmer pulled over quickly to one side of the road to provide space for passing. After or during a rain the stage was often stuck in the mud, making it necessary for everyone to climb out into the slithering mire and help to pry the coach loose with fence rails or logs in order to continue their journey.

By 1850 all the passengers, freight, and mail rumbled up Yonge Street to Holland Landing in a stage coach of the Concord type, originally built by Abbott and Downing of Concord, New Hampshire, and pulled by four, well-tended horses. These coaches were longer and lower than those built earlier, and although they were also springless, they were equipped with two through braces made of eight layers of heavy sole oxhide. Running fore-and-aft, these braces suspended the coach, making for a considerably more comfortable ride. Daily runs were made to York Mills, Thornhill, and Richmond Hill, leaving the Toronto Market Square at three and four in the afternoon and stopping at the inns to discharge passengers, and pick up those waiting to travel north.

In 1833 Rowland Burr was given a contract for improving Yonge Street. He graded the hills, straightened the road at York Mills, partially filled the bog, and drained the swamp at the foot of the hill near the mills.[3] Consequently the road went straight down the hill and up the other side, and was ready for use and prepared for "macadamizing" by 1835. This method of surfacing the road with broken stone reduced the curvature and provided better drainage, but it became very expensive. It was found that the cost was between £3,000 and £4,000 to macadamize a mile of road in Upper Canada.[4] An entry in Peter Gibson's diary[5] for November 9, 1865, throws a little more light on the macadamized roads:

> Yonge Street. While talking with roadmen on Yonge Street. They say that Gossage requires stone to be broken to pass through a two inch ring at $4.50 p. toise the men cannot do the work for such a sum they say and have given up. Gossage drives over the whole of the York roads. The roadmen are using wheel barrows they say they cannot wheel to advantage over 150 feet and that a man for a good days work should wheel one toise a day. The men are getting 75 cents p. day and board themselves.

Beginning in 1830 it was necessary for the stage coaches to pass through the second Yonge Street Toll-gate[6] which stood at the top of the southern hill near the present city limits and was known as Hogg's Hollow gate. The toll-gate house was a small building with a roof extending across the road to a small lean-to on the east side. If the gate keeper happened to be a chicken fancier, such as one Mr. Pennock, it became very fashionable for city folk to drive out to the toll-gate for fresh eggs. In 1865 York County purchased the toll-gates from the Provincial Government and leased them to the highest bidder. For instance, in 1865 Hogg's Hollow gate was leased to G. D. James for $4,300, $800 over the previous years price. Because the income received from these tolls was not used for road maintenance, the farmers tried to avoid them as much as possible. Finally, tolls were abolished in 1894, but they seem to have continued until 1896 according to the list of gate keepers. The men who leased the Hogg's Hollow Toll-gate were[7]:

G. D. James	1865	Edward Crown	1881-1884
George Lee	1867-1877	Henry Horne	1882-1883
Elias Snider	1872-1873	Alex. Brown	1884-1887
Charles McBride	1878-1880	William Richards	1890-1896

NOTES

1 In the original survey the lots on the west side of Yonge Street were 210 acres, those on the east were 190 acres in the first concessions.

2 An early district comprising the Counties of York, Ontario, and Peel.

3 Ontario, Department of Planning and Development, *Don Valley Conservation Report*, 1950, p. 122.

4 Michael S. Cross, "The Stormy History of the York Roads, 1833-1865", *Ontario History* LIV (March, 1962), 6.

5 The David Gibson Papers. Microfilm copy, North York Public Library.

6 The first Yonge Street Toll-gate stood at Yorkville just north of Bloor Street.

7 Robertson, *Landmarks of Toronto* (Toronto: C. Blackett Robinson, 1894-1914), V, 343-344.

CONC. I w.　　CONC. I E

1812 T. HUMBERSTONE　　1806 JOSEPH HARRISON

1827　WM. ALLAN　　1888 JOSEPH BALES　　14

1811 D. TIERS　　1805 C. VAN NOSTRAND　　13
1817 T. ARNOLD
1837 C. VAN NOSTRAND　DON　1808 J. VAN NOSTRAND

1814 D. TIERS　　1835 DUNC. CAMERON　　12
1815 ANDR. McGLASHAN

1809 C. ANDERSON　　11
　1828 JAMES HOGG
1844 C. VAN NOSTRAND　1813　THOS. JOHNSON
　　　　　1832　WM. MARSH　　YORK
WILSON　　　　　　　　　　　　　MILLS
AVE.　　　　　　　　　　　　　RD.

1816 ANDR. McGLASHAN　　1794 THOS. MERCER
　　　　　　　　　1819 THOS. ARNOLD　10
1876 ANDR. BATHGATE　　1824 JAMES HOGG

1819　　1823　　1797 SAM. HERON　　9
DAVID　　GEO. T.
LACKIE　DENISON　　1831 JAMES HOGG

1804 SENECA KETCHUM　1831 SENECA KETCHUM　8

1853 IGNATIUS NIGHTINGALE　1858 DR. T. COWDRY

1800 DUKE WM. KENDRICK　1834 JOS. EASTON　7
1838 JAMES NIGHTINGALE
1844 JOSEPH BECKETT　1860 WM. McDOUGALL

1824 JAMES ANDERSON　1803 JONATHAN HALE　6
　　　　　　　　　1819 JOEL BEAMAN
1836 PETER LAWRENCE　1829 PTR. LAWRENCE
　　　　　　　　　　　　　　　LAWRENCE
1808　　1804　　1808 JONATHAN HALE　AV.
RICH'D　THOS.
HERON　HILL　1836 SAMUEL A. HUSON　5

1801 JOHN McDOUGALL　1811 JONATHAN HALE　4
1833 WM. JACKES

1811 MARTIN SNIDER　1835 JESSE KETCHUM　3

1800 ROBERT BALDWIN
1835 JAMES H. PRICE　1846 JOS. HARGRAVE　2
1844 FRANKLIN JACKES

1815 FRED BARON DE HOVEN　1803 WM. ALLEN　LOT
1833 JOHN MONTGOMERY　1826 JACOB SNYDER　1

EGLINTON　EGLINTON AV.

York Mills

York mills, a mill village on the west branch of the Don River six miles from Toronto, developed around three mill sites. The first was located on the east side of Yonge and opened by Samuel Heron in 1804, the second on the west side of Yonge, was built by Thomas Arnold prior to 1817 (the site is now under the Macdonald-Cartier viaduct), and the third, also on the west side of Yonge, was erected by Cornelius van Nostrand near the foot of John Street in 1844. Four successive names bestowed upon the community all pertain to the valley south of York Mills Road. Big Creek Bridge was the first name given to the area, which was used as a division line by the various overseers of highways and fence-viewers from 1797 to 1809.[1] It was changed to Heron's Bridge from 1810 to 1822, after Samuel Heron, the miller. However, after Thomas Arnold acquired the mill site and built his mill in 1817, it became Millford Mills,[2] continuing under this name after James Hogg purchased the property in 1824. In 1836 a post office was opened under the name York Mills, also the new name of the Hogg property. It was not until the 1850's when the Hogg brothers opened their subdivision that the area became known also as Hogg's Hollow.

EARLY SETTLERS

The majority of early families in York Mills were "late Loyalists," American settlers who came for free land, or Scottish emigrants. Seneca Ketchum, an elder brother of Jesse Ketchum, the York tanner, and their uncles Joseph and James were the first members of the family to come to Canada. They made the journey on foot from Columbia County in the Catskills to Oswego accompanied by a number of settlers who travelled together for company and protection against the Indians and wild animals. At Oswego, on Lake Ontario north-west of Syracuse, they were able to obtain batteaux which carried them along the eastern shore of the lake and across the St. Lawrence to Kingston. Two crews were needed to propel a batteau; while one tramped along the shore tugging the boat by a rope, the crew on board used long poles to steer and shove the unwieldy flat-bottomed craft. Arriving in York in 1796, Seneca Ketchum leased Hiram Kendrick's property on the west side of Yonge Street at the top of the southern hill. He bought the land in 1804.[3] Having always looked forward to a church career he held Anglican services each Sunday evening in his log house. Occasionally Rev. George Okill Stuart officiated. These services marked the beginning of the congregation of St. John's York Mills.

As Yonge Street descended into the valley to the north it twisted down Heron's Hill to the east (now Donwoods Drive) to Heron's Bridge on Donino Avenue where Samuel Heron erected the first grist mill, saw mill, and distillery in York Township[4] (see Mills and Distilleries). Heron was born in Scotland, emigrated first to New York City, next to Niagara, and then to the town of York where he married Sarah Ashbridge. In 1796 he opened a shop on King Street, and became a Township collector in 1797 and an assessor in 1802, before moving to Yonge Street. In 1817, shortly before he died at the age of forty-eight, he was granted a tavern license.

Yonge Street ran north from the bridge up Old Yonge Street to the top of the hill where Thomas Mercer, an Irishman, settled and cleared his farm south of York Mills Road. The Mercer family drove all the way from Pennsylvania in 1794 in a wagon with a cow tethered on behind; when requesting land he was offered one hundred acres in exchange for his wagon.[5] Each early settler took his share of municipal responsibilities, and in 1811 Thomas Mercer was elected foreman of the Grand Jury which consisted of twenty-one men, including Samuel Heron and Thomas Humberstone of York Mills.

Cornelius Anderson, a Scot, was disbanded from his British Regiment in New Brunswick following the American Revolution. He, his wife, and nine children settled on the west side of Yonge north of the Don River about the same time as the Mercer family. During the War of 1812 Anderson lost a horse pressed into service by the Government, and many years later he received thirteen dollars in compensation.[6]

In 1800 Thomas Humberstone married the daughter of Christopher Harrison; in 1804 Thomas was elected an Overseer of Highways and Fence-viewer; and in 1805 he received five acres of cleared land on lot 13, 1 con. west of Yonge with a house in which Harrison had lived for more than three years. A barn, twenty-six by twenty feet, was also on the property and half the road allowance was cleared, fit for travelling. In 1812 Humberstone received lot 14, 1 con. west of Yonge as a Crown grant, and as the son of a Staffordshire potter, he no doubt set up his potter's wheel on both properties and operated the first York County pottery, providing brown earthenware pitchers, useful articles, and flower pots for his neighbours. During the War of 1812 he served as a lieutenant in the militia under General Brock at the Battle of Queenston Heights, and helped to carry the general's body off the battlefield. While commanding a large batteau full of American prisoners who were being transported to Kingston after the Battle of Beaver Dams, Lieutenant Humberstone was made prisoner and his captors rowed him across the lake to the United States where he was quickly jailed on October 11, 1813, and held until peace was restored.[7]

Following the war his property contained a house, thirty by fifty, a barn of the the same dimensions, out-houses, a good well, and an orchard with 200 bearing apple trees.[8] The family, like other families, had a huge fireplace for cooking, and they stoked the fire with an old Indian fowling-piece, a light gun for shooting wild fowl. One day as Humberstone's fifteen year old daughter, Elizabeth, pushed an unwieldy log to the back of the fireplace the gun exploded in her face, killing her instantly.[9]

Andrew McGlashan, a Scot, sold his property in the 2nd concession east of Yonge Street, in 1816 to William Harrison and moved to the west side of Yonge Street, south of the Don River.[10] McGlashan established a mud brick tannery in the valley below which continued to operate until the 1860's, always a very busy place after butchering time when the farmers brought their cowhides to be tanned.

Robert Lackie, a baker who supplied food for the York Ball of 1812, which included hot and cold oysters, game, chicken, and lobsters, bought the west half of the lot south of the McGlashan's house on Bathurst in 1819.[11] A baker usually built several brick ovens outside his back door to help meet the demand for his baked products.

Cornelius van Nostrand, who held a commission in the British army, brought his family from Oyster Bay, Long Island, to a farm on Yonge Street in 1800.[12] In the War of 1812 his son, Cornelius, was taken prisoner by the Americans at the capture of York, and after being paroled, served as a noncombatant doing commissariat work on the Upper Lakes. On the east side of Yonge at the top of the north hill stood Cornelius II's combined house and store in 1832. In this early period each farmer bartered what he raised for what he needed, and he settled his account once or twice a year. As a result the general storekeeper, Cornelius van Nostrand, was held in high esteem. He became a close friend of his customers, their banker by virtue of long credit, and he no doubt advised them on many occasions. Items listed in 1835 in an old van Nostrand account book for this store include:

1 lb chease	9d	1 broom	1/6
2 doz eggs	10d	3 gal brandy & 3 gal	
3 lb 10 oz butter	2/9	whiskey £1-12-7 1/2	
1 frock coat	£1-7-6	3 yds fustin[13]	3/-
1 fur cap	15/-	118 lb beef	£1-3-6
2 lb choklet	2/-	straw hat	1/8
1/4 lb mustard	7 1/2d	1 tin bason[14]	2/-
1 pair stockings	1/3	1/2 lb green tea	1/9
3 lb coffee	1/-	5 1/2 lb codfish	1/10
2 1/2 yds flannel	6/3	2 bulls eyes[15]	1d
1/2 lb Twanky[16]	3/6	1 doz tumblers	7/-
1 pair gloves	1/8	1/2 doz bowls	2/-
1 yd ribbon	1/6	2 lb cut nails	1/1 1/2
1 bed cord	1/-	1 lb candles	9d
1 velvet coat	£2	1 lb soap	6d
1/2 lb young hison[16]	2/6	10 yds Bombasette[17]	12/6
1 handkerchief	1/-	3 gal wine & 3 gal	
1/4 lb starch	3d	spirits	£1-10-0
1 doz plates, 1/2 doz cups & saucers 7/6			

One evening at the time of the Rebellion of 1837, Anna Maria Marsh, a shop assistant aged sixteen, was left alone in charge of the van Nostrand store when some rebels entered and commandeered all the ammunition they could find. A fur cap caught the eye of one of the men and he carried it off promising to pay for it later. Much to the surprise of the van Nostrands, he kept his word.[18] In 1840 Cornelius turned the store over to his son, John, aged sixteen, whose shop license allowed him to sell liquor to his customers "in quantities of no less than one quart, to be drunk out of this House," and in 1844 he opened the York Mills post office in the building. Henceforth Cornelius spent his time at his mills.

Lieutenant-Colonel Duncan Cameron, C.B., born in Scotland and a retired Peninsular War veteran with a distinguished British army career in the Low Countries, Egypt, and Denmark, was attracted to Canada by glowing accounts from his relatives. In 1836 he bought property on Old Yonge Street across from St. John's Church[19] and erected a splendid mansion, Lindally, named after the Cameron family home in Scotland, containing twenty-eight rooms, wine cellars and seven fireplaces. This house eventually became the St. Andrews Golf Club-house. The year following the Rebellion Lieutenant-Colonel Cameron, given command of the North York Militia, held his drill parade on the flat ground behind Anderson's Tavern in the valley.

THE MILLS

With three mill sites in York Mills the sound of running water over the water-wheels, the buzz of the saws cutting logs, and the noise of the stones grinding the grain echoed throughout the valley each day from 1804 until 1926. In this business district the landscape was dotted with houses, out-houses, cooper's shops, and blacksmith shops behind the tavern east of Yonge and through the valley west of Yonge where the Metropolitan Toronto Don Valley Golf Course is today.

James Hogg, one of the early millers, was an honest and energetic individual who took a prominent part in political affairs of Upper Canada.[20] In 1832 he challenged George Gurnett,[21] editor of the *Courier of Upper Canada*, to a duel. "An article in that paper had spoken in offensive terms of supposed attempts on the part of a committee in York to swell the bulk of a local public meeting, by inviting into town persons from the rural parts. 'Every wheel of their well-organized political machine was set in motion', the *Courier* asserted, 'to transmute county farmers into citizens of York. Accordingly about nine in the morning, groups of tall, broad-shouldered, hulking fellows were seen arriving from Whitby, Pickering and Scarborough, some crowded in waggons, and others on horseback; and Hogg, the miller, headed a herd of the swine of Yonge Street, who made just as good votes at the meeting as the best shopkeepers in York.' No hostile encounter, however, took place, although a burlesque account of an 'affair of Honour' was published, in which it was pretended that Mr. Hogg was saved from a mortal wound by a fortunate accumulation, under the lappel of his coat, of flour, in which his antagonist's bullet buried itself."[22]

When James Hogg died in 1839 a long account appeared in the *British Colonist*, a conservative newspaper, for April 24th:

> It was our melancholy duty, along with others of our
> fellow-citizens to attend on Monday last, the funeral of
> James Hogg, from his late residence at York Mills, to
> the burial place in the close vicinity of that village. Mr.
> Hogg was well known in this Province for many years
> as an estimable person, an enterprising public man, and
> a true friend to his country; and the estimation in which
> he was held by his friends and the public during his life,
> was well shewn, by the great concourse of people who

assembled from Toronto and the surrounding country, to pay the last tribute of respect to his memory, by accompanying his remains to the grave.

Service was performed in a house in the village formerly occupied as an Inn: but a small part only of the assembled crowd could find room in it . . . the Church was refused for the occasion! . . .

The church was built by public subscription,[23] and it was at first designed as a place of worship to which preachers of various denominations of Christians would have access: By some means or other, which have not as yet been satisfactorily explained. Dr. Strachan managed to secure the exclusive possession of the church for an Episcopal minister, contrary to the original design of the inhabitants of the place, who contributed towards its erection, and as we are informed without the sanction or knowledge of many of them.

The church in question was St. John's and James Hogg was buried in its churchyard, but feelings of bitterness and tension were apparently still evident in 1839. The widow of James Hogg was left with five children including three sons aged thirteen, eleven, and nine, all too young to carry on the milling business. As a result in 1840 the Hogg mills were leased to the Somervilles (see Mills and Distilleries).

St. John's York Mills Anglican Church

In 1797 members of the Church of England who emigrated to Canada formed the first congregation of any denomination in York, the new capital of Upper Canada. In the same year land was granted for a church and graveyard at King and Church Streets, but it was 1803 before a wooden building was begun on the site, and 1807 before the St. James' Church—the present Cathedral, was completed.

St. John's Church[24] was the first outpost or mission of St. James'. Services had been held weekly in Seneca Ketchum's log house on Yonge Street since 1796, and when the Rev. George Okill Stuart arrived in 1800 he frequently visited the Ketchum's house to conduct services for interested neighbours. In 1812 Dr. John Strachan, a young Scottish clergyman from Cornwall, Upper Canada, replaced Stuart who moved to Kingston, and following the War of 1812, during which services were held in the York Mills log schoolhouse, it was decided to build a church in the area.

Joseph Shepard and his wife, Catharine, gave two and three-quarter acres of land for the site of the new church and cemetery on Old Yonge

Street, and Seneca Ketchum gave a large donation of money as well as much of his time. The cornerstone was laid by Lieutenant-Governor Gore and Rev. Strachan on September 17, 1816, while a large crowd seated on boards and timbers around the site witnessed the ceremony.

The opening date of the new chapel is not known. The church was not mentioned in a funeral account in the *Upper Canada Gazette* on January 2, 1817, when "John Willson, (son of Stilwell Willson of Yonge Street) was killed by the fall of a log from a small house that he was assisting a poor man to raise. . . . The Remains interred on the 24th in the new Church Yard where an affecting sermon was delivered by Rev. Dr. Strachan to a large and respectable assemblage of friends and acquaintances of this much lamented young man." By August 4th Strachan reported that the church was ready for Divine Service. It was a long, wooden building, thirty by sixty feet, "with gable end and door toward the road, the roof bending down slightly with the weight of a brick chimney,"[25] and it stood facing Old Yonge Street with space cleared for a burial-ground. James Strachan, John's brother, reported that "the pews were very decent and what was much better, they were filled with an attentive audience."[26] Services were conducted each Sunday afternoon by divinity students, who were sent out from York, or by Seneca Ketchum, a lay reader. Once a month the Rev. Dr. Strachan officiated. The church was consecrated on June 17, 1829.

St. John's second building which forms the nave of the present structure, was erected at a cost of £800. The cornerstone was laid on May 30, 1843, and the official opening took place on June 11, 1844. It was designed by John George Howard, Toronto city surveyor and engineer whose home, Colborne Lodge, together with his estate, now High Park, was bequeathed to Toronto in return for a pension. In the spring of 1847 Colonel Amos Thorne and Joseph Beckett, two church-wardens, went to England to buy a barrel-organ which was installed in September, and is still in the church today even though it was replaced about 1864 with a "finger organ" which has since itself been replaced.

The first rectory, built in 1841 on Old Yonge Street, was replaced in 1878 with a large, two-storey building still standing today a short distance south of the churchyard. St. John's has continued its activities through the years, as shown so aptly by Audrey Graham in her *150 Years at St. John's York Mills*. A cloister and parish hall were added in 1939, the chancel and Memorial Chapel were erected in 1948, and the parish hall was completed in 1951. In September and October, 1966, St. John's York Mills celebrated the 150th anniversary of the first St. John's Church and it continues to be one of the leading parishes of the diocese.

THE YORK MILLS BAPTIST CHURCH

The first service of the York Mills Baptist Church was held on the second Sunday in June, 1829, when a small group of Baptists met in the home of Mrs. Herron to hear James Mitchell preach. Later meetings were held in the log schoolhouse, and by 1833 this small congregation had erected a church with burial-ground on the west side of Mercer Avenue (now York Mills Road), east of Old Yonge Street, on land given by Thomas Johnston to the Church trustees in 1832. The chapel was simple but dignified, made of clapboard painted white with three tall arched windows along each side and one on each side of the front door. Its pulpit is used today as a lectern in the Spring Garden Baptist Church in Willowdale. The church was dedicated on June 2, 1833, under the pastoral care of Rev. James Mitchell, a tailor, who was ordained in the Willowdale Cummer Meeting House on December 9, 1830. He held the office for almost twenty years, and in 1840 a parsonage was built next to the church.

Rev. Ezekiel Gooderham, the next pastor, had to resign because of ill health, and the congregation was reduced to a membership of six, becoming known as the Church of the Six Sisters: Mrs. David Gibson, Mrs. William Holmes, Mrs. Christopher Sylvester, Mrs. William Patterson, Mrs. Thomas Gray, and Miss Jennett Marquis. Between the years 1869-1874 the church made gratifying progress increasing its membership from six to twenty-one, and help was received from Deacon Latch of the Alexander Street Baptist Church in Toronto. In 1944 the church was closed; in 1948 the congregation joined the Glenforest Avenue Baptist Church in Toronto, and the little York Mills church was torn down leaving the cemetery and the 1840 parsonage still standing today. Some of the squared timbers, together with those from St. John's, were used as ceiling beams in the narthex of the present St. John's York Mills Anglican Church.

YORK MILLS PRESBYTERIAN CHURCH

Very little is known about the first York Mills Presbyterian Church, but it is certain that James Hogg was instrumental in its construction. William Marsh, who lived near St. John's Church, mentions in a letter to relatives in England on February 10, 1836, that he can see from his property "to the south in a valley a large Millpond . . . an object of admiration—there is now also a handsome Presbyterian Church building—new in addition to an Epescapealian [sic] and Baptist Church already built within ten menutes walk of our house."[27] This church stood under the hill near Ivor Road, and Rev. Thomas Wightman, who came out

Letter to Mr. Marsh in York Mills, 1835.

No. 2 —   ***Still Licence for the Year*** **1839**
DISTRICT

PROVINCE OF } SIR GEORGE ARTHUR, K.C.H. Lieutenant Governor of the Province
UPPER CANADA. } of Upper Canada, &c. &c. &c.

To all whom these Presents may concern:
This Licence is granted to *Cornelius Vanostrand*
       of the Town *ship of York*
in the County of *York & Home District* —————— District,
to have and to use **ONE STILL,** for the purpose of Distilling Spirituous Liquors,
containing *eighty* ——————————————— Gallons, and
no more.

   This Licence to be in force until the fifth day of January, one thousand eight hundred
and *forty* ———— and no longer.

      GIVEN under my Hand, at Toronto, in the County of York, this *7th*
—————— day of *January* ———————— one thousand
eight hundred and thirty *nine*   and in the second year of Her Majesty's
Reign.

By His Excellency's Command.

                        INSPECTOR GENERAL.

RECEIVED *from the said* *Cornelius Vanostrand*
the sum of *five Pounds* ————————————. *Lawful Money of*
this Province, being the full Duty of Two Shillings and Six Pence per Gallon, directed to
be paid on this Licence, by Acts of the Provincial Legislature, imposing Duties on Stills
according to the admeasurement thereof. *Alex. McDonell*
                               Inspector

Still Licence from 1839.

St. John's Anglican Church, York Mills, established in 1816 on the west side of Old Yonge Street.

Lieutenant Colonel Duncan Cameron's house on the corner of Old Yonge Street and Links Road, built about 1835.

John Conn van Nostrand's mud-brick house on the east side of Yonge, north of Lord Seaton Road. Built about 1840, torn down in 1949.

York Mills Road, looking east from Yonge Street in 1906. Board sidewalk and York Mills School, built in 1893.

Yonge Street Bridge over the Don River showing the Hogg millpond and the McGlashan tannery.

Wilfred Forsythe on York Mills Road about 200 yards east of Yonge, 1911.

Jay H. Fulton standing in front of his store and post office which opened in 1884 across from John Street in York Mills.

Looking south on Yonge Street in 1920. York Mills Hotel and store on the left and the radial tracks on the right.

Joseph Shepard's house, built in 1835, on the north side of Burndale Avenue two blocks from Yonge. Government troops upon searching the house after the Rebellion found Colonel Van Egmond, Commander of the rebels.

from Scotland in 1842, was minister at both York Mills and Fisherville from 1850 to 1856. His daughter, Sarah, became the wife of William Hogg in 1855.

Because the Church was located on a site without title, in 1859 Andrew McGlashan II, the tanner, gave two acres of land to the Church trustees. The old building north of Ivor Road was torn down and rebuilt with the same lumber on the west side of Yonge, on a plateau half way up the hill across from the Hogg store and hotel. It was a most commodious and substantial building and was opened for public worship on August 23, 1859. As there was no organ in the church, Willy Miller, the precentor, used a tuning fork to begin each hymn. The congregation was made up of many families from Don Mills who drove here to church each Sunday. They left their horses and wagons or buggies in the York Mills Hotel driving sheds and walked up a winding path to the church and cemetery. Another path gave access from Wilson Avenue on top of the hill. In 1864 Andrew McGlashan III bought a house and property on Yonge Street, north of York Mills Road, and it is believed that this building became the manse, or minister's house. Today it is an historic site, marking the home of the late C. W. Jefferys, the oustanding Canadian historical artist.

As the years passed the church members from Don Mills wanted a church in their own area, and in 1885 they decided to buy the Bethesda Primitive Methodist Church on the corner of Lawrence and Leslie. The members remaining on Yonge decided to join a congregation in Toronto and were given permission to dispose of the church in 1885. Subsequently most of the graves were removed from the cemetery. It was 1950 before another Presbyterian congregation established a church on Wilson Avenue at Saunders Street, known as Armour Heights Presbyterian Church.

POST OFFICES

The post office outlet moved up and down Yonge Street. It was established in 1836 under the name of York Mills in the Hogg's inn (see Inns and Taverns), and when the Somervilles built a general store on the north side of the Hogg inn, the postal service moved into the store. In 1844 it moved to the north hill and was located in the van Nostrand general store on the east side of Yonge Street, and in 1855 it returned to the Hogg brothers store which was rebuilt on the old inn site in the valley, following a fire which destroyed the old store and inn. In 1884 the post office moved back to the north hill again, to J. H. Fulton's general store across from John Street.

The North Hill

A new, brick, one-room schoolhouse replacing an old building on Old Yonge Street, was built half way up the north hill on the west side of Yonge Street in 1847; it still stands today as a dilapidated building, renovated some years ago. This schoolhouse served the community until 1893 when a large two-storey building was erected on York Mills Road (see Education). Across the road from the first brick school, on the east side of Yonge, William Miller ran a shoemaker's shop in another building which stands today below street level. Just to the south David Boyle ran a blacksmith shop in a convenient location for those travelling to and from the mills. George Parsons, a surgeon, who had been looking after the sick in the area since 1839, lived south of the blacksmith shop; in 1868 he turned his practice over to Dr. Thomas Armstrong, coroner for Toronto. On the very top of the hill George Harrison ran an inn in 1841, and Thomas Leach bought the old van Nostrand store to the south in 1857 and turned it into an inn. Mrs. Leach, after her husband's death, converted it back to a general store in 1869 (see Inns and Taverns).

The Valley

The sons of James Hogg took over the mills south of York Mills Road in 1848, John and William were merchants and James was the miller. In the 1850's they bought up land in the valley and had Dennis and Boulton, Surveyors and Agents, draw up a "plan of building lots in the Village of York Mills otherwise known as Hogg's Hollow, the property of J. and W. Hogg."[28] This is the first mention of Hogg's Hollow, and it appears to have been a sales subdivision name used by the brothers in 1856. As a selling point they advertised:

> The village possesses many privileges and advantages to induce Families to Purchase and Settle, viz.:—Three resident Clergymen, an experienced Physician, several Churches in the Village and Neighbourhood, a good brick School House, Stores, Post Office, two extensive Flour Mills in operation, in the hand of Capitalists, and another, to be driven by steam and water, is now in course of erection by the Proprietors, who have a Steam Saw Mill and Brick Yard in full operation, affording every facility to purchasers for Building. Three Omnibuses run through the Village daily to and from the City, one carrying daily Mail.[29]

THE TOP OF THE SOUTH HILL

John C. T. Cochrane, a Justice of the Peace and churchwarden at St. John's, settled at the top of the south hill, east of Yonge Street in 1857, and Doctor Thomas Cowdry moved into the same area in 1858.[30] He also was a St. John's churchwarden, and spent his time driving around the countryside in his buggy tending the sick in the area until 1874 when he sold his house to Thomas Humberstone. This little house stands today on Glen Echo near Mount Pleasant Road.

THE VILLAGE IN LATER YEARS

In 1870 the stages were still travelling to Richmond Hill and the population of the village was 100. J. and W. Hogg were still the leading general merchants with flourishing flour and saw mills, and their brother, John, was a Justice of the Peace and postmaster. The York Mills Hotel was vacant for a couple of years and then Wallace Carson became landlord (see Inns and Taverns). John Whitton, a butcher who moved to the district in 1878,[31] made weekly calls to the farmhouses with a supply of meat in his wagon. He built a slaughter house on the north-east corner of York Mills Road and Yonge, and his business was still operating in the 1920's. The building was pulled down in recent years to provide space for a service station.

J. H. Fulton ran a general store and post office on the north hill across from the school from 1884 to 1913. The building was destroyed by fire on Christmas Eve, 1912, and some of the presents waiting to be picked up at the post office never reached their destinations.

In 1906 Mineral Springs Limited purchased property[32] on the west side of Yonge about half way down from the city limits. From this location they dispensed bottled mineral water for nineteen years. Later the name was changed to York Springs Limited. O'Keefe Beverages took over the bottling plant in 1931 after a fire in their main building in Toronto, and erected a windmill. Their operations ceased in 1934, but the grounds around the old windmill were well kept by the caretaker until the property was sold and apartment buildings constructed on the site in the 1950's.

During the First World War an air field was built at the end of Avenue Road, a district now known as Armour Heights and used by the Air Force as a training centre. Flying in those days was very different from today. Many accidents occurred, and farmers often came upon stunned or injured pilots wandering in their fields. Today a Canadian Forces Staff College and Extension School are situated in the area.

The Rosedale Golf Club purchased 134 acres of land east of Yonge and moved from its old location in Rosedale in the spring of 1910. The golf course was built in the valley and a clubhouse erected on the south hill at the end of Doncliffe Drive. The St. Andrew's Estate and Golf Course purchased most of the old Cameron farm on the east side of Old Yonge Street in 1925 and 1926.[33] St. Andrew's College authorities planned to move to York Mills from Rosedale, but changed their minds and moved to Aurora. Instead, St. Andrew's golf course, designed by Stanley Thompson, was built. Many provincial and Canadian championship tournaments were held there through the years. The clubhouse, originally Duncan Cameron's residence was recently torn down for apartments and a new subdivision. The Metropolitan Toronto Don Valley Golf Course was built in the late 1950's on the west side of Yonge along the West Branch of the Don River. It covers the early sites of both the van Nostrand mills.

Hurricane Hazel swept the valley in 1954 changing the course of the Don River and causing extensive damage. As a result Carson Park was developed along the banks of the river in place of the old millpond, thus providing a greenbelt area for all to enjoy. Today York Mills' village atmosphere is undergoing rapid changes. The influx of newcomers to the Toronto area and the possibility of extensions of the subway system make it difficult to predict the future.

NOTES

1 Overseers of Highways and Fence-viewers elected at Town Meetings for Yonge Street: 1797, Nicholas Miller for Yonge Street; 1798, Thomas Hill and Nicholas Miller for Yonge Street; 1799, Daniel Dehart from lot 1 to Big Creek Bridge and half the bridge, Paul Wilcott from half Big Creek Bridge to lot 25; 1800, John Daniels from lot 1 to Big Creek Bridge, Malcolm Wright from Big Creek Bridge to lot 25; 1801, Duke William Kendrick from lot 1 to Big Creek Bridge, John Willson from Big Creek Bridge to lot 25; 1802, Thomas Hill from lot 1 to Big Creek Bridge, Lawrence Johnson from Big Creek Bridge to lot 25; 1803, John Kendrick from lot 1 to Big Creek Bridge, John Everson from Big Creek Bridge to lot 25; 1804, John McDougall from lot 1 to Big Creek Bridge, Thomas Humberstone from Big Creek Bridge to lot 25; 1805, Samuel Heron from lot 1 to Big Creek Bridge, Joseph Sheppard from Big Creek Bridge to lot 25; 1806, Jesse Ketchum from lot 1 to Big Creek Bridge, William Marsh from Big Creek Bridge to lot 17; 1807, George Bond from Poplar Plains to Big Creek Bridge, Thomas Mercer from Big Creek Bridge to lot 16; 1808, Thomas Hill from Poplar Plains to Big Creek Bridge, Christopher Harrison from Big Creek Bridge to lot 17; 1809 Seneca Ketchum from half of Blue Hill Bridge to half of Big Creek Bridge, Thomas Humberstone from Big Creek Bridge to lot 17; 1810, Thomas Hill from Blue Hill Bridge to lot 9 (that is centre of Heron's Bridge), Joseph Shepherd from Heron's Bridge to lot 25. Town of York, "Minute Book of Town Meetings and list of Inhabitants, 1797-1822", Toronto Public Libraries.

2 Millford Mills was also spelled Milford Mills.

3 Lot 8, 1st concession west of Yonge Street. E. J. Hathaway, *Jesse Ketchum and His Times* (Toronto: McClelland & Stewart, 1929), pp. 28-33.

4 A grist mill and saw mill were advertised for sale in the *Upper Canada Gazette* on July 6, 1809, and again on February 7, 1810. Heron is also spelled Herron.

5 *History of Toronto and the County of York, Ontario*, II, 199.

6 Lot 11, 1st concession west of Yonge Street. Ontario, Department of Public Records and Archives, *Minutes of the Court of General Quarter Sessions of the Peace for the Home District, 1800-1811*, Twenty-first Report, 1932 (Toronto: King's Printer, 1933), p. 176.

7 Lot 14, 1st concession west of Yonge Street. *History of Toronto and the County of York, Ontario*, II, 191.

8 *Upper Canada Gazette* (July 1, 1819).

9 Scadding, *op. cit.*, p. 445. According to *History of Toronto and the County of York, Ontario*, II, 191, Elizabeth was visiting her uncle Francis Lee at Talbot Settlement in Oxford Township when this happened.

10 Lot 10, 1st concession west of Yonge Street.

11 Lot 9, 1st concession west of Yonge Street.

12 Lot 13, 1st concession east of Yonge Street. Information about the van Nostrand family was supplied by Mrs. H. A. S. Molyneux and Dr. F. H. van Nostrand from their family documents including *Documentary History of the van Nostrand Family*.

13 Fustian was a coarse cloth made of cotton and flax.

14 A tin bastin was a shape for a hat.

15 Bulls eyes were large brown hard candies.

16 Twanky and Yong hison [sic]: a green tea leaf made up into different shapes called: Twankay, Hyson-skin, Hyson, Young Hyson, Imperial and Gunpowder.

17 Bombassette is a silk and wool fabric.

18 Anecdote courtesy Mrs. H. A. S. Molyneux. Anna Maria Marsh married John van Nostrand.

19 Lot 12, 1st concession east of Yonge Street.

20 Lot 10, 1st concession east of Yonge Street. In 1830 James Hogg and other inhabitants of Yonge Street petitioned the Assembly for leave to set up a Road Company. In 1834 he was nominated as a candidate to the Legislative Assembly.

21 George Gurnett, a Tory, entered Toronto City Council in 1834, served as an alderman 1834-36, 1838-47; Mayor: 1837, 1848-50; Police magistrate: 1851-61.

22 Scadding, *op. cit.*, p. 442.

23 Lists were put up on the church door and persons of any denomination could subscribe.

24 Graham, *op. cit.*

25 *Ibid.*, p. 177.

26 *Ibid.*, p. 35.

27 Correspondence of Susannah (Susan) Brown Marsh, 1819-1836. Transcript copy in the North York Historical Society files, courtesy Mrs. H. A. S. Molyneux.

28 The building lot plan is in the files of the North York Historical Society and the North York Public Library.

29 *Globe* (October 29, 1856).

30 Lot 8, 1st concession east of Yonge Street.

31 Lot 11, 1st concession east of Yonge Street.

32 Hamilton Cassels, Jr., "York Mills, 1800-1955", *Ontario History*, XLVII (1955), 189.

33 *Ibid.*, p. 188.

	CONC. II W.		CONC. I W.		CONC. I E. FINCH AV.	
	1832 WM. WREGGETT	1837 WM. IANSON	1800 JOSEPH JOHNSON 1825 JAMES DAVIS		1800 NICHOLAS JOHNSON 1807 STILLWELL WILLSON 1851 JOHN HOLMES	20
	1834 JACOB SHEPARD		1800 ABRAHAM JOHNSON 1832 JAMES BELL		1800 LAWRENCE JOHNSON 1834 WM. POOLE 1804 JACOB CUMMER	19
	1834 THOMAS SHEPARD		1805 JOHN WILLSON JR. 1831 JOHN CUMMER 1829 DAVID GIBSON		1801 JACOB CUMMER	18
	1844 ROBERT CATHCART		1805 J. SHEPARD 1837 MICHAEL SHEPARD		1830 JOHN McBRIDE	17
	1848 WM. JACKSON		1802 JOSEPH SHEPARD		1829 TERTULUS WEED 1839 ANGUS BLUE 1842 ELIHU PEASE	16
SHEPPARD AV.						
	1859 J. MORGAN	1824 JOHN BALES	1801 THOMAS HILL 1824 T. SHEPHERD		1803 JOHN EVERSON 1834 ELIHU PEASE	LOT 15

DUFFERIN ST.

BATHURST ST.

DON RIVER WEST BR.

YONGE ST. LANSING

WILLOWDALE

BAYVIEW AV.

Lansing and Willowdale.

Lansing

LANSING, EIGHT MILES NORTH OF TORONTO, DEVELOPED AS A CROSS-
roads village at Yonge and Sheppard Avenue, the latter originally
known as the side road between lots 15 and 16. Houses were widely
scattered along Yonge, and farm land separated Lansing from York
Mills on the south and Willowdale on the north. The mills situated to
the east and west at an early period made Sheppard Avenue a busy
country road.

EARLY SETTLERS

There were three very early settlers in the area. Thomas Hill, a
resident in 1797, and John Everson, a resident in 1798, ran taverns
on each of the southern corners of Yonge and Sheppard in 1802 (see
Inns and Taverns); and Joseph Shepard built a log house on the north-
west corner in 1798. The latter had come to Canada from the United
States in 1774, travelled extensively among the Indians as a fur trader,
and helped to erect the first shanties when York was founded in 1793.
During the capture of York in 1813, Shepard, a private in the 3rd York
Regiment, received a badly mangled left thigh and three broken ribs
when the grand magazine was blown up under the direction of Sir Roger
Hale Sheaffe, Brock's successor as commander of the forces in Upper
Canada and as civil administrator at Government House.[1] Besides farm-
ing and clearing his land, Joseph Shepard, as well as Seneca Ketchum,
was one of the chief promoters of St. John's York Mills Anglican
Church, and gave three acres of land for the church site and burial
ground, where members of his family are buried.

Thomas Sheppard[2] bought Thomas Hill's property and built the
Golden Lion Inn on the south-west corner in 1824 (see Inns and Tav-

erns). He advertised[3] "a grand pigeon shooting match" for Wednesday, September 26, 1833, at the Inn with three prizes for the winners: £10 for the best shot, £5 for the second, and a good rifle for the third prize. Shooting was to commence at eleven o'clock, and about 300 pigeons were provided for the occasion, having been caught in nets by the fowlers with the use of bait.

The passenger pigeon now extinct was formerly the most numerous of birds, and during migration the skies were blackened with them for about three days at a time. Alexander Wilson,[4] the father of American ornithology, mentioned a migrating flock of approximately 2,230,272,000 birds, extending 240 miles, which he calculated would consume 17,424,000 bushels of nuts, acorns or grain daily. Organized hunts, market-hunting with the use of nets, and the depletion of the forest have caused the passenger pigeon's extinction today.

A year after the pigeon-shooting match in September, 1834, the Reform Party Convention met at the Golden Lion[5] to choose the party's York County candidates for the coming election of the Legislative Assembly of Upper Canada. Robert Baldwin was chairman and the reformers nominated were David Gibson, James Davis, John Cummer, all of Willowdale, Joseph Shepard II of Lansing, and James Hogg of York Mills. All were vitally interested in the affairs of Toronto. The corrupt practices of officials, land speculation, administrative extravagance, and the question of endowments issued to one church only, were the abuses, sometimes over-exaggerated, which prompted the formation of a Reform Party, and William Lyon Mackenzie, with his printing press, was a biting leader for its radical wing.

A TANNERY

Elihu Pease moved from Newtonbrook to Lansing in 1834 and erected a small tannery on his farm on the south-east corner of Sheppard and Yonge.[6] Tanning in the thirties also meant converting leather into footwear, clothing, and harness for one's neighbours. It was purely a barter business, and Pease received half the hide he was tanning for his labour (see Early Industries). Besides being a tanner he also was interested in Township affairs. In 1836 he was elected pathmaster and in 1837, clerk of York Township, and later held the position of Inspector of Schools.

Edward Pease, Elihu's son, was apprenticed to his father who gave him property in King Township where he established the Kinghorn tannery; Elizabeth, a daughter, married Andrew Davis, a tanner and son of James Davis, a Willowdale innkeeper. Upon Elihu Pease's death, in 1854, a handbill advertised an extensive auction of the Pease property, south of Sheppard Avenue, and also Andrew Davis' tannery in Willowdale. Included were such items as agricultural and household implements, livestock, vehicles, sets of new harness, a new saddle, new bridles, a lot of carpenters and blacksmith tools, twenty pairs of new boots and shoes, and one fire engine.[7]

THE REBELLION OF 1837

Joseph Shepard Sr., one of William Lyon Mackenzie's closest friends and supporters, died a few months before the Rebellion, but his sons continued as active reformers. This was not surprising for the Township was one of the main centres of Reform strength. In the ravine near the corner of Sheppard Avenue and Bathurst, Joseph Shepard I built a water-powered saw mill in 1830. Thomas, Joseph's son, refers to the mill in his account of the Rebellion of 1837. "Mike and I then lived at the mill back of Lansing, up Yonge Street,"[8] and went to Uncle Jake Fisher's farm in Vaughan four or five times to drill with muskets. The mill was "an old structure a short distance in the rear of Gibson's farm, known as Shepard's mill which had long been a secret rendezvous for the radicals of the neighbourhood."[9]

On Monday afternoon, December 4th, 1837, the day originally chosen for the outbreak of the Rebellion, another meeting took place there. William Lyon Mackenzie and David Gibson left the house of James Hervey Price at Eglinton, and made their way to the mill separately. "According to a previous arrangement, they found several local insurgents engaged in casting bullets."[10] Not long afterwards David Gibson's servant arrived with news that Samuel Lount, Anderson and others were on their way south from Lloydtown and would reach Montgomery's during the evening.

This message accounts for Thomas Shepard's visit to his mother on Yonge Street that evening.[11] As he was cleaning his musket, Samuel Lount and about fifty-nine others knocked at the door of the little frame house built in 1835 and still standing on Burndale Avenue. They had marched thirty miles in the bitter cold and now stopped for a rest, warmth and food. After receiving a very cordial welcome they continued on their way to Montgomery's Tavern. Thomas followed the next day, and upon reaching the Tavern found there were seven or eight hundred farmers collected, a few with muskets and others with pikes.

Thomas and Michael Shepard were with Peter Matthews setting fire to the Don Bridge when Montgomery's Tavern was burned. They were captured later at the Silverthorne's house near the Humber on December 15, 1837, and sent to Kingston to await passage to Van Dieman's Land. Thomas' account of their exciting escape from Fort

Henry in Kingston to the United States may be found in *Old Toronto,* edited by E. C. Kyte.[12] Joseph Shepard II and Jacob, brothers of Thomas and Michael, were imprisoned on December 11th and finally released on May 12, 1838. Following the skirmish at the Tavern, William Lyon Mackenzie obtained a horse at the Golden Lion Hotel in Lansing, went to the Shepard's mill, and from there made his escape to the United States. Colonel Van Egmond,[13] the rebel commander from the Huron Tract, after parting from Mackenzie at the Golden Lion, felt overcome by fatigue and sought shelter on the farm of Mrs. Shepard. His hideaway was soon found, however, for the place was searched by government troops who slashed the quilts on the beds with their swords and set fire to the bedding as they hunted for rebels. If it had not been for Mrs. Shepard quickly putting out each blaze, the house would have burned.[14] Colonel Van Egmond was discovered and thrown into jail in Toronto, where he died of pneumonia contracted in the cold, damp, underground cell.

A SUBDIVISION

As the country settled down after the Rebellion, Angus Blue, a carpenter who considered himself the best dressed Highlander in Toronto, and was prominent at the Highland games every year, bought property north of Sheppard and east of Yonge in 1839. The following year he rented and operated the Royal Baths in Toronto, a small frame building on the north side of King Street where the bath-keeper lived, with the bathrooms at the rear. He advertised in 1844 that hot and cold baths were available from six in the morning until ten at night. "Entrance for the ladies on King Street. Entrance for the gentlemen on the lane leading to the Racquet court.[15] Prior to this either a dip in the lake or river, or a bath in the kitchen or a bedroom were the only means of cleanliness.

In 1847 Blue changed the name to the Toronto Baths and advertised[16] that one could have a warm bath at almost a minute's notice. The Baths were open from 8 a.m. to 10 p.m. and a family ticket was four pounds; tickets for twenty warm baths were one pound; and cold baths seven and a half pence. In 1857 he opened a subdivision on his Lansing property (on Doris Street) and, being a carpenter, no doubt built houses himself.

MILLS AND A STORE

When the Shepard men returned to Lansing after being pardoned by the Queen in 1843 for their actions in the Rebellion, Michael opened a saw mill at Oriole (see Mills and Distilleries), and built a large brick house on the farm land left to him by his father. This house stands today in the York Cemetery grounds and is used by the caretaker as a house and office.[17] Thomas Shepard took over the old saw mill in the ravine near Bathurst Street left to him by his father and enlarged his establishment by adding a grist mill (see Mills and Distilleries).

Joseph Shepard II built a large brick store on the north-west corner of Yonge and Sheppard Avenue about 1860,[18] with living quarters in the rear and upstairs, and the family rented the old farm house, and moved into the new building. The parlor and dining room were downstairs on the north side of the store, and behind them an enormous kitchen where the family gathered around a large, wood stove in winter evenings. At the back of the house a summer kitchen with a soft-water pump was used as a washroom, and outside a very deep well provided hard water for cooking and drinking. It must be remembered that at this time there were no bathrooms, running water, electricity or telephones in any of the houses.

Upstairs there were six large bedrooms, and without a furnace they were often cold. When a glass of water was taken up to one of the children, it would be frozen by morning. As a result the children snuggled into their short feather beds to keep warm. There were no springs for these beds, only a rope laced back and forth which could be tightened with a wooden bed-wrench when it sagged. A driving shed joined the summer kitchen where the cutter, buggy, surrey and wagons were kept; and the barn behind the store had a lovely hay mow enjoyed by the children, a couple of horses in stalls, feed bins, and well-polished harness hanging ready for use.

The store area was large with a friendly pot-bellied stove serving as a meeting place for those who came to buy, chat, or wait for the horse-drawn stage that ran daily from Yorkville to Richmond Hill. Long counters ran down the full length of the room on both sides, one serving for groceries and consisting of large tea caddies for black and green tea, huge drawers containing rolled oats and sugar, crackers loose in a barrel, and mild and old cheeses weighing approximately 100 pounds sat on the counter waiting to be cut into one half or one pound wedges for customers.

The dry goods section on the other side consisted of bolts of towelling, flannelette, blue denim, factory cotton, prints, and some woollens for Sunday dresses. There was no silk and very little ready-made clothing. Clothes were all made at home or by the village tailor or dressmaker. Boots were available from William Miller and later James Flynn who ran a shoemaker's shop across the road. Hardware tools and farm implements also had their place. Axes, hoes, buggy whips, shiny cow-chains, coils of rope, kegs of nails, gunpowder, bags of shot, and a shelf of common crockery were available in various parts of the store.

Many of the farmers brought butter and eggs in on Saturdays and exchanged them for needed household items. Store hours were from 7 a.m. to 10 p.m. six days a week, and once a week the horse was hitched to a loaded wagon, and a call was made to each farm in the district offering for sale bolts of gingham, linsey-woolsey, butcher's linen, and white or grey Canton flannel. Orders were also taken for additional items to be delivered later.

Wooden shutters were put up every night over the windows of the store and taken down each morning. The farmers left their milk under the veranda to be picked up later by big wagons holding fifty or sixty cans which were hauled to Toronto for distribution. In later years the radial street cars picked up the milk on Yonge Street on their trip to Toronto. Today the store is known as Dempsey's.

THE 1860's AND 70's

In 1866 Joseph Shepard II opened a post office, his daughter Saida named it Lansing,[19] and R. G. Lambert was the first postmaster. By 1870 Joseph E. Shepard had taken over his father's business, was postmaster, general merchant and operator of the flour and lumber mills near Bathurst Street[20] (see Mills and Distilleries). North of the store in 1860 stood Cornelius van Nostrand's busy carriage and wagon shop,[21] which was taken over by William Duncan in 1870 (see Early Industries).

Across the road lived Alexander McMaster, physician and surgeon, who was at the beck and call of every sick neighbour twenty-four hours a day. Next door to the doctor was the Weed's house and agricultural implement shop, where such things as shovels, rakes, fanning mills, and harrows were made by Albert Weed. His father, Tertullus Weed had moved his family to this farm lot on the north-east corner of Yonge and Sheppard as early as 1829, and Albert, his son, ran a carpenter's shop before branching out into implements.

William Miller and later James Flynn operated a shoemaker's shop and kept the people of Lansing in boots, while Robert Bestard ran a harness shop. Bestard specialized in show harness and was kept busy because most farmers had prize horses or teams requiring the finest saddlery. This shop was eventually taken over by William Gooderham, who farmed and sold agricultural implements.

MORGAN'S CORNERS

Bathurst was never a busy thoroughfare. John Bales emigrated from England in 1819, bought sixty acres of land on the south-east corner of Bathurst and Sheppard,[22] built a log house about 1822, cleared his land, and established a very good farm, according to the 1851 census. His attractive log, rough-cast house facing Bathurst is still standing in the York Downs Golf Club grounds, and his barns form part of the clubhouse.

John Morgan, in 1859, bought part of the lot on the south-west corner of Bathurst and Sheppard,[23] across the road from the Bales property. He cleared his farm and built an inn known as Morgan's Corners Hotel that was operating in the 1870's (see Inns and Taverns).

The Shepard Mills, later William Hortop's Ripley Mills, were operating in the valley to the east with a blacksmith shop near the top of the hill at Bathurst (see Mills and Distilleries). William Jackson[24] emigrated from England, married Catherine Shepard a daughter of Joseph, and owned a well-cleared farm with a large house on the north-west corner. On January 4, 1848, he advertised in the *Globe* for the owner of a brindle cow that had strayed into his premises on October 31st.

THE METROPOLITAN SKATING RINK

The Metropolitan Skating Rink was an enclosed building operated on the old Shepard farm near the present Borough offices, from 1888 to 1892. There were twelve shareholders, and general admission was ten cents. Three gay carnival nights with band music were held the first season.

THE CHURCH

The Methodist residents of Lansing had always attended the Willowdale or Newtonbrook church. When the Rev. T. W. Pickett, a retired minister, took over the old Golden Lion Hotel as a residence, he held week-night services in 1915 in the former bar-room. John Boddy began a Sunday school in his residence in 1918, and when it became too large for the house it was moved to the Pickett's home.

In 1920 a small wooden church was built on Sheppard Avenue, west of Yonge Street, called the Lansing Church School. With the adoption of Church Union in 1925, the Rev. George Waugh served as minister for Willowdale and Lansing, and the small wooden building became known as Lansing United Church. All churches suffered great financial difficulties in the thirties because the incomes of members and supporters were greatly reduced or, in some cases, non-existent during the depression years. With the nineteen-forties and the Second World War came increased prosperity and population. The old church became over-crowded and was replaced by the present edifice on Bogert Avenue, officially opened in 1951. The education wing was completed in 1955, and the new manse in 1958.

Today a few houses, including the frame Shepard house on Burndale, Michael Shepard's farm house in the cemetery grounds, and the old Shepard store, are all that remain of the very early era in Lansing.

NOTES

1 Norris Zaslow, ed., *The Defended Border* (Toronto: Macmillan, 1964), pp. 252, 257-258. This family spelled their name either Shepard or Sheppard. Their first property was lot 16, 1st concession east of Yonge Street.

2 Thomas Sheppard, whose last name was also spelled Shepard and Shepherd, may have been a brother of Joseph. He bought lot 15, 1st concession west of Yonge Street in 1824.

3 "Prescott Shooting Club, Established 4th October, A.D. 1845", *Canadian Journal of Arms Collecting*, IV, 22-4.

4 T. G. Pearson, ed., *Birds of America* (Garden City: Garden City Books, 1936), II, 10.

5 B. P. Davis and C. L. Davis, *The Davis Family and the Leather Industry, 1834-1934* (Toronto: Ryerson Press, 1934), p. 65.

6 Lot 15, 1st concession east of Yonge Street.

7 B. P. Davis and C. L. Davis, *op. cit.*, p. 78.

8 J. R. Robertson, *Landmarks of Toronto*, I, 229-233

9 J. C. Dent, *Story of the Upper Canadian Rebellion* (Toronto: C. Blackett Robinson, 1885), II, 47.

10 *Ibid.*, II, 47.

11 J. R. Robertson, *Landmarks of Toronto*, I, 230.

12 Robertson, *Old Toronto*, pp. 120-121.

13 Anthony Van Egmond, father of the Huron Tract, opened the Huron Road for the Canada Company in 1828. He reached Montgomery's Tavern on the morning of the skirmish.

14 The late Mrs. Charles Milne was told this story by her mother, Saida Shepard, a daughter of Joseph II.

15 J. R. Robertson, *op. cit.*, I, 442, 444.

16 *British Colonist* (April 2, 1847).

17 Lot 17, 1st concession west of Yonge Street.

18 This store is still standing and known today as Dempsey's Store. Details of store courtesy Mrs. E. Denby, granddaughter of Thomas Shepard, and Mrs. Philip Allen, the daughter of B. R. Brown who owned it from 1888-1921.

19 Courtesy of the late Mrs. Charles Milne.

20 County of York, *Gazetteer and Directory* (1870-71).

21 Cornelius was the son of John Conn van Nostrand.

22 Lot 15, 1st concession west of Yonge Street.

23 Lot 15, 2nd concession west of Yonge Street.

24 Lot 16, 2nd concession west of Yonge Street.

Willowdale

WILLOWDALE, ORIGINALLY KNOWN AS KUMMER'S SETTLEMENT, WAS a small village on Yonge Street, nine miles from the town of York and situated between Lansing to the south, and Finch Avenue to the north. In 1857 its population was 150.

EARLY SETTLERS

Jacob Cummer, his wife Elizabeth, and their three children were among the first settlers in the area when they chose the centre of Willowdale as their residence in 1797. They had travelled from Pennsylvania by way of Niagara with her father, Jacob Fisher, and other members of the family. The Cummers spent the winter in a log house at Eglinton until receiving their Crown grant on the east side of Yonge Street.[1] One day Elizabeth, busy with her household chores, was startled by an Indian peering through the door, his eye on a shiny kitchen-knife lying on the table. Being afraid and most anxious for him to leave, she quickly gave him the knife. Later, he returned bringing her a cradle he had made for her baby John. It was an Indian custom to return gift for gift.

Well-read, and capable of working in iron, wood, brick or stone, Cummer had an efficient workshop where he made his own implements and supplied his neighbours with scythes, cradles, flails, ploughs, harrows, wagons, carts, and sleighs.[2] The shop became a centre for the farmers to collect and discuss their common problems and, because he was also very clever in his treatment of horses and cattle, Cummer was called upon to render veterinary services. He appears to have been in demand to treat human illness as well. For bleeding his patient, widely considered a common remedy for illness, he owned a spring lance made in England which held several different blades. His grandson, Jacob, was once sent to him for treatment and it was decided that bleeding was necessary. The boy's grandmother brought the bowl, expecting to hold it, but her husband insisted that young Jacob hang on to it himself, and learn to uphold the Cummer name.[3]

The family belonged originally to the Lutheran Church, but as the Methodist denomination was the pioneer church of the time, the Cummers and other settlers around Willowdale became devoted Methodists. In 1816 the Methodist Episcopal Sunday School began in the Cummer's log house with John Rhodes as circuit rider. Camp meetings followed in a thick maple grove at the Cummer saw mill on the Middle Don River in Newtonbrook.[4]

As each of his six sons married, Cummer gave them a piece of property. When he died in 1841 he left his saw mill to John, the north half of the original 285 acre farm to Joshua, the southern half to Samuel. John, David and Daniel were very active in the temperance society formed in 1831, and John was elected to the Legislative Assembly in 1834. A Cummer house still stands today on Doris and Morton Avenues.

The Johnson family were also natives of Pennsylvania who emigrated to Canada in 1795 and settled just north of the Cummer family, on both the east and west side of Yonge.[5] According to Augustus Jones, Deputy Provincial Surveyor, Lawrence and his four sons, Abraham, Joseph, Nicholas and Thomas, were on the premises in 1797, and the following year four log houses had been built with about ten to twelve acres of land cleared on each lot. Abraham Johnson's[6] family took an active part in community affairs. Abraham I was appointed Overseer of Highways and Fence-viewer in 1806 for lots 16-25, and his son, Abraham II, was secretary of the temperance society in 1831, collector in 1836, assessor in 1837 and a Justice of the Peace in 1871. The family continued to live in Willowdale until about 1920 when their house was taken over by the Canadian Red Cross for York Cottage, a home for children.

The Willson family owned various mills and properties during the early period in North York. John Willson I[7] emigrated to America in 1752 and settled in New Jersey. In the American Revolution he served as a captain in the army on the Loyalist side, and after having his property confiscated, sought refuge in New Brunswick with other United Empire Loyalists. The family moved to Upper Canada at the time of General Simcoe's arrival, stayed a short period in the Niagara District, and then settled on Yonge Street. There were five sons: John II, Still-

Joseph Shepard's store on the north-west corner of Yonge and Sheppard. Built in 1860, it later became known as Brown's and Dempsey's.

Looking south to the Golden Lion Hotel on the south-east corner of Yonge and Sheppard in 1920. Rev. T. W. Pickett on the veranda. The door on the right was the entrance to the bar.

The south side of the O. D. Bales house on the north-east corner of Yonge and the Macdonald-Cartier Freeway. Left to right: Nellie Wilson, Allan Bales, John Bales, Mrs. J. Bishop, Douglas Bales, Eva Wilson, Mrs. Minnie Wilson, Oliver D. Bales, Mrs. O. D. Bales, Martha Pipher, Earl Bales.

Sheppard Avenue bridge over the Don River near Bathurst, between 1910 and 1918.

A barn raising on the Bales farm on the south-east corner of Sheppard and Yonge.

The Willowdale Episcopal Methodist Church and cemetery on the north corner of Church Avenue and Yonge; built in 1856, demolished in 1956. Looking south, 1914.

David Gibson's second house, standing behind the Willowdale Post Office, was finished in 1851. Peter Gibson, on the left behind his surveying equipment, with members of the family.

North York students at Whitby Ladies College. Left to right, standing: Ada Boake, Jennie Goulding; sitting: Susan Wallace, Miss Wellington, the music teacher; on the floor: Maud Wilson.

The Willowdale Episcopal Methodist Church parsonage, north of the Gibson house, where Mrs. Gibson brought her children when her house burned during the Rebellion. Demolished in 1967.

James Davis' Hotel, built in 1825 on the west side of Yonge south of Finch.

George Goulding's threshing crew and steam engine, about 1900. George is standing left on the machine. Front row: W. O. James and his dog, George Hackett, ———?, Steve Middleton, William James, Albert Montague, ———?, Jack Beck, ———?, Manuel Chapman.

well, William, Isaac, and Jonathan, all prominent in York.

John Willson II served as a lieutenant in the Loyalist army during the American Revolution, settled on lot 18 west of Yonge about 1805, and was appointed with Seneca Ketchum and Joseph Shepard as a trustee for building St. John's Anglican Church. It was his grandson, John Willson IV, who, still living in Willowdale, was elected York Township clerk in 1836 and held the office until his death in 1866, and his great-grandson Arthur, who followed his father as clerk and later became reeve.

Stillwell settled on Joseph Johnson's original lot 20 on the east side of Yonge in 1807. On June 10, 1823, the *Upper Canada Gazette* carried a notice of a sale of the family property at public auction. It was described as 240 acres with a large and well-finished barn, a house, out-houses and an orchard. Stillwell had to give it up because, like many others, he could not meet his payments. The property was taken over by William Allan, the first president of the Bank of Upper Canada, a member of the Legislative Council, financial genius of the Family Compact and possibly the richest man in the province.

The McBride family originally emigrated from Ireland to Pennsylvania, fought on the side of the English during the Revolution, and came to Canada in 1793 receiving land on King Street in York and farmland to the north.[8] Sergeant John McBride Sr. and his wife were caterers to the House of Assembly, and he was also door-keeper to the Legislative and Executive Councils. He died in 1801 and his widow opened a tavern in York which was patronized by members of the Legislature. John II and his wife Eleanor were living in Willowdale on the east side of Yonge Street as early as 1806 when they were summoned by their neighbour to the north, Jacob Cummer, on a charge of assault and battery. John was found not guilty, but his wife was fined five pounds and placed on one year's probation to keep the peace.[9]

Following the War of 1812 when Canada was going through a period of hard times, John II went to Ireland with the approval of the Government to promote immigration to Canada. He drove to New York, sold his horses, and set sail accompanied by three Indians. He remained away for over a year, demonstrating the friendliness of the Indians and trying to convince the Irish that they should move to Canada, a land of opportunity. A great many were enthusiastic and emigrated to Canada. When John returned home he was very surprised to find that the two horses he had sold in New York had found their way back to his farm on Yonge Street.[10] John II's grandson Charles became proprietor of Prospect House at Eglinton in 1858 and later built and operated the Bedford Park Hotel (see Inns and Taverns). Two McBride houses still remain in Willowdale; a frame house that was moved from Yonge near Empress to Spring Gardens, and a brick house on Yonge now owned by Dr. Ralph P. Johns.

AN INN AND A TANNERY

James Davis built and operated a large two-storey inn on the west side of Yonge, south of Finch Avenue, in 1825.[11] This became a temperance inn and a favourite rendezvous for Mackenzie's rebels (see Inns and Taverns). About 1834 Davis also opened a small tannery. No capital was necessary for purchasing tanning materials as the hemlock and oak bark used in the process was obtainable on the farm. All that was needed was a vat and a hammer to crush and grind the hemlock. Later a small mill to be propelled by a horse was erected to crush the bark. The finishing process was done by hand.[12] As his son Andrew grew older it was decided that he should become a tanner and take over the business his father had started. Andrew, too, may have become more interested in the work due to his frequent visits to the Pease family and their tannery at Lansing. The real purpose of his visits, however, was to court Elizabeth Pease, whom he later married.

The tanning business evidently progressed sufficiently to warrant the construction of a separate establishment; a small frame building was built on the corner of Finch and painted red to match the house. In 1849 this structure, the first Davis Leather Company building, was sold to Andrew with an acre of land.[13] When Elihu Pease died in 1854 the Pease property and Davis tannery on Yonge Street were both put up for auction and the commodious Davis tannery was bought by Jacob Lawrence of Lawrence Avenue, and sold two years later to James Hugo, a tanner and currier.

DAVID GIBSON AND THE REBELLION

The 200 acre lot north of the Shepard property was divided in half. In 1829 David Gibson bought the southern portion from John Willson III and a huge elm marked the gate of his farm.[14] Gibson was the first professional landholder in Willowdale having come from Scotland as a qualified surveyor-engineer. The most common method of determining the length of survey lines in those days was by measuring with the Gunter's chain, and Gibson's chain is still in the family's possession. One chain equalled a mile and ten square chains equalled an acre. Distances were recorded in chains and links. As a land surveyor and farmer, Gibson became very prominent in Township affairs. In 1831 he was elected President of the temperance society, and in 1834 and 1836 a member of the Legislative Assembly. At the municipal meeting of the Township of York in January, 1836, he was chosen secretary, and in the following year officiated as chairman. He was a man well liked by his neighbours and held in high favour as one of the Reform leaders.

Caucus meetings were often held at the Gibson house and 200 volunteers held training manoeuvres on his farm.[15] During the uprising at Montgomery's Tavern, Gibson was in charge of the Tory prisoners, who were released when the Government forces set fire to the inn. He escaped to the east and a price of £500 was offered for his capture. Government soldiers, leaving Montgomery's went directly to the Gibson farm and, acting on orders from Sir Francis Bond Head, immediately set the house on fire.[16] Mrs. Gibson and her four small children fled from the building into the cold December weather. She wrapped the baby, Peter Silas, in a blanket and left him in a snow bank by the fence with the children while she collected a few things, including the face and works of a grandfather's clock. The family found shelter at the parsonage nearby and later moved in with John Cummer's family. The hired men let the horses loose, and they escaped to the woods at the back of the property while the soldiers slaughtered the pigs and chickens and carried them off across their saddle-bows.[17]

David Gibson, after days of December exposure, finally arrived at the house of a friend near Oshawa where he spent four or five weeks in a haystack waiting for an opportunity to cross the lake to the United States. This was finally accomplished in an open boat with several other fugitives.[18] When William Lyon Mackenzie, living also in the United States, tried to obtain Gibson's support to send raiding parties into Canada, Gibson refused, and was severely criticized openly by Mackenzie. However, after obtaining a certificate as to his character and professional ability from Marshall Spring Bidwell, one time Assembly Speaker who had fled to New York, Gibson "obtained professional employment at Lockport where important public works, including the enlargement of the locks on the Erie Canal, were then in progress."[19] His family joined him shortly afterwards, and they later moved to Rochester.

The Cummers were Reformers and personal friends of William Lyon Mackenzie. Following the uprising, John Cummer, the Newtonbrook miller, was under suspicion. The morning after Gibson's house was burned, Cummer went down to see the ruins. He had just arrived home when a band of Government soldiers appeared at his door demanding his surrender. One soldier rode up on the veranda, banged on the door with the butt of his pistol, and, when Cummer reluctantly appeared, his wrists were tied and he was roped to other prisoners; then the party marched down Yonge Street on foot to the jail in Toronto.[20] The next day he was released thanks to his Tory friends: Peter Lawrence, his brother-in-law, and Sir Allan Napier MacNab, who had purchased large quantities of lumber from the Cummer mill. Samuel Cummer, a rebel in sympathy and brother of John, was drafted into the Government army and locked up for the night, but released in the morning because of his youth.

William Poole, a son-in-law of Abraham Johnson II, lived north of the cemetery and was an ardent rebel. His house was also set on fire by the troops following the Gibson fire but it was put out quickly and the damage was not great.[21] He was arrested on December 11, 1837, and released July 13, 1838, giving his word to keep the peace and be of good behaviour for three years. However, he and his wife, and other rebel friends found it convenient to move to the United States.

Shortly after Lord Durham's report was published on October 15, 1839, the leading Reformers held a meeting at James Davis' Inn to consider the document. Many leading statesmen were present, including the Hon. Robert Baldwin, his father Dr. Baldwin, and Francis, afterwards Sir Francis, Hincks. The meeting ended in confusion when a raiding party, headed by Sheriff Jarvis, arrived from Toronto; during a heated skirmish one of the Reformers was killed by a flying stone.[22]

THE CHURCH

In 1834 Jacob Cummer gave a half-acre of his property on the east side of Yonge to the community for church purposes. At the same time the Johnson family gave part of Lawrence Johnson's original land next to the church property for a cemetery. A Methodist Episcopal log meeting house was built on Yonge Street with Jacob Cummer doing most of the work himself. The sabbath school was held promptly at 9:00 a.m. and the church service at 2:00 o'clock, with another service following in the evening. At the time of the Rebellion Jacob Cummer assembled the men in the church for prayers before they went down to Montgomery's Tavern.

In 1856 the small, log Methodist Episcopal chapel was replaced with a substantial yellow brick structure with gabled front and buttressed walls. The artistic spire built by Samuel Cummer could be seen for many miles on Yonge Street until it was blown down in the 1920's, never to be replaced. The formerly picturesque church lost most of its character in 1931 when a large section at the front was removed to widen Yonge Street. The adjacent cemetery was also encroached upon, and many of the pioneers were disinterred by their descendants and removed to other cemeteries. A few stones in some of these old cemeteries use a poetic approach. A favourite seems to have been:

> Remember all, As you pass by,
> As you are now, So once was I
> As I am now, So you will be
> Prepare yourself to follow me.

Finally in 1954 a new spacious modern building was erected on Kenneth Avenue. The old church on Yonge was sold to the Seventh Day Adventists Communion who used the building for services until its demolition on September 21, 1956. A park has been designed for the cemetery as a joint project of the Borough and some of the descendants. It is very fitting that they have preserved the memory of the early Methodist pioneers who wrested a livelihood from the wilderness and shaped a community of rich, productive farms along with successful, commercial and industrial enterprises.

The 1840's

An interesting development of early industry by absentee control is revealed in an agreement between David Gibson, then living in Lockport, in the United States, and Henry Neal, of Toronto, to make "133,333 good merchantible Stock Bricks, to be made on the South Half of Lot Number Eighteen on the West Side of Yonge Street . . . The said Henry Neal doth agree to chop his own wood on Mr. Gibson's said lot . . . and draw all the sand necessary for making said brick. . . ."[23] The kiln was built and the bricks made under the inspection of neighbours John Cummer and his brother-in-law, Robert Irwin. Enough were stored to build a new home for the Gibson family which was finished in 1851, and recently restored by the Borough of North York. The remainder of the brick was purchased by various neighbours living on Yonge Street. Jacob Cummer, for instance, bought 2,300 bricks for a shingle machine, and bricks were also supplied for the school in 1842.

There were three schools built on the west side of Yonge Street near the corner of Ellerslie Avenue. Children from as far away as Bathurst and Sheppard Avenue met their friends and talked and laughed as they walked through the snow or along the dirt roads and wooden sidewalks to school (see Education).

An interesting comparison can be made between today's land values and those of 1846. The settlers and their sons were given land grants of

200 acres with the obligation to clear the trees and help with roads. In 1846 James Hervey Price, the lawyer in Toronto handling Gibson's affairs, wrote to Hickory Corners, Lockport, informing him that William Mathers of Toronto had offered £1,200 for the Gibson farm, provided he could have twenty trees off other Gibson acreage for rails, the bricks left on the property, and wheat growing in the ground. In his letters[24] to Gibson, Price refers to properties for sale on Yonge Street:

> "I sold 100 acres all cleared except 15 acres of wood just 4 miles from Town for a thousand pounds this was as clear of stumps as yours. . . . I sold 200 acres the Ruggles Farm with a House that cost 1800 with barns stables and 16 acres of wheat for £2800. . . . Michael Shepherd [Shepard] offered me his 200 acres with building and all for 2400£ well fenced and in good condition . . . Montgomery was offered £1250 for his farm a side line running on its south & a good new cottage built thereon within the last two years or so . . . I think property has arrived on Yonge St. to its ultimate value . . . therefore you may conclude that I am sincere in my view of the value of your Farm. Several persons have called & have been thunder struck at the price a thousand pounds they all say is more than its worth. . . ."

While David Gibson was in Lockport his father lived in Willowdale, and letters were written back and forth as his father tried to settle his interests. Finally in 1848 David returned to Yonge Street, in 1851 his brick house, that is still standing, was completed, and in 1853 he was appointed Crown Land Commissioner, Inspector of Crown Land Agencies, and Superintendent of Colonization Roads. With his two eldest sons, James and William, shouldering some of the responsibility they supervised the building of roads and bridges in the developing Province of Canada West. In 1856 they built and owned a saw mill in Parry Sound and employed Joseph and Michael Shepard to help them. Peter Gibson, David's son, received his engineering degree from the University of Michigan, at Ann Arbour, in 1864, the year of his father's sudden death in Quebec. He built an office building near the back door of his father's house and carried on as a professional surveyor while continuing to farm.

THE FIRST POST OFFICE

Jacob Cummer was a jack of all trades. At the request of David Gibson he cut the timber on the Gibson property and hauled it to Yonge Street to provide lumber for the Gibson house. In the forties he built a shingle mill and later, with his son Joseph, built a small shop on Yonge and carried on the business of tin and coppersmiths, selling such things as pots, pans, and stove pipes. On December 3, 1847, J. Cummer advertised in the *Examiner* for a pedlar to sell his tinware and obtain orders:

PEDLAR WANTED

Jacob Cummer, tinsmith, anxious to engage a person to
pedal tinware. Liberal wages given.

David Gibson petitioned the government to open a post office and suggested the name Willow Dale, because of the numerous willow trees in the district. It was established on March 28, 1855, in the tinsmith's shop and Jacob Cummer was appointed the first postmaster. When the shop burned in 1865, Peter Gibson went immediately to Toronto to see the Post Office Inspector and obtain duplicate post office papers in order to continue mail service. A couple of days after the fire a benefit social was held at the Golden Lion for the unfortunate father and son. The proceeds amounted to $27.

SOCIETIES

The Cummers, the Davises, the Gibsons and the Johnsons were all very active in the temperance society formed in 1831. Members from Willowdale and other North York chapters attended the first great temperance rally in Canada held in Weston in January 1843, when the Wesleyans led the total-abstinence movement in its sweep across the country. The roads were thronged with people in sleighs, on horseback, and walking, all converging to support the cause. Peter Gibson records in his diary[25] in 1865 that the "Sons of Temperance met fortnightly to accommodate the Literary Association." In the same year "the Literary Association appointed at its first meeting of the year, Miss Hayes, Miss Johnson and Peter Gibson to edit the *Willowdale Clip*, perhaps the first local paper.

An active missionary society was functioning in the 1860's and probably earlier, providing numerous speakers who held their audiences spellbound. However, one young man's comments may reveal problems similar to those of today regarding the gap between the generations. Peter Gibson records, "Went to Missionary Society but heard only one decent speech." After paying a three dollar subscription for his mother, and accompanying two young ladies back to their farms, he returned home to pursue his reading of Edward Gibbon's *Decline and Fall of the Roman Empire*.

THE STORE

In 1883 Ludwig Lehman opened a general store and post office located on the west side of Yonge, north of both the Gibson's house and the parsonage. It was a small frame building with the store and post office at the front of the building, and the family quarters in the rear and upstairs. As there was no well on the property, it was necessary for the family to carry water from a well across the road at the Flook's house. The creek close by, however, was a constant menace to the merchandise kept in the cellar. William Stevenson became postmaster in 1887 and eventually erected a new brick store in 1914 to replace the old building. An ice-cream parlor on the back veranda, grew into a gathering place for young people. The building still stands today across from Parkview Avenue.

LATER YEARS

An account in the *Globe* for December 3, 1913, stated that the Gibson farm had been sold to the Ontario Estates Limited who planned to subdivide the land for building purposes. The price, a record for the district, was approximately $1,000 an acre. This sale anticipated the modern trend of subdividing farmland along Yonge Street. Due to these developments along Yonge Street, two new churches were opened following the formation of the Township: St. George's Anglican Church, a small frame building erected by its parishioners, which opened in 1922 on the corner of Yonge and Churchill; and the Westminster Presbyterian Church (later Willowdale Presbyterian), which in 1925 held services in the Township Hall and in 1929 opened a new building on Empress Avenue.

During the First World War a Canadian Red Cross branch, formed on October 16, 1914, under the able leadership of Mrs. Arthur van Nostrand, carried on the necessary home-front tasks of rolling bandages, knitting socks, and sending parcels overseas. Money was raised by concerts, tag days, donations, and sales. A Flax Festival was held in August 1918 in the fields behind the William Wallace house on Ellerslie Avenue, where the Government was experimenting with 160 acres of flax. Demonstrations of different processes required to turn flax into linen drew sizeable crowds and proceeds from refreshments, games of all kinds, and the sale of home-made food added $1,708.50 to the Branch funds. Linen was recognized as one of the best materials used in the manufacture of airplane wings. When Belgium and Northern France, large producers of flax fibre, were captured by Germany, linen manufacturers faced a tremendous shortage of raw material and efforts were made to develop the product in various Allied countries. Canada's production was admirable, as displayed at the Wallace farm; after further experiments following the war it was found that Canadian flax growers could produce an excellent quality of seed, which was sold to

Ireland. During the Second World War the Canadian Red Cross once more embarked on an active programme which has since led into other fields. On October 16, 1964, the Branch celebrated its fiftieth anniversary at Newtonbrook United Church.

The Willowdale story is similar to that of the other districts in North York in portraying the industrious character of its people whose philosophy of mutual support and assistance developed a stable, thriving and lively community spanning three or four generations. The Gibson House is being restored to the 1851 period in which it was built. As a teaching museum its revelation of the past, with an accent on surveying, will provide vision for the future.

NOTES

1   Lot 18, 1st concession east of Yonge Street. Cummer was also spelled Kummer.

2   W. W. Cummer and C. L. Cummer, *Cummer Memoranda* (Cleveland: 1911), p. 24.

3   *Ibid.*, p. 25.

4   Lot 22, 3rd concession east of Yonge Street. See Newtonbrook.

5   Lawrence Johnson: lot 19, 1st concession east of Yonge. Nicholas Johnson, lot 20, 1st concession east of Yonge. Thomas Johnson: lot 21, 1st concession east of Yonge. Thomas did not build a log house, and only 6 acres were cleared by 1798. Abraham Johnson: lot 19, 1st concession west of Yonge. Joseph Johnson: lot 20, 1st concession west of Yonge.

6   Abraham Johnson I, 1767-1840; Abraham II, 1807-1892; Abraham III, 1848-1942.

7   *History of Toronto and the County of York, Ontario*, I, pt. 2, 84.

8   Lots 4 and 5, 2nd concession west of Yonge Street and lot 4, 3rd concession west of Yonge.

9   Lot 17, 1st concession east of Yonge Street. Patent was not registered until 1830. *Minutes of the Court of General Quarter Sessions of the Peace for the Home District, 1800-1811*, p. 83.

10 F. A. Mulholland, *The Mulholland Family Tree* (Toronto: Ontario Publishing Co., 1937), p. 70.

11 Lot 20, 1st concession west of Yonge Street.

12 B. R. Davis and C. L. Davis, *op. cit.*, pp. 60-61.

13 *Ibid.*, pp. 75-80.

14 Southern half of lot 18, 1st concession west of Yonge Street. John Willson II died in 1816.

15 David Gibson Papers. Microfilm copy, North York Public Library.

16 Dent, *op. cit.*, II, 130-131.

17 Courtesy of the late Miss Lina Gibson, descendant.

18 Dent, *op. cit.*, II, 147.

19 *Ibid.*, p. 236.

20 W. W. Cummer and C. L. Cummer, *op. cit.*, pp. 29-30.

21 Robertson, *Old Toronto*, p. 112.

22 B. R. Davis and C. L. Davis, *op. cit.*, p. 73.

23 David Gibson Papers.

24 *Ibid.*

25 *Ibid.*

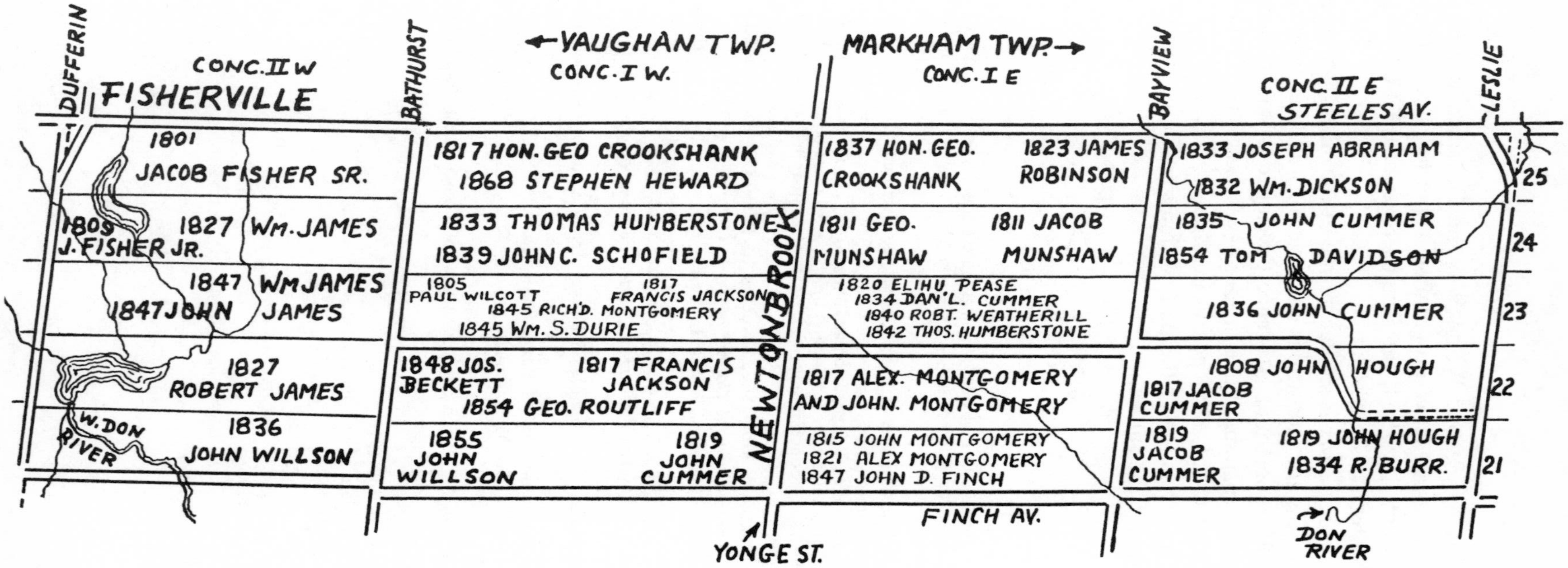

Newtonbrook.

Newtonbrook

NEWTONBROOK, ON NORTH YORK'S NORTHERN BOUNDARY, SOUTH OF Vaughan and Markham, was a thriving village of 200 people by 1870, centred at Yonge and Drewry. In 1819 its roads extended to the east as far as the Middle Don River where the Cummer Mills were located, and by 1820 to the West Branch of the Don at Dufferin and Steeles where the Fisher Mills were erected and Fisherville developed. The name, Newtonbrook, was derived from the Newton Brook Wesleyan Methodist Church, and until the early twentieth century was spelled as two words. Mary Gapper, travelling from Thornhill to York on October 26, 1829, noted the district in her diary: "The fences are universally zig zag rails which are generally untidy and at all times perhaps more picturesque than neat; the cottages are more or less distant from the road. Mostly of plank with barns at hand . . . but with seldom more than a wild sort of attempt at a garden."[1]

EARLY YEARS

The brook running through the community has been known for over 150 years as Wilket[2] Creek. Its source was west of Yonge and north of Drewry, and the swampy area at Yonge Street made it necessary for the road to turn west for easier crossing until an arch bridge was erected. The property at the interesection of Yonge and the creek, in 1805, belonged to Paul Wilcot, who emigrated from Pennsylvania in 1793, applied for a tavern license but was refused. He was elected, however, an Overseer of Highways and Fence-viewer for Yonge Street from Big Creek Bridge, now York Mills, to Steeles Avenue.

John Mills Jackson of Jackson's Point returned to Canada from

England and settled for a time in Newtonbrook where he owned a saw mill on Yonge Street just north of Drewry that was sold to George Playter[3] (see Mills and Distilleries).

Elihu Pease, whose ancestors emigrated from England on the Puritan ship *Francis* and landed at Boston in 1634, grew up in the United States and was educated as a civil engineer and land surveyor. He came to York in its early days, settled in Thornhill and taught school in 1811 in the first schoolhouse in York County at Langstaff. When asked to take the oath of allegiance at the beginning of the War of 1812, Elihu refused, left Canada, and went to Buffalo, where he served in the post office and custom house. After the war, however, he returned to York, pledged allegiance, and assisted in rebuilding the old garrison. In 1819 he married Jacob Cummer's daughter, Katherine, and in 1820 moved to Newtonbrook, where he taught school. In 1821 he moved back to Buffalo, but returned in 1825 and took over his father-in-law's property in Newtonbrook, where he farmed for nine years before moving to Lansing.

CAMP MEETINGS

John Cummer, son of Jacob Cummer of Willowdale, owned a farm on the north-west corner of Finch and Yonge. A side road, now Cummer Avenue, ran through to the Don River, east of Yonge Street in 1819. Here John operated a saw mill owned by his father who came to Canada from Reading, Pennsylvania, with his wife and family.

Camp meetings were held at the mill site for many years and the area became known as Scripture Town, a name later changed to Angel Valley by those who lived there. The Rev. Peter Jones, a part-Indian Wesleyan missionary, mentions in his journal spending three days at a camp meeting at the mill. "Monday, July 12, 1826 started with a number of the Indians to attend a Camp meeting on Yonge Street, where we arrived the next day about noon. During the meeting, a number of both whites and Indians professed to experience a change of heart, at the close, several Indians received the solemn ordinance of baptism. The name of the Lord be praised!"[4]

The following year another meeting is mentioned which lasted for four days. "Saturday 16th. Arrived at the Camp meeting this morning, where I met about sixty Indians, mostly from Lake Simcoe. I spoke to them the words of eternal life; they paid great attention and were much affected. Sunday 17th. I addressed the white people on the state of the Indian Missions. Monday 18th. This morning the ordinance of baptism was administered . . . total number 36, 20 adults and 16 children."[5]

Later in 1828 the journal states:

Tuesday June 10th. About noon started for the Camp ground.
When we arrived we found between two and three hundred Indians
from Lake Simcoe and Schoogog [sic] Lake. Most of those from Lake
Simcoe have just come in from the back lakes to join with their
converted brethren in the service of Almighty God. They came in
company with Brother Law, and all seemed very glad to see us,
giving us a hearty shake of the hand. The Camp ground enclosed
about two acres, which was surrounded with board tents, having one
large gate for teams to go in and out, and three smaller ones. The
Indians occupied one large tent, which was 240 feet long and 15 feet
broad. It was covered over head with boards, and the sides were
made tight with bushes to make it secure from any encroachments.
It had four doors fronting the Camp ground. In this long house, the
Indians arranged themselves in families, as is their custom in their
wigwams. Divine service commenced toward evening. Elder Case
first giving directions as to the order to be observed on the Camp
ground during the meetings. Brother James Richardson then
preached from Acts 11.21; after which I gave the substance in Indian,
when the brethren appeared much affected and interested. Prayer
meeting in the evening. The watch kept the place illuminated during
the night.[6]

This camp meeting continued until Friday the 13th when Peter Jones
left with the Indians for Lake Simcoe.

Religion continued to play a very important part in the lives of the
settlers, and camp meetings continued at the Cummer mill during the
summer. The following notice appeared in the *Christian Guardian*,
June 10, 1840: "A camp meeting will be held on Yonge Street Circuit,
in the vicinity of Cummer's Saw Mill, two miles east of the street, and
twelve miles from the city,—commencing on Friday the 26th of June.
Arrangements are made with a person near the place to provide 30
board tents, for the convenience of families from a distance. Some are
expected from the adjoining circuits and from the city. Several Ministers
are fully expected, in particular Rev. Messrs. J. Ryerson, D. Wright,
H. Biggar, and J. Musgrove. George Poole, Superintendent. June 5,
1840."[7]

The Church

James Agar came to Newtonbrook in 1844, settling on the east
side of Yonge, north of Wedgewood Avenue. The first Primitive Methodist services were held in his house,[8] and afterwards in the log schoolhouse. Sunday school and class-meetings were held in the morning and
the preaching service in the evening. This congregation became known
as Agar's Appointment.

About the same time the Parsonage congregation was established by Abraham Johnson II and John Willson IV. Services were held on Sunday afternoons in two joined wooden buildings on Finch Avenue, just west of Yonge,[9] where the men sat on the east side of the building and the women on the west side. This congregation had a reputation for promptness; the minister always found his flock waiting quietly for his arrival.

In 1857 Thomas Davidson,[10] a lumber merchant, provided land for a church about a quarter of a mile south of Cummer Avenue, on the east side of Yonge. A new white brick building was erected through the combined efforts of the Parsonage congregation and Agar's Appointment, which united to form the Newton Brook Wesleyan Methodist Church, named after the late Rev. Robert Newton. Young and old worked on the building. Bees were held to haul brick and stone, and the men made seats, tables, lamps, and boxes with long handles to replace the hats used to collect the offerings. The women provided hymn books, and made cushions and a carpet for the pulpit and altar.

The church was remodelled about 1887, and a horseshoe-shaped gallery, a pipe organ, crimson wool carpet, new cushioned pews and an elaborate chandelier of sixteen lamps were added to the furnishings. The old frame church stood behind the new building and became the Sunday school. In 1888, before the debt for all the improvements was cleared, a fire broke out and completely destroyed the church. However, immediately steps were taken to rebuild, and services were held in the parsonage[11] near Hounslow Avenue until a shed was erected.

The circuit minister held service at three churches each Sunday, driving many miles in his one-horse buggy to cover his territory. On his visits to members of his congregations, he seldom left without a gift of a bag of feed for his horse, a bag of potatoes, or a choice piece of fresh meat. Edwin Arthur Pearson was the Newtonbrook circuit minister in the 1890's. His son, the Rt. Hon. Lester Bowles Pearson, was born in the old parsonage on Yonge Street in 1897, received the Nobel Peace Prize in 1957, and became Prime Minister of Canada in April, 1963.

Prior to 1870 William Goulding, son of Thomas Goulding of Downsview, moved to Newtonbrook[12] and became a prominent local preacher and Sunday school superintendent. Through the years the tea and missionary meetings became outstanding events, and great rivalry developed between Newtonbrook and Downsview as to who could supply the best oyster suppers during the winter months, or the most elaborate tea table.

TAVERNS

John Montgomery's first inn, The Bird in Hand, was opened on the west side of Yonge, about a quarter of a mile north of Finch, in the 1820's. It was leased to John Finch in the 1830's, and ceased to operate about 1847 when he opened his own inn on the north-east corner of Yonge and Finch Avenue.

The first inn at Steeles and Yonge stood on the north-east corner and was called The Green Bush, run by Joseph Abrahams. In 1847 John Morley opened his tavern on the north-west corner and it was taken over later by Thomas and John Steele (see Inns and Taverns).

MILLS ON THE MIDDLE DON

Milling was one of a variety of active concerns for John Cummer, who also farmed and organized camp meetings. Since horses were needed in his business, when one disappeared it must have seemed a great loss. The following advertisement was placed in the *British Colonist* for October 11, 1838:

STOLEN OR STRAYED

On last Sat. week, near John Cummer's Yonge Street,
a Brown Mare seven years old, a white stripe down her
face, white hind feet, her mane hangs on the off side,
she is narrow behind, and rather sharp and light off
the belly. Whoever will bring her to John Cummer or
inform him of her, shall be handsomely rewarded.

John and his son, Jacob, enlarged their business to include a grist mill, saw mills, and a woollen mill (see Mills and Distilleries).

Two saw mills were also operating to the north-east near Leslie, one owned by Thomas Davidson, who provided land for the church, and the other by Samuel Hammil in Markham; and a grist mill and saw mill owned by Benjamin Fish were producing flour and lumber at the corner of Steeles and Bayview Avenues (see Mills and Distilleries). The miller's house is still standing but has been moved back from the road.

THE NEWTON BROOK POTTERY

Thomas Humberstone Jr., apprenticed by his father in York Mills as a potter, moved to Newtonbrook, married Sarah Wilson of Markham Township in 1835, and opened a pottery of his own on the west side of Yonge, about a quarter of a mile south of Steeles. Here he made such items as earthenware pitchers, flower pots, vases, and bricks. Humberstone's pottery business was disrupted by fire three times, and each time he rebuilt and struggled back to prosperity. In 1870 he turned the business over to his second son, Simon Thomas, who, besides operating the Newton Brook Pottery, became Reeve of York Township from 1890-1893, and through his interest in astronomy printed a pamphlet entitled *Antiquity Revealed or Philosophy of the Solar System*.[13] Thomas Allan Humberstone inherited the pottery from his father in 1915, but before the end of the First World War he decided to close down the kilns, and the building stood empty until 1919 when it was gutted by fire.

DREWRY AVENUE OPENED

The opening of Drewry Avenue[14] in 1847 brought those living on Bathurst, particularly the James family, into closer contact with Yonge Street. William S. Durie, a retired English army officer who emigrated to Canada in 1836, developed a subdivision on lot 23 west of Yonge, and opened what later became Drewry Avenue on the southern edge of the property. This new road first became known as Pope's Lane because of the number of Roman Catholics who moved into the area and built houses along it. William Durie continued his interest in the army, and in 1860 was appointed lieutenant-colonel of the 2nd Battalion, Volunteer Rifles of Canada, which became the Queen's Own Rifles of Toronto. In 1848 Joseph Beckett divided his property on the south side of Drewry and opened his subdivision. Joseph, a chemist and Warden of St. John's Episcopal Church, lived on Yonge Street, north of Lawrence Avenue.

Three schools were built on Drewry Avenue. A brick building was erected in 1847 to replace a log school on Yonge Street south of Steeles Avenue; another was built in 1878 close to Yonge, and another in 1928 across the road on the north side of Drewry, where it stands today (see Education). At the west end of Drewry Avenue across Bathurst Street, Robert James built a house as early as 1827 when he and his family moved from Newmarket to lot 22, 2nd concession, west of Yonge. His three sons farmed and were very active: Joseph ran a saw mill near Dufferin Avenue (see Mills and Distilleries), John was one of the pillars of Newtonbrook Wesleyan Methodist Church, and William who built his house on lot 24 in 1848 was a Justice of the Peace, a member of York Township Council when it was formed in 1850, and as reeve he was very influential in the early development of the Township for nine years.

THE CENTRE OF NEWTONBROOK

Newtonbrook developed into a community in the 1860's and 1870's. George Routliff,[15] the butcher, lived in a mud brick house nearly a

Yonge Street looking north from the Gibson house. From left to right: corner of Mrs. William Holmes' house, William Stephenson's store and post office, built in 1865, the third school built in 1892, and above the radial car is the Willowdale Episcopal Methodist Church steeple.

John Cummer's house on the north-west corner of Yonge and Finch, built about 1819. Government troops captured John Cummer here after the Rebellion. (above)

William James' house built in 1848 on the west side of Bathurst, about a quarter of a mile south of Steeles. James was reeve from 1852 to 1860. (above right)

Daniel Flynn, a shoemaker, built this house south of Drewry on Yonge in 1858. It was moved to Black Creek Pioneer Village in 1959. (right)

A Cummer house on the east side of Yonge across from Patricia Avenue. Occupied by Elihu Pease and family in 1820, and David Cummer and family in 1832.

Demolition of same house in 1964. Note vertical plank construction.

Newtonbrook Wesleyan Methodist Church manse on Yonge, south of Hendon Avenue, in 1908. The birthplace of the Rt. Hon. Lester B. Pearson.

Newtonbrook store and post office in 1920, at the corner of Drewry and Yonge. Thomas Clark Street's coal team in centre of road, fence on right is in front of the Humberstone's house.

Keele Street in 1902, site of Northwestern General Hospital on right. Farmers doing statute labour: team 1, J. A. Macdonald with son, John, driving; team 2, John Holmley, standing in front of team with arms folded; team 3, belonged to Bentom Parsons who took picture, Charlie Yeatman driving, George Fox with shovel.

Fairbank Wesleyan Methodist Church built in 1889 on the west side of Dufferin about half a mile north of Eglinton. (top)

Mrs. Thomas Mulholland by the house erected by Henry Mulholland in 1826 on the west side of Bathurst, about a quarter of a mile north of Lawrence. Photo taken in 1895; house demolished in 1950's. (centre)

John Perkins Bull's house, Downsview, on Rustic Road west of Keele; now a nursing home. Small room off porch was his courtroom. (left) quarter of a mile south of Drewry on Yonge, across from the Methodist Church. Weekly visits were made to the neighbouring farmhouses in his covered rig with an assortment of meat. A horn was blown to announce his arrival and the housewife came out with her platter to make the purchases.

Daniel Flynn's house and his shoemaker's shop stood north of the butcher's property, south of Drewry,[16] in 1858. A skilled bootmaker, he produced a wide range of styles, from the high-cut dress boot to rough work boots. Flynn died at the age of ninety-six and his buildings now stand in Black Creek Pioneer Village as examples of an artisan's house and shoemaker's shop.

On the north-west corner of Drewry and Yonge stood a frame general store.[17] A post office opened in the building in 1863 with M. Richardson as the first postmaster. William W. Cummer, son of John and originally a miller, took over the store in 1867, and George Goulding, a pillar of the Newtonbrook Methodist Church, took it over in 1886. It burned to the ground in 1907 and was replaced with a new, brick building still standing today.

North of the store, on the west side of Yonge, lived Dr. George H. Husband,[18] who advertised in the Miles *Illustrated Historical Atlas of the County of York* in 1878 as a practical dentist who "will attend to the duties of his profession as follows: Weston on the 9th of every month, Woodbridge on the 22nd of every month, office every Saturday at Newton Brook, Yonge Street." Wilket Creek ran under the old arch bridge in front of his house.

Across the road, on the east side of Yonge, stood Peter Weatherill's blacksmith and wagon shop.[19] The Weatherill family, ardent Methodists, had lived in Newtonbrook since 1840. The shop was eventually taken over by his neighbour, William Street, whose son John built wagons. The Street family moved to Newtonbrook in 1854 and built a log house on their farm, replacing it later with a frame house and a brick house, both still standing today. Thomas Clark Street, William's son, later ran a coal business.

James Agar, a shoemaker and local preacher of the Primitive Methodist Church, lived south of the Street's house and built a store and shoemaker's shop in front of his house.[20] Agar was very fond of singing and played the flute. As a result, the family generally spent Sunday afternoon in sacred song. Mrs. Agar's philosophy of life, as described by her daughter, was intriguing: "Above all things she desired godliness for her children. After godliness and industry came education. How she did prize it before wealth, social position, dress or accomplishments. Life was a most interesting thing to mother, because she had a purpose and lived in its fulfillment. Labor in her mind was a moral tonic, and she kept us employed to keep us from evil. She was always busy at home, but she performed many loving ministries in other homes."[21]

The old picturesque quality of Newtonbrook has all but vanished in recent years with the disappearnce of the century-old houses and impressive rows of chestnut trees that used to line both Yonge and Steeles Avenue at their intersections. Some lonely lilac hedges and the old blacksmith shop north of Wedgewood have had an inexplicable stay of execution, but they too are doomed as their homes have been demolished.

NOTES

1 Mary S. Gapper O'Brien, journal, October 26, 1829.

2 Wilket was also spelled Wilcott and Wilcot. Paul Wilcott owned lot 23, 1st concession west of Yonge Street in 1805-1818, and Jonathan owned lot 22, 1st concession east of Yonge Street in 1799-1816.

3 Lots 22 and 23, 1st concession west of Yonge Street.

4 Peter Jones, *The Life and Journals of Kah-ke-wa-quo-na-by* (Toronto: Anson Green, 1860), p. 70. Peter Jones was the son of Augustus Jones, the King's Provincial Surveyor who opened Yonge Street.

5 *Ibid.*, pp. 89-90.

6 *Ibid.*, pp. 149-151.

7 John Ryerson, 1799-1878. Yonge Street Circuit 1823, book stewart 1837-41; David Wright, 1792-1872. Methodist Episcopal. Yonge Street Circuit 1831-32; Hamilton Biggar, 1806-83. Yonge Street Circuit 1836-37; James Musgrove, 1816-63. Yonge Street Circuit 1850-51.

8 Lot 23, 1st concession east of Yonge Street.

9 Lot 21, 1st concession west of Yonge Street.

10 Davidson was also spelled Davison. The church was on lot 22, 1st concession east of Yonge Street.

11 Lot 21, 1st concession west of Yonge Street.

12 Lot 24, 1st concession west of Yonge Street.

13 North York Public Library, Scrapbook. The Humberstones owned forty acres of lot 24, 1st concession west of Yonge Street in 1833, and another acre in 1840, and twenty-eight and a half acres of lot 23, 1st concession east of Yonge Street in 1842.

14 For some unknown reason the street was called Drewry instead of Durie.

15 Routliff was also spelled Rutileff. Lot 22, 1st concession west of Yonge Street. This mud brick house was torn down by the North York Hydro.

16 Lot 22, 1st concession west of Yonge Street.

17 Part of lot 23, 1st concession west of Yonge Street.

18 *Ibid.*

19 Part of lot 23, 1st concession east of Yonge Street.

20 *Ibid.*

21 Hopper, *op. cit.*, pp. 255-256.

Eglinton

THE COMMUNITY OF EGLINTON EXTENDING NORTH FROM EGLINTON Avenue along Yonge Street, took its name from a notorious, mock-medieval tournament held in France, in the castle of the 13th Earl of Eglinton, in August, 1839.[1] When news of the fête reached Canada it generated wide discussion since, not only was Louis Napoleon, the future Napoleon III, a participant, but the scandalous sum of £30,000 to £40,000 was expended in bringing it off. Although the street became part of North Toronto in 1912, the rear half of the farm lots from about half way to Bayview on the east, and almost to Avenue Road on the west, are within the North York boundary. The village was very early linked through common interest to North York, inasmuch as Yonge Street was the main artery to Toronto; many landowners held property in both communities; and, of course, the skirmish at Montgomery's Tavern, headquarters for Mackenzie's rebels in 1837, played an important part in North York history.

WAR OF 1812

Martin Snyder, a United Empire Loyalist of German descent who live in Nova Scotia before coming to York Township, settled and cleared his land on Yonge Street in 1811.[2] Jacob Snyder, Martin's son, was very active during the War of 1812, pressing teams of horses into service for conveying stores, ammunition, and troops to Holland Landing and other likely places where foreign troops might land. One Sunday he went to Newmarket and, while the Quakers were at church, commandeered the teams of horses left in the driving shed.

The Hon. William Allan offered his farm for sale on the east side of

Yonge at Eglinton in 1810. The advertisement stated that the property was well cleared, fenced and under crop, with a good frame house, barn and other buildings.[3] Sales were slow, apparently, because it did not sell until 1826 when Snyder bought it for £400, or approximately $1,600.

When York was captured by the Americans in 1813, Elizabeth Russell[4] with four other adults, and four children escaped to Baron de Hoen's farm at Eglinton on the west side of Yonge. Before leaving York, Miss Russell loaded her phaeton so full of personal belongings that the whole party had to walk, and the youngest boy was carried by his mother most of the way. The de Hoen log farm house must have been very crowded with its nine extra visitors, as there were only two rooms, one above the other. After a period of three days, two of the ladies walked back to York and arrived just in time to prevent Miss Russell's house from being looted by the soldiers.

THE CHURCH

Early religious services were held in the log schoolhouse erected in 1816 on Bayview Avenue (see Education), and on October 16, 1830, Jesse Ketchum, a farmer and philanthropist of York and Buffalo, conveyed a half acre of land to the trustees of the Eglinton Methodist Church.[5] However, it was not until 1834 that a brick church was built by a small group of Wesleyan Methodists. Before completion a fire broke out and so blackened the building that a coat of plaster had to be added to make it presentable.

A small library was presented to the Sunday school by Jesse Ketchum, who later endowed the Upper Canada Bible Society with a fund for providing Bibles for Toronto Sunday school scholars. The library tablet was inscribed:

> If the Dear Children who may read Books of this small Library should feel grateful & wish to make any return the most exceptable return they can make will be to abstain wholly from the use of all Intoxicating Liquors and Tobaco. 1839. *Jesse Ketchum*[6]

THE 1830's AND 40's

There were only four early inns in Eglinton: Thomas Hill's small hostel in 1811, the Nightingale's Durham Ox in the 1840's, and Montgomery's two taverns, one built in the 1830's and destroyed by fire in the Rebellion and the other built after his return to Yonge Street about 1845 (see Inns and Taverns).

James Hervey Price, an English gentleman admitted to the bar in

1833, built his house, Castlefield, north of Montgomery's Tavern, and the street bearing the same name led to the house.[7] Though a moderate politically, he contributed a large sum of money to Mackenzie's cause. The Rebellion lost, he was forced to sell Castlefield to Franklin Jackes, a baker, in 1842.

Samuel A. Huson, Davidson M. Murray, and later John G. Nanton, each from the West Indies, settled in the district.[8] The Murray and Nanton property was known as Pilgrim's Farm and had a long avenue of evergreen trees leading to the house. In 1855 James Beaty, M.P.P., bought the farm and turned it into a summer retreat, renaming it Glen Grove. The trees along his lane in later years bordered Glengrove Avenue.

Eglinton had three saw mills on the West Branch of the Don River north of Lawrence Avenue, operating from 1820 to 1860 or after. One belonged to William McDougall,[9] a Father of Confederation (see Mills and Distilleries).

LATER YEARS

Joseph Hargrave opened the Eglinton Post Office in 1856.[10] His little shoemaker's shop had already expanded to sell groceries. It was in the centre of the district, with the Wesleyan Methodist Church and Jacob Lawrence's tannery to the north, the hotel to the south, and a school was built across the road in 1879.

James Metcalfe, M.P.P., in 1856 owned one of the show places of Yonge Street, and delighted the country children with his Australian birds. Cockatoos, magpies, pheasants and peacocks wandered freely around the grounds on the west side of Yonge, north of Lawrence. In his younger days, he had been a builder and contractor. His business failed with heavy liabilities, and he departed for Australia where he accumulated a large fortune. Upon returning to Canada he gave a banquet and invited all his old creditors. On the table, under the plates, each guest found a cheque in full for his account, with interest added to date.[11]

Charles McBride ran two hotels in the area. He bought Montgomery's Tavern in 1858 and it continued operating under the name of Prospect House until it was destroyed by fire in 1881. Oulcott House replaced it on about the same site. In 1873 Charles McBride opened his Bedford Park Hotel, still standing today south of Fairlawn Avenue (see Inns and Taverns).

Finally by 1891 houses had been built on the east and west side of Yonge Street and the Bedford Park post office was established with Philip W. Ellis as the first postmaster.

NOTES

1 H. Scadding, *Toronto of Old*, abridged and edited by F. H. Armstrong (Toronto: Oxford University Press, 1966), p. 320.

2 Lot 3, 1st concession west of Yonge Street. His name is spelled Snider and Schneider. Robertson, *Landmarks of Toronto*, VI, 588.

3 *Upper Canada Gazette* (February 1, 1810).

4 Miss Russell was the sister of the Hon. Peter Russell, President of the Government of the Province, 1796-1799, Receiver General, and Member of the Executive and Legislative Councils, who died in 1808. H. Scadding, *Toronto of Old* (Toronto: Adam, Stevenson, and Co., 1873), p. 434.

5 Lot 4, 1st concession east of Yonge Street.

6 Eglinton United Church, Archives.

7 Lot 2, 1st concession west of Yonge Street in 1835.

8 The Huson family bought part of lot 5, 1st concession east of Yonge Street in 1835. The Nanton family bought part of lot 4, 1st concession west of Yonge Street from the Murrays in 1847. H. Scadding, *Toronto of Old* (Toronto: Adam, Stevenson and Co., 1873), pp. 433-434.

9 His grandfather John McDougall was proprietor of a hotel in York, and owned lot 4, 1st concession west in 1801 which he sold to his son Daniel in 1826. William grew up on this farm.

10 Lot 2, 1st concession east of Yonge Street.

11 Newspaper clipping in scrapbook belonging to Mrs. Alan Sumner. North half of lot 6, 1st concession west of Yonge Street.

THE COMMUNITIES WEST OF YONGE STREET

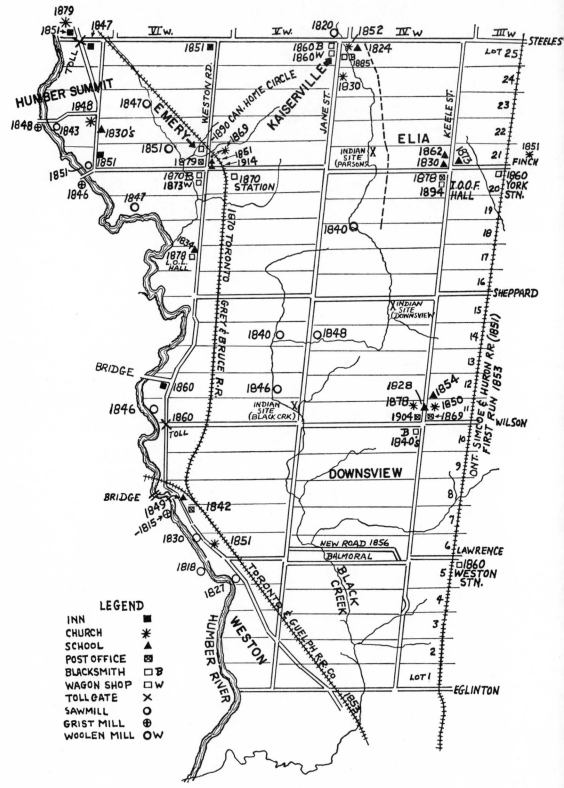

Communities west of Yonge Street.

Fairbank

Fairbank, a community bordering York Township, was situated along busy Dufferin Street near the Eglinton and Vaughan Road corners. The name of Matthew Parson's farm, located on the west side of Dufferin in North York, was selected for the post office when it opened in 1874. In the early days people travelling from Toronto to Fairbank reached it by going along Davenport to the Vaughan Road, which ran diagonally from Bathurst to Dufferin across the third concession from the bay.

Early Settlers

Captain William Moore, an early pioneer of Fairbank, built his house on the corner of Eglinton and Bathurst following the War of 1812, in which he was severely wounded in the face by a musket ball during the battle of Queenston Heights.[1] He and Henry Mulholland, a neighbour who lived on Bathurst north of Lawrence, tired of walking a mile and a half east on Eglinton to Yonge Street when travelling to York, decided to blaze a south-easterly trail through the woods to St. Clair. As they walked through the forest from the Moore's house they cleared a path and notched the trees at intervals with an axe in order to find their way home again. This trail became very popular with the Bathurst Street residents and became known as the Serpentine Road because of its winding nature. Today it is called Forest Hill Road.

Another pioneer, Daniel Tiers, a Pennsylvania German, settled about 1794 in William Berczy's German settlement in Markham, later moved to York, and finally settled in Fairbank in 1832.[2] In York he turned his hand to chair making and advertised on January 23, 1802, in the *Upper Canada Gazette*:

> The Subscriber returns his sincere thanks to his Friends
> and the Public for the great encouragement he has
> hitherto met with, and begs leave to inform them, that
> he now intends carrying on his business in all its
> branches without delay—armed chairs, Sittees, and din-
> ing ditto, fan-back and brace-back Chairs. He very
> shortly expects a quantity of different paints; it will then
> be in his power to finish his Chairs in the best manner,
> and by his great attention to perform his promises,
> hopes to merit protection and support.
> N.B. He also expects a quantity of common Chairs
> from below, which he will dispose of on reasonable
> terms.

That the chairs were expected "from below" implies that Tiers was im-
porting from Lower Canada. Possibly he did not receive the support
he solicited because in 1808 he opened the Beefsteak and Beer House
in York, and a little later the Red Lion Hotel at the corner of Yonge
and Bloor, a hostelry famous for its political gatherings and the starting
point for the Yonge Street stage coaches.

Jacob McKay, a farmer living at Humber Summit in Vaughan, was
a very early property owner.[3] His daughters married Matthew Parsons
and Joseph Watson, both from Humber Summit. The Parsons moved
to the McKay farmland on the west side of Dufferin, where they built
a large house made of brick fired on the property, and cleared and
cultivated a large farm which they named Fairbank.

The Watsons were given another part of the McKay property on
the east side of Dufferin, north of Eglinton, which they called Spruce-
grove.[4] Joseph Watson was very active in the development of Fairbank
Methodist Church as well as assisting with the Emery Church. He was
also a member of York Township Council for twelve years, and his
farm remained in York Township when the North York boundary was
formed in 1922.

One of the best known characters in Fairbank was Isaac Dollery,[5]
who was part Indian and lived to be ninety-five. He was a house mover
and carpenter, and served for nine years as a member of Council, beginning in 1877. Well known for his marksmanship, it was said that he
could hit a three inch nail three times on the head and drive it into a
board from across the street. He taught most of the local boys in the
area how to handle a gun properly, which was no mean task. In the
early days the only gun in use was the old flint-lock musket which
served as both shotgun and rifle, shot being used for shooting birds and
small animals, and bullets for large game. The proper method of loading these guns was an art, and if the powder was the least bit damp the
gun would not go off.

One day Isaac returned home from a hunting trip with a bear cub. He kept it as a pet, boxing with the animal and taking it for walks on a chain. Someone offered him $200 for the cub if its weight could be increased. In those days $200 was a lot of money, and Isaac set out to earn it. Much to his chagrin, however, he fed the poor beast so much that it died before he could collect the money.

THE CHURCHES

Methodist Church services were first held about 1844 in the log schoolhouse on the Dollery property north of Eglinton with Mr. Needham, a schoolteacher, as class leader. In 1863 when the brick school was built on the Watson lot across from the Parsons' farm (see Education), services were held in the new building. Finally through the combined efforts of the neighbourhood, the Fairbank Wesleyan Methodist Church was built on land given by the Parsons' family, and bricks for the building were made in their kiln. William Clarke's diary records the following: "June 27, 1889—Thursday, fine in forenoon. Heavy rain in the afternoon. Boys went to Fairbank to see the corner-stone of the new church laid . . . Oct. 11, 1889—Friday a nice fine day. Fred, George and Richard ploughing in forenoon and others picking apples. All went to Fairbank Church Opening and Tea Party in the afternoon. Tickets, Collection etc. $3.00."[6] As there was no music in the church for a number of years, a tuning fork was used by the precentor to start the singing.

The Presbyterians in the area became very active in 1888, and in November began to meet in McFarlane's Hotel. On March 10th, 1889, the congregation was referred to as the Five Points Mission Station, and in July their new church was opened on the Vaughan Road. By March 4, 1890, the name was changed to Fairbank Presbyterian Church, and their minister also officiated at Fisherville (see Steeles Avenue Communities). Later a new church was erected on the south-east corner of Dufferin and Eglinton and in 1925 when the members voted for Church Union, those wishing to remain Presbyterians broke away. In 1927 the Fairbank Presbyterian Church, which has been greatly altered since, was built on Ramsden Road west of Dufferin, north of Eglinton.

Residents of Fairbank picked up their mail in Yorkville until a post office was established south of Eglinton in 1874 with William Todd as the first postmaster. Francis McFarlane's Hotel (see Inns and Taverns), operating since 1867 took over the postal service in 1877.

The Belt Line Railway was finished and operating north of Eglinton between Yonge and Dufferin in 1888, and the Davenport station south of Eglinton made transportation very easy for commuters to Toronto. The service was not as popular as was expected, however, and operations ceased in 1894. In fact, all that remains of the early Fairbank community is the brick Methodist Church, now Fairbank United, still standing on the west side of Dufferin.

NOTES

1 Lot 1, 2nd concession west of Yonge Street. Bull, *op. cit.*, p. 163.
2 Lot 1, 3rd concession west of Yonge Street.
3 The Parsons were on Jacob McKay's lot 3, 3rd concession west of Yonge Street.
4 The Watsons were on Jacob McKay's lot 2, 2nd concession west of Yonge Street.
5 Lot 2, 3rd concession west of Yonge Street.
6 *Fairbank United Church, 1889-1939*, Golden Jubilee Anniversary Services, October 1, 3, 5, 1939. 50th anniversary pamphlet.

Dublin

DUBLIN, A CROSSROADS VILLAGE NAMED AFTER WILLIAM DUNCAN'S farm, developed at the corner of Sheppard Avenue and Dufferin Street. There were very few merchants in the surrounding area and the Watson's store became a central point for community activities. A road to the Shepard's mills east of Bathurst was very accessible for the farmers, and the construction of the Gore and Vaughan Plank Road provided a better approach to the mills to the north.

DUBLIN FARM

Dublin Farm, running from the north-west corner of Sheppard and Dufferin to Keele Street, was purchased by William Duncan III on the second trip he made to Canada to sell linens from his flax mills in Ireland. The cost of 200 acres in 1827 was $3.50 an acre, and Duncan also bought farms in Emery for his four brothers, James, George, Adam, and John.[1] Years later property was acquired for each of his nine sons, and Henry, the second son, became reeve of York Township.

Near the Dufferin corner of the property a log shoemaker's shanty was built, and Tim and his wife Bridget, an elderly Irish couple, made boots, leather articles, and carpet bags for the neighbourhood. On the corner a frame general store was constructed in the late 1830's and James Watson who lived across the road became an active proprietor. The shop was well stocked, and maple syrup, butter, eggs, and cowhides were accepted in lieu of money. Watson took "whatever the settlers had to offer except cordwood, timber, hay, grain and other farm products too heavy and bulky for a small village store to handle."[2]

When the Duncan children reached school age, their father, who

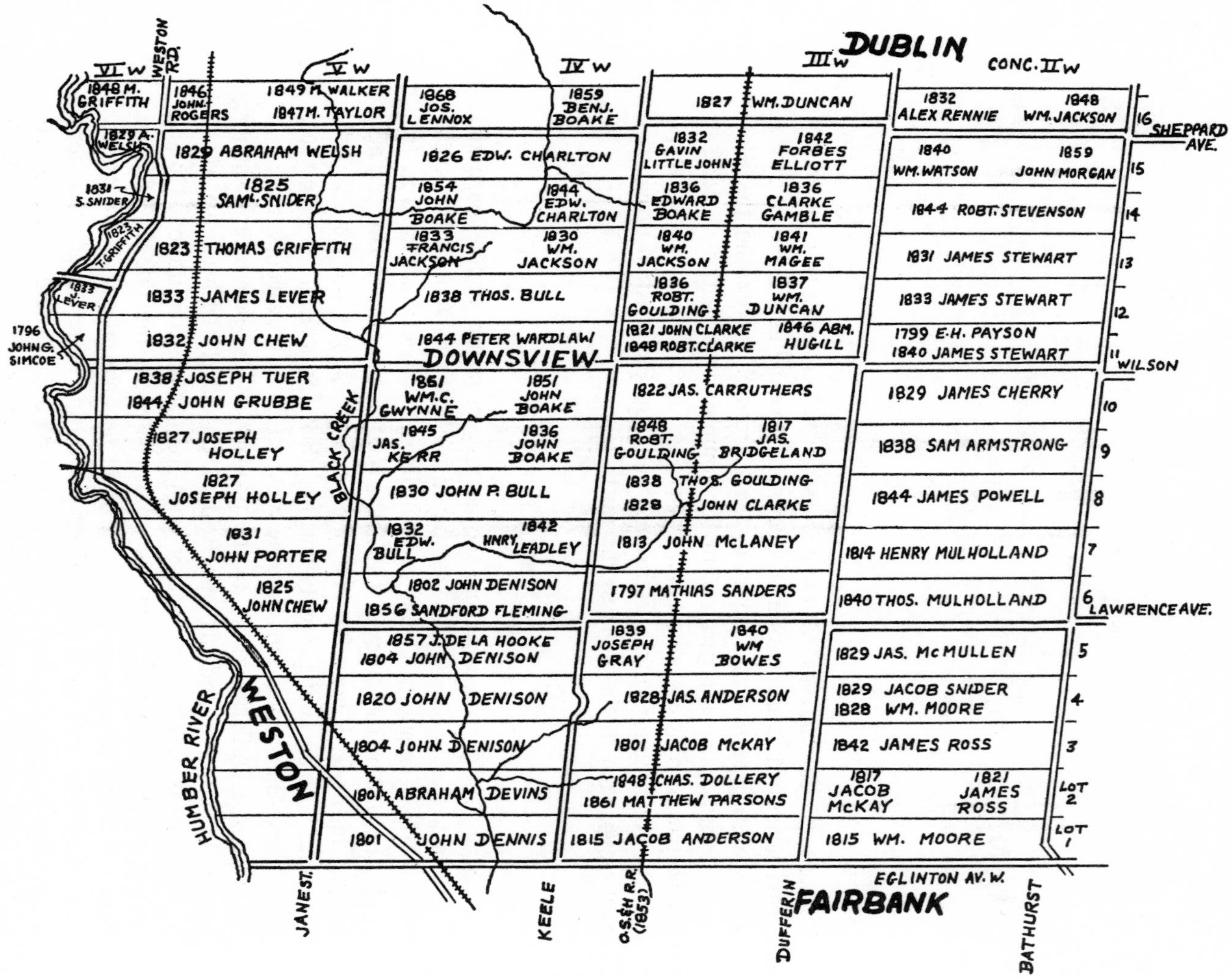

Downsview, Fairbank and Dublin.

had had a liberal education in Ireland, built a one-storey frame school-house on the west side of the cobblery, and hired a schoolmaster for his growing family and the neighbourhood children. In later years two other schools were built on Sheppard, east of Dufferin (see Education).

Although in Ireland the Duncan family were members of the Church of England, William became a Wesleyan Methodist and trustee of York Church in Downsview. One evening at a meeting the preacher, Dr. Bredin, a persuasive Irishman, needed money for an unpopular con-nexional fund. He looked around the room and announced in a loud voice, "Brother Duncan is prepared to head the subscription list with fifty dollars."

"Make it twenty," came the loud and clear response.

The preacher nodded his head affably. "Thank you, Brother Duncan. Brother Duncan leads the list with fifty dollars." Duncan accepted his defeat graciously and gave Dr. Bredin his money.[3]

OTHER SETTLERS

Thomas Farr purchased the east half of the property north of Dublin Farm in 1831, and developed a large farm.[4] His father, James, had built a grist and saw mill on the York side of the Humber River in 1815. The community of Weston had developed on the Etobicoke side of the river, but it was forced to relocate on the east side, near Farr's Mills, follow-ing the freshets of 1842 and 1850, when all the buildings on the west side were washed away (see Mills and Distilleries).

Across Dufferin, on the east side, Alexander Cathcart established a farm on a King's College reserve lot which he leased in 1819 and which his son Robert finally bought in 1844.[5] The Cathcarts belonged to the Church of England and drove to St. John's Church in York Mills for service each Sunday. Cathcart's son Joshua died in the Battle of Vicksburg and was the only Downsview person known to have lost his life in the American Civil War.

Many landowners did not develop their land but lived in Toronto or the vicinity. This meant quarter-mile stretches of bush land along the roads, and sometimes the statute labour was lacking on road main-tenance. Clarke Gamble, Q.C., was an absentee landowner who bought property about a quarter of a mile south of Sheppard on Dufferin in 1836.[6] He was City Solicitor from 1840 to 1863, and a promoter and director of the City of Toronto and Lake Huron Railway. His father, Dr. John Gamble of Enniskillen, had served in the Queen's Rangers during the American Revolution and then moved to Saint John, New Brunswick, before coming to Upper Canada.

William Watson and his family emigrated from County Monaghan, Ireland, in 1834 and settled on the south-east corner of Sheppard and Dufferin.[7] They were staunch Presbyterians and held services in the schoolhouse each Sunday. Francis, Watson's son, an extremely tall man who eventually took over the farm, was instrumental in the building of the Fisherville Presbyterian Church in 1856 on Steeles Avenue, east of Dufferin, in Vaughan Township.

James Watson later constructed a new general store on the Watson corner, and in 1854 opened a post office under the name of Carronbrook. Apparently the community must have requested that the name be changed, because in 1878 the postal area was altered to Dublin, the name of the Duncan's farm. A toll-gate was opened on the corner opposite the store prior to 1878 to collect fees for the upkeep of the Gore and Vaughan Plank Road.

The west end of the little district of Dublin was cut off in 1928, when the De Havilland Aircraft of Canada closed Sheppard Avenue for its airstrip (see Downsview). However, the community continued to grow, and a new public school was built in 1944 with the old 1872 cornerstone mounted in the wall of the main entrance (see Education).

NOTES

1 Lot 16, 3rd concession west of Yonge Street; lots for his brothers: Lots 17, 18.
2 Bull, *op. cit.*, p. 44.
3 *Ibid.*, p. 207.
4 Lot 17, 3rd concession west of Yonge Street.
5 Lot 17, 2nd concession west of Yonge Street.
6 Lot 14,, 3rd concession west of Yonge Street.
7 Lot 15, 2nd concession west of Yonge Street.

Robert Clarke's house, built in 1844 on Paxtonia Blvd., north of Wilson. Small ell on right built for Downsview post office, opened in 1869.

The John Goulding family in front of their house on the east side of Keele about half a mile south of Wilson Avenue. Built prior to 1878.

Looking north at Keele and Wilson Avenue. York Wesleyan Methodist Church, built in 1870, in background.

First Weston, later Downsview, Station on the south side of Lawrence, east of Keele.

Downsview Gun Club: Left to right, front row: Joseph Carruthers, George Deacoff, Robert Carruthers, George Carruthers, Edwin McDonald, John Alpine; second row: Frank Griffith, Harry Bagg, Frank Carruthers, Herbert Deacoff, Bert Carruthers, Rev. Robert A. Spencer, Ernie Bagg, Harold Shirley; third row: Percy Smithson, James Alpine, Stanley Bagg, Morris Morgan, John Holmley, Harry Barnard, Robert Barnard.

Isaac Harrison's barn, erected in 1893 by Riddell & Sons on the east side of Dufferin about half a mile south of Finch. Albert Slaney in wagon. Thomas Feeny at horse's head, Mrs. Harrison and family in buggy, Isaac standing beside them.

Dublin House, built by William Duncan about 1831 on the north-west corner of Dufferin and Sheppard. (top left)

Cherry's Hotel in Fisherville, on the south-east corner of Dufferin and Steeles. (top right)

Elia Episcopal Methodist Church, built in 1901 on Finch, east of Keele and the C.N.R. railway tracks. (left)

Centre of Elia at Keele and Finch, looking south. Left to right: Boynton house, the Canadian Order of Foresters Hall, Elia general store and post office.

Downsview

DOWNSVIEW DERIVES ITS NAME FROM JOHN PERKINS BULL'S FARM, Downs View. Two schools, two Methodist churches, and St. Phillips Anglican Church in Weston served the community. The well-established mills, general stores, shoemakers, harness makers, and taverns in the Village of Weston provided a centre for shopping, and as a result Downsview remained an agricultural area.

LAWRENCE AVENUE

Along Lawrence Avenue, west of Dufferin, Mathias Sanders, a noted shipbuilder, was granted property in 1797. He settled on this property in 1801 after spending a few years in Markham with other pioneers in William Berczy's Pennsylvania German settlement. Sanders was killed at the caupture of York in 1813 when the powder magazine exploded, and his property went uncultivated until his son, Andrew, was old enough to farm in 1824. The family remained on the property well into the 20th century.[1]

John Denison owned two lots south of Lawrence and west of Keele in 1804,[2] which were inherited by members of his family upon his death in 1824. His son, George Taylor Denison I, had leased and wanted to buy the Clergy Reserve lot north of Lawrence which many years later was owned by Sandford Fleming. A request was made following the War of 1812, in which George served, but it was denied. Finally he was able to purchase the property in 1840 for £175 because of his efforts during the Rebellion of 1837. Around this same period he organized the "Denison's Horse," a volunteer corps which played an important part in the formation of the volunteer militia of Canada. This unit later became known as the Governor-General's Body Guard.

The Bathurst and Lawrence Crossroads

On the eastern border, about Lawrence Avenue and Bathurst Street, a small settlement developed around a school and a Methodist Church on a road open in 1825, but never improved. In 1814 Henry Mulholland sold his eastern farm on Leslie, below Sheppard, and bought a farm on the west side of Bathurst, a quarter of a mile north of Lawrence.[3] During the War of 1812 Mulholland served in Captain Samuel Ridout's Company of the 3rd York Militia and participated in the battles of York, Stoney Creek, and Lundy's Lane.[4] He was a typical red-headed Irishman, musical and humorous, with the true fighting spirit of an Ulsterman. By 1826 he had built a large house of bricks, made and sun-dried on the farm. The walls were fourteen inches thick, or three bricks deep; the timber was hewn from his own forest; the shingles were hand-made; the nails were forged by his blacksmith; and the eaves-troughs were carved out of logs forty-four feet long. The house was finished inside in the old Colonial style, with a centre hall wide enough for a team of horses and a very fine staircase to the second floor. Each room had a large fireplace and the basement kitchen contained an old-style, chimney bake-oven. In later years his grandchildren lined the driveway to the house with evergreen trees.[5]

Mulholland made two or three trips to Ireland to try to persuade people to emigrate to Canada. While on one of these journeys, with an added purpose of borrowing money to acquire more land, he wrote to his wife, Jane Armstrong Mulholland, from New York before sailing:[6]

Mrs. Jane Mulholland and Family:

I take this opportunity with great pleasure of letting you know our progress in passage so far.

We were eight days before we got to New York. Our passage was very pleasant. We spent about Nine Dollars. You may think our grog bill was very high, but we had but one Quart till we came to New York. We were temperance after as we made great resolution against it, as you thought that we were so addicted to it.

Our boarding is heavy, it is five and sixpense a day. We take shipping tomorrow in the Ship *South A* to Liverpool, which is a new packet, never sailed before and is a beautiful ship. And our fare is eighteen dollars, and I think it will take about ten sovereigns to carry us to Liverpool, this and other things with care—that will be the whole amount. The journey I hear was too long as we could do no better. I have health ever since I left home. Thank God for it. But I am anxious in mind. Tallentrie is healthy, but Breaden is not.

Mack Moore is in good health, but low in circumstances. Him and I travelled two days through the City trying to find my brother's children. They are all dead but one and Hugh is mate of a ship gone to the Chinas. He is doing well, he has £25 in the savings Bank in

New York. He made his will before he left and left it all to me if he never returns, as he is single.

John Simons is dead twelve years ago. I left nothing undone that I could do with respect to information. I think I have nothing more to say, but I will write as soon as I get to Liverpool, if God spares me, and if He thinks fit to call me away, O may I share of his Kingdom; O help us all to rely on Him for he is our refuge, our stay and fortress, and may we on Him rely.

Dear children, I desire you will be obedient to your dear Mother;

Dear wife, I remember well the last charges between you and I when we parted. I shall never forget them. Dear wife, I remain your ever loving husband, *Henry Mulholland.* Oct. 6, 1832.

Remember to fence the orchard from the dooryard, and do not let any of the trees be destroyed.

In May, 1833, Mulholland sailed for home on the *Lady of the Lake.* Early one morning the ship ran into an ice field and was struck by an iceberg. Only one lifeboat was launched and its fifteen survivors were picked up by a passing brig and brought to Quebec. Mulholland, however, was not among them. A cairn has been erected to his memory by his descendants on the original Crown land, east of Leslie Street in Oriole.

Thomas Mulholland inherited the Bathurst Street farm and accumulated large tracts of land in Innisfil, King, York Township and Toronto.[7] In 1849 he owned the north-west corner of Lawrence and Bathurst, where he built a blacksmith shop.[8] Robert Askelon Raynor, who later became the toll-gate keeper at Dufferin and Wilson, was hired in 1874 by Thomas as the blacksmith. Raynor lived in a rented rough-cast cottage surrounded by lilac bushes next to the shop.

A clear spring of drinking-water flowed on another piece of Mulholland property about a half a mile north of Eglinton. In 1852 water was piped to a large trough installed on Bathurst Street for the convenience of the horses and cattle as they passed. It was known as the "Thomas Mulholland Public Water Trough on the 2nd,"[9] meaning 2nd concession road, and was still in use in 1941.

THE BATHURST STREET SCHOOL AND CHURCH

Thanks to the efforts of Henry Mulholland a log school was established on the south-east corner of Lawrence and Bathurst in 1817. This building not only served for educational purposes during the week, but became a church on Sundays, with Elijah C. Bens as class leader. The log school was replaced by a new brick structure on the south-east corner of Bathurst and Glencairn Avenue, and in 1921 a third school was built (see Education).

Mrs. Henry Mulholland in 1845 gave three-quarters of an acre of farm land near Lawrence Avenue to provide a site for the Asbury Wesleyan Methodist Church. A frame clapboard building, approximately thirty by forty feet, was erected in 1845 and named after Francis Asbury, the first man to be ordained a Methodist minister in America. He was born in 1745, and this church was built in the year of the centenary celebration of his birth. It was destroyed by fire in 1898, and replaced by a brick church the following year on a site also given by the Mulholland family located a short distance north of the old church. The cost was $2400. In 1947 the Asbury congregation invited the West United Church to join them. The latter had sold its College Street building and planned to move to North Toronto. A new stone church, built around the brick church, was dedicated in 1951 and became the Asbury and West United Church of Canada, the former West minister, Rev. Harold C. Vernon, became the first minister.

THE DUFFERIN AND WILSON CORNERS

Dufferin Street in 1825 ran north to Wilson Avenue and then west to Keele Street. On the north-east corner Ephraim Holland Payson, a government bricklayer in 1799, was given property to complete his military claim. However, "in 1804, he was fined £1.5.0 for nonperformance of statute labour and non-payment of his 'composition money'—a tax of 1/8 of a penny per acre imposed on absentees in lieu of statute labour."[10]

There were a number of early settlers in this area. James Carruthers originally built his house facing an Indian trail on the south-west corner lot at Dufferin and Wilson,[11] and called it Petherhill Farm after the family home in England. The large living room, thirty-two by twenty-seven feet, contained a huge fireplace with a crane to hold various iron kettles used for cooking. It also would accommodate eight sets of lancers on festive occasions. Invented by Laborde in Paris in 1836, the lancers' quadrille became very fashionable in London in 1850. Eight or sixteen couples formed a set, dancing five intricate figures to operatic and popular tunes.

The five Carruthers men were very active in sports, particularly hunting and target shooting. They attended various "shoots" during the winter, with turkey, geese and partridge as "victims" and prizes. At one of these on December 18th, 1891, George and his sons went to "Fisher's Shooting Match" and returned home with four turkeys for the price of their $2.05 admission fee. George Carruthers was president of the Downsview Gun Club in 1910-11.

James Bridgland, an Englishman, settled in York, became Assistant Messenger to the House of Assembly and was also attached to the Court of the King's Bench. After his wife died, the family moved to Downsview. Clark B. Bridgland, a son, farmed the property[12] south of the Carruthers, served as a school trustee, a York Church trustee and a Justice of the Peace.

James Stewart, an Irishman, farmed land on the east side of Dufferin above Wilson in 1831. He contracted with the other settlers to cut wood on their property, haul it out of the woods, and pile it near the road. In winter he supplied fuel to King's College, Osgoode Hall and Upper Canada College. "In this way his hired help, oxen and horses, used on the farm in summer, were also gainfully employed in winter."[13]

The Gore and Vaughan Plank Road

The Gore and Vaughan Plank Road[14] was built about 1850 following a decision that planking would reduce road construction costs. Stringers three inches by six to fourteen inches wide, and eight feet long were laid on the west side of the road parallel to traffic. On these were placed three-inch, white pine planks. The heavy carts headed toward Toronto with their produce had the right of way, and those going north had to turn off the planks to pass, or use the dirt road all the way. The lip formed by extended boards made it easier for the carts to get back on the plank road.

Toll-gates were placed at various corners to collect fees for the upkeep of the road. One gate stood at Wilson Avenue and another at Sheppard. A sign stood at the toll-gate indicating the cost:

Under the Authority of Parliament, The Gore and Vaughan Plank Road rate of Tolls to be collected thereon for each time passing whether loaded or otherwise

	£	S	D
For every Vehicle drawn by two Horses or other Cattle	0	0	6
for every additional horse or beast	0	0	2
for every Vehicle drawn by one horse	0	0	3
for every Horse Ass or Mule	0	0	2
for every score of Neat Cattle	0	0	1
for every score of Sheep or Swine	0	0	1

By order of Directors

Date January 1, 1851.[15]

Thomas Roy reported that the planks heaved and broke after six or seven years, and were dangerous for the horses.[16] Gravel was used to fill the holes, and as the condition of the roads became worse, travellers were even less willing to pay high tolls. William Jackson, for instance, upset a load of hay three times on his way to market.

In 1876 William Geddes married a daughter of John Boake and ran a blacksmith and wagon shop on the south-east corner of Wilson and Dufferin. Askelon Raynor the blacksmith at Bathurst and Lawrence, later leased the toll-gate; his wife collected the toll, and he ran the blacksmith shop. Those living north of the gate often tied their horses up the road and walked through the gate without charge, carrying any equipment that needed sharpening or repairing to the shop to avoid the toll. Mrs. Raynor had definite ideas about collecting toll. She refused to take it on Sundays even though it was supposed to be collected, because she wanted Sundays to herself, and she also refused to stay up past her bedtime.

The toll-gates closed in 1891 because the plank roads were in such bad repair, the railways provided an easy means of transportation, and the crossroads became more important as connecting links with the railway.

THE KEELE AND WILSON CROSSROADS

Very few settlers were living in Downsview in the 1820's and Keele Street, in 1825, was the western thoroughfare for north and south travel. The John Clarke family settled on a Crown Reserve lot in 1821 at Keele and Wilson, but fearing it might become a King's College lot and not for sale, they moved three-quarters of a mile south on Keele Street.[17] Clarke died in 1832 leaving his widow to look after seven children and a partly cleared farm. Robert, the eldest, was thirteen at the time, and soon took over his father's responsibilities.

In the spring of 1821 Thomas Goulding and his family arrived in Downsview, and settled east of Keele Street.[18] He was a veterinary surgeon in the Peninsular War, and practiced his profession in York Township. His rough-cast house, Pine Cottage, frequently boarded a schoolmaster who taught his ambitious students after school hours in his room. Church services were also held in the house, and Goulding's Appointment became very popular.

The three Griffith brothers from Ireland, Matthew, Thomas, and Joseph, and Abraham Welsh, a brother-in-law, were the next pioneers to open up farms, settling west of Jane.[19] Each built a log cabin on his farm, and later Matthew built a house of red bricks, made and burnt in the Humber Valley, just north of the house which stands today on Weston Road. The walls were two feet thick and there were twelve rooms. Thomas built a white, rough-cast house with eleven rooms; and

Joseph built one of stone hauled from the Black Creek, also with eleven rooms. This latter house is now replaced by the Workmen's Compensation Board buildings near Highway 400. Between the years 1823 and 1878 these brothers owned about 1,000 acres.

Then Edward Charlton bought the property on the south-west corner of Keele and Sheppard Avenue in 1826 for £100 and, like the others, his house was made of bricks burned on his farm.[20] The family was very active in church affairs, and as early as 1835 the local preaching appointment was known as Charlton's Settlement.

During the 1830's with the increase in immigration, more people settled in the area. When William Jackson and his wife, Jane Duncan, set out for their farm on the west side of Keele Street,[21] their wagon became mired in the mud crossing a small creek just north of Lawrence, and they were forced to sleep at the side of the road. The next day the Clarkes and the Gouldings pulled them out and helped them on their way. Jackson, a tall, powerful, hard-working man, like other farmers cleared his land with his axe and oxen, and brought the first team of horses to Downsview.

John Boake married his cousin, Rebecca Bull, from Davenport, in 1832. "The ceremony over, the groom and his bride drove up to the Checkered Store[22] in the Town of York and purchased bunk bedding, tin dishes, cups, dipper and pail, knives, forks and spoons, hammers and nails, axe, broad axe, shovel, gun, flour, salt, sugar, soap and such other goods as were needed to start housekeeping and farming. Having piled on their wagon all it would carry and all the oxen could pull, they set out to create a home on a lot on which man never lived before. They drove out Bull's Road, up the 2nd, and along the York and Vaughan Road to the Fairbank side road, then across to the 4th, where they again turned north. All went well until they reached the creek. There they were stuck fast in the mud. This hollow already had a bad name as William Jackson and his bride, Jane Duncan, had been mired here.

"The hospitable Clarkes and Gouldings, who had a clearing a few rods further on, each invited the newlyweds to pass the night in their cabins, but they declined as all their worldly possessions were on the wagon. They tethered their oxen and slept on an improvised bed under an old beech tree. At daybreak, Tommy Goulding arrived at the top of the hill. His wife alighted with kettle and frying-pan, matches, some tea, maple sugar, buckwheat flour and a jug of maple syrup. Meantime her husband drove his oxen down the hill, over the creek and pulled up alongside the Boake wagon. They transferred half the load to the Goulding wagon, and with both yolks of oxen, pulled the wagon out of the mire, across the creek and up the hill to the level ground where Mrs. Goulding and Mrs. Boake had tea and pancakes ready."[23]

After breakfast they all went on together. Thomas Goulding helped his new neighbour throw together a little shelter of poles, bark and hemlock and fixed up a mattress of balsam boughs on which to make their bed, and Mrs. Goulding brought out sandwiches of cold boiled venison and tea for their dinner.

During the Rebellion of 1837, the pioneers of Downsview were all very loyal. Thomas Mulholland was a Captain with the King's Troops; George Taylor Denison I founded "Denison's Horse," a militia regiment which served under him; Robert Clarke served as an ensign in the York Militia; Thomas Griffiths fought with the Government troops; and Abraham Welsh was captured by the Rebels and later released.

In the 1840's the sons of the early families acquired their own farms, and a few new families moved into the area. When John Perkins Bull left college, his father, Bartholomew, gave him property[24] across from the Gouldings and Clarkes on Keele Street. John put a cabin on the lot, and in 1842 took from home a saddle-horse, a yoke of oxen and a wagon, and began to clear his land. After his marriage in 1844, he followed the Bull tradition and opened his house, Downs View, for religious services. As an active Justice of the Peace for over thirty-five years, he was known as "Squire Bull," and court was held in his house and the jail was located in the cellar. Later he built a courtroom on the south-west corner of the veranda.

Keele Street and Wilson Avenue gradually became the centre of Downsview. Thomas Charlton ran a blacksmith shop on the south-west corner. Robert Clarke bought his father's first farm on the north-east corner where the old log schoolhouse built about 1828 straddled the road.

York Church

Services held at Goulding's and Charlton's Appointments formed York Church in 1844 and met in the home of John Bull, later moving to the old schoolhouse. By 1850 the school was considered no longer suitable and Robert Clarke, an Anglican, offered a piece of his land to the Wesleyans. A building bee was organized to clear the site, and build the rough-cast meeting-house,[25] which was small but adequate.

The new church was opened before the 1850 harvest. A letter dated "Downs View, February 6th, 1863," written to Brother Jeffers, who delivered the opening sermon for York Church, reads: "Ten years ago our church was dedicated. There is no store, post office or public building—only church and school house within miles. Some people think that a tavern would pay well, as there is a great deal of traffic on our road; but, Sir, I am glad to say that I do not believe a site for one could be bought in our neighbourhood. A post office we expect shortly."[26]

The cornerstone for a new brick church was laid on June 28, 1870, on property given by the Wardlaw family across the road from the old church.[27] Joseph Lennox of Hillcrest Farm[28] cut a white pine to be used as the backbone of the steeple. From this he shaped a twelve-inch square, sixty-foot, straight and flawless core for the graceful spire, itself 112 feet high. The church, built at a cost of $6,500 and still standing today, measured thirty-seven by thirty-eight feet, with Gothic windows fitted with stained and frosted glass, and heavy timbers and woodwork, stained and varnished. It was heated by two large coal furnaces in the eastern angles of the building, with short stove pipes joining flues under the gallery. Ten days after the opening the trustees decided to rent the pews annually: double pews were $4 each, side pews were $2, under the gallery $1.50, long pews in the centre $2.50, short ones $1.50, and those under the gallery in the centre were $2 and $1.

When the church was nearly finished the minister heard of a large dinner-bell in Markham which was so loud that it disturbed the neighbours. He sent two young men to try to obtain it from the farmer. They set off full of enthusiasm, but on the way stopped at a wayside inn and joined friends for refreshments. A poker game followed and two days later they arrived home in their "democrat" without the bell. However, they were able to raise a little money, set off again to Markham, this time returning joyfully with the bell.

Bartholomew Bull and his wife from Balquehollie Farm arrived at church one Sunday morning in a top buggy, the first in the Township. Everyone was excited, and for some time afterwards it aroused the interest of those who expected its arrival or saw it coming down the road. The reaction, no doubt, was similar when the automobile first made its appearance.

THE DOWNSVIEW SCHOOL

The old school was found to be unsanitary after the church was built in 1851 so the farmers decided classes should be held in the new church building. About twenty years later, when another church was built the old one was bought by the school trustees and later enlarged. It was 1948 before a new schoolhouse was erected (see Education).

POST OFFICE

When Robert Clarke opened the Downsview Post Office it was necessary to build a small addition to his house for the purpose. Prior to 1869, people in Downsview went to Weston, York Mills, or to York-ville for mail. John Earson Clarke followed his uncle as postmaster, and in 1904 Mrs. Benjamin Boake added the post office to her shop on the north-west corner of Keele and Wilson Avenue.

THE RAILWAY

The Ontario, Simcoe and Huron Railway, known later as the North-ern, ran through the centre of the 3rd concession between Dufferin and Keele in 1851, and the Weston Station, later changed to Downsview, stood on the south side of Lawrence Avenue. The railroad made it easier for the farmer to transport his produce to Toronto and also provided a market for cordwood, used to stoke the train. These small piles of wood were placed at intervals along the track, and when required the train stopped and picked them up. However, the wood-burning trains were definite fire hazards, sparks from the smoke-stack often causing grass fires during the dry season.

BALMORAL

Sandford Fleming, Chief Engineer of the Ontario, Simcoe and Huron Railway, bought land on Lawrence Avenue between Keele and Dufferin in 1856 and opened a subdivision called Balmoral. The ad-vertisement for the project sounds very like those we read today. It stressed the advantages of ownership, and emphasized the compensa-tions of living in the country: " . . . a house, not squeezed in between others, not dimly lighted in front and rear, not looking out upon pave-ments and brick walls and narrow yards, but standing by itself, sur-rounded by the free, pure air, with a grass plot on which your children can play; with flowers and shrubs, and shade trees of your own planting, and fruits and vegetables of your own raising. . . . The taxes charged on the property are those of the Township of York, amounting to a mere trifle when compared with those paid in Toronto."[29] Nevertheless, the development was a failure and the lots that sold were repossessed.

Colonel Fred A. Fleming, of the Body Guards, took over the prop-erty in 1881, and became engaged in the importation and breeding of Hereford cattle. Park Farm became one of the finest stock-breeding farms in the country. His father was knighted in 1897 for his work on universal standard time, which he first publicly proposed to the Cana-dian Institute at Toronto in 1878. Following the International Prime Meridian Conference in 1884, Canada adopted standard time. Before this the world operated on "Sun Time," and the railroads found it very difficult because the time differed from town to town. An ardent imperialist, Fleming also proposed as early as 1879 the laying of the Pacific cable to link Canada and Australia. A submarine telegraph was completed in 1902.

MILLS

During the 1840's three saw mills were operating along the Black Creek between Wilson and Sheppard Avenue, but there were no grist mills in Downsview. The Weston mills supplied the needs of the farmer and there were four sites with grist mills, saw mills, and a woollen mill, and the Chew's saw mill on the Humber north of Weston (see Mills and Distilleries).

INNS AND THE PLANK ROAD

Weston's inns catered to the Downsview farmers who went to Weston regularly for their supplies (see Inns and Taverns). The Albion Plank Road running through Weston, was constructed by a company formed in 1848 consisting of Matthew, Thomas and Joseph Griffith, John Chew, and John Grubbe, the president, all Downsview farmers. A toll-gate at the corner of Wilson Avenue and Weston Road collected fees for its upkeep, but it was no more satisfactory than the other plank roads built at the same time, since the horses hooves wore it out too. On a very busy corner about half a mile north of the gate where the Albion Road crosses into Etobicoke stood Downsview's only inn, operating in 1860 under Robert Hiscocks.

As the Downsview families prospered they acquired more land, enlarged their farm buildings and improved their livestock. Many fine herds of purebred shorthorn and Jersey cattle as well as Clydesdale horses were developed. The area continued to be farmland until 1928 when the De Havilland Aircraft of Canada built a plant and airstrip at Sheppard and Dufferin Street. During the Second World War this was taken over and later expanded by the Government, and, in spite of much agitation for its removal, it is still in operation.

On February 26, 1964, Yorkdale, an enclosed shopping centre east of Dufferin Street and south of the Macdonald-Cartier Freeway, was opened for business. Built at a cost of twenty million dollars on eighty acres of Samuel Armstrong's original farm, it provides 1,296,754 square feet of floor space for approximately one hundred stores. An auditorium with 419 seats and parking space for 6,600 automobiles are among its facilities. The Downsview United Church, the first post office and a few houses are all that remain of the early period.

NOTES

1 Lot 6, 3rd concession west of Yonge Street. Bull, *op. cit.*, p. 67.

2 John Denison owned lots 3 and 5, 4th concession west of Yonge Street. His son wanted to lease lot 6, 4th concession west of Yonge Street.

3 First farm was on lot 14, 3rd concession east of Yonge Street. Second farm was on lot 7, 2nd concession west of Yonge Street.

4 Mulholland, *op. cit.*, p. 1.

5 *Ibid.*, opposite p. 3.

6 *Ibid.*, p. 3.

7 *Ibid.*, p. 56.

8 Lot 6, 2nd concession west of Yonge Street.

9 The concession roads north and south were known by the concession they separated. Yonge Street was considered the first for both east and west; i.e., Dufferin, the third, Keele, the fourth.

10 Bull, *op. cit.*, p. 94. Lot 11, 2nd concession west of Yonge Street.

11 Lot 10, 3rd concession west of Yonge Street.

12 Lot 9, 3rd concession west of Yonge Street.

13 Lot 13, 2nd concession west of Yonge Street. Bull, *op. cit.*, p. 84.

14 Dufferin Street, when planked, became known as the Gore and Vaughan Plank Road. However, it is much more often referred to as the York and Vaughan Plank Road or the Yorkville, 3rd Concession West and Vaughan Plank Road.

15 Bull, *op. cit.*, p. 121.

16 M. S. Cross, "The Stormy History of the York Roads 1833-1865", *Ontario History*, LIV [March, 1962), 8.

17 First property was lot 11, 3rd concession west of Yonge Street in 1821, moved to south half of lot 8, 3rd concession west of Yonge in 1828.

18 North half of lot 8, 3rd concession west of Yonge Street. The Gouldings were living in Downsview in 1821 but the property was not registered until 1838.

19 The Griffiths settled on lot 13, 5th and 6th concession west of Yonge Street and the Welsh's on lot 15, 5th concession west of Yonge Street.

20 Lot 15, 4th concession west of Yonge Street. Bull, *op. cit.*, p. 183.

21 Lot 13, 4th concession west of Yonge Street.

22 The Checkered Store stood on the north-west corner of Toronto and King Street. J. R. Robertson, *Landmarks of Old Toronto*, I, 81.

23 Bull, *op. cit.*, pp. 87-90. Lot 9, 4th concession west of Yonge Street.

24 Lot 8, 4th concession west of Yonge Street. In 1867 John Bull gave his son, B. H. Bull, the east half of lot 14, 4th concession west of Yonge Street for a wedding present, and the son bought the east half of lot 15.

25 Lot 11, 3rd concession west of Yonge Street.

26 *Christian Guardian* (March 4, 1863).

27 Lot 11, 4th concession west of Yonge Street.

28 Lot 8, 3rd concession west of Yonge Street.

29 Lot 6, 4th concession west of Yonge Street. "Land Boom in Early Fifties, Subdivision Still Pasture", *Telegram* (November 2, 1923). North York Public Library Scrapbooks.

Elia

ELIA[1] (PRONOUNCED E-LI'-A) IS THE DISTRICT BETWEEN DUFFERIN AND Jane Street and from north of Sheppard to Steeles Avenue, including a four hundred year old Indian site north of Finch and west of Keele (see Pre-Settlement). The original lot owners in 1800 were mostly members of the Queen's Rangers, who accompanied Governor Simcoe from Niagara to York in 1792. Later the property was sold to Pennsylvania Germans who left Lancaster, Franklin, and Bedford Counties in Pennsylvania and came overland with their families to take up residence in Upper Canada.

THE PENNSYLVANIA GERMANS

The ancestors of these people were originally from the Palatine, a German province on the upper Rhine generally influenced by Martin Luther.[2] After the seventeenth century war between the Catholics and Protestants, 40,000 Palatines left the country in search of civil and religious liberty. Many went to London, where Queen Anne offered them a home in Pennsylvania or along the Mohawk Valley in New York State. Here, under British rule, they were joined by thousands of other Palatines from their homeland. By the time the American Revolution broke out in 1776, the original pioneer farms were comparable to those they had left on the Rhine in 1709. By the 1790's many were becoming disturbed by the Anglo-American settlers' influx into their territory. William Berczy's migration from the Genessee Valley in New York State to Markham was the greatest influence in their coming to Upper Canada. Beginning in 1798 and streaming along until 1805, the solemn trek to a new country moved on, night and day. The covered wagons

STEELES.
DUFFERIN
CONC. III W.
FINCH AV.
KEELE ST.
CONC. IV W.
JANE ST.

Elia.

LOT 25 | 24 | 23 | 22 | 21 | 20 | 19 | 18 | 17

1835 JOHN BRACK
1853 MICHAEL FISHER
1811 JOHN.M. JACKSON
1833 MICHAEL KURTZ
1852 JOHN LEVITT
1812 CONRAD GRAM
1850 JOHN GALE
1811 JOHN SHUNK
1818 MICHAEL KURTZ
HORD
1829 THOMAS JACKSON
1831 THOMAS FARR

1838 EBER WHITE
1837 JOHN DANBY
1842 GEO JACKSON
1853 HENRY SNIDER
1839 ISAAC
O.S. & H.R.R. (1853)

1803 JACOB FISHER
1816 DANIEL STONG
1846 PETER ERLIN KAISER II
1811 PETER ERLIN KAISER I
1826 CHRISTIAN HOOVER
1855 JOHN BOYNTON
1834 GEO. STONG
1848 JACOB STONG
1840 SAML. SNIDER
1826 SAML. SNIDER
1830 HENRY SNIDER
1830 SAML. SNIDER
1830 HENRY SNIDER
1812 SAML. SNIDER
1835 JOHN SNIDER

BLACK CREEK

were drawn by oxen with a few cattle walking behind, making about eight miles a day for 500 miles, along the Allegheny River, around Lake Erie, across Niagara, bound for Upper Canada.

The Conestoga wagons carrying these hardy people were originally designed about 1755 in the Conestoga Valley, Lancaster County, Pennsylvania, and were ideally suited for travel on the early stumped roads through the woods. They were long and deep, with a sag in the middle, and held about five tons of freight. When travelling over rough and hilly ground the contents shifted toward the centre rather than towards the ends. Rivers were not a problem since each wagon was well caulked and made an excellent boat. The homespun cover, about twenty-four feet long, fitted over the ribs of the wagon in a bonnet shape about eleven feet from the ground in front, and a little shorter in the rear. The wheels, on the other hand, were about five or six feet high in the rear and smaller in the front. The driver often rode on the "lazy board," a sliding board that could be pulled out on the left hand side of the wagon, from which it was easier to control the oxen and work the heavy brake. As a result, in order to get a clear view of the road ahead, the driver began to keep his vehicle to the right.

Samuel Snider[3] and his family came from Pennsylvania in 1806 and settled near Black Creek south of Finch Avenue in a small log cabin. A typical, progressive Pennsylvania German farm developed, with a bank barn built on a hill. Its stone foundation housed a root cellar, and it had an overhang at the rear of the main floor. There were also fully equipped carpenter and blacksmith shops, and a smoke house where hams and bacon were hung for four to six weeks in a smudge of burning beech or maple wood. In the sugar bush stood a maple syrup house where the sap was collected and boiled in iron or copper kettles each spring. The Sniders also had a saw mill in 1851 and their second house on the hill overlooked the mill pond.

Conrad Gram,[4] another Pennsylvania German, married Catherine Fisher and settled on Finch Avenue west of Dufferin Street prior to 1812. His second house on the west side of Dufferin is still standing today. His will, dated 1860, provides some interesting arrangements for his wife. She was to receive all the household furniture, beds, bedding, linen and exclusive use of his house and four acres of land including the garden and out buildings. Besides an annuity of sixty dollars a year during her life time, she was also to receive sufficient fuelwood suitably prepared for fuel and delivered for her use, as well as enough good wheat flour and as many good quality apples as she might desire for her own use.

Michael and Elizabeth Cober Kurtz[5] and their five sons and four daughters built a log house on Dufferin Street south of Finch about 1818. Their family burying ground was on the farm, and in 1965, when the land was opened for subdivision, the remains were reinterred. Jacob Kurtz, a son of Michael, built a hotel in 1848 on the diagonal section of Dufferin Street about half a mile south of Steeles.[6] When the Gore and Vaughan Plank Road was constructed and straightened, the Kurtz Hotel was by-passed, lost its patronage, and, forced to close in 1855, it opened in another location at Dufferin and Steeles (see Inns and Taverns).

The Hoover family[7] were Mennonites. Christopher and Maria Troyer Hoover built a log cabin in the ravine east of the Black Creek, near the Kaisers in 1826. They brought rose bushes, plants and fourteen different kinds of apple trees from Lancaster, Pennsylvania. Their house stands today on York University grounds.

Scottish and English Settlers

Immigration, in the 1830's, brought people of other nationalities to the area. John Brack[8] from Scotland settled on Steeles Avenue in 1835. When the Ontario, Simcoe and Huron Railway went through his property in 1852 their log house was six feet from the tracks! This original house was not replaced until 1910 when the house standing today was built of cement blocks made in the stable during the winter. John Danby, Isaac Hord, George Jackson I, and John Boynton[9] were all English farmers. George Jackson emigrated to Canada in 1798 and settled in Elia, where it is said he acquired his land in exchange for a logging chain. The latter was a valued possession, as it was made by hand, one link at a time. John Boynton also owned the Weston Hotel, run by his son-in-law, John Kemp.

Prior to 1860 a lane ran through the fourth concession from the Snider farm north to the Boynton, Hoover, Kaiser and Stong farmhouses which were situated along the east bank of the Black Creek. This road provided a short cut to the old log house on the Boynton farm used for dances, oyster suppers, and paring bees.

The Crossroads at Dufferin and Finch

On the north-west corner stood a blacksmith shop run by John Gram as early as 1837, which he operated later as a carriage and wagon shop. In 1853 William Troyer, another Pennsylvania German from Vaughan, had a blacksmith shop on the south-east corner. As a result, at these crossroads it was possible for a farmer to pick up lumber at John Willson's saw mill[10] north of Finch on the West Branch of the Don

River, or have equipment repaired and his horse shod while waiting for his grain to be ground at William Wreggitt's grist mill[11] south of Finch (see Mills and Distilleries). Wreggitt apparently became so alarmed over the Fenian Raids in 1866 that he buried all his gold money on the farm. Shortly afterwards he was killed without disclosing the location of the treasure, and in the intervening years, many people have searched for it unsuccessfully.

THE CHURCH

Until Conrad Gram donated land for an Episcopal Methodist log church and cemetery on Finch Avenue east of the railway tracks, early church gatherings were held in the home of John Boot,[12] a house west of Keele recently pulled down by the Roman Catholic Church. The church may have been erected in 1832, the date of the earliest gravestone. However, the deed for the land was not signed by the Church trustees until March 31, 1851, when a new frame building was erected.

A new, brick, Episcopal Methodist Church was built in 1901 at a cost of $2,700, although bricks were only $6.40 a thousand, and in 1903 it became part of the Downsview Circuit. By 1942 the building was too small, and an addition, twenty-four by twenty-six feet, was added at the rear. Bricks were donated by George C. Jackson, and the congregation assisted with the labour. The oil industry moved into the area in the Fifties and people used to the country air moved away. The last regular service was held in December 1956, and on January 1, 1962, the building was sold to the Dutch Reformed Church which is still using it today. The gravestones in the cemetery around the church were attractively arranged on a bank of earth behind the building.

THE CROSSROADS AT FINCH AND KEELE

A log school erected as early as 1830 on the Jacob Stong property,[13] was replaced in 1851 with a frame building, and a new brick school was erected across the road on the north-east corner in 1873 (see Education). Finch Avenue jogged to the south at Keele Street, and it was on the south-west corner that the general store and post office was built and run by William Snider in 1878. In 1860 the mail, previously collected at Yorkville, was picked up south of Finch Avenue at a railway station called York. After the opening of the post office the name was changed to Elia. Social activities through the years had been carried on in the school and in the church. Preparations were made weeks in advance for these gala events. On August 1, 1894, the Canadian Order of Foresters instituted Court Elia No. 524 and built a hall south of the general store. This property was owned by Abraham Snider and leased for ninety-nine years or as long as the building was retained by the Foresters. The hall was the scene of many oyster suppers, minstrel shows, Christmas concerts and dances. At election time, municipal voting for the area took place in the building. The Court was disbanded on March 15, 1946, and the building demolished ten years later.

Today the church stands alone surrounded by huge oil tanks. The old school, which closed in 1956, has been replaced with many new school buildings, and York University opened its doors in September, 1964, on the Boynton, Hoover, Kaiser and Stong farms.

NOTES

1 Elia was composed of lots 17 to 25 inclusive in the 3rd and 4th concessions west of Yonge Street. This also includes what is now Black Creek Pioneer Village, but the corners at Steeles and Jane have been treated separately.

2 T. E. Kaiser, *The Kaiser Families of the County of York, Ontario* (Oshawa: 1933), pp. 5-6.

3 Snider is also spelled Schneider and Snyder. Lot 19, 4th concession west of Yonge Street.

4 Lot 21, 3rd concession west of Yonge Street.

5 Lot 19, 3rd concession west of Yonge Street.

6 Lot 23, 3rd concession west of Yonge Street.

7 Lot 23, 4th concession west of Yonge Street.

8 Lot 25, 3rd concession west of Yonge Street.

9 Danby: lot 24, 3rd concession west of Yonge Street; Hord: lot 18, 3rd concession west; Jackson: lot 22, 3rd concession west; Boynton: lot 22, 4th concession west.

10 John Willison IV, J. P. and Clerk and Treasurer of York Township, owned a saw mill on lot 21, 2nd concession west of Yonge Street in 1851.

11 William Wreggitt ran a grist mill on lot 20, 2nd concession west of Yonge Street in 1851. "Time Marches on in Elia", an account in the files of the North York Historical Society.

12 Lot 20, 4th concession west of Yonge Street.

13 Lot 21, 4th concession west of Yonge Street.

Emery

EMERY CIRCUMSCRIBED THREE MAIN AREAS; ONE AT WESTON ROAD and Finch Avenue, another at Finch and Islington, and a third at what later became Humber Summit. Isaac Devins,[1] a Pennsylvania German, was the first settler. Before coming to Emery he served as a road superintendent, contributing to the extension of Yonge Street to Lake Simcoe, and in 1795 he was associated with his brother-in-law, Nicholas Miller, in building the first saw mill on the Humber at Lambton Mills. He bought a lot on the east side of the Humber River, south of Finch Avenue, and the family transported their possessions to the site by boat.[2]

The next settler, John Crosson, arrived about 1799.[3] He and his family walked from Pennsylvania with all their household goods on the back of a two-year-old colt. Crosson was able to obtain one hundred acres from Devins in exchange for his horse. The Crosson family, like all other pioneers, had to cope with Indians who came frequently to their door requesting food and anything else that caught their fancy. The original farm is now divided by Highway 400; the family cemetery was on the east side, and the old homestead, with its apple orchard planted with seeds brought from Pennsylvania, was on the west side.

These Pennsylvania German settlers, like those who settled in Elia, chose their farms well, using their knowledge of the soil and noting the trees growing on the property. "Three things cannot be overemphasized in considering these people; they were physically equipped both in knowledge of what to do in the wilderness and the strength to do it; they came with money and equipment; and they aided one another, whether Quaker, Huguenot, Lutheran, or Mennonite. Religious or racial differences meant little in a community."[4]

Canadians can trace much of their folk-lore back to these hard-

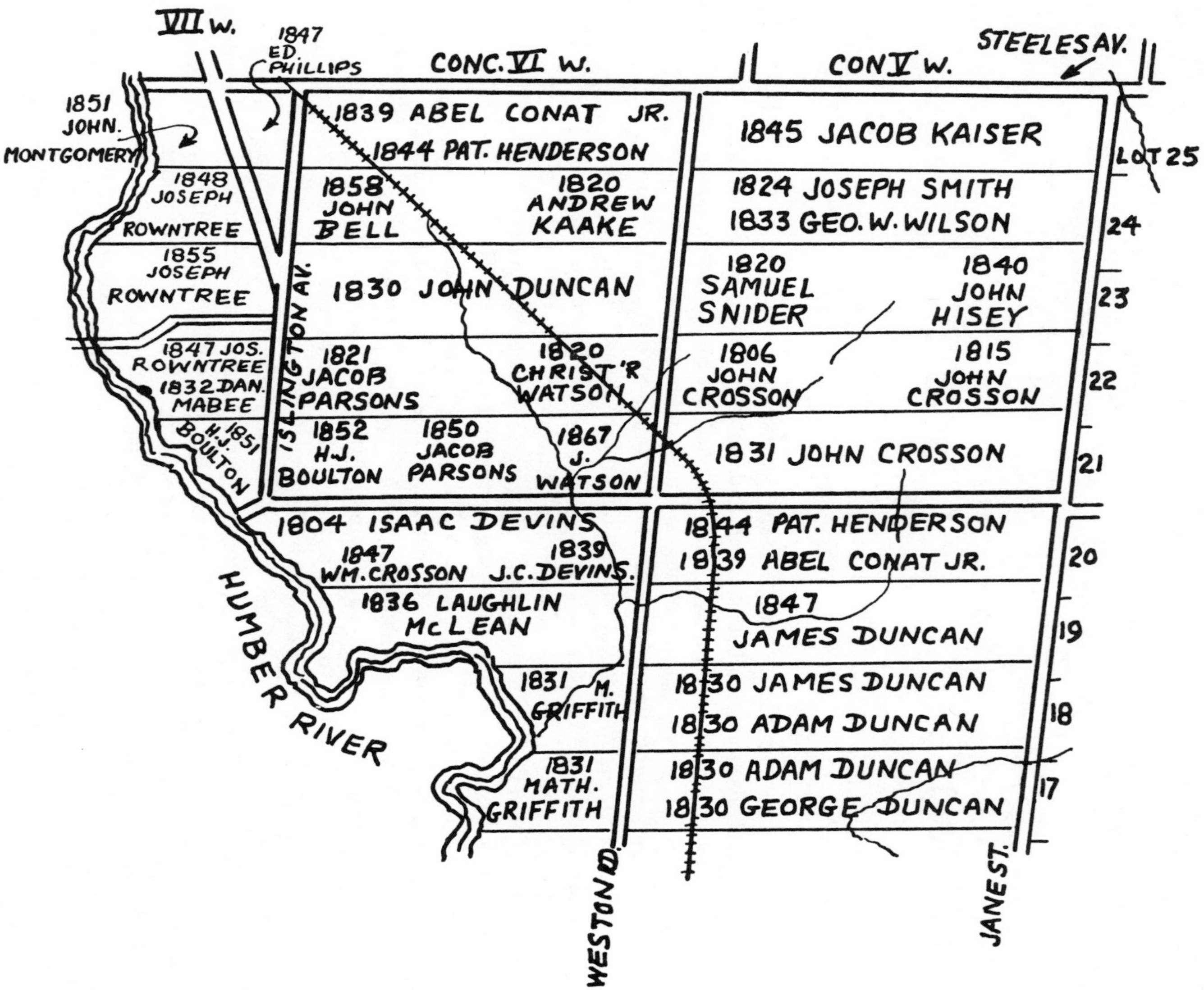

VII W.
1847 ED. PHILLIPS
CONC. VI W.
CON V W.
STEELES AV.
LOT 25
24
23
22
21
20
19
18
17
1851 JOHN. MONTGOMERY
1839 ABEL CONAT JR.
1844 PAT. HENDERSON
1845 JACOB KAISER
1848 JOSEPH ROWNTREE
1858 JOHN BELL
1820 ANDREW KAAKE
1824 JOSEPH SMITH
1833 GEO. W. WILSON
1855 JOSEPH ROWNTREE
1830 JOHN DUNCAN
1820 SAMUEL SNIDER
1840 JOHN HISEY
ISLINGTON AV.
1847 JOS. ROWNTREE
1832 DAN. MABEE
1821 JACOB PARSONS
1820 CHRIST'R WATSON
1806 JOHN CROSSON
1815 JOHN CROSSON
1851 H.J. BOULTON
1852 H.J. BOULTON
1850 JACOB PARSONS
1867 J. WATSON
1831 JOHN CROSSON
1804 ISAAC DEVINS
1847 WM. CROSSON
1839 J.C. DEVINS.
1844 PAT. HENDERSON
1839 ABEL CONAT JR.
1836 LAUGHLIN McLEAN
1847
JAMES DUNCAN
HUMBER RIVER
1831 M. GRIFFITH
1830 JAMES DUNCAN
1830 ADAM DUNCAN
1831 MATH. GRIFFITH
1830 ADAM DUNCAN
1830 GEORGE DUNCAN
WESTON RD.
JANE ST.

working people, who felt it was bad luck to open an umbrella in the house, or spill salt, and seven years' bad luck to break a mirror. However, they anticipated good luck if they found a four-leaf clover, or a horseshoe. Their predictions of the weather were based on signs. It would rain if some one killed a toad or if a cock crowed after sundown, and if it rained on Whitsunday it would rain for seven Sundays in succession. If a large number of crows were seen flying about in winter, the weather would soon be milder. If squirrels gathered large quantities of nuts in the fall, a long cold winter would be expected. Cats, they believed, had nine lives, and when one washed its face, visitors were expected.[5]

There were also various quasi-magical cures for illness. A child with asthma stood against a tree and a hole was made above his head. When the child grew past this hole, he lost his asthma. A child with mumps was cured by rubbing his jaw on the pig trough.[6] A cholera remedy consisted of a tincture of opium, red pepper, rhubarb, peppermint and camphor which were mixed in equal parts. The dose was from ten to thirty drops in three or four teaspoons full of water.

English Settlers

By 1820 Christopher Watson moved his family to a site on the west side of Weston Road across from John Crosson.[7] Watson, who was injured while helping a neighbour build his log house, died in 1827 leaving his wife and five children. Mary, the eldest daughter, learned to handle the axe, hoe, crowbar, and handspike, and spent all her time on farm work, helping to chop down the trees, sow the grain, plant the seeds, and gather the harvest. Her younger sister, Betty, did the housework. She carded the wool, and spun the yarn, preparing it for the weaver who came to the house to do the weaving.

Jacob Parsons settled on the west half of the Watson lot in 1821.[8] After being widowed twice, with two families of his own, he married Mrs. Watson, who moved into the Parsons' house with her five children. By 1833 Richard Parsons, the eldest of the fourth family, was born. The following story might have pertained to this complicated household: One day when the man of the house came in from the barn, he heard quite a racket in the next room, and enquiring of his wife the cause of the noise, she replied, "Oh, it's only your family and my family, having a row with our family."

FINCH AND WESTON ROAD CROSSROADS

The centre of Emery in the 1870's became the intersection of Finch and Weston Road. Three schools were built on Weston Road: the first one, a log school, was erected about a half a mile south of Finch, it was replaced with a new brick school at the crossroads in 1851, and a third school was constructed next to the old one in 1914 (see Education). The Methodists in the district worshipped in the one-room brick school-house as soon as it was built. However, by 1868 the members felt a church building was needed on Weston Road and a meeting was called to discuss the matter. John Duncan and Joseph Watson, an old member of the community who had moved to Fairbank, became instrumental in the planning and in collecting the money. In 1869 the Claremont Wesleyan Methodist Church was erected north of the school. This active congregation was often occupied with plans and preparations for one of its many church socials. The tradition of active participation continued; in 1945 a full-course, dinner-strawberry garden party was held on the lawn with 200-300 people attending. Admission was fifty cents.

In 1870 the Toronto Grey and Bruce Railway built a narrow gauge line through Weston, north to Emery, and across to Humber Summit. It was taken over by the C.N.R. in 1881 and the tracks were moved very close to the church. The former line, south of Finch Avenue, was easily distinguishable until 1966 when the land was subdivided for business. Isaac Devins, son of John C. Devins, ran a blacksmith shop on the south-west corner, and his brother, John R. Devins had a carriage shop to the south. Originally the mail brought out from Toronto was left at the blacksmith shop, to be picked up by each family.

In 1878 M. S. Burkholder, an ex-teacher, was proprietor of a store built on the north-west corner across from the school and church, and Frank Bunt's shingle mill stood to the west of it on Finch Avenue. The store opened a post office in 1879 under the name of Dayton, which was used by the flag station of the Toronto Grey and Bruce Railway located on the south side of Finch Avenue. Apparently in June the name was changed to Grouse Hill, the name of the Griffith property, and in August changed back to Dayton. However, the railway officials found that "Dayton, Ontario" became confused with "Dayton, Ohio," so in September 1880, the name was changed again, this time to Emery.

Grouse Hill L.O.L. No. 91 was the name of the first Orange Lodge situated on the Thomas Griffith farm on Weston Road.[9] Of log construction, its dimensions were eighteen by twenty-four feet, and it was built by the three Griffith brothers, Thomas, Matthew, and Joseph. The charter was issued to Joseph Griffith on March 25, 1845. In later years over a dozen oxen shoes were found tacked to the log walls, no doubt intended as decoration.

By 1890 a more elaborate meeting place for the Emery community activities was established on Weston Road north of the store and the log lodge became an ice house. The new building was called the Canadian Home Circle Hall and provided a large room on the second floor, with a stable underneath. In 1922 the community bought the building from the insurance society which built it, and appointed a board of trustees to manage it. Besides being an active community hall for Orange Lodge and temperance meetings, church socials and public meetings, it was used in later years for a short time to handle the overflow of the school built in 1914.

In the 1960's Emery developed into a suburban community with new subdivisions and light industry. Nothing remains of the past except the school bell that has been mounted in a cairn on the grounds of Emery Collegiate Institute.

NOTES

1 Devins is spelled Devaynes, Devans, and Devens.
2 Lot 20, 6th concession west of Yonge Street.
3 Lot 22, 5th concession west of Yonge Street.
4 G. E. Reaman, *The Trail of the Black Walnut* (Toronto: McClelland & Stewart, 1957), p. 147.
5 W. J. Wintemberg, "German-Canadian Folk-lore", Ontario Historical Society, *Papers and Records*, III (1901), 86-96.
6 North York Historical Society, family histories, "Crosson".
7 Lot 22, 6th concession west of Yonge Street.
8 Lot 22, 6th concession west of Yonge Street.
9 Lot 18, 6th concession west of Yonge Street.

Steeles Avenue Communities

THREE SMALL VILLAGES SPRANG UP WEST OF YONGE STREET ALONG Steeles Avenue, North York's northern boundary. Two, Fisherville and Kaiserville (now Black Creek Pioneer Village), were drawn toward the villages in Vaughan to the north; the other, Humber Summit, was more closely linked to Emery, and not until 1937 had the village established a post office of its own.

FISHERVILLE

Fisherville was named after Jacob Fisher, who brought twenty-two members of his Pennsylvania German family to Canada in 1797 and received land from the Crown in Vaughan Township and North York, bordering Steeles Avenue. The settlement grew up around a mill site on the West Branch of the Don River, east of Dufferin Avenue.[1] The Fisher family ran a saw mill as early as 1820, and then a grist mill (see Mills and Distilleries), and in 1836 the property around the mills was divided into small lots. Three houses were built, and a blacksmith shop to accommodate the farmers visiting the mill, and later the inn was completed.

About 1855, after the Gore and Vaughan Plank Road (now Dufferin Street) was built, Jacob Kurtz moved into a hotel on the south-east corner of Steeles and the Plank Road. This highly regarded inn was always very popular (see Inns and Taverns). About the same time that Kurtz opened his hotel, William Jackson bought property on the south side of Steeles, east of the river,[2] and eventually built a large house. It is still standing and is known as The Four Winds Restaurant.

The Fisherville Presbyterian Church, a fine example of Greek

Revival architecture in Canada, was built in 1856. Prior to this services had been held in private homes, such as John Brack's house, and in the Dublin School under the guidance of Francis Watson. The little church, transported to Black Creek Pioneer Village in 1960, stood among the trees overlooking the West Branch of the Don River in Vaughan, at the Dufferin and Steeles crossroads. A monument encasing the grave stones from the cemetery was erected in memory of the early settlers. It stands on the church site, built by Vaughan Township in 1967.

In 1809 Christian Troyer, a Mennonite minister, petitioned for 200 acres in Vaughan Township, stating that he had returned twelve times to Pennsylvania and was responsible for bringing about thirty-five people to Upper Canada. Some of the families settled on the north-west corner of Dufferin and Steeles, where an octagonal barn may be seen today. Others eventually bought land in North York and ran blacksmith shops in Elia and York Mills.

As Concord in Vaughan Township developed into a community, the people in the little district of Fisherville turned northward to pick up their mail and buy groceries rather than travel eastward to Yonge Street.

KAISERVILLE

Kaiserville was the unofficial name the Kaiser family gave to the settlement where they lived. Other families in the district may not have accepted the name, but for lack of a better one, it is used to distinguish this early community, part of which is now known as Black Creek Pioneer Village.

Land was often settled much earlier than the recorded registration date. Peter Erlin Kaiser,[3] an army officer from Frankfurt-on-Main, settled south of Steeles on Jane prior to 1803, but the Crown grant was not registered until 1846. Shortly before the American Revolution he had settled in Johnstown, Pennsylvania, and like other British sympathizers his land was confiscated. In 1785 he moved to Niagara with other Pennsylvania Germans, but hoping to regain his property, he returned to Pennsylvania. By 1798, his civil rights still denied, he came back to Upper Canada and settled in Kaiserville with his wife and three children. He died in 1824 and was buried on the east bank of the Black Creek which flowed through his farm. A large, black cherry tree marked the place of interment,[4] and the stump was located recently on York University campus. Daniel and Elizabeth Fisher Stong,[5] John Fisher's daughter, built their log house and cleared their land on the corner of Jane and Steeles in 1816. Their buildings stand today as part of Black

Creek Pioneer Village. Stong's school, erected on Steeles Avenue in 1824, was discontinued in 1839 (see Education).

In order to meet the need for a church and community hall, the Kaiser Chapel[6] was erected in 1830 on Jane Street, and it served many purposes. It was open to all itinerant preachers including the spiritualists. It is said that during one spiritualist meeting, while waiting for the spirit to answer, the table was deliberately overturned, revealing a human "spirit" who quickly escaped. When the Townline Church was established, the old Kaiser Chapel was used as a temperance hall, and in 1870 it was dismantled. Families were large, but baptisms and marriages could only be performed when the itinerant preacher appeared. According to Rev. William Jenkins' marriage records,[7] couples from North York often travelled at least ten miles to the Richmond Hill Presbyterian Church to be married. Since money was scarce the minister was often paid in such produce as vegetables or sausages.

The Townline Church,[8] a log building, was erected on the Stong property, adjoining the school, in 1852, and the Evangelical Association held church and Sunday school services regularly for twenty years. In 1859 land was purchased west of the church for a cemetery. The congregation was under the ministration of the Episcopal Methodist Church of Canada from 1870 to 1885. With the union of all Methodist Churches in Canada and the Bible Christian Church in 1884, the old Townline Church was closed. Sunday school continued for many years superintended by Abraham Hoover and, later, by John E. Kaiser. The cemetery is now in Black Creek Pioneer Village.

John Dalziel's saw mill was the centre of industry in the community. In the immediate vicinity stood a blacksmith shop and a carpenter shop, as well as a wagon shop on Jacob Kaiser's lot, on the south-west corner of Jane and Steeles Avenue. Another blacksmith shop stood across the road on the Stong property. Meanwhile the community was gradually turning northward to Edgeley, where a school was opened about 1839, a post office in 1872, and finally a Methodist church in 1877.

HUMBER SUMMIT

Situated in the north-west corner of North York, between Finch and Steeles on Islington Avenue, Humber Summit was a bustling mill district in the early years of its existence. Mills developed along the Humber River beginning in 1843, when Joseph Rowntree built the Green Holme Mills, a saw mill and a grist mill, in the area known as Rowntree Mill Park, half way between Steeles and Finch Avenues. These and the Kaitting, Boulton, and Crosson mills on the Humber, near Finch, lent considerable colour to community life (see Mills and Distilleries). Along Islington Avenue, among the tall pine trees, a log schoolhouse was erected (see Education), and three inns were open for business in 1851 (see Inns and Taverns).

John Duncan, a brother of William Duncan of Dublin Farm, built his farm-house in 1830 on Burns (or Duncan's) Creek, a small tributary of the Humber River, flowing through the sixth concession.[9] Keenly interested in erecting the Pine Ridge Methodist Church, he built a saw mill on the creek and supplied lumber for its construction. The church was actually created by a bond drawn up by Joseph Rowntree, a miller, and Duncan and other interested neighbours in 1845. It was situated on the south-west corner of the road leading to the Rowntree mills from Islington Avenue, and was enclosed by its cemetery which is all that remains today.

Islington Avenue, at the time, a plank toll road, later was reconstructed of stone, which made it more durable, in spite of the clatter of hooves and wooden wagonwheels. Nevertheless, the toll-gate at the corner of Steeles Avenue became a source of deep consternation to the neighbourhood on Sundays, for at the same time that the Pine Ridge Church was pulled down, the church in nearby Thistletown was moved north of Steeles. Much to their chagrin, those in the congregation who lived south of the toll-gate were forced to pay a toll to get home from church each Sunday. Rather than pay the unpopular fee, the people soon met in a log house south of Steeles. When the stove was lit in winter the bedbugs came out of the wood, and the church became known as the Bed Bug Church. This building was used for two years, the tolls were abolished, and the people returned to their church north of Steeles Avenue.

Humber Summit in the 1940's was a summer resort known as Riverbank Park. There were cottages on each side of the river road and Miss Chesterton's School ran a girls' camp near the river. The area was badly hit in Hurricane Hazel, when twelve houses were washed away. The old Rowntree mill site, once suggested as a good place for the Township dump, has fortunately been turned into a lovely Metropolitan Toronto park.

NOTES

1 Part of lot 25, 2nd concession west of Yonge Street.
2 *Ibid.*
3 The name Erlin was a prefix similar to "Mac" in MacDonald, meaning "son of".

It appears frequently in connection with the Kaiser family and was written originally Erlin Kaiser. M. Burkholder, "Palatine Settlement in York County", Ontario Historical Society, *Papers and Records*, XXXVII (1945), 92.

4 *Ibid.*

5 Lot 25, 4th concession west of Yonge Street.

6 Lot 24, 4th concession west of Yonge Street.

7 A. J. Clark, "Reverend William Jenkins of Richmond Hill", Ontario Historical Society, *Papers and Records*, XXVII (1931), 17-76.

8 T. E. Kaiser, *The Kaiser Families of the County of York, Ontario* (Oshawa: 1933), p. 12. Daniel A. Stong, *The Stong Genealogy of Canada and U.S. 1800-1958* (Toronto: 1958), pp. 11-12.

9 Lot 23, 6th concession west of Yonge Street.

THE COMMUNITIES EAST OF YONGE STREET

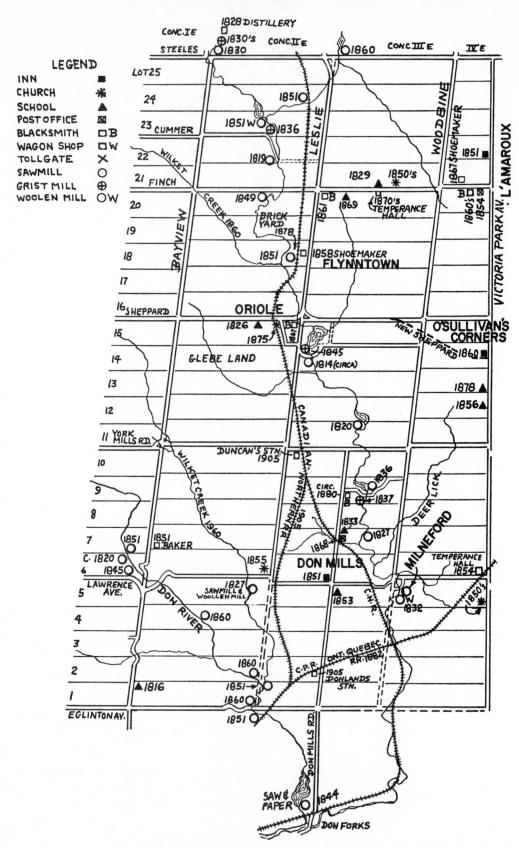

Communities east of Yonge Street.

Don Mills

THE DON RIVER WAS NAMED AFTER THE DON IN YORKSHIRE, ENGLAND, in 1793. Originally it was known by various Indian names, such as "Nechinquakakonk." Don Mills, or Don, as it was first called, is the area extending along the Don River Valley from Bayview to Victoria Park, and from south of Eglinton Avenue to York Mills Road. In the early days the route to Toronto was by way of Lawrence Avenue, through the Bayview ravine to Yonge Street. Finally the farmers agreed to give sufficient land to open the Don Independent Road, now Don Mills Road, to Plains Road or O'Connor Drive. Each farmer on the east side of the proposed route gave half the road allowance, and each farmer on the west side matched it, making what is termed a "given" road. By 1825 it was an improved road, and by 1852 it was macadamized as far as Todmorden.

SETTLERS

One of the earliest settlers in the area was James Gray, who arrived from Scotland in 1816, built his log cabin on the site of the present Beth El Synagogue, on the east side of Don Mills Road, and established a farm overlooking the Middle Don River.[1] His two brothers emigrated about 1820; Alexander built a house and saw mill on the east side of the river, and William erected his house and grist mill in the valley on the west side (see Mills and Distilleries). A large mill pond stretched up the valley, and its dam made a convenient crossing for family and friends. The grist mill continued into the twentieth century, and in 1914 the property was sold to David A. Dunlap, a mining magnate, who built a summer residence overlooking the old mill pond where beautiful,

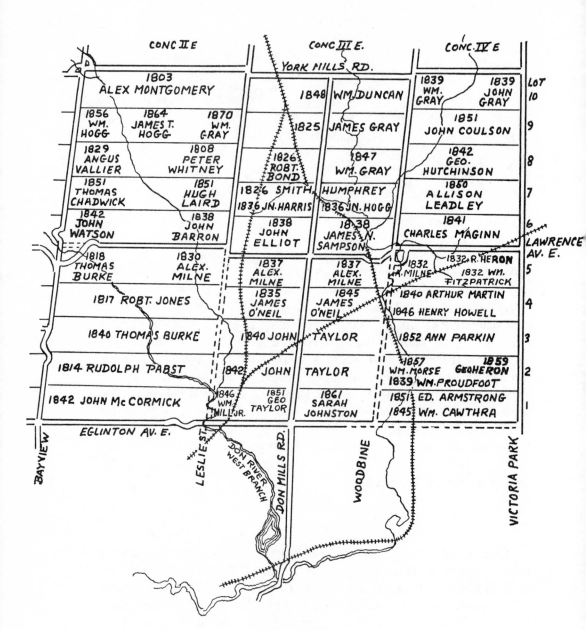

Don Mills.

Collecting sap from the maple trees in 1890.

Emery station on the south side of Finch, east of Weston Road.

Emery schools on the north-east corner of Weston Road and Finch; trustees, teacher, and others. Opening day 1914 for the school on left; one on right built in 1851.

Jennie Crosson with her Claremont Wesleyan Methodist Church Sunday School class, Joe Crosson, Superintendent, on right. Church erected north of school in 1869.

Rowntree Mill Road bridge over the Humber River in Humber Summit. A sawmill was built on the right in 1843, and a grist mill on the left in 1848. (left)

John Crosson's log cabin, built about 1815 and demolished in 1956, stood on the west side of Victoria Park about a quarter of a mile south of York Mills.

Milneford Mills, the Milne woollen mill built following the flood of 1878, and a Milne house built in 1832. They stood south of Lawrence, east of the Don Valley Parkway.

Mill dam at Milneford Mills.

Don School built 1837. S.S.No 9 York

The first Don School, built in 1837, stood on the east side of Don Mills Road, about half a mile north of Lawrence. Artist, Owen Staples.

Aggie Hogg's general store, Do post office, and library, wi James Hogg on the steps. Ne site of log school, on the east si of Don Mills Road, north of th C.N.R. bridge. Looking south.

white swans swam majestically all summer. He also operated a model
dairy farm on the site which was named Donalda, after his wife. A huge
barn was added to the old grist mill, as well as other farm buildings,
cow stalls were tiled, electric fans whirled to distract flies, and music
was piped into the barn to provide contentment for the herd. When
Dunlap died in 1924 his wife sold the farm, and she and her son presented an observatory built at Richmond Hill to the University of
Toronto. Donalda Farm was finally taken over by the Don Mills Development Company and became the Donalda Golf Course with the
Dunlap summer home serving as a clubhouse. Three of the original
Gray houses and the flour mill are still standing on the club grounds.

Alexander Milne, a Scottish weaver, emigrated to Long Island in
1801, came to Canada in 1817, and went into partnership with Jacob
McKay of Humber Summit, carrying on a carding and fulling business.[2]
When this enterprise dissolved Milne went into partnership with his
brother, Peter, in Markham, and finally in 1827 the Alexander Milne
family moved to York Township and erected a saw and woollen mill of
their own in what is now Edwards Gardens (see Mills and Distilleries).
Some of the family continued to live on the old site, but in 1832 a new
mill and house for William, Alexander's son, was built in the valley, south
of Lawrence, on the Middle Don River. In 1836 William married Jane
Weatherston, who had arrived in Canada in 1832 after a short, four-
week Atlantic crossing; her sister's ship took nine weeks to cross. Jane
completed her journey from Montreal to York by Durham boat, going
ashore each evening to sleep. The Milne lot ran along Lawrence Avenue
from the Edwards Gardens site east to the river.[3] The second Don School
(see Education) was erected on what was originally Milne property, on
the south-east corner of Don Mills Road and Lawrence, and in 1860
an inn stood across the road, on the north-west corner (see Inns and
Taverns).

Smith Humphrey's farm and saw mill, north of Lawrence, was purchased in 1836 and run by John Hogg, another Scot, who stayed with
his brother, James, on Yonge Street before settling on Don Mills Road
near the railway bridge.[4] The Hoggs were a very musical family, with
Robert and James playing the cello and violin while other members of
the family sang. Much of the social life of the community was centred
around musical evenings, enjoyed with family and neighbours, and
"fiddle nights" were known to last until dawn.

The first school had been erected on Hogg property on the east side
of Don Mills Road, north of Lawrence. John Hogg built a frame general
store south of the school location and became postmaster when the Don
Post Office opened in 1868. His daughter, Agnes, later operated a new,

brick general store and post office located at the railway bridge, south of the first store. It was known in the neighbourhood as Aggie Hogg's store and was a hub of community activity. Teachers often boarded with the Hogg's, who lived in the building, which also housed the first Don library.

Children dropped in on their way home from school to buy "sweeties," or maybe just to torment Aggie, who had a kind heart but a sharp tongue.[5] Packaged foods had not made their appearance on the market, and open boxes and barrels were tempting. A box of icing sugar stood on the counter near the door. While one boy diverted Aggie's attention, the others would grab a fistful of icing sugar and bolt. The system failed one day when Aggie substituted Epsom salts for sugar. A copper would buy a couple of "bull's eyes" or a coloured sugar stick. Daily, Aggie's patience was severely tried when she was summoned all the way from the garden or house by the store bell only to be confronted by a small customer with a copper to spend. Aggie had two pairs of glasses and would often wear one on top of the other, much to the amusement of the children. In her very broad Scottish accent she would greet the children with "Well, aye, aye, how are you the day?" and to the mothers she always enquired after the "wee 'uns." John Hogg and his wife lived over the general store during the last years of their lives while their son, Robert, farmed the land east of the Don River and built the second Hogg frame house. Another son, James, farmed the land west of the Don, and for convenience, a swing bridge was built over the river between the two farms in 1890.

Charles D. Maginn, a Welshman, came to York County about 1832 from Beamsville, Ontario, and he and his Irish wife, Margaret Fitzpatrick, settled on a Crown grant north of Lawrence, between Woodbine and Victoria Park, in 1841.[6] As devout members of the Connexion, the Maginns gave a warm Irish welcome to the Methodist Church ministers who preached or visited in the area, and often lent their grove for church camp meetings. Maginn, a general merchant in Don village in 1869,[7] was a man of fine build with a pleasant, open countenance, willing to take on community responsibilities, such as serving on York Township Council from 1861 to 1864, and as a School trustee, advocating a free Don School in the fifties and sixties. He also had a reputation for being very adept at spearing salmon in the Deer Lick, a small stream running near his farm.

The Sons of Temperance Harvest Home Division No. 317, organized in 1851,[8] erected a temperance hall in 1854 on the Maginn property, west of the present C.P.R. tracks, near Victoria Park. This Division and the Wexford Wesleyan Methodist Church were closely allied, and the hall was frequently used for the church business meetings of the Scarborough Circuit Quarterly Board. It was also known as Maginn Hall. Although the records are not too clear, it appears that the Temperance Division also met in the church. The question of whether to repair the old hall, build a new one or stay at Wexford is mentioned from time to time in the minutes. The last meeting recorded in the minute book was held at the Milne residence in 1910.

John Coulson, an Englishman, emigrated to Canada when in his teens and settled on a rented King's College lot north of the Maginn property about 1833.[9] He built a log house, farmed, and was finally able to buy the property in 1839. Among the Coulson papers are many samples of early documents indicating that he may have drawn up agreements for his neighbours who were not as capable. The Coulson frame house was not built until 1891 and stood a quarter of a mile south of the log cabin, which was demolished in 1956.

THE CHURCHES

William Fitzpatrick, a Methodist preacher who lived on Dawes Road (Victoria Park), near Wexford, sometimes preached at Davenport, and his route to Toronto was a path through the bush, indicated by a blaze on the trees. Travelling at night was extremely hazardous, as Fitzpatrick must have known, because one could so easily become lost in the woods. One day he set out for Davenport on horseback, and near the Don found a tree had fallen across the path. Noting the direction he must take to get around the tree when coming home, he continued on to church. On his return after dark, he went around the tree, trying first one way and then another to get back on the path. Becoming bewildered and losing his sense of direction, he tethered his horse and sat to wait for daylight. It was a long night; he could not sleep for fear of attack by wild animals, and as soon as it was light he found the path, mounted his horse, and continued his journey home.[10]

On October 20, 1851, Fitzpatrick granted land for the construction of a Wesleyan Methodist Church, later surrounded by a cemetery, on the west side of Victoria Park Avenue. These devoted Methodists met occasionally for field meetings in C. D. Maginn's grove or James Ionson's "bush" in Scarborough. The church was still open in 1878, but today all that remains is the small cemetery, the building having been moved across the road to the Roman Catholic Church grounds near St. Jude's Episcopal Church in Wexford.

Don Mills Road ran through the centre of the community. To the west, on the north-west corner of Lawrence and Leslie Street, Barron's

Chapel, a frame Primitive Methodist Church, was erected on land donated by Mrs. Barron, "a small woman with a clear white complexion and a spiritual appearance. She was earnest, sincere, whole-hearted and sympathetic, a mother to all the ministers in kindly offices and with encouraging words. The key-note of her life was unselfishness; the unseen world was intensely real to her, and the cause of God had the supremacy in her thought and affection."[11] In 1854 a committee was formed to acquire the deed for the chapel, and the following week the name Bethesda was proposed. In the spring of 1859 a Sunday school was established under the leadership of Isaac Hutchinson. However, many residents of the district attended churches outside the area such as York Mills Baptist Church, St. John's Anglican Church, and York Mills Presbyterian Church, all situated near Yonge Street in York Mills.

The Don Mills residents of the York Mills Presbyterian Church were interested in having their own church; so in 1885 they bought the Bethesda Methodist Church at Leslie and Lawrence for about $400 and called it Bethesda Presbyterian Church. The church pews consisted of a straight board for the back and another for the seat, each made from a single, wide board. These seats had one advantage from the minister's point of view—no one could get sufficiently comfortable to go to sleep during the sermon. Mrs. Gray bought her small boy a pair of soft leather moccasins so he would not make a noise when he kicked the back of the seat in front of him in his efforts to get comfortable.

In 1904 a new, red brick church replaced the old frame building on the same location. Bees were held by the men of the congregation to haul materials and to erect the building. Through the years, the church was very active, and in 1925 the congregation joined the United Church of Canada. With the growth of Don Mills, the building became too small, and in 1958 a modern Bethesda United Church was built on Larkfield Avenue. The old church on Lawrence was used by the Lions Club and finally torn down in 1961.

THE DUNCAN PROPERTY

To the north, along the south side of York Mills Road between Leslie and Woodbine was the farm of Henry Duncan,[12] son of William Duncan of Dublin. When he became of age, his father gave him this farm of 200 acres, and his house on Don Mills Road was built in 1868 with bricks made on the property. A large willow tree, still standing, was originally near the house. Henry was elected to York Township Council in 1870, served as reeve for a number of years, and was an active member of the community (see Political Growth). His brother,

David Duncan, settled on the farm north of York Mills Road known as Moatfield.[13] This handsome brick house, still owned by the family, stands today just west of Don Mills Road. David was a well-known dairyman and breeder of Jersey cattle.

THE FLOOD OF 1878

The great flood of 1878 swept away all the bridges along the Don River as well as the saw mill, the logs in the mill pond, the woollen mill in Milne Hollow, and the Gray's Mill dam. Miss Janet Hogg recalled seeing a dog house being swept down the river. A howling dog tied to his kennel sat on the roof, unable to swim to shore.

James Hamilton Smith, postmaster at Aggie Hogg's store, made sure the mail got through, if a day late. He picked it up at the Lombard Street Post Office in Toronto and made his way up Dawes Road and across the farms on horseback as far as he could go on the first day. By the next morning the water had receded sufficiently for him to go through the river on horseback.

At the end of Don Mills Road a house in the flats was carried away by the flood. The occupant was able to get his wife and baby to safety on a hill before their home was washed away. The cradle went merrily down the river with a hen perched on top.

THE TAYLOR PROPERTY

In 1880 George Taylor's three sons, owners of extensive property north and south of Eglinton, established the Don Valley Pressed Brick Works in East York which produced twelve million bricks a year. Still operating in the Valley, the plant is known as the Toronto Brick Works. The Taylor family was staunchly Anglican, but also contributed to the Methodist cause. Their houses, such as Thorn Cliff in Todmorden, were estates with well-kept gardens, orchards and stables.

In 1904 W. F. MacLean, one time Conservative Member of Parliament for York and proprietor of the *Toronto World*, took over part of the Taylor property north of Eglinton and gradually extended his holdings to nine hundred acres of farmland including the Milne property. This was known as the Donlands Farm. A brick house, formerly the Taylor's, was used to board the hired men, and MacLean built a large frame summer cottage for his family. When the Dillamore property was acquired, their stone house, situated in a grove of trees, was renovated for the MacLeans, but it was destroyed by fire in 1940. A small flag station named Valleydon adjoined the C.P.R. near the MacLean house, which was most useful for commuting to and from Toronto. In

1922, the farm was taken over by R. J. Fleming, a name always associated with the fine grey barns on Don Mills Road near the C.P.R. lines, where herds of cattle roamed the pastures.

Public Library

A public library was opened by the Don residents in 1896, and the first books were bought with money raised by the Literary Society concerts. Aggie Hogg provided still another service to the community when the library books were placed on shelves in her store. In 1918 James Hamilton Smith, Postmaster, wanted to be relieved of the responsibility of caring for the books, and James Muirhead offered the use of an abandoned First World War military hut located on his property, donated a Quebec heater, and supplied firewood.[14]

The Public Libraries Branch of the Department of Education sent out Miss Spearman, who assisted Pearl Muirhead and Mary Duncan with cataloguing the books. Although there were numerous town public libraries at this time, there were only two rural public libraries. An annual County grant of $25 and a Provincial grant, supplemented by the proceeds from oyster suppers or concerts, provided the yearly budget of about $125, which was used to buy new books.

The Canadian Northern Railway

In 1905 the Canadian Northern Railway was built through Don Mills between Leslie and Woodbine, on the west side of the Don River. Duncan Station was erected on the property of Henry Duncan, just south of York Mills Road, and was very convenient for local farmers wanting to ship their produce. The railway was finally taken over by the C.N.R., and the station was later changed to Oriole.

Don Mills remained predominantly farm land until 1954, when the Don Mills Development Company began the first planned community in Canada. It covered nearly 3,000 acres of rolling fields and provided for houses, apartments, a shopping centre, schools, churches, and industries on the perimeter.

1 Lot 9, 3rd concession east of Yonge Street.
2 *History of Toronto and the County of York, Ontario*, I, pt. III, 189.
3 Part of lot 5, 2nd concession east of Yonge Street; lot 5, 3rd concession east of Yonge Street, and part of lot 5, 4th concession east of Yonge Street. The Milne Cemetery is in a corner of the Edwards Gardens.
4 East half of lot 7, 3rd concession east of Yonge Street.
5 Helen Hickman, "The Dawn of Don Mills", a paper in the North York Historical Society files.
6 Lot 6, 4th concession east of Yonge Street.
7 It is not known where this store was located, but Maginn is listed as a general merchant, 1869-71, in the directories.
8 Records available courtesy of Miss Marion Coulson.
9 Lot 9, 4th concession east of Yonge Street.
10 Hopper, *op. cit.*, pp. 182-183.
11 *Ibid.*, p. 235.
12 Lot 10, 3rd concession east of Yonge Street.
13 Lot 11, 3rd concession east of Yonge Street.
14 West half of lot 7, 3rd concession east of Yonge Street.

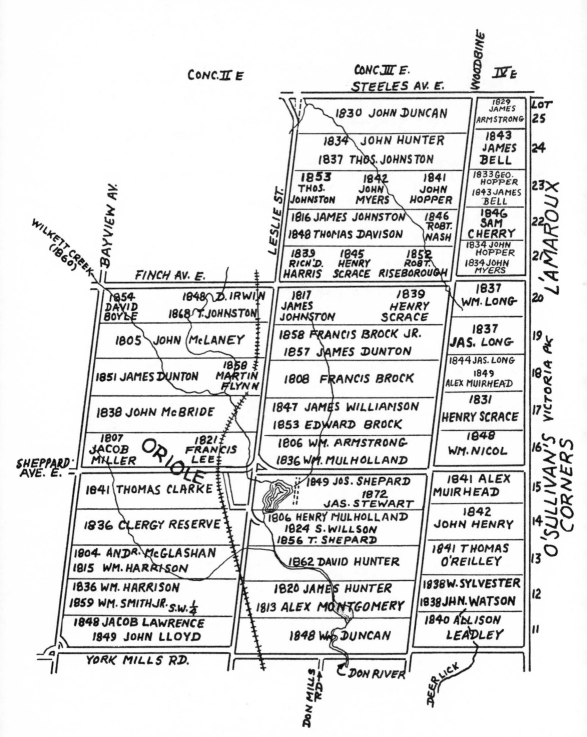

Oriole, L'Amaroux and O'Sullivan's Corners.

Oriole and Flynntown

ORIOLE

ORIOLE, A SMALL MILL COMMUNITY, DEVELOPED AROUND LESLIE AND Sheppard Avenue. It was named after George S. Henry's farmhouse, Oriole Lodge, so called because of the numerous, orange-coloured birds with black heads that occupy the area all summer.

EARLY SETTLERS

Henry Mulholland, a native of County Monaghan, Ireland, emigrated to Canada in 1806 with his wife. He secured two lots from the Crown, between Leslie and Woodbine, just south of Sheppard Avenue.[1] A log house was built on the southern lot, where they cleared the land and farmed. Five children were born before they moved to property on Bathurst, north of Lawrence, in 1814 (see Downsview).

Another settler, Andrew McGlashan, emigrated from Scotland with his family and procured property east of Bayview, north of York Mills Road, as early as 1804.[2] He built a log house and cleared his land with the help of his wife and five young children. In 1815 he moved to York Mills and sold the southern half of his property containing houses, out houses, woods and water to William Harrison for £100.

The Christopher Harrison family, United Empire Loyalists, had settled in Nova Scotia following the American Revolutionary War. They moved to York and in 1806 settled on Yonge Street, north of the line of the Macdonald-Cartier Freeway, where Joseph Harrison and his family continued to live,[3] and George constructed his inn in 1841. It was after his father's death that William bought the McGlashan farm and eventually built a brick house facing Bayview Avenue, still standing at the north end of Harrison Road. Other Harrison family homes are on Forest Heights Boulevard and on Windfields Farm, north of York Mills Road, near Leslie.[4]

William Harrison was a keen Reformer and supporter of William Lyon Mackenzie. After taking part in the skirmish at Montgomery's Tavern, he escaped to the United States where he died in February of 1838, of wounds received in the fighting. His eldest son, Joshua, then twenty-two years of age, went to the United States to bring back his father's body for burial. The authorities opened the coffin three times on Joshua's return trip, suspecting smuggling, but Joshua continued his journey, frightened, but determined that his father should be buried in St. John's cemetery, York Mills.

William Armstrong, a brother-in-law of Henry Mulholland, owned a farm north of Sheppard Avenue, east of Leslie. When he died without a will, the property fell into the hands of relatives in England.[5] William Mulholland, Henry's son, went to England in May of 1832 to negotiate with the Armstrong heirs. He landed in Liverpool twenty-three days after leaving New York, having experienced only one storm during the journey. He was able to buy the property for fifty pounds, and on his return home, settled down on the farm. He became a Warden for York Township in 1845, a member of Council from 1850 to 1853 and again from 1865 to 1866, and the first Justice of the Peace in East York.

In 1841 Thomas Clark bought and farmed the lot on the south side of Sheppard Avenue between Bayview and Leslie.[6] His wife died in 1844, leaving him with seven children. He then married Nancy Miller and, because of his increasing family, built his second house, Barberry Place, in 1855. This large brick house with two gable windows is still standing among its evergreen trees near Bayview Avenue across from a shopping plaza. The eighteen-inch foundation of field stone and mortar encloses the basement and provides an inside wall running the length of the house. The floor is paved with brick. The walls are three courses of red brick, painted white. The second floor is also supported by an inside brick wall. Two large fireplaces provided most of the heat for the entire house. Logs of white pine were cut on the farm from trees at least two feet in diameter and hauled by oxen to the Shepard saw mill to be cut. The hand-split laths, three by ten inch joists, and floorboards an inch and a half thick, were all of clear white pine. The trim varies from room to room and is an example of fine, mid-nineteenth century carpentry.

MILLS

Saw mills developed along the Middle Don River beginning as early as 1814 and lasting until after 1878. The mill south of Sheppard Avenue provided flour and lumber between 1856 and 1869 under the proprietorship of Thomas Shepard (see Mills and Distilleries).

THE CHURCH

Thomas Clark's first house was the meeting place for the Wesleyan Methodists of Oriole, and in 1853 the small group, which had been meeting as a class, formed Clark's Congregation. Sunday services were held in the log school built in 1826 and later in the 1848 brick school (see Education) and William Mulholland helped with the Sunday school. There were several gangs terrorizing the district, one being the Markham Gang. William received threatening notes left under a stone on top of the gate by the Markham Gang saying they would burn his house and barns if he continued to teach Sunday school. Fortunately, they did not carry out their threat.[8]

In 1873 land was sold by Thomas Clark to the trustees of Clark's Wesleyan Methodist Congregation, and a church was erected on the south-west corner of Leslie and Sheppard. It was not large, about thirty by fifty feet, and was built of yellow brick with three Gothic shaped windows on each side and two on the east wall flanking the front door. The simplicity of the interior seemed to reflect the tastes of its Methodist congregation. An ancient, foot-pumped, reed organ, polished like glass, stood in one corner, and there were two big box stoves on either side of the church requiring two double chimneys. The wood, given by members of the congregation each year, was hauled to the church, where a chopping bee was held to split it for Sunday use.

During the short period when Rev. Edwin A. Pearson, the father of Prime Minister Lester B. Pearson, was preacher of the Newtonbrook circuit, Oriole was under his charge. After meetings he often invited part of the congregation home for coffee and croquinole. On one such occasion two sleighs set out, everyone dressed warmly in his "Sunday best." On the way one team of horses became excited, shied, and ran away, and the sleigh turned over dumping its occupants and the croquinole board into a snowbank. As the flustered and dishevelled passengers picked themselves up they heard loud guffaws from their friends in the other sleigh who had come to their rescue.

A final candlelight service closed the church that had served the community for many years; on Sunday, May 12, 1957, the Oriole Congregation transferred its services to the Harrison Road Public School.

Sunday school classes were carried on in the old church for some time, and in due course the new Oriole-York Mills United Church held its first service on December 17, 1961. The old church building, unused for a number of years, was finally dismantled in 1965 to make way for shops.

GEORGE S. HENRY

George S. Henry, Premier of Ontario from 1930 to 1934, bought the James Stewart property in 1898 and established Oriole Lodge farm, a dairy farm of about eighty or ninety prize Holstein cattle.[9] His residence, built originally around a very early house with an outside wall of two-inch pine planks, is still standing, facing west on the Henry Farm subdivision on George Henry Boulevard.

A cairn commemorating the memory of Henry and Jane Mulholland, who settled on the property in 1806, was erected by the Mulholland, Duncan, Stewart, White, Francis, and McBride descendants of the family in October of 1937. The cairn was moved in 1966 from its original location at Woodbine and Sheppard Avenue to make way for the Don Valley Parkway. The natural stone monument now stands in a park across the street from the Henry house.

THE POST OFFICE

The residents of Oriole went to Lansing to shop as there were no stores in their own community. George Summers, the blacksmith, opened the Oriole Post Office in 1908; it closed in 1913, and the blacksmith shop was taken over by John Reid in 1918. During one period the blacksmith was so busy with continual repairs to wagons and farm implements, as well as with shoeing horses, that it was necessary to employ five assistants. In their spare time they made ornamental pieces.

FLYNNTOWN

North of Sheppard on Leslie was a district known as Flynntown, named after Martin Flynn, the shoemaker, who had a small general store and cobblery beside his house in 1858.[10] This house is still standing on the west side of Leslie Street, half a mile north of Sheppard.

Francis Brock moved into the district in 1808, on the east side of Leslie. The family remained on the property, farming until approximately 1871. On December 9, 1824, Brock advertised in the *Upper Canada Gazette*:

A Stray Cow. A large Yellow Cow, with a short tail and
gathered Horns. The Owner is requested to bring her
from No. 18 in the 3rd concession, Township of York.

In later years, some members of the family moved to York Mills where
they ran a store.

Saw mills were flourishing on the west side of Leslie (see Mills and
Distileries), and Thomas Johnston, an Irishman, had a blacksmith shop
on the south-east corner of Finch Avenue. By 1878, however, the mills
and blacksmith shop had vanished and James Andrews, an Englishman, was proprietor of a brick and tile manufactory near the mill site.
His advertisement in Miles' *Illustrated Historical Atlas of the County
of York*, stated that he had white and red brick of superior quality, as
well as drain and roofing tiles made to order and kept on hand.

Today the North York General Hospital has been opened on the
west bank of the river, and subdivisions have opened housing for suburban living. All that remains of the rural past is the Henry house on
the east side of the river, and the Flynn house in Flynntown.

NOTES

1 Lots 14 and 15, 3rd concession east of Yonge Street.
2 Lot 13, 2nd concession east of Yonge Street.
3 Lot 14, 1st concession east of Yonge Street.
4 Two houses are on lot 13, 2nd concession east of Yonge Street and the Windfields
   Farm house is on lot 11, 2nd concession east of Yonge Street.
5 Lot 16, 3rd concession east of Yonge Street.
6 Lot 15, 2nd concession east of Yonge Street.
7 W. C. Rean, "The Homestead", a talk given to the North York Historical Society
   in January, 1961.
8 Mulholland, *op. cit.*, pp. 20-21.
9 Lots 14 and 15, 3rd concession east of Yonge Street.
10 Lot 18, 2nd concession east of Yonge Street.

L'Amaroux and
O'Sullivan's Corners

VICTORIA PARK AVENUE, FORMERLY DAWES ROAD OR THE BORDER LINE, is the eastern boundary between North York and Scarborough. As an early road it was so rough that in winter the farmers used to take down sections of their fences so that travellers could drive their sleighs through the fields rather than along the country lane.

L'AMAROUX

L'Amaroux, a border community located at Victoria Park and Finch, was named after the French Huguenot family of Joshua Lamoreaux. Following the American Revolution, the family moved first to New Brunswick as United Empire Loyalists, and then to York County where they settled and farmed in Scarborough.[1]

The early farmers in the area were emigrants from Ireland and England. Thomas Johnston, an Irishman, settled in the area in 1837[2] and, according to his family, was the first man in York County to own a threshing machine. As an active supporter of the Government during the Rebellion of 1837, Johnston, James Armstrong, and three other men captured Peter Matthews and other Mackenzie followers hidden in the house of two bachelors, John and William Duncan,[3] near Steeles Avenue. The prisoners were all taken down to the jail in Toronto and the captors collected the bounty of £500 for turning in Matthews. Samuel Lount of Lloydtown and Matthews, both leaders during the Rebellion, were executed on scaffolding built in front of the Toronto jail on April 12, 1838.

In 1843 John Bell, another Irishman, married Martha Cherry from

Wilson and Bathurst, and settled on his Spruce Lane Farm[4] in the north-east corner of the Township. He will long be remembered for the spruce trees still standing along the lane to his house, which was destroyed by fire, as well as for those he planted at St. Paul's L'Amoreaux, and at Zion School. Bell was one of Ontario's best known breeders and stockmen, specializing in high class Clydesdales, Tamworth swine, and Shropshire sheep.

Twenty-three relatives came to Upper Canada in 1837 with Robert Nash from Guysboro, Nova Scotia. He settled and farmed in L'Amaroux in 1846, and erected a frame house, still standing, facing Woodbine Avenue about a quarter of a mile north of Finch.[5] The house was built by William Murphy, a carpenter, who also built the general store.

Robert Risebrough came to Canada in 1837 with six children after a voyage of thirteen weeks on a sailing vessel. Their food was almost exhausted on the trip and the family had to subsist on salt pork and sea biscuit. They eventually settled south of the Nash family on Finch Avenue.[6]

A store, and an inn which stood on Victoria Park a quarter of a mile north of Finch, were both vacant by 1851, at which time James Long opened his general store near the south-west corner of Finch, incorporating the L'Amaroux Post Office in 1854, with James Taylor[7] as postmaster. It was taken over in 1878 by William Nash, a brother of Robert, who was postmaster and agent for agricultural machinery, and the building still stands as a residence today.

Jesse Richardson's blacksmith shop stood west of the store, and Archibald Wright was wagon maker. By 1867 John Myers, a Yorkshireman, owned a shoemaker's shop which stood in front of his house on the north side of Finch Avenue, and James Flynn looked after the leather repairs in 1870.

The residents of L'Amaroux built two schools on Finch between Woodbine and Leslie. A log school was raised as early as 1829 near the Zion Church site, and another, a brick building still standing east of Leslie, was erected in 1867 (see Education).

The Churches

The Anglicans attended services at St. Paul's L'Amoreaux in Scarborough, where a frame church was erected in the fall of 1840; and James Long, the storekeeper, helped to build it. Paul Sheppard of Scarborough, whose daughter married George Scrace, did the carving on the church, as well as on the steeple of St. James Cathedral, and the

Golden Lion statue for the hotel at Lansing. The L'Amoreaux Church burned down in December 1935, and was replaced by a new brick building.

Early Primitive Methodist church services were held in the home of David Erwin on the south-west corner of Leslie and Finch in 1848. Later the congregation moved to the home of James Johnston, and finally to a Primitive Methodist log church built on the north side of Finch Avenue on Henry Scrace's property. The exact date of this church is not known, but in 1854 Samuel Cherry, a farmer in the community, was buried in the cemetery, and the church is listed on Tremain's Map of 1860.[9]

Because it was so easy to become lost in the bush after dark, the Church held its services in the afternoon. The congregation was divided so that the men sat on one side of the church and the women on the other. By 1873 Henry Scrace had granted an acre of land for a church, sabbath school, and burying ground,[10] and a new red brick building was erected and called the Zion Primitive Methodist Church. After much effort on the part of the congregation, an organ was installed to supply the music. The anniversary sermon was preached on July 3rd each year; field-meetings were held every summer in the open air[11]; and Harvest Home Suppers, another yearly event, added to the social life of the community.

By 1878 a temperance hall[12] had been built on the property of Sam Kennedy on the south side of Finch, east of Zion School. As in other communities, it was used for meetings, church socials, and temperance society programs which included recitations, singing and debates.

All that remains of this North York community is Zion Church standing high on the hill, and the last "little red schoolhouse," unoccupied and still unaltered on its original site east of Leslie, at present owned by the North York Public Library.

O'SULLIVAN'S CORNERS

O'Sullivan's Corners, also a border community, was situated south of L'Amaroux at the corners of Sheppard Avenue, or the Lansing Cut Off, and Victoria Park Avenue, west of Agincourt in Scarborough. The community was made up of English farmers such as Allison Leadley, Henry Scrace, and George Hooper; Scotch farmers such as Alexander Muirhead, William Nicol, and John Henry; and an Irish farmer, John O'Reilly. In the early 1850's the crops were exceptionally good throughout the district and the old log or frame houses were replaced with fine,

Gray grist mill on the east side of Don Mills Road, half a mile south of York Mills Road by the river.

Thomas Clark's house, built in 1855 on the east corner of Rean Drive and Sheppard.

Moatfield, David Duncan's home on the north side of York Mills Road west of Don Mills Road.

Oriole Lodge, the George S. Henry residence, stands south of Sheppard, east of the North York General Hospital, in the Henry Farm subdivision. Part of the house may have been built by Stillwell Willson about 1824.

Spruce Grove, the William Nicol house, built in 1855 on the north side of Old Sheppard Avenue, west of Sandra Blvd. Recently demolished. (above)

Home of Martin Flynn, shoemaker, on the west side of Leslie, half a mile north of Sheppard. Built about 1858. (right)

O'Sullivan's Corners, Sheppard Avenue and Victoria Park. O'Sullivan's Hotel in the background was opened by Patrick and Ann O'Reilly O'Sullivan in 1860. Also post office in 1892.

The O'Sullivan Hotel veranda. Left to right: Mrs. Parker (proprietor) in doorway, Hilda Benson, Bert White, Mamie Zimmers, Shirley White.

Zion Primitive Methodist Church and cemetery, built about 1873 on top of the Finch Avenue hill, west of Woodbine.

John Duncan's house, the scene of Peter Matthews' capture during the Rebellion. Located between Leslie and Woodbine, about an eighth of a mile south of Steeles.

brick homes, and larger barns were added to the establishment. The William Nichol house, Spruce Grove, on Old Sheppard Avenue, was a fine example of an 1855 house.

Two schools were erected in the area. The first one in 1856 about a quarter of a mile north of York Mills Road, and the second was erected on the lot to the north in 1873 (see Education).

Patrick O' Sullivan, a native of County Cork, Ireland, emigrated to Canada with his parents, and his father, Daniel O'Sullivan, established an inn in Norway on the north side of the Kingston Road at Lee Avenue. Patrick married Ann O'Reilly; in 1860 they ran a hotel on her father's property on the north-west corner of Victoria Park and Sheppard. Their son, Michael, opened the O'Sullivan's Corners Post Office in the hotel and became the first postmaster in 1892 (see Inns and Taverns).

Real estate developments and road changes have completely altered the appearance of O'Sullivan's Corners and the schools, inn, and farm houses along Victoria Park have gradually disappeared.

NOTES

1   The spelling of the name has always been a problem. In 1776 the family spelled their name Lamoreaux; the church on Finch Avenue in Scarborough is St. Paul's L'Amoreaux; Martha the wife of James L'Amoreaux, is shown on the gravestone as Lamoraux; the Anglican Church at York had a missionary station at Hogg's Hollow and later at L'Amoureux settlement in Scarborough; in 1840 Isaac Lamoureux gave land for this Scarborough Anglican Church; and the post office and Tremaine's Map of the County of York 1860, list L'Amaroux.

2   Lot 24, 3rd concession east of Yonge Street.

3   Beers, op. cit., pp. 433-434. The Duncans lived on lot 25, 3rd concession east of Yonge Street. James Armstrong lived on lot 25, 4th concession east of Yonge Street.

4   Lot 24, 4th concession east of Yonge Street.

5   Lot 22, 3rd concession east of Yonge Street.

6   Lot 21, 3rd concession east of Yonge Street.

7   Lot 20, 4th concession east of Yonge Street.

8   Lot 21, 4th concession east of Yonge Street.

9   G. E. Tremaine, Map of the County of York, Canada West (Toronto: 1860). Lot 21, 3rd concession east of Yonge Street. Samuel Cherry was the son of James Cherry of Wilson and Bathurst.

10   Lot 21, 3rd concession east of Yonge Street.

11   Hopper, op. cit., pp. 118-119.

12   Lot 20, 3rd concession east of Yonge Street.

PART THREE

POLITICAL EVOLUTION

Political Growth
From Township to Borough

Political Growth

LORD DORCHESTER, FORMERLY SIR GUY CARLETON, RETURNED TO Canada as governor in 1786, and, to provide local government for the Loyalists, in 1788 he issued a proclamation forming four administrative districts in the western part of the old Province of Quebec. These were Luneburg, extending from the present Quebec border to the Gananoque River, Meckleburg, reaching to the Trent River, Nassau, covering the area to Long Point, and Hesse covering the rest of the western region.[1] When John Graves Simcoe became lieutenant-governor of Upper Canada in 1791, he divided the original districts into nineteen counties for the purposes of parliamentary representation and military organization. York County was one of the original counties of 1792.

In the same year the old districts were renamed: Eastern, Midland, Home and Western. The Home District, which contained the Town and Township of York, was gradually reduced in size; by 1850 it comprised only the counties of York, Ontario and Peel. Management of local affairs in each district was vested in the District Court of General Quarter Sessions of the Peace, composed of the magistrates or Justices of the Peace.[2] They controlled all local moneys such as wages for members of the House of Assembly, fees for poundkeepers, parish clerks, and jailors; they laid out and improved the highways; appointed district and township constables, surveyors, and inspectors of weights and measures; established and regulated markets and ferries; erected and managed courthouses, jails, and asylums; and granted licenses to sell liquor. The magistrates also granted licenses to ministers of the Church of England, the Presbyterians, the Lutherans, and the Calvinists, authorizing them to perform marriages. Methodist ministers were excluded deliberately because they were suspected of having republican sentiments. Finally an act in 1829 validated marriages performed by all ministers, but required that all but those of the Church of England obtain certificates for each marriage from the Court of Quarter Session in their districts. Bans and licenses were necessary and proper returns had to be made.[3]

According to an act of 1793 the magistrates were required to call town meetings once a year for the election of officers, and when vacancies occurred replacements had to be appointed. The officers elected were: town clerk, assessors, collectors, overseers of highways, pathmasters, fence-viewers, poundkeepers and town wardens. Each officer had to carry out the laws enacted by the Upper Canada Assembly, and was responsible to the Justices in Quarter Sessions. Two town wardens represented the Township, and had the power to sue and defend on behalf of the inhabitants.[4]

The first recorded town meeting was held on March 4, 1797. It included the townships of York, Markham and Vaughan and the wardens, assessors, and overseers of highways were elected for all three as a unit. Separate poundkeepers, pathmasters and fence-viewers were, however, elected for separate areas, such as the "Circles of the Don and Humber," specified sections of Yonge Street and the German settlement of Markham. The Town of York was included with York Township until 1804, when it was listed as a separate unit but continued to hold joint meetings with the Township.[5]

In the beginning, the magistrates and the settlers were bound together by a strong bond of interest, and the magistrates were guided by public opinion. After the War of 1812, this happy feeling was less and less apparent, and the inhabitants complained of incompetence, selfishness and high-handedness among the administrators of Upper Canada. By 1830 the population of the Home District had reached 17,020 with 3,127 in York Township and 2,860 in the Town of York. Immigration was greatly accelerated by the unrest in the British Isles and Europe brought about by the stirrings of liberalism and nationalism following the Napoleonic War. Finally, on March 6, 1834, York became the City of Toronto, acquiring its municipal status by special legislation.

THE DISTRICT COUNCILS ACT

Because the country had outgrown the system of magistrates, the District Councils Act was passed in 1841 forming a district council for each of the Ontario districts. Each council was elected directly by those qualified to vote in the township. It had all the powers of the courts of Quarter Sessions relating to roads, bridges and other public works, schools, expenses for the administration of justice, payment of township officers, and the collection of taxes for these purposes. Clerks, treasurers, and wardens were appointed by the Crown until 1846.

Franklin Jackes, an Eglinton baker, represented York Township from 1842 to 1849. He also owned a shop on King Street in Toronto where he specialized in fancy buns and gingerbread men. He bought James Hervey Price's house north of Eglinton following the Rebellion and named it Castlefield. When the new Municipal Act was passed Jackes became the first reeve and was also elected county warden.

THE BALDWIN MUNICIPAL ACT

In 1843 an attempt was made to replace the District Councils Act with another act providing for the incorporation of municipalities. Legislation was delayed by opposition until 1849, when the Municipal Corporations Act was passed and a system of municipalities set up, the basis of our present organization. The new act, put into effect January 1, 1850, abolished the districts, then 20 in number. The unit of organization for both judicial and municipal purposes became the county, and the town meeting was replaced by an elective township council headed by the reeve. York Township became part of the united counties of York, Ontario, and Peel, the successor to the Home District.

John Willson IV of Willowdale, who had been clerk of York Township since 1836, continued as both clerk and treasurer after 1850. Township meetings were held regularly in the three Eglinton hotels[6]: Prospect House, John Miller's Hotel, and the Bedford Park Hotel. A central place was essential because a trip by horse and wagon to Eglinton for meetings and home again usually took an entire day. North York residents predominated as members of Council during the last half of the nineteenth century. William Tyrrell of Weston followed William James of Bathurst Street, and was very prominent in the early period serving on Council from 1851 to 1878 and as a reeve for twelve of those years. In 1879 Henry Duncan, son of William Duncan of Dublin Farm, a hard working conservative and resident of Don Mills became reeve. York Township East was his special interest, but he also had an intimate knowledge of the Township as a whole. He was very popular, wielded a remarkable local influence, and arbitrated disputes about bridges, line fences, sales, neighbourhood and family undertakings, and matters of inheritance. When he retired the first time in 1886, he was presented with a gold watch, and the following citation was made: "The affairs of the Township are now left by you satisfactory to the entire number of rate-payers. The rate of taxation is lower than for years, and the roads, bridges, and walks are in an efficient state."[7]

In 1880 Arthur L. Willson, York Township Clerk and Treasurer since the death of his father in 1866, resigned due to differences of opinion with Reeve Duncan. This led to the separation of the offices of clerk and treasurer, and John Knox Leslie became clerk, and William Jackes, treasurer. During this period three communities left York Township and became incorporated villages: Parkdale in 1878, and Brockton and Weston in 1882.

On Sunday night, November 20, 1881, a disastrous fire broke out in the stables of the Prospect House. The hotel and the adjoining Masonic Hall containing the Township offices were destroyed. The clerk's records, kept in a wooden box, were completely obliterated and consequently much valuable information is not available for research today.

THE RADIAL

The Metropolitan Street Railway Company electric car line was extended from the Canadian Pacific crossing north of Bloor Street to York Mills in 1890.[8] It was continued in 1896 to Richmond Hill and replaced the old stage coach line that had been carrying the mail to and from Toronto. In 1904 the Toronto and York Railway Company took over the line and opened it as far north as Jackson's Point carrying passengers, freight, mail, milk, and newspapers en route. Built like railway coaches, the long black or dark green, double-ended street cars were comfortable, heated electrically, and equipped with a smoking compartment. The track ran along the west side of Yonge Street as far as the top of the hill north of York Mills, where it crossed to the east side. Switches were placed at intervals with sidings to the various industries for unloading freight without interrupting regular service. The drive down into the valley at York Mills was always breathtaking. The driver frequently did not apply the brakes going down, and as the crowded car gained speed on the grade it often rocked and lurched, much to the consternation of the passengers. On October 10, 1948, the street cars were removed from service and a diesel bus line was installed. As North York increased in population all public transportation was taken over by the Toronto Transit Commission.

THE ROADS

In 1896 the County Council transferred the roads to the local municipalities. Some roads deteriorated rapidly and the upkeep and maintenance varied with the prosperity of the township or village through which they passed. In 1903 George S. Henry, of Oriole, a graduate of the Ontario Agricultural College, with a keen appreciation of the farmer's needs, entered York Township Council and remained in public life until he retired as Premier of Ontario in 1934. In 1910, as Reeve of York Township, he proposed that the main roads of the electoral districts of East and West York be formed into a county road system with a uniform standard of construction.

In 1916 a county wide system was ratified by the legislature with the county, city, and province sharing the cost of constructing permanent roads within York County. The name given the representative body was changed from York Highway Commission to Toronto and York Roads Commission, and Edgar A. James, whose grandfather Joseph James owned a saw mill between Bathurst and Dufferin north of Finch, was the first engineer.

NOTES

1 G. W. Spragge, "The Districts of Upper Canada, 1788-1849", *Ontario History*, XXXIX (1947), 91-100.

2 *Ibid.*

3 W. R. Riddell, "The Law of Marriage in Upper Canada", *Canadian Historical Review*, II (1921), 226-248.

4 Ontario, Department of Planning and Development, *Don Valley Conservation Report*, 1950, pp. 97-100.

5 "Minutes of Town Meetings and Lists of Inhabitants of York, 1797-1822", Toronto Public Libraries.

6 J. C. Boylen, *York Township, An Historical Summary* (The Municipal Corporation of the Township of York and The Board of Education of the Township of York, 1954), pp. 7-49.

7 Resolution passed by Council reproduced on a decorated scroll for Henry Duncan when he retired on December 28, 1886.

8 J. F. Due, *Intercity Electric Railway Industry in Canada* (Toronto: University of Toronto, 1966), pp. 82-83.

Township to Borough

NORTH YORK IS A BUSTLING, VITAL, BURGEONING COMMUNITY. VIGOROUS growth in the last twenty years has changed this rural farm land into one of the most advanced municipalities in Canada, but in a very real sense it remains a pioneering community. Since World War I, North York has been the northern frontier for Toronto. It was here that veterans of both wars found inexpensive land for their young families, and immigrants from many different lands and cultures settled. While in 1947 its population was 33,167, by Canada's Centennial year the figure had shot up to 411,517, and it is now Canada's fourth most populous community.

At the end of World War II, North York was still little more than a constellation of tiny settlements separated by miles of farms. By Centennial, however, only a handful of farms remained. In their place one now finds vast residential tracts, a wide variety of industries, office buildings, many of striking architectural design, high-rise apartment buildings, shopping plazas, and numerous churches and synagogues. Yorkdale, a forty million dollar enclosed shopping mall, is so unique that Walt Disney included it in his Bell Telephone Expo film of Canada. Of the hundreds of high-rise apartment buildings springing up, Flemingdon Park apartment city contains the highest, two twenty-eight-storey towers. Higher buildings are on the drawing boards, including one of thirty-four storeys in another apartment city near Yonge Street and Steeles Avenue. The kind of foresight and strategic planning exemplified by the development of Don Mills has won the respect of town planners and builders the world over. York University, Seneca Community College, and a tri-level school system, noted for its experimentation, illustrates how North York's educational system has kept pace with its vast expansion.

Of course, getting to this point has not been easy. North York would never have been born as a self-governing municipality if a group of dissatisfied farmers had not managed to secede from York Township. In the Great Depression of the 1930's, North Yorkers suffered from hunger and other inconveniences, the same as their early forebears. After World War II, water became so scarce that stories spread of babies being bathed in ginger ale, and traffic jams were gigantic, as thousands of new residents, living in "strawberry box" houses, filled roads originally built for horses and buggies.

A New Municipality

Prior to 1922, York Township included what are now the boroughs of North York, York and East York, plus Forest Hill and Swansea. In the years following the turn of the century both York and East York had grown as lunch-pail suburbs, areas close enough to street car lines for men to commute to Toronto factories. With the return of the veterans from World War I, the house building boom was accelerated in these areas.

What is now North York was still a community of farms, not growing much in population. Every year the balance between the new urban dwellers and the old farmers shifted more in favour of the newcomers. By 1915 Reeve Thomas Griffith, who farmed near Downsview, was the only member of council to come from North York. By 1919, all members of the five-man council were from the urban parts. Some 75,000 were city dwellers compared to 6,000 on the farms. The farmers were paying almost twenty-three percent of the taxes, but the council's interest was in urban problems, such as streets, lighting and sidewalks, and the farmers' demands for gravelled roads and other repairs were mostly ignored.

Roy Risebrough, who still lives in the old farmhouse on Cummer Avenue next to the St. John's Convalescent Hospital, was then a young fellow in his late twenties. He was brought into the leadership of the farmers' cause because he had a Model T Ford and could drive, something none of the other leaders could do. He drove them from farm to farm as they collected names on petitions of protest, and cash to hire a lawyer after their candidate W. J. Buchanan, a farmer from Finch Avenue, west of Dufferin Street, was defeated in the election of 1920. The next year Buchanan, Risebrough, and three other farmers, James Muirhead, John Brummel and W. C. Snider, brought in a petition asking for secession. A private member's bill was organized. The only hold-up was a delay of one year, until 1922, to readjust the York-North York border so that more farmers could be included. The private bill ordered York to conduct a plebiscite in the area requesting secession, with the result that North York became a separate municipality on June 13, 1922. On August 12, R. F. Hicks, a Bathurst Street farmer, was elected its first reeve.

North York had three settlements of commuters when it became independent. Two were small pockets north of Weston, one of which was called "Little Europe" by the predominantly Anglo-Saxon farmers. The third and largest community was along Yonge Street, which was actually a series of villages, each with its own distinct pride and its own baseball team. Between York Mills, Lansing, Kingsdale, Willowdale, Northmount, Newtonbrook and the Steele's corner were narrow farms whose houses fronted on the street. The older villages fanned out around a group of stores as they had in pioneer times, but the stores now opened at 6:30 A.M. for the commuters. Men dropped in orders on their way to catch the radial to work, then picked them up at night when they returned. Farmers came into stores such as Dempsey's at Lansing, and Stevenson's at Willowdale, to barter eggs and butter for other groceries. Wages were low. A farm hand could be hired for twenty-five dollars a month in the summer or fifteen dollars in the winter.

In addition to the radial, the communities were linked by board sidewalks, and a two-lane crushed stone road. Piles of big stones were stacked at regular intervals along the edge of the road where hired men could easily reach and break them up for the highway. Other roads were either dirt or gravel. Farmers, still doing statute labour, had to make themselves and their wagons available for the municipality three days a year to haul gravel for the roads.

Council meetings were held in the Brown (Willowdale) School and later in the old bar room of the former Golden Lion Hotel at Yonge and Sheppard Avenue, until an office was set up in two apartments above a block of three stores on the east side of Yonge in Lansing. This building was destroyed by fire in February 1923[1]; and most of the Township records were destroyed. The newly formed Suburban-Yonge Businessmen's Association had just started to investigate the possibility of organizing a volunteer fire brigade. Lansing had neither trained men nor equipment when the fire broke out about 8:30 A.M. One of the first businessmen to reach the scene was Bill Dempsey, new owner of the Dempsey General Store, who ran across Yonge Street carrying a shovel and began shovelling snow into the blazing basement. The fire spread to the first and second floors and gutted the building despite all efforts. Dr. Carl Hill, who had settled in Lansing in 1921, owned a house and office, three houses to the north. Next to the burning building stood a shingled house, and Dr. Hill was convinced that if it caught fire, the blaze would sweep on to his house. Blankets were thrown over the shingles and neighbours with a bucket brigade threw pails of water over them to keep them wet. Dr. Hill recalled pumping a well dry to supply the water, and because he was not hopeful for success, he had his bride remove most of their wedding presents from their house. But, the fire was contained in one building.

Plans were immediately drawn up for the construction of a municipal office building. A site was purchased at the corner of Yonge and Empress Avenue. The $35,000 building, which still stands today and now houses the Emergency Measures Organization, was opened on December 19, 1923. The council chamber on the second floor also served as a community hall and was rented to local organizations such as the Orange Lodge, the Horticultural Society which was established in 1924, and the Canadian Legion B.E.S.L. organized in 1926. Today it is a courtroom for the trying of municipal offenses such as the breaking of construction safety laws.

Murray Brown, who designed the building, also designed a seal and crest for the corporation. The words "Progress with Economy" surround an ornamental shield on which are emblazoned the Canadian beaver, a full sheaf of wheat and the scales of justice. It was meant to symbolize a community of industrious people living in prosperity from the fertile land and dispensing justice and square dealing.

The New Pioneers

Veterans from Vimy Ridge, Ypres and the Somme were heading up Yonge Street in the early 1920's to attack the meadows, trees, clay, marsh and swamp with frontier ferocity. These vets were staking claim to land they had just defended. North York could not afford to put in roads. The new land owners did that themselves, then they covered them with cinders and ashes that the Township provided. Streets built in this manner, such as Byng and Hillcrest, are still in existence and remain basically a patch-over job of tar on top of the cinders. The same weed-filled ditches carry off the storm water. Other veterans established themselves on farmland along Avenue Road, Bathurst, and up the Humber River north of Weston. But primarily North York remained a farm community, run by farmers.

Shortly after the new municipality was formed, Roy Risebrough, the youngest of the five who petitioned for secession, became its chief constable and one-man police force, and stayed in office until one month before the police force was amalgamated as part of the Metropolitan Toronto Police in 1957 (see Appendix). Reeves and other politicians came and went, but Chief Risebrough, who only twice wore a police uniform, was an important advisor to every one until the new breed of young politicians arrived following World War II. As a knowledgeable and respected member of the community, his recommendation was important to the election of candidates, at a time when municipal employees did not hesitate to take part in civic politics. As a police officer, he was dealing mainly with families that he knew well. A boy who had gotten into trouble was treated to a friendly chat that contained a warning, and several times each year he was called upon to settle arguments between neighbours. Chief Risebrough recalls the occasional house burglary near the city, a steady flow of raids on farms by chicken thieves, and a much smaller series of raids by cattle rustlers. As there were no cars, people didn't travel much outside their area, which made it easier to control law and order. If there was not much crime for the chief to fight in the 1920's, that picture changed by the 1950's when suburban banks were favoured by robbers. His police officers captured the famed Boyd gang in a Don Valley barn after they had broken out of the Don jail for the second time.

W. J. Nelson was chosen as North York's first fire chief in 1923 because he operated the Pioneer Garage, located where the Willowdale Volkswagen now stands. This made it possible for the Township's one fire truck to have a garage and be under the control of a proven mechanic who had had as much fire-fighting experience as the volunteer business-men, his neighbours. The original volunteer brigade had one Model T Ford fire truck in Lansing and four hand reels, one in each of four sub-fire stations located in the urban areas (see Appendix). In spring, the roads were flooded and the fire truck answering a call east or west of Yonge often could not get there. Most barn fires were impossible to fight because of a water shortage, so the firemen just sat and watched them burn. Fre-quently, in an attempt to reinforce the firemen, somebody would hitch a hand reel onto the back of a Model T and go speeding over the dirt or gravel roads. Hand reels were not built to be pulled this way and the wheels would fall off. Passersby would find firemen frantically unravelling hose from the collapsed rig and loading it into the back seat of the car. In the mid-1930's Chief Nelson's volunteers were paid $1.50 a call for every fire, and by 1942 the fire department became a fulltime professional operation.

THE MARKET

York outdoor market opened with twenty-eight producers on June 19, 1926. It was located at the present bus terminal at the city limits on Yonge Street. Each Saturday crowds of workmen, farmers, storekeepers, men, women and children thronged the market, laughed and joked with their friends, caught up on the gossip, and enjoyed the noise and bustle as about eighty farmers sold their products. Mingling with the laughter and voices of the buyers could be heard the quacking of ducks, the cluck-ing of hens, and even the meowing of kittens as one farmerette offered pure bred Persian kittens for two dollars each. Fruits, vegetables, seasonal flowers, butter, eggs, maple sugar and syrup, sausage, bacon and other cuts of meat were all for sale. Housewives sold home baked cakes, pies, bread, preserves and pickles. Other wives offered needlework, aprons, braided and hooked rugs, and patchwork quilts. In 1931, under W. G. Scrace, as superintendent, the market moved into the old car barns, now used as a garage and car lot, just to the north of the bus terminal area, and remained there until 1952 when it was sold by the municipality because the stalls were not used by the farmers, but by merchants. The farmers moved to Finch and Yonge for a short time, and then in 1953, under the name of York Farmers Marketing Limited, they moved into the new Thornhill market on Yonge Street.

THE ENTERPRISE

On November 11, 1926, Robert Rankin, a North York printer, and T. Austin Osborne, a linotype operator, founded *The Enterprise*, a four-sheet weekly newspaper printed in Lansing to serve the Yonge Street corridor. In 1928, Rankin bought out Osborne who, however, continued to work with the paper until 1960. In the midst of the Depression, in 1936, Rankin acquired another partner, William A. Stowe, who had been doing finer type printing for *The Enterprise*. In 1938, Rankin sold his half of the weekly to the Dempsey Brothers, owners of the general store. At this time, the weekly circulation had reach almost 900, although about half the copies had to be given away in order to maintain the advertising. Bertram Long, now publications officer for the North York Board of Education, was managing editor for the next twenty-two years. In 1941, the Dempseys took over the paper completely, and in 1948, one of the brothers, William A. Dempsey, became sole proprietor. His son, Douglas, has been the editor since 1959, and the circulation now is about 15,000. Other weeklies were established in the Township during its rapid expansion period: the *Mirror*, formerly the *Don Mills Mirror* and *York Mills Mirror*, opened in Don Mills in 1957 to provide service to the eastern section of the Township; the *News* established in 1959 covers Downsview and Weston; and the *Yorkdale News*, which began in 1964, covers the Bathurst-Dufferin area.

SCHOOL SYSTEM

The early school systems continued unchanged in the 1920's, after North York's secession. Each school had its own board. However, as time went on the Provincial Government began encouraging newly built-up areas to form unified school systems. North York was the first to respond.

By 1928 the Yonge Street area was a fairly continuous community even though narrow farms still had frontage on it. Three school areas—York Mills, Willowdale and Newtonbrook—with a total of five schools were united into the first Township School Area (see Appendix). In the same year, North York's first high school board was established. Before that pupils attended classes in other municipalities such as Weston, Richmond Hill, and Toronto. The Lansing-Willowdale Arena, located on Burnett Avenue behind the present Municipal Offices, was used for classes the first year. During the next two years they were held in the old Brown School, the two-storey elementary school building that served the Willow-dale-Lansing area before Queen Mary (now McKee Avenue) and Duke of Kent (now Spring Garden) Schools were built. Earl Haig, North York's first secondary school built for that purpose, was opened in the fall of 1930. It served more than 300 pupils from not only the Willowdale area but also from Armour Heights, the farms east of Downsview Airport, Thornhill, and as far east as the Scarborough border. High school students from other parts of the Township continued to attend schools in other municipalities. Since this early period, North York education has become the third largest educational system in Canada (see Appendix).

FLYING

Little airfields, some just a farmer's open field, sprang up in North York following World War I. The field which had been used by the air force during the war continued to operate at the end of Avenue Road, where Highway 401 passes it today. On September 23, 1926, the Richmond Hill *Liberal* reported that there had been complaints to North York Council about Sunday flying from this field. Huge crowds watched the planes, and it was argued that this was not a proper Sunday pastime.

In 1925 Barker Field, named after Colonel W. G. Barker, V.C. of the First World War, was opened on the west side of Dufferin, north of Lawrence Avenue. During the Depression this field fell behind in taxes and barely managed to stay ahead of being seized. It was used until 1953 when the property was sold for housing. Yonge Street was a favorite for fliers because the fields were next to a well-travelled highway, which provided good publicity for pilots hiring out their planes. One little field was located where the Memorial Community Hall now stands, south of the Public Library. A couple of pilots set up another field on George B. Elliott's farm on the east side of Yonge north of Finch beside the Algonquin Tavern, in 1928. They gave flying lessons, as well as observation trips for five dollars. Whenever an accident occurred Dr. Carl Hill, who had been appointed the Township Medical Health Officer, was called to the scene to look after the unfortunate aviator and his passenger.

Top of the Don Valley; intersection of the Don Valley Parkway and York Mills Road, Highway 401 in the background.

Don Mills; intersection of the Don Valley Parkway and Eglinton Avenue.

*Hogg's Hollow today; a section of Yonge Street, with the Jolly Miller
Tavern at the left, and 4000 Yonge Street at the right.*

Inn on the Park.

Yorkdale shopping mall.

SAVAGE

Yorkdale shopping mall.

SAVAGE

Civic Garden Centre.

RAYMOND MORIYAMA

Japanese Canadian Cultural Centre.

RAYMOND MORIYAMA

The biggest and best known field developed around the De Havilland Aircraft of Canada plant which opened in 1928 between Dufferin and Keele, near Sheppard Avenue. After war was declared, the Federal government requested that Sheppard Avenue be completely closed between Dufferin and Keele so that land could be leased to De Havilland to extend their facilities. In May, 1953, the R.C.A.F. opened a supply depot at the field (now Downsview Airport) which housed the storage and repair facilities for all of Eastern Canada. Runways were lengthened to accommodate all types and sizes of aircraft and De Havilland Aircraft of Canada moved into a new building south of its earlier site. About three months after this reorganization, the Township began to receive many complaints from residents living adjacent to the field, and the question of closing it has been prominent ever since.

PLOWING MATCHES

The first Provincial Plowing Match was held in 1913 at Sunnybrook Farm, the present hospital site, owned by Joseph Kilgour. One tractor and twenty-seven teams of horses competed. Interest in the event increased and the annual competition moved to other farms with large acreage. By 1926, the fame of the contest had spread so that American plowers entered and the name was changed to the International Plowing Match and Farm Machinery Demonstration. In 1934 the match returned again to North York. This time the site was Maryvale Farm owned by Frank P. O'Connor (later Senator O'Connor), about a quarter of a mile north of Lawrence, on the west side of Victoria Park. O'Connor founded the Laura Secord Candy Shops in 1913 and the Fanny Farmer Candy Shops in the United States, and O'Connor Drive was named for the family.

In 1928 the Kilgour estate deeded Sunnybrook Farm to the City of Toronto as a park which officially opened in September of that year. Covering 380 acres of fields, woods, and ravine, it was a favourite picnic ground for families, and a camp ground for many Boy Scout troops. Purchased by the Department of Veterans' Affairs at a cost of fourteen million dollars, Sunnybrook Veterans' Hospital opened on September 26, 1946, and continued to serve the armed forces of Canada until 1966 when it was opened to the public.

THE DEPRESSION

The Great Depression, following the stock market crash of 1929, hit North Yorkers brutally. Estimates of the number of wage earners unemployed in the municipality ranged from one third to more than forty percent. The word welfare had not been invented as a term for paying the unemployed; men were on relief, or more scornfully, "on the pogey." The number of unemployed was exceptionally high because Toronto firms paying Toronto taxes fired suburban workers first to save on city relief payments; and people who lost their homes in Toronto often moved north because land was cheap and sometimes even available for squatting. Many, particularly in the west end, put up shacks or dug basements and covered them over. North York had almost no industries, which meant their tax base was shaky. Homeowners on the pogey stopped paying taxes, so did land speculators who during the good times had picked up and subdivided hundreds of lots in Willowdale and Armour Heights. Most of those employed had their pay cut. Farmers were having difficulty selling their products and had little money for taxes. Only thirty-three to thirty-five percent of the taxes were collected in the worst years.

To collect relief the unemployed had to walk to an office on the east side of Yonge and line up. Many who had never before been out of work found this degrading, as passersby, including passengers on the radial cars, could see them. Ben Ross, the relief officer, with the aid of the Canadian Red Cross, the Salvation Army, the Canadian Legion, and the churches set up depots to hand out all varieties of new and used clothing. For every dollar spent by the Township on such items, the sum of three dollars was received from the Ontario Department of Welfare. Unemployed married men with wives and a couple of children were given fourteen dollars a week, with extra for fuel depending on how many stoves there were in each household. In 1931 *The Enterprise* published a list of suggested foods that a family with four children could obtain for their weekly food coupons—worth $6.33. It pointed out they could buy twelve quarts of milk for $1.20, four pounds of oatmeal or corn meal for twelve cents, and fourteen loaves of bread for eighty-four cents.

Every council meeting attracted a seething mass of bitterly discontented men who had given up hope of finding work. Tempers flared. But real violence was avoided, probably because in 1931 so many in a community of 11,006, including women and children, knew each other. The unemployed were bitter and frustrated. They worked off some of their feelings at council meetings with catcalls and jeers, and by stomping down the stairs. After a particularly frustrating meeting they would crowd around the stairs and threaten to prevent the councillors from leaving. Council, on the other hand, cut the pay of their civil servants in 1931 by fifteen percent, and their own salaries from $8.00 per meeting to $6.50. Members recall that it was not profitable for most of them to attend a council meeting because they usually handed out something to old friends down on their luck.

Dr. Hill suggested that it was very demoralizing for these men to sit around their houses day after day without hope or activity, and requested Council to insist that they work for their relief money. Shovels and rakes were provided for the men to clean out the ditches along the streets. This was so successful that it was decided each man should dig a certain number of feet each day on the watermains, an effort which resulted in the development of the waterworks department. Each man had so many feet to dig in a week to be eligible for his pogey. Farm boys and labourers did their allotment in an hour or two. Unemployed office workers and elderly men were facing a job that they did not have the muscles to cope with; but Chief Risebrough recalls that the stronger almost always pitched in to help their neighbours. Unfortunately this work programme was all but dropped early in the 1930's because it was driving the Township toward bankruptcy. It cost the taxpayers more than straight relief because pipe and other supplies had to be bought.

These were critical years for the Township Treasurer, Frank H. Brown, who succeeded J. A. Bathgate in 1931 and held the position until his recent retirement on December 31, 1967. In October 1933, North York reached the point where they had to default both principle and interest payments to their bond holders. Until then they had managed to pay them by borrowing from the bank, but this source of credit was cut off. Other municipalities throughout Ontario were having the identical problem, and the Ontario Government for the first time set up a Department of Municipal Affairs to help them. On February 1, 1935, North York and all the municipalities in the metropolitan area, except Toronto, Forest Hill Village, and Swansea, were placed under the supervision of the Government. This meant that all North York expenditures needed Provincial approval, and it protected the Township from bond holders launching court actions to force repayment. It also meant that politicians could not be persuaded to spend money for political reasons. Reeve R. Earl Bales[2] and his council worked unceasingly to give assistance to the needy and endeavoured to lift the district out of its financial difficulties. In December, 1937, they paid off the full contractual amounts of the bonds plus the accrued interest by floating a new issue which was taken by the bond holders. On July 25, 1941, almost two years after the Depression, North York was released from supervision. It was one of the few municipalities in Ontario that paid all its debts, including accrued interest.

THE BOOM STARTS

George Mitchell was the reeve when prosperity returned and the land boom started. During the Depression North York did not seize either homes or farms for non-payment of taxes, although they sometimes pressured mortgage companies to pay up and add the amounts to the home mortgages. What they did seize were hundreds and hundreds of lots held by land speculators. Some had been subdivided before and after World War I, but they were never built upon because of the Depression Years. Reeve Mitchell saved a few to be kept as playgrounds. One of these, Mitchell Field, bears his name, but he was able to sell most of them to new speculators. The price started at $2.00 a foot, which meant that fifty-foot lots in Willowdale and Armour Heights sold for $100. If the same lots were vacant today, they would be worth $17,500 to $20,000 according to real estate evaluators. The demand for lots was strong, so Mitchell slowly but steadily raised the price, and within less than two years the price was raised to $8.00 a foot. The first to start speculating were people familiar with buying a product, such as poultry, drygoods or junk, for a low price and selling for a small profit; a few, such as poultryman Harry Ungerman and dress-seller Jake Mandell, grew with the industry and now are major developers.

With little house building during the fifteen year period of depression and war, few builders knew what they were doing. They started with simple and identical "strawberry boxes." Some had Federal Government aid because they were for veterans who could get Government loans at low interest rates to establish small farms. The biggest of these Veterans' Villages in North York was just east of Weston. It was a time when few would say "no" to a veteran, so many bought land and started to build their own houses. They dug basements, covered them over, then paused to regroup their finances, and as the idea became known, others followed suit. They were somewhat derisively called "cave dwellers". Slowly, these houses have been finished, sometimes after a nudge from the municipal authorities, but for a number of years "cave dwellers" walked daily to a pump near the centre of the community for water.

With the population more than doubling within ten years, and the new real estate developments very patchy, a number of small communities were created in various parts of the Township. Ratepayers' Associations were soon formed in each district to take up the cry for water, the spraying of mosquitoes, roads, and better bus service. In order to consolidate their efforts a Central Community Council was established on September 7, 1945, to coordinate all district organizations interested in promoting social, cultural, recreational, and educational activities in the Township. Up to this time communities had no shopping facilities, bus service was infrequent, and there were no entertainment or recreational facilities. People borrowed from their neighbours, and there was much visiting back and forth. Representatives from each Ratepayers' Association took their local problems or suggestions to the Community Council, which acted as the liaison in bringing the matter before Council. A Southern Community

Council, formed later in the south-west section of the Township near Weston, eventually joined the earlier body which changed its name to North York Community Council.

Most roads to the city were still only two lanes wide. One of the few exceptions was Yonge Street, and the two-lane bridge on it was an effective bottleneck. Side streets were often covered with cinders, but by 1947 builders had to provide gravel roads in new subdivisions. The Yonge Street hills on each side of York Mills were very slippery in winter. This difficulty was overcome in 1929 when the first Hoggs Hollow Bridge[3] over the Don River Valley was completed in only nine months, and Yonge Street joined Yonge Boulevard on the west end, providing a road around the valley. The Bayview Avenue bridge north of Lawrence, similar in construction but smaller, also opened in the same year to relieve north-south traffic.

There were still no arterial roadways developed to facilitate inter-municipal transportation, and with the increasing automobile traffic this became a necessity. In 1951 the Barrie Highway (later 400) was finished. In the following year a section of Highway 401 (now the Macdonald-Cartier Freeway) was ready for use west of Yonge, but it was not completed east of Bayview until 1959. Finally in 1956 the widening of Yonge Street was completed, providing one good road south for commuters. It was not until 1963, however, that the mammoth road building programme began to relieve many congested areas: Sheppard Avenue was widened for the second time and its new high bridge over the valley west of Yonge was completed; a section of the Don Valley Expressway was opened; and a multi-million dollar project was started to provide for twelve lanes of traffic on Highway 401, six in the centre for through traffic and three on each side for service traffic. Within the past few years major road construction has been completed on all north-south, east-west concession roads, and in addition, in 1965, a section of the Spadina Expressway was opened between Lawrence and 401.

RECREATION

The Lions Club was formed in 1945, followed by the North York Kiwanis in 1951, and the Rotary in 1952. Since this period many branches of all service clubs have been established, and each has contributed much to the community, particularly in the field of recreation. Under the Planning Act of 1946, approved by the Ontario Legislature, municipalities were given power to require a subdivider to deed five percent of his land holdings for municipal purposes which has been generally interpreted for parks and playgrounds use. The first summer playgrounds opened in 1946 through the efforts of Rev. A. W. Jones, youth activities convener of the

North York Central Community Council, and in the years following various service clubs took responsibility for individual parks. Countless hours, money and effort went into providing play areas, benches, ball parks, bleachers, field houses and rinks for the youngsters of North York.

In 1950 a Recreation Commission was established and Harry W. Moreland became the first director with a budget of $5,500. In 1954 operations were expanded and John Hannant became Director of Recreation and H. W. Moreland, Director of Parks with a combined budget of $37,000. Finally in 1957 steps were taken to merge Parks and Recreation activities under D. W. Snow, Commissioner, and since then parks, arenas, rinks, community centres, swimming pools, tennis courts, and summer playground programmes were developed extensively throughout the Township.

The Edwards Gardens, situated on the south-west corner of Lawrence Avenue and Leslie Street in Don Mills, is perhaps the most highly developed park in North York. In 1944 R. E. Edwards purchased the original site of the first Alexander Milne woollen mill. Realizing the potential beauty of the property, he erected a five-hundred-foot rockery, dammed the creek to provide an adequate water supply, and installed a large steel water wheel to pump the water to various points throughout the grounds. Later another dam was built to increase the water reserve. In 1955 the twenty-seven acre property was sold to Metropolitan Toronto as a park which opened to the public in June, 1956. Gardens which change with the season and walks have been greatly enlarged to join Wilket Creek Park to the south, and a large parking area is provided behind Raymond Moriyama's beautifully designed Garden Centre building.

In 1964 North York claimed international fame when E. P. Taylor's beautiful thoroughbred, Northern Dancer, won the Kentucky Derby, two weeks later the Preakness Stakes at Baltimore, and upon returning home, the Queen's Plate at Woodbine Race Track. Winfield Farms, the Taylor estate, contains 350 acres of rolling fields situated on both sides of York Mills Road between Bayview and Leslie. It provides a luxurious landscape with its distinctive looking stables, practice track, numerous paddocks and fields where thoroughbred race horses and Black Angus cattle graze in a lovely country atmosphere. Part of the farm was sold recently to a sub-divider who plans to develop the area over a four-year period.

BILL 80

Frederick J. McMahon, who had moved to North York in 1950, became reeve during a period of major significance. With the inception of Bill 80, which provided for the formation of Metropolitan Toronto in 1954, the Township began planning vigorously for the future. The most significant acquisitions received from each area municipality were: the issuing of debentures; the assessment of properties, provision for the production, treatment and storage of water; control of all sewage treatment plants; upkeep of certain main arterial highways; and the Toronto Transit Commission. On January 1, 1957, all thirteen police forces were combined into one metropolitan force. Two important educational boards (see Appendix) were set up following the establishment of Metropolitan Toronto. Under the new act the first amalgamated Board of Education in the Township was elected in 1954, and S. J. Kelner, a young lawyer, was the first chairman. The following year a Public Library Board was appointed with Richard Stanbury (later Senator Stanbury) as its first chairman. Over a ten-year period North York's population had increased by 105,666, and as a result, a change was required in the number of councillors to provide better representation: five councillors, one from ward one, and two each from wards two and three were elected instead of one councillor as previously.

1953 marked the beginning of apartment buildings. They were not high rise, but low apartments which had been almost completely absent from the area previously; 245 apartments were built in comparison to twenty-two the year before. In addition, the first shopping centre in the Toronto suburbs opened at Lawrence Plaza, on the corner of Lawrence and Bathurst, on October 29th. Previously citizens had to go to the corner store or downtown Toronto for all shopping. This was a completely new concept. People were introduced to one-stop shopping with free parking for over 2,000 cars in a floodlit area open for night shopping. The Plaza included a Loblaws Food Store, two restaurants, two banks and thirty-one retail stores. In August, 1955, another first was added: Henry Morgan & Co., a Montreal firm later bought out by the Hudson's Bay Company, opened the first suburban department store in the Plaza. Here was shopping deluxe, and this was the beginning of a turn of the tide from downtown to suburb shopping.

Later, a broader concept of the shopping centre was introduced when Yorkdale opened in 1964 (see also Downsview). The Spadina Expressway with its rapid transit from downtown Toronto meets Highway 401 east of Dufferin Street, and it was at this location that Eaton's real estate department bought land in the early 1950's for a major suburban store. In 1960 they got together with Simpson's and decided to develop it jointly. New York developer, William Zeckendorf of Place Ville Marie fame, joined them. Yorkdale was the result, attracting shoppers and tourists from all over southern Ontario and northern New York. One of the secrets of Yorkdale's appeal is that it offers variety—from the biggest department stores to a tiny kiosk selling art objects from India. With its

120 stores, it has made the old style shopping centres obsolete in proving the charm and efficiency of enclosed malls. It has attracted architects, planners and businessmen from the far corners of the world, including New Zealand and the Union of South Africa.

THE WATER CRISIS

It was during the McMahon years that stories spread of babies being bathed in ginger ale for lack of water. Summer after summer for nine years hoses dried up, and the grass and flowers burned. Families in North York visited friends in Toronto or Scarborough in order to take a bath. Many mornings they were able to make coffee only by coaxing a few cups of water from the hot water tank. The problem was that North York had no major source of water. Wells were drilled wherever there was any prospect, but usually water had to be bought from municipalities that had access to Lake Ontario. Scarborough was paying for much of its development by charging high rates.[4] North York grew more slowly than Scarborough and Etobicoke because of the water shortage (see Appendix). Sewage was another problem. Thousands of septic tanks still exist, a holdover from those early days, and according to medical advice the clay soil is not really suitable for them.

Vernon Singer, who followed McMahon as reeve, was elected with the promise to end the chronic, recurrent water shortage. At this time Metro was three years old, and North York hoses were still drying up with each hot spell. Every year Metro civil servants promised that some watermain would do the job—but each year they failed. Largely due to Singer's determination and persistence, after 1958 there was no shortage.

THE PUBLIC LIBRARY

During the 1920's and 30's North York Council gave a small grant to Don Mills to set up a little library (see Don Mills). But North Yorkers until well into the 1950's depended on the Toronto Public Libraries for books. Mrs. Gladys Allison, who still lives on Hounslow Avenue in Willowdale, helped stimulate an interest in the need for libraries while she was a member of the Queen Mary Home and School Association. Her first attempt to organize bookmobile service was dropped during the war years because of gasoline rationing. The Ontario Government operated a travelling library service in which boxes of books were loaned to outlying municipalities for a few months and then exchanged for other titles. In 1945 Mrs. Allison arranged for travelling library books to be loaned from the Willowdale United Church two evenings a week. At the same time she was the main pusher for the building of the Memorial Community Hall on Yonge Street in memory of the Township men who served in World War II. When the building opened in 1950, one room was set aside for a library. A theatre night was held to raise money and publicize the need for donations of books, and when Eaton's closed their lending library, Gladys Allison arranged for North York to buy the books for fifty cents a piece. In 1953, she headed a Library Planning Commission, and out of their recommendations came the purchase of a bookmobile, the buying of a school portable for a children's library and the appointment of a Library Board. North York's first permanent library building opened in 1959 and was named the Gladys Allison Building (see Appendix), and Mrs. Allison, who was named woman of the week in 1953 by Bob Hope on his radio programme, "Hope for the Ladies", was an active Library Board member from its formation in 1955 until 1966.

DON MILLS

It is hard to believe, but Don Mills was something to scoff at when it was first conceived. Everyone on North York Council was opposed, with the exception of Reeve McMahon. Mortgage money was difficult to get because the lending companies could not visualize it. The heads of industries objected to controls that prevented outside storage, undue noise, and unsightly signs, and that insisted on large parking lots, on the kinds of materials to be used in construction, and on architecture. The first plants to come in were Barber-Greene Canada Limited and Philco. Years later, when a new industrial subdivision was being planned to the north of Don Mills, the same industrialists who had complained about the restrictions were so won over that they petitioned North York to impose them on their neighbours. House buyers, used to the old style boxes, were reluctant to accept the more imaginative architecture of Don Mills. However, once it was accepted, this type of house was immediately built in other subdivisions.

At the end of World War II, O'Keefe Breweries obtained land near the corner of Don Mills Road and Lawrence Avenue to build a brewery. Eventually it was decided not to go ahead with it and E. P. Taylor, president of the brewery, urged them to buy more land and develop a new community. At first it was called Yorktown, then Don Mills. It was built as an almost self-contained district, bringing together new industries, housing (selling from $12,000 to $50,000), and apartments into a balanced region. It pioneered new concepts in row housing at a time when municipalities were banning it because of the poorly designed row housing in Toronto. Don Mills won a multitude of awards including three Massey Silver Medals for design, one for row housing, a second for industrial design, and the third for its shopping centre. In addition, Don Mills captured five national and eighteen regional Canadian Housing and Design Council awards. The community was completed in 1960, and there are more than 27,000 people living in the area, seventy industrial plants and nine churches. There were no high-rise apartments because at that time North York by-laws limited the height of buildings in the Township to thirty-five feet. Getting rid of this law was one of the final contributions of McMahon before he retired in 1956. The restriction was lifted in 1957.

CULTURAL INFLUX

Thousands of new Canadians moved into North York following World War II. The ethnic groups in the 1961 census listed the British as the largest group followed by Italians, Germans, Poles, French, Dutch and Belgians, Russians, Ukrainians, Scandinavians, Asians, and other Europeans. Since then their number has increased steadily. Besides those moving into the area from abroad, many families, uprooted from Toronto due to the construction of the east-west subway, moved into the suburbs. Opened in Don Mills in 1963 by one of the smallest minority groups, the Japanese Canadian Cultural Centre has successfully introduced its culture to the citizens of Metropolitan Toronto. Other new Canadians, each in his own manner, have helped to create a better understanding of human relationships in the expanding Township.

Before this period of rapid expansion North York had been a community of Methodists, almost entirely. With the immigration influx, the religious face of the area became more diversified. Beginning in 1942, when St. Edward's Roman Catholic Church became a parish, numerous churches of all denominations and synagogues mushroomed throughout the Township. Separate schools, a Jesuit seminary, a Dutch Reformed School, Jewish schools and a rabbinical college as well as buildings for youth organizations have been established. Baycrest Home and Hospital for the Aged, opened in 1954, is reputed to be the finest of its kind in Canada, and Comfort Lodge, a Christian Science retirement home completed in 1968, has a most attractive setting.

INCREASED OPPORTUNITIES

Doors began to open slowly to provide increased opportunities for North Yorkers. The Don Valley and Humber Valley Conservation Authorities had been publicizing the importance of conservation in their reports, but it took Hurricane Hazel to speed up the formation of a fairly effective Metropolitan Toronto Conservation Authority. The Humber Valley Conservation Authority acquired fourteen acres of land on the north-west corner of Steeles Avenue and Jane Street in Vaughan Township in 1954, and the Dalziel Pennsylvania German bank barn built in 1809 was opened as a museum. Lots were also expropriated along the Humber and Don rivers where houses had been washed away, and laws were passed to prohibit building in the flats as much as possible. In 1957 the Authorities of the Humber Valley, Don Valley, Etobicoke-Mimico, and R.D.H.P. (Rouge, Duffin, Highland, Petticoat streams) merged to become the Metropolitan Toronto and Regional Conservation Authority. The following year this new Authority acquired the Stong farm on the south-east corner of Steeles and Jane with a nucleus of buildings to provide a village, and on June 1, 1960, Black Creek Pioneer Village opened with seven buildings in addition to the Dalziel Museum. The village has continued to grow each year as other restored buildings have been added, and it now represents a small community developed around a grist mill prior to Confederation. Its extensive teaching programme in connection with the North York schools provides a substantial base for those interested in Ontario and Canada.

Ontario's Centennial Centre of Science and Technology, a thirty million dollar provincial Centennial project, is nearing completion. The site consists of 180 acres of rugged ravine land running south from Eglinton Avenue between Don Mills Road and the west branch of the Don River. More than twenty acres were set aside for three large inter-connected buildings, on three different sites, surrounded by Ernest Thompson Seton Park, named after the famous naturalist-author who enjoyed the area during his boyhood. The buildings of textured cement were designed by architect Raymond Moriyama. The reception building on Don Mills Road will have a 250-foot enclosed bridge to the core building, and the third and largest building, located on the valley floor, will be reached by elevator or a series of escalators. The accent is on the future, and the objective is to stimulate the young people who will study here by demonstrating the extensive possibilities of science and technology.

York University held its first classes in Falconer Hall at the University of Toronto in the fall of 1960 with Dr. Murray G. Ross as President. The following year the faculty moved to Glendon Hall, a former University of Toronto Campus, at Bayview and Lawrence Avenues. Several new buildings were erected, but the student enrolment increased so rapidly that it became necessary to acquire another site. As a result, a new main campus comprising 475 acres of farm land located between Jane and Keele, south of Steeles, was opened in the fall of 1965. Eventually the University will invest a hundred and nine million dollars in buildings on the new site, and construction of a college and residence is scheduled for each year, which is really not fast enough to handle the enrolment. Glendon College is a small undergraduate, residential, co-educational, liberal arts college, oriented towards the development of an interest in and an understanding of public affairs, with special emphasis on skill in the use and appreciation of English and French. York, as a new institution, had an opportunity to open its doors to meet the needs of adults through evening and part-time degree studies. Joseph E. Atkinson College, situated on each campus, was appropriately named in honour of a man whose objective in life was to help individuals and the general public keep abreast with the progress and developments in our changing world.

In September, 1967, Seneca College of Applied Arts and Technology, one of the new Ontario community colleges, was opened in Willowdale. The response was very rewarding: 959 students attended the day classes, and 1,100 enrolled for evening classes. The building was outgrown in less than a year and a new one will be opened in September, 1969, on the north-west corner of Finch and Woodbine. Until it is completed Seneca will remain on Sheppard Avenue with additional temporary quarters on the new site. Students are now provided with post-secondary educational opportunities for high school graduates not bound for university and for adults who wish to continue their education, whether or not they possess formal educational prerequisites, as well as those interested in qualifying to enter regular college programmes.

In Retrospect . . .

The forty-five years in which North York existed as a township show spectacular development, in radical contrast to the slowly evolving towns and villages which preceded it. Following World War I, North York entered a truly dynamic phase in its history. The enormous problems stemming, primarily, from the massive influx of new families put grave responsibilities on the shoulders of public officials. Crises, as well as resultant pressures from those who made their homes here, gave rise to an awareness of the need for sound planning in the development of the community. A slower evolution toward urbanity might well have caused the kind of laxity or complacency, both on the part of municipal leaders and North Yorkers generally, which would have allowed errors of judgment or in policy to mushroom into impossible snarls.

Each administration during this period attempted to cope with the forces of change, and each made contributions the results of which can be seen today. During the early years, R. F. Hicks, W. W. Anderson, and James Muirhead assisted in the formation of policy, the building of a municipal office, and the acceptance of a seal for the corporation. Secession from York and establishing a new township reflected their "pioneer" spirit, at the same time the rural school boards had the foresight to establish the first Township School Area in Ontario.

George B. Elliott struggled through the early years of the Depression, knowing there was precious little that could be done for those in need, in view of the international scope of the crisis.

R. Earl Bales led the Township out of its financial difficulties into the beginning of the boom period of the war years, and George H. Mitchell's council introduced the idea of a planning board and the development of an official plan and zoning by-law. Albert Standing was also appointed clerk-administrator.[5] Nelson Boylen was forced to cope with a staggering population increase[6] of 34,071 in a three-year period. Crowded schools, septic tanks, and a water shortage became serious problems. At the same time the Ontario Municipal Board held public hearings on amalgamation, resulting in the Cumming Report.

Fred J. McMahon put council meetings on a more businesslike basis, setting up committees to discuss items, in place of the less formal methods used previously. Bill 80 was his greatest concern. The formation of a central Board of Education and a Public Library Board, as well as the opening of Don Mills, all took place under his guidance.

Vernon Singer followed demanding a high-level performance from his civil servants. Thanks largely to him, new people moving into the Township, unaware of the early shortages, did not have to worry about using plenty of water to keep their new shrubs, trees and lawns alive. Crosswalks were introduced in 1958.

When Norman C. Goodhead became reeve his policy of planned progressive development kept him in office for six years. During this period the population increased by 131,347 and again the municipal services were pushed to capacity. It was in Goodhead's administration that the subdivision builders were forced to agree to pay for all municipal services except school sites. These regulations have been a model for North York ever since, as well as being copied by other municipalities throughout Canada.

Three World War II memorials have been erected on Yonge Street. Started in George Mitchell's administration, the Memorial Community Hall was completed in 1950, north of the entrance to York Cemetery (see Appendix). After many years of argument, Reeve Vernon Singer opened the Memorial Swimming Pool beside the Memorial Community Hall. An active swimming programme was inaugurated, and the therapeutic swimming bath is in constant use. In 1963, under Goodhead, a fifty-foot memorial was constructed on the York Cemetery grounds facing the entrance gates on Yonge Street. In the summer of 1968, when the entrance gates to the cemetery were moved west and a new street was put through from Parkhome to Burnett in order to avoid Yonge Street traffic, the memorial stands in much closer proximity to the gates.

The following statistics will clarify and show distinctly the work and effort that has gone into making North York what it is today:

	1922	1966
Population	6,000	382,792
Churches and synagogues	15	115
Schools in North York system	14	135
Teachers in North York System	18-20	3,450
Pupils in North York system	500-600	81,500
Industries	6	1,200
Roads (in miles)	150	720
Watermains (in miles)	11	700
Sidewalks (in miles)	10	350
Street lights (in miles)	5	670
Storm and sanitary sewers (in miles)	7	1,095

THE BOROUGH OF NORTH YORK

On January 1, 1967, North York became a Borough of Metropolitan Toronto under the revised Metropolitan Act. North York and Scarborough were the only municipalities under the reorganization that retained their old boundaries. North York has an area of 69.44 square miles, and is bounded on the north by the Townships of Vaughan and Markham; on the east by the Borough of Scarborough; on the south by the Borough of East York (including the former Leaside area), the City of Toronto and the Borough of York; and on the west by the Town of Weston, now part of the Borough of York, and the Humber River.

The Council is the governing body of the Municipal Corporation and upon it rests the responsibility for carrying out the duties and exercising the powers of the Corporation. Council's main activities fall into two groups: legislative and administrative. The legislative activities consist of passing by-laws for the benefit or protection of the people of the municipality, or by-laws necessary to conduct the Corporation's affairs. The administrative activities include carrying out the responsibilities and duties of the Corporation and controlling and directing public services. The Board of Control is the executive committee of Council. Its duties are assigned to it by statute and include: the preparation of the annual estimates; the calling of tenders and awarding contracts; the nomination of all heads and sub-heads of departments and other permanent employees; and the suspension or dismissal of department heads. The Mayor, four members of the Board of Control, and one Alderman represent the Borough on the Metropolitan Council. A Mayor, four members of Board of Control, and two Hydro Commissioners are elected at large; and twelve

Aldermen and twelve School Trustees are elected from twelve wards in place of the old nine-man Council. The term of office was changed from two to three years.

Mayor Service has endeavoured to provide a maximum of services with a minimum of expenditures, and his interest is in still further expansion. In 1967 the building permits issued by the Borough exceeded 200 million dollars. This increase was not due to single-family dwellings as in the past, but primarily due to the volume of high-rise apartment building and extensive industrial construction. During the year the Mayor's exciting future plans for the redevelopment of the Yonge Street Corridor was disclosed. John B. Parkin and Associates and Murray Jones and Associates presented a stimulating development for the new-born Borough, based on the extension of the subway coming north to Sheppard Avenue and subsequently to Finch. It will cost $600,000,000, and take twenty years to complete. The possibilities for North York's future are, therefore, exciting and unlimited.

NOTES

1   There seems to be some difference of opinion as to the date of the fire. A date written in the first township minute book is February 20th, 1923. Dr. Carl Hill insists on February 13, as this date is written in his annual report as first president of the Suburban-Yonge Businessmen's Association.

2   R. Earl Bales was only thirty-seven when he was elected reeve in 1934. He was the youngest reeve in North York history. Second youngest was Vernon Singer, also thirty-seven, but eight months older than Bales. Mayor James Service at thirty-eight trailed Singer by ten months. Bales was a member of York County Council for eight years and its warden in 1940. He was appointed to North York's first planning board in January, 1947, and has been a member ever since (1968). He has been the chairman for fifteen years.

3   The Hoggs Hollow Bridge was 1,225 feet long, sixty-eight feet wide, well lighted with double street railway tracks along the centre and sidewalks on both sides.

4   According to former Reeve Vernon Singer, now the deputy leader of the Liberal Party in Ontario.

5   In 1946, the year Albert Standing was appointed, Deputy Reeve W. I. Hearst introduced the idea of a planning board to formulate land policy for the Township. The Planning Act, approved by the Ontario Legislature, resulted in the formation of the Planning Board on September 25, 1946.

6   In 1950, 17,000 people moved into the Township. Because of previous limited budgets, in 1952, Boylen's last year in office, the tax rate jumped sixteen mills to provide money for schools, street lighting, additional police, road improvement, and a county tax increase.

York University.

SAVAGE

PANDA ASSOCIATES

SAVAGE

SAVAGE

Municipal Offices of the Borough of North York.

MAX FLEET

North York Public Library.

SAVAGE

North York General Hospital.

Edwards Gardens.

SAVAGE

Ontario Centennial Centre of Science and Technology, Don Mills.

Bata International Centre.

APPENDIX

Township Services

*Reeves and Council Members of
York Township 1850-1921*

*Reeves and Council Members of
North York Township 1922-1967*

Board of Education Trustees 1954-1968

North York Hydro Commission 1923-1968

Early Post Offices and Postmen

North York Population 1922-1968

TOWNSHIP SERVICES

Board of Education

BECAUSE NORTH YORK WITH A POPULATION OF 9,510 WAS CONSIDERED TOO LARGE to be served by various rural school boards, the Hon. G. Howard Ferguson, Premier of Ontario, in 1928 established the first Township School Area in Ontario. It comprised five schools between York Mills and Newtonbrook, and its board of trustees consisted of G. R. Goulding, R. E. Bales, P. J. Vigrass, W. Cox, and F. E. Odlum, who met in the Duke of Kent (Spring Garden) School. District boards, however, continued to serve the areas east and west of Yonge until the Thirties when two more areas were created. The first high school district was also established in 1928 and its board of trustees consisted of O. D. Bales, W. C. Spracklin, R. H. MacDonald, J. V. Batchelor, G. R. Goulding and J. Cruickshanks. The old Willowdale School was converted into a continuation school, and in 1929 became a high school until Earl Haig, North York's first high school, was completed in 1930.

During the population explosion following the Second World War further improvements were needed in the educational structure. As a result the first Township School Area was expanded in 1950 to include those living from the city limits to Steeles Avenue and from Bayview west to Humber Summit. This amalgamated seven School Section Boards and Township School Area 3 with the First Township School Area. Public education in North York was now administered by six school boards: the newly-created First Township School Area (23 schools), Township School Area No. 2 (3 schools), School Section No. 2 (one school—pupils attended Toronto schools), School Section No. 18 (one school), School Section No. 19 (one school), and a High School Board (one school).

At the first meeting of the expanded First Township School Area Board held in Armour Heights Public School a committee was set up to study plans for further amalgamation. Board officials at the time were: T. J. Rowson the Supervising Principal, H. M. Brownlee the Business Administrator, and Kenneth Crawley the Assistant Business Administrator. Later in the year the present Administration Building was opened, and many one- and two-room rural schools were closed such as Emery, Elia, Zion, Oriole, and Don. Many students were also attending schools

283

in adjacent townships because they were nearer to their homes, or because a number of secondary school courses were not available in North York.

Among the famous names in education during this early period was George S. Henry who was a school trustee at Oriole, a councillor, reeve of the Township, a warden of York County, and a member of the Ontario Government who held the portfolios of Agriculture, Public Works and Highways before he acceded in 1930 to the offices of Premier, Provincial Treasurer, and Minister of Education. C. B. Parsons who served on school boards for almost forty years, George R. Goulding a trustee at Newtonbrook for thirty-six years, and Nelson A. Boylen who served for twenty-eight years on the board at Maple Leaf School.

The present Board of Education was established by the Municipality of Metropolitan Toronto Act in 1953, and assumed authority for all public and secondary education in the Township on January 1, 1954. This was a busy period. The Township School Area Boards met weekly in 1953 in order to integrate the work of the former boards, and pave the way for an amalgamated board of education. When this first Board took office it had jurisdiction over two secondary schools and forty-five public schools employing a total of 728 teachers, and providing accommodation for an enrolment of 23,271. The 1954 expenditures for the Board totaled $4,854,000.

The first Director of Education was Dr. F. W. Minkler. In 1944 he had been appointed the first public school inspector for North York's sixteen schools. In 1948 and 1949 he acted as educational adviser to the Royal Commission on Education under Mr. Justice John A. Hope; in 1951 he was a special instructor in philosophy of education at the University of Alberta summer school; and in 1953 he accepted a similar post at the University of Saskatchewan. As Director of Education for North York, Dr. Minkler guided a study of the educational needs of the Township and in 1956 established the tri-level system of education whereby junior high schools were introduced as an integral part of the educational system. As the population increased, school services were improved and their structure altered so that the quantity and quality of instruction continued to rank with the best. In 1956 D. L. Tough became Superintendent of Secondary Schools succeeding G. A. Preston, and Dr. H. R. Partlow was appointed Superintendent and Chief Inspector of Public Schools succeeding T. L. Rowson. Like Dr. Minkler both men have given outstanding service to the Board and their positions, and like those of many teachers under them, have changed to meet the increasing needs of a large urban community. The establishment of two vocational schools rounded out the educational system. Yorkdale Vocational School opened in 1963 and Lewis S. Beattie Vocational School in 1966 in order to provide ungraded programs especially suited to student abilities which will lead to service occupations.

Effective January 1, 1965, the Board of Education was composed of fourteen members, twelve trustees elected by public school supporters, and two representatives appointed from the Metropolitan Toronto separate school system. The chairman is elected annually from among the trustees. In 1967 North York operated 144 schools in its system. These include 105 elementary schools, twenty-one junior high schools, sixteen secondary schools and two vocation centres. The expenditures for the Board totaled $57,045,000. In addition there were thirty-five Roman Catholic schools, twenty-one Jewish schools, and a number of other religious and private schools for the pre-schoolers, retarded and disturbed children.

The Health Department

The Health Department was formed in 1922 following the formation of the Township, and the members of the first Board were Reeve R. F. Hicks, Frank G. Hassard and Dr. Carl E. Hill, the first medical health officer. The work of the department includes the following services: public health nursing, water and sewage control, food control, quarantine and communicable disease control, environmental sanitation, and school dental service which began as early as 1939. The statutory duties of the department are set by the Ontario Health Act, augmented by local by-laws, and its function is to protect the health of the public from a community and environmental standpoint.

Medical Services and Social Agencies

Hospitals were slow to develop, but the situation is improving rapidly. Branson Hospital opened in 1957. Sunnybrook became a University of Toronto teaching hospital in 1966, the North York General opened in 1968, and York-Finch General will open in 1969 as a York University teaching hospital. Social agencies were essential to provide health, welfare and recreational needs for this large urban area, and each year new buildings are built and new agencies opened to promote the orderly development of well-balanced community services.

The following table shows the hospitals and the diversified range of agencies available in the Township with the date they opened:

1914   Canadian Red Cross. North York Branch.

1920   York Cottage, a children's centre opened by the Red Cross.

1923   Salvation Army.

1926   Canadian Legion, B.E.S.L. "Royal" added to their name in 1960.

1937   St. John's Convalescent Hospital run by the Anglican Sisterhood of St. John the Divine. 210 beds.
       North York Victorian Order of Nurses.

1946   Sunnybrook Veterans' Hospital. 1966 University of Toronto. 1,200 beds.
       Bethesda Private Chronic-care Centre. 1952 active treatment hospital. 23 beds. 1968 moving into North York General Hospital.

1948   Shadowbrook, an alcoholic clinic run by Dr. R. G. Bell. 1954 moved to Willowdale. 1966 became Donwood Foundation in Leaside or East York.

1952   North York Advisory Committee for Canadian National Institute for the Blind.

1953   Sunny View, a school for crippled children, run by the Toronto Board of Education.
       Probation office.

1954   Baycrest, Jewish home and hospital for the aged.
       St. Bernard's Private Convalescent Home run by the Dutch Missionary Sisters of the Precious Blood. Originally Shadowbrook. 1956 60-bed public convalescent home.

1955   Social Planning Council of Metropolitan Toronto, North York Branch.
       Canadian National Institute for the Blind.

1956   North York and Weston Family Service Centre.
       Y.M.C.A. and Y.W.C.A.

1957   Branson Hospital run by the Seventh Day Adventists. 507 beds.

Canadian Cancer Society, North York Branch.

Jewish Family and Child Service Centre, North York Branch.

1958 Children's Aid Society built next to their children's centre, York Cottage.

Workmen's Compensation Hospital and Rehabilitation Centre.

1959 Rotary School for Mentally Retarded Children.

1960 Boy's Village, a centre for emotionally disturbed children.

First Day Centre for Senior Citizens in the Community Hall.

Y.M.H.A. and Y.W.H.A.

1962 Salvation Army William Booth Memorial College for Officers.

Emergency Measures Office.

Ontario Crippled Children's Centre.

1963 Toronto Rehabilitation Centre.

1965 Mental Health Clinic.

1968 North York General Hospital, including children's hospital. 601 beds.

1969 Marina Lodge, a home and workshop for the handicapped, in progress.

York-Finch General Hospital. 200 beds in progress.

Fire Department

Fire protection in 1923 was provided by a volunteer fire brigade organized under Chief W. J. Nelson. The fire fighting equipment consisted of one Model "T" Ford truck fitted with hose and chemical tanks, and four hose hand reels located at strategic positions. The first truck was housed at the Pioneer Garage, the centre of operations, on the corner of Elmhurst and Yonge. The hand reels were located at Drewry and Yonge, Lillian near Steeles, Glencairn and Dufferin, Bedford Park near Ledbury, Harding near Jane, Albion Park, and Humber Summit. Chief W. J. Nelson remained as leader of the volunteer brigade until his retirement in 1931. He was succeeded first by Harry Ryder, and in 1935 by his son Ivan Nelson.

The Department continued to operate on a volunteer basis until 1941, when the development and growth of the Township indicated the need for a full-time operation with permanent staff complement. On January 1, 1942, the first fire station was opened in Willowdale, with a five-man permanent force and two pumper trucks. Volunteers augmented the regular staff, and by the end of 1949 there were 21 members on the permanent force and vehicles were fitted with mobile telephones to allow greater mobility of operation.

The tremendous increase in population following the Second World War from 18,205 in 1939 to 30,114 in 1946, indicated that the fire-fighting service had to expand if it was to provide adequate protection. The first major step was the construction of a second fire station on Lawrence Avenue, just east of Bathurst Street in 1952. A new triple-combination pumper was purchased to operate from this location and thirteen men were hired to man the station. The total strength of the Department had reached 49 members.

Two new fire stations opened in 1956, one on the west, and one on the east side of the Township, and the headquarters station on Yonge Street had to be enlarged to provide accommodation for offices and increased personnel. Since that time expansion has been very rapid, with new fire halls providing service as subdivisions open in the Borough. Today, the total complement reaches 352 men.

Police Department

In 1922 the North York Police Department comprised one constable, Roy D. Risebrough, who became the first Chief of Police. From 1922 until 1931 the police office was located in the first Municipal Building on Yonge, then, due to lack of space, they were forced to move into other quarters until a building was erected. On January 7, 1950 the first police building was opened at the corner of Princess and Yonge. It cost about $70,000 and provided ample office space, garage facilities, and a cell block.

John Harrison, who joined the force in 1930, was appointed deputy-chief in 1946, and became district chief when the Department was taken over by Metropolitan Toronto in January, 1957. At this time there were nearly 200 policemen in North York. A police college opened on the corner of Maplehurst and Longmore in the spring of 1959, with a parade ground in front of the building on Maplehurst. This school helps to provide personnel for an ever-expanding area today. There are six Divisions serving North York.

Magistrate's Court

Until after the Second World War, North York traffic act violators and criminal code miscreants were required to appear in court at 57 Adelaide Street East, Toronto, and at Newmarket to answer charges. In 1947, due to the increase in population, a Magistrate's Court was opened in Willowdale with Magistrate O. S. Hollingrake presiding. Court was held in the Memorial Community Hall when it opened in 1950, and moved to the Willowdale School in 1952 when it was purchased from the trustees of the First Township School Area to provide more extensive quarters. Later plans were made for a new building, and in July, 1960 the first session of the Magistrate's Court was held in the new premises behind the old schoolhouse, later razed to provide parking facilities. Probation service was established in September 1953. The first office was in the North York Municipal building, but later was located on the lower floor of the new Magistrate's Court.

Hydro

Prior to 1922 North York's supply of electrical power was provided from the Toronto and York Metropolitan Railway lines, with service extended to the Yonge Street area. Hydro supply was under Council's jurisdiction until December 7, 1923, when a Public Utilities Commission was formed and the privately owned transmission lines were purchased.

In 1925 the first Hydro building was constructed at a cost of $3,650. It was located on the north-east corner of Empress and Yonge and was used as a warehouse for equipment. The Commission purchased a team of horses and a wagon, with E. Kelly in charge of the operation, and the first truck was obtained in 1928. A one-storey office building, in front of the warehouse, was built and officially opened in 1929. In December, 1956, the Hydro offices moved into the former Municipal Building on the corner of Empress Avenue, and in 1965 into the $1,139,000 Hydro Building in Newtonbrook. At present, the Hydro is administered by a three-man commission comprised of two commissioners, elected every three years, and the mayor.

Following approval of the Ontario Hydro Commission in 1926, work of installing lights on every pole from the city limits to Old Yonge Street was commenced.

at an approximate cost of six cents per foot frontage per year for the first five years followed by three and a third cents per year. The first underground distribution system was installed in 1958 to add to the aesthetic appearance of the area. By 1961 the Hydro Commission was encouraging subdividers to install underground wiring at their own expense, and the Township was amongst the first to adopt the 13,800 volt distribution system.

Public Library

The North York Public Library system was established through the efforts of the residents of North York. A survey was conducted in 1940 to ascertain library needs, and a bookmobile service was recommended. However, the Second World War with its gas rationing and manpower shortage necessitated postponement of the project. The Central Community Council appointed Mrs. W. W. Allison and Rev. George Kelly in 1945 to arrange for deposits of books to be sent to the Willowdale United Church from the Public Libraries Branch of the Department of Education. Ladies of the Queen Mary (now McKee) Home and School Association volunteered to run the library, and it was open one evening a week.

After the war, when the Memorial Community Hall opened in May, 1950, a library room was made available, and a committee was chosen. A municipal grant of $1,807 was received, and a professional librarian appointed on a part-time basis. The committee, realizing the library did not comply with the Public Libraries Act, took steps to organize an association library, which became effective January 1, 1951. A second survey made in 1953 recommended the following to Council: Increased financial support from the general levy; purchase of a portable building for a children's library; and the appointment of a Public Library Board. In 1954 a building was placed at the corner of Park Home Avenue and Yonge to provide children's library service and a bookmobile service was inaugurated to augment the service in the Memorial Community Hall.

Council established a Public Library Board in 1955 and appointed the following members: R. J. Stanbury chairman, Mrs. W. W. Allison, Mrs. F. A. Pryal, Lloyd Sawyer, and Reeve Fred McMahon. William L. Graff, a man with foresight and vision, was appointed first Chief Librarian and Secretary-Treasurer of the Board. During 1956 land was acquired for the main library and three branch libraries, but construction plans were postponed when capital expenditures of the municipalities were limited by the Ontario Municipal Board. By 1957 the bookmobile service had expanded to three units and the adult and children's libraries moved to three attractive rented stores north of the post office while the main library was being built. The new building on the corner of Park Home and Yonge was officially opened on October 18, 1959. The demand for library service in North York increased steadily. The Don Mills Area Branch opened in 1961 and the Bathurst Heights and Downsview Area Branches in 1962. Each of these area branches and Willowdale provide full reference and circulating service with a film and record loan service at Willowdale.

In July 1963, John E. Dutton of Lethbridge, Alberta, was appointed Chief Librarian of the North York system. Under his active leadership community branches with collections of 20,000 adult and children's books for general reading with a small reference collection were established. The community branches opened in each area include: three in Downsview—one at Woodview Park in 1964, one at Amesbury Park in 1967, and one at Black Creek in 1968; one in Bathurst

Heights at Yorkdale in 1966; two in Willowdale—one at Centennial Centre and another at Bayview Village both in 1966; and two in Don Mills—one at Victoria Village in 1967 and one at Brookbanks in 1968. Four bookmobiles helped to serve the outlying districts for nine years. One was discontinued in May 1967, leaving three to carry books to adults and children living in new areas, some distance from the branches. In 1967 the North York Public Library system circulated 3,415,980 books and 39,659 phonograph records to 108,570 borrowers, and at least 133,196 patrons received information they were seeking.

Memorial Community Hall

In 1945 the residents in an area bounded by Steeles Avenue, Bayview, Bathurst and York Mills Road agreed by plebiscite to the financing up to $70,000 for a Memorial Community Hall to be built on the Yonge Street frontage of York Cemetery. A building committee was formed comprised of Mrs. A. N. Martin, Mrs. W. W. Allison, Rev. A. W. Jones, R. S. Rackham, Mrs. L. A. Reeves, Ellis Galbraith and Reeve George H. Mitchell.

The first and only unit was completed in 1950, and since then it has been used constantly as a meeting place for a service club, the North York Branch of the Canadian Red Cross Society, lodges and associations. The Magistrate's Court held its early sessions in the building, and the North York Public Library occupied a room for its circulation centre. When the library moved into other quarters their room became a senior citizen's centre.

Waterworks Department

North York residents obtained water from various sources prior to and following the formation of the municipality. Many of the rural residents and some of the suburban property owners maintained wells on their land. With the establishment of a filtration plant and pumping station on the Middle Branch of the Don River at Oriole, and the construction of a tower reservoir at Bayview and Sheppard Avenues, a water supply system was installed which served the Yonge Street district for some years. This tower was removed by Metropolitan Toronto in 1960.

Continued growth necessitated a search for other sources of supply. In 1939 North York's first deep well was drilled on Leslie, just south of Steeles. It tapped an underground stream and provided 1,000,000 gallons of water daily. Other wells and reservoirs followed as new subdivisions were opened and a second tower was built to stabilize water pressure in the Bathurst-Wilson area. In 1954 Metropolitan Toronto assumed all water production processes, filtration plants, towers and reservoirs and proceeded to instal a system of trunk mains to supply the entire Township with water from Lake Ontario to the extent of 60,000,000 gallons daily.

YORK TOWNSHIP REEVES AND COUNCIL MEMBERS

1850   Reeve, Franklin Jackes; Councillors, William James*, John ——, William Mulholland*, James Duncan*.

1851   Reeve, Franklin Jackes; Deputy Reeve, William James*; Councillors, William Mulholland*, William Lea, William Tyrrell.

Indicates residents of what is now North York

1852   Reeve, William James*; Deputy Reeve, William Mulholland*; Councillors, Joseph McMullin*, William Tyrrell, William Lea.

1853   Reeve, William James*; Deputy Reeve, William Mulholland*; Councillors, William Tyrrell, William Lea, Joseph McMullin*.

1854   Reeve, William James*; Deputy Reeve, William Tyrrell; Councillors, William Lea, Joseph McMullin*, Thomas Clarke*.

1855   Reeve, William James*; Deputy Reeve, William Tyrrell; Councillors, Joseph McMullin*, William Lea, Thomas Clarke*.

1856   Reeve, William James*; Deputy Reeve, William Tyrrell; Councillors, William Lea, Joseph McMullin*, John Henry*.

1857   Reeve, William James*; Deputy Reeve, William Tyrrell; Councillors, Joseph McMullin*, William Lea, David Boyle*.

1858   Reeve, William James*; Deputy Reeve, William Tyrrell; Councillors, William Lee, David Boyle*, Barth. Bull.

1859   Reeve, William James*; Deputy Reeve, William Tyrrell; Councillors, David Boyle*, B. Bull, Jr., William Morse.

1860   Reeve, William James*; Deputy Reeve, William Tyrrell; Councillors, David Boyle*, B. Bull, Jr., William Morse.

1861   Reeve, William Tyrrell; Deputy Reeve, William Morse; Councillors, B. Bull, Jr., Joseph Shepard*, C. D. Maginn*.

1862   Reeve, William Tyrrell; Deputy Reeve, William Morse; Councillors, B. Bull, Jr., Joseph Shepard*, C. D. Maginn*.

1863   Reeve, William Tyrrell; Deputy Reeve, B. Bull, Jr.; Councillors, R. E. Playter, C. D. Maginn*, Joseph Shepard*.

1864   Reeve, William Tyrrell; Deputy Reeve, B. Bull, Jr.; Councillors, R. E. Playter, William James*, C. D. Maginn*.

1865   Reeve, B. Bull, Jr.; Deputy Reeve, R. E. Playter; Councillors, William Tyrrell, William James*, William Mulholland*.

1866   Reeve, B. Bull, Jr.; Deputy Reeve, R. E. Playter; Councillors, William Tyrrell, William Mulholland*, James A. Duncan*.

1867   Reeve, B. Bull, Jr.; Deputy Reeves, R. E. Playter, William Jackes, William Tyrrell; Councillor, James A. Duncan*.

1868   Reeve, B. Bull, Jr.; Deputy Reeves, R. E. Playter, William Jackes, William Tyrrell; Councillor, George Jackson*.

1869   Reeve, B. Bull, Jr.; Deputy Reeves, R. E. Playter, William Jackes, William Tyrrell; Councillor, George Jackson*.

1870   Reeve, B. Bull, Jr.; Deputy Reeves, R. E. Playter, William Jackes, William Tyrrell; Councillor, Henry Duncan*.

1871   Reeve, William Tyrrell; Deputy Reeves, J. P. Bull*, Joseph Watson, Henry Duncan*; Councillor, Elijah Armstrong*.

1872   Reeve, William Tyrrell; Deputy Reeves, Henry Duncan*, Joseph Watson, J. P. Bull*; Councillor, Elijah Armstrong*.

1873   Reeve, William Tyrrell; Deputy Reeves, Henry Duncan*, J. P. Bull*, Jos. Watson, George Leslie, Jr.

1874   Reeve, William Tyrrell; Deputy Reeves, Henry Duncan*, J. P. Bull*, George Leslie, Jr., Jos. Watson.

1875   Reeve, William Tyrrell; Deputy Reeves, Henry Duncan*, J. P. Bull*, Jos. Watson, George Leslie, Jr.

1876   Reeve, William Tyrrell; Deputy Reeves, Henry Duncan*, J. P. Bull*, Jos. Watson, George Leslie, Jr.

1877 Reeve, William Tyrrell; Deputy Reeves, Henry Duncan*, Jos. Watson, Geo. Leslie, Jr., Isaac Dollery.

1878 Reeve, William Tyrrell; Deputy Reeves, William Jackes, Charles L. Denison*, William Clarke*, William Goulding*.

1879 Reeve, Henry Duncan*; Deputy Reeves, William Jackes, Isaac Dollery, John Hamilton, Alex. Gibb.

1880 Reeve, Henry Duncan*; Deputy Reeves, Isaac Dollery, Jos. Watson, John Hamilton, Alex. Gibb.

1881 Reeve, Henry Duncan*; Deputy Reeves, Isaac Dollery, Jos. Watson, John Hamilton, Alex. Gibb.

1882 Reeve, Henry Duncan*; Deputy Reeves, Isaac Dollery, Jos. Watson, John Hamilton, Alex. Gibb.

1883 Reeve, Henry Duncan*; Deputy Reeves, Frank Turner, Jos. Watson, H. R. Frankland, Alex. Gibb.

1884 Reeve, Henry Duncan*; Deputy Reeves, Frank Turner, Jos. Watson*, H. R. Frankland, Jos. Davis.

1885 Reeve, Henry Duncan*; Deputy Reeves, Isaac Dollery, S. T. Humberstone*, H. R. Frankland, Jos. Davis.

1886 Reeve, Henry Duncan*; Deputy Reeves, Isaac Dollery, S. T. Humberstone*, H. R. Frankland, D. W. Clendenan.

1887 Reeve, H. R. Frankland; Deputy Reeves, Isaac Dollery, S. T. Humberstone*, George Wood, D. W. Clendenan.

1888 Reeve, Arthur L. Willson*; Deputy Reeves, Isaac Dollery, Jas. H. Austin, George Wood, Jas. C. Ross.

1889 Reeve, Arthur L. Willson*; Deputy Reeves, John Morgan*, S. T. Humberstone*, Chas. Peterman, William Clarke*.

1890 Reeve, S. Thos. Humberstone*; Deputy Reeves, John Morgan*, George Wood, Charles Peterman, William Clarke*.

1891 Reeve, S. Thos. Humberstone*; Deputy Reeves, John Morgan*, George Wood, Chas. Peterman, William Clarke*.

1892 Reeve, S. Thos. Humberstone*; Deputy Reeves, Henry Welsh*, Jno. A. Macdonald, Chas. Peterman, John Fogg.

1893 Reeve, S. Thos. Humberstone*; Deputy Reeves, Henry Welsh*, Jno. A. Macdonald, Chas. Peterman, John Fogg.

1894 Reeve, William J. Hill; Deputy Reeves, John Goulding*, William Sylvester*, Jno. L. Heslop*, William H. Lucas.

1895 Reeve, William J. Hill; Deputy Reeves, John Goulding*, William Sylvester*, Jno. L. Heslop*, Wm. H. Lucas.

1896 Reeve, William J. Hill; Deputy Reeves, John Goulding*, William Sylvester*, Robert J. Bull*, William H. Lucas.

1897 Reeve, William J. Hill; Deputy Reeves, John Goulding*, William Sylvester*, Robert J. Bull*, Frederick C. Miller.

1898 Reeve, Henry Duncan*; Deputy Reeves, John Goulding*, William Sylvester*, George Syme, Frederick C. Miller.

1899 Reeve, Henry Duncan*; Councillors, John Goulding*, Frederick C. Miller, William Sylvester*, George Syme.

1900 Reeve, Henry Duncan*; Councillors, John Goulding*, William Sylvester*, George Syme, Frederick C. Miller.

1901 Reeve, Henry Duncan*; Councillors, John Goulding*, William Sylvester*, George Syme, Wallace Maclean.

292 PIONEERING IN NORTH YORK

1902   Reeve, Henry Duncan*; Councillors, William Sylvester*, John Wanless, Jr., George Syme, Wallace Maclean.

1903   Reeve, William Sylvester*; Councillors, George S. Henry*, Wallace Maclean, George Syme, John Wanless, Jr.

1904   Reeve, William Sylvester*; Councillors, George Syme, George S. Henry*, John T. Watson, John Wanless, Jr.

1905   Reeve, George Syme; Councillors, John T. Watson, George S. Henry*, F. J. Dunbar, Thos. J. Armstrong.

1906   Reeve, George Syme; Councillors, John T. Watson, George S. Henry*, Robert Barker, Thos. J. Armstrong.

1907   Reeve, George S. Henry*; Deputy Reeves, John T. Watson, Robert Barker, J. Nelson, Jr.; Councillor, Jas. W. Jackson.

1908   Reeve, George S. Henry*; Deputy Reeves, John T. Watson, Robert Barker, J. Nelson, Jr.; Councillor, Jas. W. Jackson.

1909   Reeve, George S. Henry*; Deputy Reeves, John T. Watson, Robert Barker, J. Nelson, Jr.; Councillor, Jas. W. Jackson.

1910   Reeve, George S. Henry*; Deputy Reeves, John T. Watson, Robert Barker, George Syme, Jr,; Councillor, Thos. Griffith*.

1911   Reeve, John T. Watson; Deputy Reeves, Robert Barker, George Syme, Jr., Thos. Griffith*; Councillor, Frederick H. Miller.

1912   Reeve, John T. Watson; Deputy Reeves, Robert Barker, George Syme, Jr., Thos. Griffith*; Councillor, Fred. H. Miller.

1913   Reeve, George Syme, Jr.; Deputy Reeves, Thos. Griffith*, Frederick Miller, John Buchanan*; Councillor, William M. Graham.

1914   Reeve, George Syme, Jr.; Deputy Reeves, Thomas Griffith*, Fred H. Miller, John Buchanan*; Councillor, William M. Graham.

1915   Reeve, Thos. Griffith*; Deputy Reeves, Frederick H. Miller, Robert Barker, William M. Graham; Councillor, Charles McKay.

1916   Reeve, Thos. Griffith*; Deputy Reeves, Frederick H. Miller, Robert Barker, William M. Graham; Councillor, Charles McKay.

1917   Reeve, Thos. Griffith*; Deputy Reeves, Frederick H. Miller, Robert Barker, William M. Graham; Councillor, Charles McKay.

1918   Reeve, Thos. Griffith*; Deputy Reeves, Frederick H. Miller, Robert Barker, William M. Graham; Councillor, Charles McKay.

1919   Reeve, Frederick H. Miller; Deputy Reeves, Robert Barker, William M. Graham, Jno. A. Macdonald; Councillor, Jas. A. Syme.

1920   Reeve, Frederick H. Miller; Deputy Reeves, Robert Barker, William M. Graham, Jno. A. Macdonald; Councillor, Jas. A. Syme.

1921   Reeve, Frederick H. Miller; Deputy Reeves, Robert Barker, William M. Graham, Jno. A. Macdonald; Councillor, Jas. A. Syme.

NORTH YORK REEVES AND COUNCIL MEMBERS

1922   Reeve, R. F. Hicks; Deputy Reeves, O. D. Bales, W. G. Scrace, James Muirhead; Councillor, W. J. Buchanan.

1923   Reeve, R. F. Hicks; Deputy Reeves, O. D. Bales, W. G. Scrace, James Muirhead; Councillor, W. J. Buchanan.

1924   Reeve, R. F. Hicks; Deputy Reeves, James Muirhead, W. G. Scrace, W. J. Buchanan; Councillor, W. W. Carson.

1925   Reeve, R. F. Hicks; Deputy Reeves, James Muirhead, W. G. Scrace, W. W. Anderson; Councillor, W. W. Carson.

1926   Reeve, R.. F. Hicks; Deputy Reeves, James Muirhead, W. G. Scrace, W. W. Anderson; Councillor, W. W. Carson.

1927   Reeve, W. W. Anderson; Deputy Reeves, Jas. Muirhead, Dr. E. J. Hambly, Reuben Phillips; Councillor, Jos. C. Bales.

1928   Reeve, W. W. Anderson; Deputy Reeves, Jas. Muirhead, Dr. E. J. Hambly, Reuben Phillips; Councillor, St. Clair Hurlbut.

1929   Reeve, James Muirhead; Deputy Reeves, R. Phillips, Goldwin O. Fleming, St. Clair Hurlbut; Councillor, George B. Elliott.

1930   Reeve, James Muirhead; Deputy Reeves, George B. Elliott, W. J. Boddy, R. Phillips; Councillor, W. W. Carson.

1931   Reeve, George B. Elliott; Deputy Reeves, W. J. Boddy, W. W. Carson, J. C. Bull; Councillor, R. E. Bales.

1932   Reeve, George B. Elliott; Deputy Reeves, W. J. Boddy, W. W. Carson, R. Phillips; Councillor, R. E. Bales.

1933   Reeve, George B. Elliott; Deputy Reeves, R. E. Bales, J. C. Bull, W. J. Boddy; Councillor, W. T. H. Boyd.

1934   Reeve, R. Earl Bales; Deputy Reeves, W. J. Boddy, St. Clair Hurlbut, R. Phillips; Councillor, H. R. Mountain.

1935   Reeve, R. Earl Bales; Deputy Reeves, J. C. Bull, St. Clair Hurlbut, W. J. Boddy; Councillor, H. R. Mountain.

1936   Reeve, R. Earl Bales; Deputy Reeves, St. Clair Hurlbut, W. J. Boddy, J. C. Bull; Councillor, H. R. Mountain.

1937   Reeve, R. Earl Bales; Deputy Reeves, W. J. Boddy, Reuben Phillips, St. Clair Hurlbut; Councillor, H. R. Mountain.

1938   Reeve, R. Earl Bales; Deputy Reeves, Reuben Phillips, St. Clair Hurlbut, W. J. Boddy; Councillor, H. R. Mountain.

1939   Reeve, R. Earl Bales; Deputy Reeves, W. J. Boddy, St. Clair Hurlbut, George H. Mitchell; Councillor, H. R. Mountain.

1940   Reeve, R. Earl Bales; Deputy Reeves, St. Clair Hurlbut, George H. Mitchell, W. J. Boddy; Councillor, H. R. Mountain.

1941   Reeve, George H. Mitchell; Deputy Reeves, H. R. Mountain, N. A. Boylen, W. I. Hearst; Councillor, F. W. Kemp.

1942   Reeve, George H. Mitchell; Deputy Reeves, H. R. Mountain, W. I. Hearst, N. A. Boylen; Councillor, F. W. Kemp.

1943   Reeve, George H. Mitchell; Deputy Reeves, W. I. Hearst, N. A. Boylen, Leslie Ross; Councillor, F. W. Kemp.

1944   Reeve, George H. Mitchell; Deputy Reeves, N. A. Boylen, Leslie Ross, W. I. Hearst; Councillor, F. W. Kemp.

1945   Reeve, George H. Mitchell; Deputy Reeves, Leslie Ross, W. I. Hearst, N. A. Boylen; Councillor, F. W. Kemp.

1946   Reeve, George H. Mitchell; Deputy Reeves, W. I. Hearst, Ward 1, Leslie Ross, Ward 2, J. A. Quigley, Ward 3; Councillor, F. W. Kemp.

1947   Reeve, George H. Mitchell; Deputy Reeves, N. G. S. Ingram, Ward 1, T. R. Deacon, Ward 2, N. A. Boylen, Ward 3; Councillor, F. W. Bartrem, Ward 2.

1948   Reeve, George H. Mitchell; Deputy Reeves, N. G. S. Ingram, Ward 1, T. R. Deacon, Ward 2, N. A. Boylen, Ward 3; Councillor, F. W. Bartrem, Ward 2.

1949   Reeve, George H. Mitchell; Deputy Reeves, N. G. S. Ingram, Ward 1, T. R. Deacon, Ward 2, N. A. Boylen, Ward 3; Councillor, F. W. Bartrem, Ward 2.

1950   Reeve, N. A. Boylen; Deputy Reeves, N. G. S. Ingram, Ward 1, E. W. Grose, Ward 2, F. J. McMahon, Ward 3; Councillor, E. J. Carter, Ward 2.

1951   Reeve, N. A. Boylen; Deputy Reeves, N. G. S. Ingram, Ward 1, C. C. Holmes, Ward 2, F. J. McMahon, Ward 3; Councillor, A. H. Hollingworth, Ward 2.

1952   Reeve, N. A. Boylen; Deputy Reeves, N. G. S. Ingram, Ward 1, C. C. Holmes, Ward 2, Maurice T. Hook, Ward 3; Councillor, A. H. Hollingworth, Ward 2.

1953   Reeve, Fred J. McMahon; Deputy Reeves, N. G. S. Ingram, Ward 1, C. C. Holmes, Ward 2, Maurice T. Hook, Ward 3; Councillor, T. J. Graham, Ward 2.

1954   Reeve, Fred J. McMahon; Deputy Reeves, H. S. Honsberger, Ward 1, T. J. Graham, Ward 2, Maurice T. Hook, Ward 3; Councillors, K. Burn, Ward 1, F. A. Douglas, Ward 2, V. M. Singer, Ward 2, N. A. Boylen, Ward 3, J. E. Walker, Ward 3.

1955   Reeve, Fred J. McMahon; Deputy Reeves, H. S. Honsberger, Ward 1, T. J. Graham, Ward 2, Maurice T. Hook, Ward 3; Councillors, K. Burn, Ward 1, F. A. Douglas, Ward 2, V. M. Singer, Ward 2, N. A. Boylen, Ward 3, J. E. Walker, Ward 3.

1956   Reeve, Fred J. McMahon; Councillors, H. S. Honsberger, Ward 2, 1st Vice-Chairman, V. M. Singer, Ward 4, 2nd Vice-Chairman, J. E. Walker, Ward 7, 3rd Vice-Chairman, D. D. Aldcorn, Ward 1, Norman C. Goodhead, Ward 3, F. Young, Ward 5, I. A. Paisley, Ward 6, A. H. Bartlett, Ward 8.

1957-   Reeve, Vernon M. Singer; Councillors, Richard H. Rohmer, Ward 1,
1958   H. Stanley Honsberger, Ward 2, Norman C. Goodhead, Ward 3, Basil Hall, Ward 4, Fred Young, Ward 5, Irving A. Paisley, Ward 6, James E. Walker, Ward 7, William D. Lyon, Ward 8.

1959-   Reeve, Norman C. Goodhead; Councillors, Donald Aldcorn, Ward 1,
1960   Dalton Bales, Ward 2, Ken Gariepy, Ward 3, Basil Hall, Ward 4, Fred Young, Ward 5, Irving Paisley, Ward 6, J. D. Service, Ward 7, W. D. Lyon, Ward 8.

1961-   Reeve, Norman C. Goodhead; Councillors, D. D. Aldcorn, Ward 1,
1962   D. A. Bales, Ward 2, K. A. Gariepy, Ward 3, B. H. Hall, Ward 4, F. M. Young, Ward 5, I. A. Paisley, Ward 6, J. D. Service, Ward 7, W. D. Lyon, Ward 8.

1963-   Reeve, Norman C. Goodhead; Councillors, J. R. Williams, Ward 1,
1964   F. E. Watson, Ward 2, G. G. Hurlburt, Ward 3, B. H. Hall, Ward 4, M. H. Chusid, Ward 5, I. A. Paisley, Ward 6, J. D. Booth, Ward 7, J. A. Gould, Ward 8.

1965-   Reeve, J. D. Service; Board of Control, G. G. Hurlburt, F. E. Watson,
1966   I. A. Paisley, B. H. Hall; Councillors, J. D. Booth, Ward 1, J. A. Gould, Ward 2, R. F. Yuill, Ward 3, P. Godfrey, Ward 4, M. H. Chusid, Ward 5, J. A. McGivern, Ward 6; I. M. Rogers, Q.C., Ward 7, W. G. Cassels, Q.C., Ward 8, K. A. Lund, Ward 9, H. A. Black, Q.C., Ward 10, W. Sutherland, Ward 11, J. R. Williams, Ward 12.

1967- Mayor, James D. Service; Board of Control, G. G. Hurlburt, B. H.
1968- Hall, F. E. Watson, Paul Hunt; Aldermen, J. D. Booth, Ward 1, J. A.
1969   Gould, Ward 2, R. F. Yuill, Ward 3, Paul Godfrey, Ward 4, M. H.
       Chusid, Ward 5, J. A. McGivern, Ward 6, I. M. Rogers, Q.C., Ward 7,
       W. G. Cassells, Q. C., Ward 8, K. A. Lund, Ward 9, H. A. Black,
       Q.C., Ward 10, W. Sutherland, Ward 11, J. R. Williams, Ward 12.

The Board of Education Trustees

1954   Chairman: S. J. Kelner; Trustees: F. C. Stinson, J. H. Gregg, Dr. N. H.
       Tayler, Mrs. M. Mahon; Separate School Representative, R. B. Bradley.
1955- Chairman: F. C. Stinson, Ward 4; Trustees: A. Becker, Ward 1, J. H.
1956   Govan, Ward 2, Mrs. J. Pearce, Ward 3, Dr. N. H. Tayler, Ward 5,
       J. H. Gregg, Ward 6, F. E. Watson, Ward 7, R. Hastings, Ward 8;
       Separate School Representative, R. B. Bradley.
1957- Chairmen: A. Becker, Ward 1, in 1957, R. Hastings, Ward 8, in 1958;
1958   Trustees: F. E. Watson, Ward 2, Mrs. J. Pearce, Ward 3, C. Tooze,
       Ward 4, Mrs. D. Bishop, Ward 5, S. Cowan, Ward 6, Mrs. I. Walker,
       Ward 7; Separate School Representative, R. B. Bradley.
1959- Chairman: F. E. Watson, Ward 2; Trustees: Mrs. J. Dodds, Ward 1;
1960   Mrs. J. Pearce, Ward 3, C. Tooze, Ward 4, Mrs. D. Bishop, Ward 5,
       S. Cowan, Ward 6, Mrs. I. Walker, Ward 7, R. Hastings, Ward 8,
       succeeded during year by R. D. Hoag; Separate School Representative,
       R. B. Bradley.
1961- Chairmen: R. B. Bradley, Separate School Representative, in 1961;
1962   Mrs. I. Walker, Ward 7, in 1962; Trustees: R. T. Hazell, Ward 1,
       R. D. G. Stanbury, Ward 2, Mrs. J. Pearce, Ward 3, Mrs. S. Darnell,
       Ward 4, Mrs. D. Bishop, Ward 5, succeeded during year by S. Moscoe,
       S. Cowan, Ward 6, R. D. Hoag, Ward 8; Separate School Representa-
       tive, R. B. Bradley.
1963- Chairman: R. D. G. Stanbury, Ward 2; Trustees: P. R. W. Tacon,
1964   Ward 1, Mrs. J. Pearce, Ward 3, succeeded during year by R. P.
       Leitch, Mrs. S. Darnell, Ward 4, S. Moscoe, Ward 5, S. Cowan,
       Ward 6, Mrs. I. Walker, Ward 7, J. V. Newton, Ward 8; Separate
       School Representative, R. B. Bradley.
1965- Chairmen: S. Cowan, Ward 4, in 1965, P. R. W. Tacon, Ward 10, in
1966   1966; Trustees: G. Risk, Ward 1, J. V. Newton, Ward 2, Mrs. I.
       Walker, Ward 3, S. Moscoe, Ward 5, D. R. Malcolm, Ward 6, Mrs.
       M. Mahon, Ward 7, B. C. Bone, Ward 8, R. P. Leitch, Ward 9, Mrs.
       S. M. Darnell, Ward 11, Dr. K. Wang, Ward 12; Separate School
       Representatives, R. B. Bradley, J. M. Clancy.
1967- Chairman: P. R. W. Tacon, Ward 10; Trustees: R. V. Scott, Ward 1,
1968- J. V. Newton, Ward 2, G. R. McCleary, Ward 3, S. Cowan, Ward 4,
1969   S. Moscoe, Ward 5, D. R. Malcolm, Ward 6, Mrs. M. Mahon, Ward 7,
       B. C. Bone, Ward 8, Mrs. L. Deane, Ward 9, G. R. Burns, Ward 11,
       Dr. K. Wang, Ward 12; Separate School Representatives, R. B. Bradley,
       J. M. Clancy.

NORTH YORK HYDRO COMMISSION

On December 7, 1923, a Commission, made up of the Reeve and two elected commissioners, was created to administer the Hydro. From 1924 to 1956, the term of office was one year. From 1957 to 1966, the term of office was two years. In 1967 the term of office was changed to three years.

Members of the Commission

1924 Reeve R. F. Hicks, Robert Risebrough, F. Danby.
1925 Reeve R. F. Hicks, Dr. E. J. Hambly, F. Danby.
1926 Reeve R. F. Hicks, Dr. E. J. Hambly, Robert Risebrough.
1927 Reeve W. W. Anderson, Robert Risebrough, H. V. Bowden.
1928 Reeve W. W. Anderson, Robert Risebrough, H. V. Bowden.
1929 Reeve James Muirhead, Robert Risebrough, H. V. Bowden.
1930 Reeve James Muirhead, Robert Risebrough, H. V. Bowden.
1931 Reeve George B. Elliott, Robert Risebrough, R. C. Jackson.
1932 Reeve George B. Elliott, Robert Risebrough, R. C. Jackson.
1933 Reeve George B. Elliott, Robert Risebrough, R. C. Jackson.
1934 Reeve R. Earl Bales, Robert Risebrough, R. C. Jackson.
1935 Reeve R. Earl Bales, Robert Risebrough, G. K. Summers.
1936 Reeve R. Earl Bales, G. K. Summers, Dr. R. P. Johns.
1937 Reeve R. Earl Bales, G. K. Summers, Dr. R. P. Johns.
1938 Reeve R. Earl Bales, G. K. Summers, Dr. R. P. Johns.
1939 Reeve R. Earl Bales, G. K. Summers, Dr. R. P. Johns.
      (G. K. Summers succeeded during year by J. A. Orr)
1940 Reeve R. Earl Bales, Dr. R. P. Johns, J. A. Orr.
1941 Reeve George H. Mitchell, Dr. R. P. Johns, R. S. Brown.
1942 Reeve George H. Mitchell, Dr. R. P. Johns, R. S. Brown.
1943 Reeve George H. Mitchell, Dr. R. P. Johns, R. S. Brown.
1944 Reeve George H. Mitchell, Dr. R. P. Johns, R. S. Brown.
1945 Reeve George H. Mitchell, Dr. R. P. Johns, R. S. Brown.
1946 Reeve George H. Mitchell, Dr. R. P. Johns, R. S. Brown.
1947 Reeve George H. Mitchell, Dr. R. P. Johns, R. S. Brown.
1948 Reeve George H. Mitchell, Dr. R. P. Johns, R. S. Brown.
1949 Reeve George H. Mitchell, Dr. R. P. Johns, R. S. Brown.
1950 Reeve N. A. Boylen, Dr. R. P. Johns, J. A. Orr.
1951 Reeve N. A. Boylen, Dr. R. P. Johns, J. A. Orr.
1952 Reeve N. A. Boylen, Dr. R. P. Johns, J. A. Orr.
1953 Reeve Fred J. McMahon, Dr. R. P. Johns, J. A. Orr.
1954 Reeve Fred J. McMahon, Dr. R. P. Johns, J. A. Orr.
1955 Reeve Fred J. McMahon, Dr. R. P. Johns, J. A. Orr.
1956 Reeve Fred J. McMahon, Dr. R. P. Johns, J. A. Orr.
1957-
1958 Reeve Vernon M. Singer, Dr. R. P. Johns, J. A. Orr.
1959-
1960 Reeve Norman Goodhead, Dr. R. P. Johns, J. A. Orr.
1961-
1962 Reeve Norman Goodhead, Dr. R. P. Johns, A. K. Meen.
1963-

1964 Reeve Norman Goodhead, Dr. R. P. Johns, A. K. Meen.
1965-
1966 Reeve James Service, Dr. R. P. Johns, A. K. Meen.
1967-
1969 Mayor James Service, A. K. Meen, John Dunn.

EARLY POST OFFICES AND POSTMEN

Don, Ontario, situated on Don Mills Road, North of Lawrence Avenue. Established: 1-8-1868. Closed: 31-3-1913 and became R.R. delivery from Todmorden. On 19-1-1954 the Don Mills Post Office was established.

Postmaster	Period of Service	
John Hogg	1- 8-1868	?
Miss Agnes Hogg	1-10-1879	27- 6-1898
Joseph Atkinson	1-10-1898	26-12-1904
Timothy Gray	1- 3-1905	11- 5-1905
William Shaw	3- 6-1905	23- 4-1906
James H. Smith	26- 2-1907	28- 6-1910
J. C. White	18- 7-1910	31- 3-1913
David Drew (acting)	19- 1-1954	21- 1-1954
D. J. Lawrie (acting)	21- 1-1954	26- 1-1954
Chas. Frederick Prince (acting)	26- 1-1954	28-11-1955
C. J. L. Day	28-11-1955	

Downsview, Ontario, situated at Keele Street and Wilson Avenue. Established: 1-1-1869.

Postmaster	Period of Service	
Robert Clarke	1- 1-1869	4- 5-1885
John E. Clarke	1- 7-1885	2- 1-1895
W. F. Boake	3- 4-1895	31- 1-1929
John Alfred Quigley	4- 2-1929	26- 3-1953
Ross Douglas Quigley	27- 3-1953	April 1955
G. S. Dearle	April 1955	17- 5-1962
T. H. Clarke	18- 5-1962	

Dublin, Ontario, situated at Sheppard Avenue and Dufferin Street. Established: 1-1-1854 under the name of "Carronbrook". Name changed to "Dublin": 1-5-1878.

Postmaster	Period of Service	
Uzziel C. Lee	1- 1-1854	20- 6-1862
Joseph Kidd	1- 9-1862	July 1872
G. J. Kidd	1- 8-1872	11- 7-1888
Louis J. Kidd	1- 9-1888	11- 3-1889
Matthew Williams	1- 6-1889	21- 5-1906
James Jordon	19- 6-1906	12-11-1934
David McConnell	14- 8-1935	28- 8-1955
Miss Monica May Byrne	1- 9-1955	

Elia, Ontario, situated at Finch Avenue and Keele Street, south-west corner. Established: 1-2-1878. Closed: 30-6-1916 on inauguration of Rural Mail Delivery.

Postmaster	Period of Service	
William S. Snider	1- 2-1878	17-11-1879
Jacob Snider	1- 4-1880	1880
James C. Ross	1-10-1880	4- 9-1884
John H. Snider	1- 1-1885	30- 6-1916

Emery, Ontario, situated at Weston Road and Finch Avenue. Established: 1-2-1879 under the name of "Dayton". Name changed to "Grouse Hill": 1-6-1879. Name changed to "Dayton": 1-8-1879. Name changed to "Emery": 1-9-1880. Closed: 1-2-1913 on inauguration of Rural Mail Delivery.

Postmaster	Period of Service	
M. S. Burkholder	1- 2-1879	11- 2-1884
John Watson	1- 4-1884	24- 2-1912
Mrs. Margaret Jane Gillies	20- 4-1912	31- 1-1913

Fairbank, Ontario, situated on Dufferin Street at Eglinton Avenue. Established: 1-10-1874. Status and name changed to Toronto-Fairbank sub-office: 1-11-1927.

Postmaster	Period of Service	
William Todd	1-10-1874	8-11-1875
R. D. Macpherson	1- 1-1876	8- 3-1877
Francis McFarlane	1- 4-1877	8- 3-1894
Andrew Watt	1-12-1894	15- 7-1913
Charles Lacey	24- 4-1914	4- 1-1915
J. J. Little	22- 2-1915	30- 5-1927
Ellis Endicott (acting)	31- 5-1927	4-12-1927
John Crawford Gould (acting)	5-12-1927	13-12-1927
Richard Atherley (acting)	14-12-1927	2- 4-1928
Albert Oscar Slade	3- 4-1928	12- 3-1929
Arthur William Cooper	13- 3-1929	14- 5-1929
Mrs. Hilda Elizabeth Alford (acting)	15- 5-1929	9- 7-1929
William Lewis Bettridge (acting)	10- 7-1929	31-10-1929
Frederick Barlow Holmes	1-11-1929	8-12-1930
Ross James Hern	9-12-1930	30-11-1960
Mrs. Mabel Hern	1-12-1960	

Humber Summit, Ontario, situated at Islington and Steeles Avenues. Established: 1-6-1937 as a summer Post Office. Status changed to "All-Year-Round" Office: 2-11-1938.

Postmaster	Period of Service
William George Evans	1- 6-1937

L'Amaroux, Ontario, situated at Finch Avenue and Victoria Park Avenue. Established: 1-4-1854. Closed: 30-11-1913 on inauguration of Rural Mail Delivery.

Postmaster	Period of Service	
James Taylor	1- 4-1854	28-12-1871
William Long	1- 7-1872	12-11-1873
William Nash	1- 4-1874	21- 9-1882
Alfred Mason	1- 6-1889	1- 3-1897
Charles Murphy	1- 9-1897	24- 3-1900
S. Arthur Hill	20- 6-1900	4- 7-1902
William Kennedy	1- 1-1903	6- 2-1913
Alfred John Shadlock	28- 4-1913	30-11-1913

Lansing, Ontario, situated at Sheppard Avenue and Yonge Street. Established: 1-10-1866. Status and name changed to: "Willowdale Sub Office No. 1": 5-9-1960.

Postmaster	Period of Service	
R. G. Lambert	1-10-1866	2- 9-1868
Joseph Shepard	1- 4-1869	2-11-1876
James McGlashan	1- 4-1877	23- 2-1881
Thomas McGlashan	1- 4-1881	17-10-1883
Joseph French	1- 7-1886	16- 3-1889
Thomas A. Lackie	1-11-1889	2- 4-1890
B. R. Brown	1- 6-1890	18-11-1921
George A. Dempsey	22-12-1921	30-11-1949
A. Munro (acting)	1-12-1949	9- 1-1950
R. B. Gibson (acting)	10- 1-1950	4- 9-1950
William Herbert Stokes	5- 9-1950	12-12-1953
Mrs. Olive Stokes	12-12-1953	31- 5-1954
James Gerald McGinn	1- 6-1954	18- 7-1960
Donald St. Clair Archer	25-10-1960	7-12-1961
Howard Strader	18-12-1961	

Newtonbrook, Ontario, situated at Drewry Avenue and Yonge Street. Established: 1-5-1863. Closed: 15-5-1954.

Postmaster	Period of Service	
M. Richardson	1- 5-1863	4- 9-1867
W. W. Cummer	1-10-1867	9- 7-1883
H. H. Cummer	12- 7-1883	23- 8-1886
Geo. R. Goulding	1- 4-1886	18- 4-1906
R. A. Wilson	14- 5-1906	20- 9-1907
John Grice	23-11-1907	17- 2-1917
G. C. Charlton	5- 5-1917	27- 1-1927
O. Cyril James	3- 9-1927	18- 3-1930
Sidney Castle Smith	2- 6-1930	27- 9-1933
James A. Varcoe	5-12-1933	8- 2-1936
Francis Phee MacFarlane	18- 3-1936	14- 4-1937
Wm. Talmage Adair	4- 5-1937	20- 8-1939
Mrs. Emily May Adair	25- 8-1939	9-10-1947
Norman Wade Fry	21-10-1947	23-11-1948
Elwood Patrick McNamara (acting)	6- 1-1949	1- 5-1949
Albert Henry Holliwell (acting)	2- 5-1949	16- 6-1949
Miss Frances G. Risebrough (acting)	17- 6-1949	21- 8-1949

Phillip Armados Blais (acting)	22- 8-1949	13- 9-1949
Hanley Emerson McBride (acting)	14- 9-1949	31- 7-1950
Edward A. Rowsell (acting)	1- 8-1950	16- 8-1950
Horace Edwin Rewald	16- 6-1950	4-12-1953
Alex MacGregor (acting)	5-12-1953	15- 5-1954

Oriole, Ontario, situated at Sheppard Avenue and Leslie Street. Established: 1-7-1908. Closed: 1-4-1913 on inauguration of Rural Mail Delivery.

Postmaster	Period of Service	
George Summers	1- 7-1908	31- 3-1913

O'Sullivan's Corners, Ontario, situated at Sheppard and Victoria Park Avenues. Established: 1-6-1892. Closed: 19-11-1912.

Postmaster	Period of Service	
Michael O'Sullivan	1- 6-1892	2-10-1902
J. W. Ward	1-11-1902	4- 3-1905
C. E. Mitchell	1- 4-1905	29- 3-1911
John W. Graham	31- 3-1911	19-11-1912

Toronto—No. 12, Ontario. Established: 6-9-1906. Closed: 14-9-1922. Reopened: 8-1-1923. Closed: 1-6-1945. Reopened: 25-11-1946.

Postmaster	Period of Service	
S. M. Green	6- 9-1906	20- 1-1922
Leslie C. Waters	10- 5-1922	14- 9-1922
James Joseph Stuart	8- 1-1923	9- 4-1945
Mrs. Elizabeth Stuart (acting)	11- 4-1945	31- 5-1945
Samuel Beber	25-11-1946	7- 1-1947
Samuel Pearson Dime	8- 1-1947	

Toronto—No. 15, Ontario. Established: 13-3-1912. Closed: 4-7-1912. Reopened: 28-12-1921. Closed: 29-5-1924. Reopened: 20-3-1931.

Postmaster	Period of Service	
Mrs. John Stratton	13- 3-1912	4- 7-1912
Charles R. Mills	28-12-1921	29- 5-1924
William Stewart	20- 3-1931	23- 9-1931
Herbert Lea	16-11-1931	21- 2-1935
William Stewart	1- 4-1935	

Toronto—No. 19, Ontario. Established: 2-3-1912. Closed: 31-7-1916. Reopened: 12-2-1923. Closed: 16-1-1925 on suspension of Murray-Kay business. Reopened: 1-3-1932.

Postmaster	Period of Service	
Mrs. Ettie Wright	2- 3-1912	19- 3-1914
Samuel Levinter	27- 3-1914	31- 7-1916
Wilson Fenton	12- 2-1923	16- 1-1925
Arthur Clifford Marshall	1- 3-1932	1- 5-1962
Joseph Donald Gordon	1- 5-1962	

Willowdale, Ontario, situated on Yonge Street between Sheppard and Finch Avenues. Established: 1-4-1855. Letter Carrier Delivery Service: 28-8-1950. Staff Post Office: 5-9-1950.

Postmaster	Period of Service	
Jacob Cummer	1- 4-1855	1- 5-1880
Samuel Cummer	1- 4-1880	4- 4-1882
L. Lehman	1- 1-1883	5- 2-1886
Spencer Pickering	1- 7-1886	11- 3-1887
William Stevenson	1- 7-1887	12- 5-1936
William Ambrose Stevenson	14- 5-1936	15- 8-1940
Mrs. Myrtle Stevenson	16- 8-1940	14- 8-1941
Charles Anthony Corcoran	15- 8-1941	5- 9-1950
R. B. Gibson	1-10-1950	

York Mills, Ontario, situated on Yonge Street near York Mills Road. Established: 6-1-1836. Closed: 31-10-1918. Reopened: 2-12-1918. Closed: 27-1-1928 on inauguration of Rural Mail Delivery.

Postmaster	Period of Service	
James Hogg*		1839
W. Hamilton	1839	No record between
John Somerville	6- 4-1842	6- 4-1842
		1842 and 1844
C. van Nostrand	1844	March 1855
John Hogg	1- 4-1855	1870
William Hogg	1- 4-1871	August 1879
John Arkell	31-10-1879	No record between
		1879 and 1884
J. H. Fulton	1-10-1884	24-10-1913
W. H. Thornborrow	26-11-1913	20- 7-1915
Norman McBride	6- 9-1915	24- 1-1918
George F. Wolfe	9- 5-1918	31-10-1918
Mrs. Nellie Crowe	2-12-1918	27- 1-1928

*Not known whether James Hogg was the first Postmaster.

POPULATION

1923	6,303	1933	13,964
1924	7,187	1934	14,295
1925	8,375	1935	14,600
1926	8,800	1936	15,464
1927	9,006	1937	16,006
1928	9,510	1938	16,912
1929	10,332	1939	18,205
1930	11,006	1940	20,382
1931	12,263	1941	21,962
1932	13,236	1942	22,953

1943	24,528	1956	165,544
1944	25,100	1957*	182,942
1945	26,432	1958	200,185
1946	30,114	1959	228,374
1947	33,162	1960	247,764
1948	37,932	1961	260,319
1949	45,783	1962	279,323
1950	62,646	1963	303,577
1951	80,771	1964	331,113
1952	96,717	1965	359,721
1953	110,311	1966	382,792
1954	130,766	1967	411,517
1955	148,258	1968	425,016

*From 1957 to 1968 September figure given.

INDEX

INDEX

Page numbers appearing in *italics* refer to information in illustration captions.

William Munshaw

Robert Gordon

Tho? Armstrong

William Robinson

Eber White

Oliver

GREEN BUSH INN

Geo. Crookshanks

I.S.S.

Geo Crookshanks

W? Robinson

POTTERY

Geo. Crookshanks

John Woods

Jo? Shepard

Scholfield, Property

Newtonbrook

Jo? Neal

Nicholas Munshaw

Geo. Davis

W? Street

David Mulholland

Rich? Montgomery

Thomas Humberstone

POTTERY

W.M. Ch.

Tho? Davison

Tho?

W? James

Ja? Mear

R.B. Woodcott

Joseph James

Tho? Harper

M? Speirs

Ashton Fletcher

George Routliff

Ashton Fletcher

John

Peter Lawrence J?

John Wilson 4th J.P.

Locke & Johnson

Finck

HOTEL

Jonathan Dunn

W? Janson

Emanuel Bowes

W? Holmes

Davi

John Kirby

Abraham Johnson

John Kirby

Jonathan Dunn

Tho? J. Lackie

Joshua Cummer

Nichol

John Cummer

Joshua Cummer

David Gibson P.L.S.

Samuel Cummer

WILLOWDALE

Heirs of Daniel McBride

Michael Shepard

Heirs of Daniel McBride

McBride

David Gibson

Jacob Miller

Joseph Shepard

WAGGON STORE

Edw? Pease

John Bales

John Sheppard

Edward Pease

Andrew McGlashan

Christopher Harrison

John Bales

I West

Andrew McGlashan

I Con East

McDougall

James Harrison

John Vannostrand

J. Steward

STAFFORDSHIRE HOUSE

John Vannostrand

Moffatt Murray & C?

Cap? Peebles

John Armour

M.M. & C?

M? Cameron

W? Smith

W? Green

W? Smith

John Armour

M? Johnson

John

Jos? Penrock

TANNERY

Tho? Lackie

Andrew McGlashan

Thomas Mercer

YORK MILLS

John Lawrence

STEAM & WATER

W? Bell

Lackie

Rich? L. Denison

Daniel Brooks

Alex? Whitney

Geo. Grainger

Alex? Patterson

Dr Cowdry

John Street